G000124345

Inside Concentration Camps

201299748

Inside Concentration Camps

Social Life at the Extremes

Maja Suderland
Translated by Jessica Spengler

polity

**WEST SUSSEX
LIBRARY SERVICE**

201299748	
Askews & Holts	11-Feb-2014
940.5317	

First published in German as *Ein Extremfall des Sozialen* © Campus Verlag GmbH, Frankfurt/Main, 2009

This English edition © Polity Press, 2013

Polity Press
65 Bridge Street
Cambridge CB2 1UR, UK

Polity Press
350 Main Street
Malden, MA 02148, USA

All rights reserved. Except for the quotation of short passages for the purpose of criticism and review, no part of this publication may be reproduced, stored in a retrieval system, or transmitted, in any form or by any means, electronic, mechanical, photocopying, recording or otherwise, without the prior permission of the publisher.

ISBN-13: 978-0-7456-6335-7
ISBN-13: 978-0-7456-6336-4 (pb)

The translation of this work was funded by Geisteswissenschaften International – Translation Funding for Humanities and Social Sciences from Germany, a joint initiative of the Fritz Thyssen Foundation, the German Federal Foreign Office, the collecting society VG WORT and the Börsenverein des Deutschen Buchhandels (German Publishers & Booksellers Association).

A catalogue record for this book is available from the British Library.

Typeset in 10 on 11.5 pt Palatino by
Servis Filmsetting Ltd, Stockport, Cheshire
Printed in the USA by Edwards Brothers Malloy, Inc.

The publisher has used its best endeavours to ensure that the URLs for external websites referred to in this book are correct and active at the time of going to press. However, the publisher has no responsibility for the websites and can make no guarantee that a site will remain live or that the content is or will remain appropriate.

Every effort has been made to trace all copyright holders, but if any have been inadvertently overlooked the publisher will be pleased to include any necessary credits in any subsequent reprint or edition.

For further information on Polity, visit our website: www.politybooks.com

Contents

Foreword

This book addresses a central issue in sociology, namely, the question of humanity's fundamental sociality and how it can be precisely defined. Sociology has taken different approaches to answering this question. The idea of the social contract, the twentieth-century concept of acting in social roles, and rational choice theory all assume the existence of a pre-societal individual who enters into relationships with other individuals at various opportunities and thus constitutes "the social" – in other words, society. Another line of sociological thinking, which stretches from Karl Marx through Norbert Elias to Pierre Bourdieu, holds that individuals are social creatures from the outset. Following this argument, "concepts such as 'individual' and 'society' do not relate to two objects existing separately but to different yet inseparable aspects of the same human beings," as Norbert Elias puts it in his criticism of Talcott Parsons, the leading proponent of role theory (Elias 2000: 455).

Maja Suderland tackles this controversy by exploring an extreme case of social life, namely, relations in the Nazi concentration camps – the "societal" nature of which has been debated by sociologists and historians alike. She focuses in particular – though by no means exclusively – on the hidden social practices of the inmates, that is, the social activities that existed beneath and beyond the official rules dictated by the SS. The data she draws on consist primarily of literature of memory – autobiographies, diaries, and the reflections of former prisoners and those close to them who recorded what they had been told; this material is supplemented with scholarly research.

The study at hand follows up on the work of Paul Martin Neurath, who documented his experiences in German concentration camps as early as 1943 in the form of a dissertation submitted to Columbia University. Neurath spoke of a camp society – a "society of terror" – in which he recognized the "basic concepts" that characterized society outside the camp. With the help of a broad conceptual horizon encompassing Bourdieu's praxeology, Foucault's theory of power, Goffman's idea of the total institution, Bauman's concept of culture, Weber's thoughts on notions such as ethnicity and caste, and Dumont's theories on modern individualism, Suderland assembles a set of analytical tools which she applies to her empirical material to distill these "basic concepts" of society. The theoretical connections that she reveals and her critical reflections on concepts of ethnicity and caste, for example, are new, stimulating, and provocative.

Ultimately, Suderland is able to demonstrate that the social world of the concentration camps was an outpost of the social space of the surrounding society, an outpost which shared that society's lines of conflict, but in a cruelly distorted way: In a "normal" society, lines of differentiation are associated with greater or lesser disadvantages and discrimination for certain individuals and groups of individuals, but in the camps they always represented "a simple and terrible alternative between survival and death" (p. 205). Maja Suderland also shows that human beings possess a fundamental sociality, a type of social *libido* which spawns social order (i.e., society) even under the most extreme conditions and which therefore also spawns individuals – at least in the modern age, and her findings indicate that the social world of the concentration camps is a modern one. This social libido manifests itself in the general notions associated with concepts such as human dignity, individuality, and reason, but also in the distinctions that individuals make to identify similarities and establish boundaries in their everyday lives. These include distinctions in social position based on gender, on social class, on apparent ethnic background, and on new classification principles unique to the social world of the concentration camps.

It is tremendously challenging to approach the question of humanity's fundamental sociality as a question which can (also) be answered empirically. When the "case study" used to answer this question documents the most violent, destructive, and dehumanizing events in human history, there is an added complication: By turning the cool and, in its own way, merciless analytical gaze of the sociologist upon these oppressed, tortured, and murdered people, do you not run the risk of debasing them all over again? Avoiding this risk demands a high degree of reflection – and self-reflection – as well as great sensitivity to the material, which consists by and large of personal documents that were not created for the purposes of empirical social research. The meticulous examination of the complex reality of the concentration camps which forms the backdrop to the prisoners' testimonies, the balanced analysis and careful reading that enable the finest nuances to be detected, and, finally, the clear, precise, and differentiated language make Suderland's study an outstanding sociological work that sets new standards. This book impressively demonstrates that it is possible to carry out a concise sociological analysis of life and death in the Nazi concentration camps and simultaneously, as stated in the opening chapter, "make the polyphonic lament of the people [. . .]

audible once again and, in doing so, identify both the unwritten musical score of the whole and the improvised melodies of the individuals" (p. 6).

I hope Suderland's work finds attentive readers – her study will help them better understand the social world of the modern age.

Beate Krais
Darmstadt, November 2008

Preface

Though it is certainly not critical to the reader's understanding to explain the personal motivations for addressing a research question, I would like to do so in this case anyway. There are two main reasons for this: First, I am often asked why I have dedicated myself to this kind of topic. Although the subject in question is undoubtedly of great concern to many different academic disciplines, I also have personal reasons for wanting to explore it, and in the interest of transparency I feel I should reveal these factors. Second, I am just as often asked how I can bear to "voluntarily" plunge into the dark chasm of this subject and examine it in detail instead of shying away from it in horror.

The answer to both questions is essentially the same: I have been regularly confronted with the Holocaust since I was a child – in the words of Gustave Flaubert, "one does not choose one's subjects, they force themselves on one" (cited in Pfäfflin 1996: 265). There is hardly anyone on either side of my family whose life – and very often death – was not affected by this historic event. As a result, the terrible and the incomprehensible have always been within touching distance for me. Like so many people of my generation, I heard my parents and grandparents speak frequently of war, destruction, loss, and displacement. Of the surviving protagonists in my family's stories, most had managed to emigrate to Argentina, the USA, or Australia just in time. Some – the minority – were concentration camp survivors. But the names of many other family members were mentioned in conjunction with failed attempts to hide, to emigrate, or to escape in some other way. Horrifying stories were told of deportations to places known and unknown, of a relative's last signs of life or exact circumstances of death. Until just a few years ago, I still used the monogrammed damask table napkins belonging to my great-aunt Irene, who had stashed them away together with her dishes, cutlery, and other things prior to being deported as a sign of her hope that she would return.

In other words, while my friends had family members who could celebrate birthdays and other occasions together with them in person, my family gatherings were populated largely by absentees – relatives who either lived on the other side of the world or who had been murdered long before I was born. And from a very early age, I knew that I wanted to find out what exactly had happened.

After so many years of dealing with this terrible subject I had become fairly accustomed to it, so it was a key moment for me when I discovered, through Zygmunt Bauman (1989), a very special way of looking at this topic (see chapter 1), one which would become the basis of my own scholarly research. While I was initially interested primarily in the importance of education and culture to the action strategies of concentration camp inmates (cf. Suderland 2003, 2004, 2005), I found myself being drawn more and more to the nuanced descriptions of diverse aspects of the prisoner society which are given a considerable amount of attention – alongside depictions of the horrors – in the memoirs and reports of survivors. Although it is frequently claimed that the mass of prisoners did not constitute a society in the true sense, former prisoners themselves place great value in explaining the finest social distinctions in their accounts. I therefore felt compelled as a sociologist to address this apparent contradiction, to reconstruct the inmates' perspectives and study the descriptions of former concentration camp prisoners to find an explanation as to why, even in the face of starvation, disease, misery, and death, it was so important to portray the social diversity within the prisoner society. I discovered the answers in references made by former prisoners to the "hidden social world of the Nazi concentration camps" which is the focus of this work.

When dealing with the events of the "Third Reich," you are forced to engage with the world-view of the Nazis and, in order to explain their goals and the resulting conflicts, make use of terminology you fundamentally reject. For me, this extreme discomfort regularly goes hand in hand with the need to distance myself from the interpretations of meaning lurking behind these terms. For this reason, I have put distancing quotation marks around any such terms whose meaning I view skeptically (even if these terms did not originate with the Nazis, such as "ethnicity"; see below).

In closing, I would like to thank some of the people who, through their support, have made it possible for me to complete this work. First, I must thank Beate Krais for encouraging me to pursue this topic, for giving me the space in which to do so, and for asking the critical questions that continually spurred me on in my thinking and research. My friend and colleague Ragna Schümann (1969–2010), who passed away far too young, not only cast a critical eye over parts of the manuscript and gave me useful feedback, she also valiantly tackled many of the day-to-day workings of the Institute and therefore was a tremendous help to me.

I owe her my thanks for this. Very special thanks go to Jakob, David, and Detlev for always supporting my decision without a grumble. The patience they have shown me over the years helped me find the strength I needed to stick with this subject. Finally, I want to thank Hartmut Gante for his helpful publishing advice and Jessica Spengler for her excellent translation.

Maja Suderland
Darmstadt, August 2012

Translator's Note

Wherever possible, English editions of texts have been used as the source for the quotations in this work. If no English edition of a text was available, I translated the respective quotations from the German text myself. In cases where the English edition was a revised or abridged version of a foreign-language text, I have supplemented the available English text with my own translation of any additional passages where necessary; these additional translations are placed in brackets when they occur within quotations. This particularly applies to the works by Tadeusz Borowski (1992, 2006), Ruth Klüger (1999, 2001), Eugen Kogon (1946, 2006), Leon Szalet (1945, 2006), and Krystyna Zywulska (1980, 2004).

Thank you to Georg Felix Harsch for his careful reading of the translation and his invaluable linguistic advice.

Jessica Spengler

Acknowledgments

The publisher gratefully acknowledges the permission granted to reproduce the following copyright material in this book:

From THE DROWNED AND THE SAVED by Primo Levi, translated by Raymond Rosenthal, reprinted with the permission of Simon & Schuster Inc. Copyright © 1986 by Giulio Einaudi editore S.P.A. English translation © 1988 by Simon & Schuster Inc. All rights reserved.

From IF THIS IS A MAN (SURVIVAL IN AUSCHWITZ) by Primo Levi, translated by Stuart Woolf, translation copyright © 1959 by Orion Press Inc., © 1958 by Giulio Einaudi editore S.P.A. Used by permission of Viking Penguin, a division of Penguin Group (USA) Inc.

From THIS WAY FOR THE GAS, LADIES AND GENTLEMEN by Tadeusz Borowski, translated by Barbara Vedder, translation copyright © 1967 by Penguin Books Ltd. Original text copyright © 1959 by Maria Borowski. Used by permission of Viking Penguin, a division of Penguin Group (USA) Inc.

Every effort has been made to trace copyright holders and to obtain their permission for the use of copyright material. The publisher apologizes for any errors or omissions in the above list and would be grateful if notified of any corrections that should be incorporated in future reprints or editions of this book.

[There was no] way that you'd ever really become nobody for everybody.
Robert Antelme

Part I
Introduction

1

Topic and Research Question

In his book *Modernity and the Holocaust*, first published in 1989, Polish-British sociologist Zygmunt Bauman proposes that the Holocaust should be seen *"as a rare, yet significant and reliable, test of the hidden possibilities of modern society"* (Bauman 1989: 12, emphasis in original). He claims it is almost imperative to view our society through the "window" of the Holocaust (ibid.: viii), as this can offer a glimpse of things which would otherwise remain invisible. According to Bauman, not only can the social sciences shed a light on the Holocaust, the Holocaust can shed a new light on present-day concerns (ibid.). Picking up on Bauman's thesis, I propose that insights into *our* society can be gained by peering critically through the "window" of the Holocaust and examining the social relationships between the prisoners in Nazi concentration camps.

Bauman's viewpoint is rather unusual in today's Holocaust research. The unspoken mission of Holocaust research is to analyze what is abnormal, monstrous, and "evil" (cf. Safranski 1997: 267ff.), to explore the suffering of the victims and distill the unique aspects of this historical event. Such research is therefore considered absolutely necessary but also highly specialized. Bauman, who naturally questions neither the uniqueness of the Holocaust nor the suffering of its victims, nonetheless concludes that if we want to find out something about our society, the Holocaust must not only be the object of our research, it should also determine the perspective of our research.

He thus opposes a core tenet of many academic studies of life inside the Nazi concentration camps which emphasize one thing above all: that this was *not* a society in the conventional sense because all of these people were forced to live together in unprecedentedly inhumane conditions and were therefore in a situation which would not normally be described as a society.

The phrase "prisoner society" is certainly used in Holocaust research, but it is often flanked by distancing comments that explain why it is "actually" completely inappropriate (in more recent literature, see Pätzold

2005, for example). In other cases, scholars emphasize that within the body of prisoners as a whole there were distinctions between the better-off prisoner functionaries who formed a kind of prisoner elite and the mass of regular prisoners who had no influence over anything (cf. *Abgeleitete Macht* 1998; Brzezicki et al. 1987; Orth 2000). Another viewpoint can be found in works dealing with the social characteristics of particular groups of prisoners – but because of their tight focus, such works tend to overlook the complex structure of the totality of prisoners, as this is beyond the scope of their intent (cf. Benz and Distel 2005b; Moller et al. 2002; Quack 2003; Streibel and Schafranek 1996).[1]

There is no doubt that the Nazi concentration camps were designed to dehumanize and annihilate their inmates through open and extreme brutality. In light of this overwhelming, crushing violence, it seems logical at first glance that the forced community of prisoners would be shaped solely by the imposed structures of the camps and the wretched and threatening living conditions found there. Historical and sociological studies of the Holocaust therefore frequently argue that concentration camp inmates could not constitute a "prisoner society" because their community was based on direct, open violence and the relations within it were not voluntary.[2] For example, an introductory essay on "prisoner societies" in the first volume of the series *Der Ort des Terrors* (Benz and Distel 2005a) states:

> The prisoner societies were the product of arbitrariness, violence, and terror. All of the rules and standards still applicable outside of their fences and walls between 1933 and 1945 had been abolished within them. [. . .] The drawback of the term prisoner society is that it does not express the relationship [between the enforcers and the enforced], and it is deceptive in that it makes the prisoners appear to be the active agents and shapers of this society. (Pätzold 2005: 110–11)

This position assumes that the Nazis largely succeeded in annihilating the concentration camp prisoners as social entities. Apparently the only exceptions to this are the exemplary resistance fighters, whose political motivation and strategic planning enabled them to oppose the brutal violence – and who sometimes also resorted to draconian measures against their fellow prisoners in order to achieve their goals (cf. ibid.).

While the term "prisoner society" is not typically found in the memoirs of former concentration camp prisoners, even the testimonies from regular prisoners clearly reveal that the inmates did assert their human-ity and sociality in the camps through a hidden and usually symbolic dimension of social life. In their memoirs, former prisoners often mention the commendable and particularly brave "heroic acts" of others, but they frequently place an even greater emphasis on their own efforts to main-tain continuity with their prior social experiences in order to distance themselves from the new, terrifying, and alienating experiences in the concentration camps.

Scholarly analyses of the Holocaust focus on the violence, atrocities, and abnormalities in order to highlight the inhuman aspects of the world in the camps – and for good reason. But this focus has a startling effect: If we follow the reasoning behind Pierre Bourdieu's[3] concept of "symbolic violence" (cf. Bourdieu 1991a, 1993b; Bourdieu and Passeron 1990), then by rejecting the term "prisoner society," the scholarly perspective described above unwittingly commits a type of "symbolic violence" itself. By denying the prisoners' fundamental sociality on the basis of the violence of the SS, we limit our perception, thus obscuring the hidden social dimensions of the prisoner society and making it practically impossible to discuss them without simultaneously turning a blind eye to the unbridled violence. Using Bourdieu's tools, however, we can reveal the multifaceted nuances of this symbolic dimension of a social life under compulsion and adversity and demonstrate that *not* "all of the rules and standards [. . .] had been abolished" (see above; Pätzold 2005: 110). This approach also portrays the prisoners as "the active agents and shapers of this society" (ibid.: 111) – though ones with extremely restricted freedom of action – and thus restores their human dignity (cf. Suderland 2008).

While the memoirs of former prisoners frequently stress the shocking discrepancy between life in the camps and "normal society," they also describe a multitude of complex and sometimes contradictory social relations. These had a lasting impact on the prisoners, but this impact can be easily overlooked in the face of the brutal violence that dominated the camps. In their recollections, former concentration camp prisoners depict these multifaceted interpersonal relationships in their own words, which they themselves often feel are inadequate. But by illustrating the social context for us and describing what they felt, thought, and did, they explain which aspects of society were particularly important to them under the extraordinary conditions of camp life. The authors of these texts seem to feel the need to convey that the world in the camps was "topsy-turvy" (Klüger 2001) and that they used any available means in their steadfast attempts to restore a certain degree of "rightness" within it. On the one hand, they vividly describe the traumatic violence of the Nazis and the powerlessness and helplessness they felt in the face of it. But this powerlessness is precisely what compels them to present themselves as actively engaged individuals who, at least on a small scale, tried to restore the familiar and necessary social order – even if only by deliberately holding on to familiar patterns of perception and evaluation. Each personal account reconstructs an individual viewpoint which is nuanced by virtue of its integration in various social contexts and which gives the author a recognizable identity. These reconstructed viewpoints can thus also be viewed as individual conceptions of society. The abnormality in the concentration camps is described as an alternative world in which everything the prisoners themselves felt to be right was not allowed to exist and therefore had to be reconstructed – as much as possible – in secret and using whatever means were available.

The leitmotif in this polyphonic and by no means always harmonious choir of memories appears to be the need for differences and similarities. These were apparently essential to the prisoners as individuals and were based on just a few principles of differentiation, even under these extraordinary conditions. Paul Martin Neurath, who was imprisoned in Dachau and Buchenwald in 1938 and 1939 and later became a sociologist, observed this phenomenon himself and made a sharp sociological analysis of it early on (Neurath 2005: 261). However, his exceptional dissertation entitled "Social Life in the German Concentration Camps Dachau and Buchenwald," which he completed in 1943 after emigrating to the USA, was of no immediate interest to anyone and was therefore not published until 2004 (as *The Society of Terror*).[4]

In this book, I have adopted Zygmunt Bauman's research perspective and directed my sociological gaze through the "window" of the Holocaust to examine the prisoner society within the concentration camps[5] in order to learn something about both the prisoners and their view of the world from the former inmates themselves. The main goal of my study is to *understand the points of view of the concentration camp prisoners* (cf. Bourdieu 1994, 1999) and to *reconstruct* and *describe* them with the help of sociological theories focusing on the social practices of real social agents.

To express this goal another way, allow me to draw on a metaphor used at various times by Bourdieu: I want to make the polyphonic lament of the people who were imprisoned in Nazi concentration camps at least partially audible once again and, in doing so, identify both the unwritten musical score of the whole and the improvised melodies of the individuals (cf. Bourdieu 1993a: 56). This will involve examining the recurring leitmotifs and elucidating the sharps and clefs that fundamentally modify all of the determining factors (cf. Bourdieu 1997b: 222), thereby revealing the structures created by the social agents themselves that form the basis of both the unwritten musical score and the improvised melodies of everyone who participates in it.

Academic studies of the Nazi concentration camps and autobiographical accounts from former prisoners leave no doubt that the camps were places of horror where their victims were robbed of their dignity, dehumanized, and ultimately murdered. This physical destruction was usually preceded by psychological destruction; neither the body nor the mind, neither individuality nor community was tolerated in the camps. In his dissertation submitted to Columbia University in New York in 1943, Neurath writes of his experiences and observations in Dachau and Buchenwald:

A man is thrown into a concentration camp as a means of cutting him out of human society like a rotten piece of flesh out of the living body. He shall have nobody to speak or listen to. [. . .] His life, as long as it is left to him, shall be only a physical vegetating, with no memories about the past, no meaning to the present, and no goals for the future. He shall be only a cog in the huge mechanism of Nazi terror, pressed by other cogs and the weight of the whole machinery, seldom repaired, but used until worn out, when finally the late individual, now a number, will be written off the inventory. (Neurath 2005: 132–3)

There were no limits to the harassment and torment meted out to this end by the Nazi bureaucrats and guard squads. The situation was made all the worse by the prisoners' strict isolation from the world outside. The Nazis wanted the rules of normal life to hold no sway over life in the concentration camps.

Since one of the main tasks of a concentration camp is to break the prisoner as a human being, two of the first prerogatives of a human being are withdrawn from him: the right to expect that there shall be some reason in the way he is treated, and the right to influence his own fate by reasonable behavior. Instead he is subject to completely arbitrary treatment. (Neurath 2005: 86)

This arbitrary treatment plainly corresponded to the values of the Nazis, but the prisoners felt it to be a reversal of their concept of humanity and of all conventional values. It is no coincidence that former prisoners often speak of a "topsy-turvy world" (e.g., Klüger 2001). The Nazis' enormous experiment to dehumanize their opponents and all other undesirables seemed, to the prisoners, to be an attempt to turn them into wild animals who would fight and tear each other apart in their desperation.

Though it may seem cynical under the circumstances, a closer look reveals that even in the concentration camps there was a social life that corresponded to that of a normal society in many respects, although the opportunities to express differences and nuances were drastically restricted. Regarding the "social status" (Neurath 2005: 261) of the prisoners and their respective sense of honor, Neurath writes: "The difference between the two societies, that outside and that inside the camp, seems [. . .] one of *rules of behavior* rather than *basic concepts*" (Neurath 2005: 261; emphasis added). Inherent in this realization is the minimal scope the prisoners had to continue to feel like human beings, that is, to feel like individuals and members of a human society in which the "basic concepts" still applied, while adhering to the relevant "rules of behavior." In light of the transparent desires of the SS regime, this was existentially important to the prisoners if they wanted to resist being dehumanized.

This raises the following questions: What ideas can be considered "basic concepts" of society, and which measures were necessary in the Nazi concentration camps to express these ideas in a way appropriate to the situation?

I suggest that the "basic concepts" of society must include those ideas that:

- first, pertain to the characteristics considered typical of individual members of a society or of social groups and their relations with one another;
- and, second, were so important to the prisoners, even in the extremely restricted and oppressive conditions in the concentration camps, that former inmates continually addressed them in various ways in their accounts of their imprisonment.

If these concepts were inessential trivialities, they would have lost their significance under the enormous pressure of the situation and given way in the prisoners' memoirs to other subjects which were more important in this context.

With regard to the subject of the work at hand, we must look for the distinctions made by the prisoners in Nazi concentration camps – distinctions made not solely on account of the particular situation in these camps, but because they represented the last thread of continuity with the inmates' former lives.

I am most interested in the hidden social practices of the prisoners in Nazi concentration camps which sometimes made it possible for them to preserve their human dignity by striving to realize certain aspects of their social identity. On the basis of autobiographical material and memoirs as well as academic literature, I will explore the conditions and opportunities for such social situations in the camps and their significance to the prisoners. I intend to look at both the concepts that served as templates for social identity and the means employed to manifest and maintain this social identity in the camps. My theory is that the "basic concepts" of society are hidden behind these notions of social identity, and that the means of putting these concepts into practice reveal something about the special "rules of behavior" in the camps.

How could concentration camp prisoners create a sense of individuality and social position, and what role did their bodies and minds play – despite their physical and psychological destruction? What value was placed in the social structural characteristics of class and gender – characteristics considered to be fundamental in sociological theory – and how did other criteria such as "ethnic" affiliation influence the prisoners' interactions with one another?

Human sociality appears to be a trait extinguished only in death and one which is a driving force in life, even under the most adverse conditions. Bourdieu refers to this type of social urge as "social libido."[6] Following

Bourdieu's arguments, my study reveals that even in the concentration camps, people were driven by "socially constituted interests which only exist in relation to a social space in which certain things are important and others don't matter and for socialized agents who are constituted in such a way as to *make distinctions* corresponding to the objective differences in that space" (Bourdieu 1998: 79; emphasis added). In connection with this, I view the concentration camps as outposts of the social space in which the prisoners must also be considered agents who – though their scope for action was extremely restricted – continued to make socially relevant distinctions that were important to them. But how is this "social libido," this "impulse" toward the social, expressed in a realm in which all connection to the outside world and to your own individual, social past appears to have been cut off? And what remains of the various types of social differentiation when you are as fundamentally restricted in your personhood as the concentration camp prisoners were?

A historical overview is needed in order for these questions to be addressed. Paul Neurath's thesis that the "basic concepts" of society were still effective in the concentration camps necessitates that we examine the society of the "Third Reich," as it was this society that made possible in the first place the establishment of camps for interring or annihilating its opponents and anyone else considered "useless." This fact alone reveals that within this society there were apparently antagonistic forces at work that must be described. In the following chapter (chapter 2), I turn my attention first to the origins of the concentration camps in order to set the stage, so to speak, for the aspects of interest to us here. I will look at the historical and social conditions at the time as well as the camps' organizational structure and staff.

Following this historical introduction to the topic, part II introduces the basic methodological and theoretical sociological considerations that lay the groundwork for examining the empirical evidence presented in part III. This detailed sociological reflection is necessary because the general scholarly consensus – namely, that concentration camp prisoners did not constitute a society – demands that we give careful consideration to the social differentiation criteria used by social agents to describe different social positions. In order to take a *new* approach to the well-trodden path of concentration camp research, we first need to determine the key differentiation criteria in modern European societies in the twentieth century. Only then can we see whether the empirical materials provide sufficient evidence that the camp prisoners can actually be viewed as social agents because, independent of any coercion arising from their situation, they made social distinctions of their own accord which correspond to the fundamental differentiation principles of Western societies.

The grim reality of the concentration camps was so unprecedented that it is tempting to view them as utterly beyond comparison in every respect. But the singularity of the crime must not blind us to the fact that it was committed by people against other people. If we want to investigate what people do in such a situation to defend their human dignity, we must not ignore what the concept of human dignity actually means and how deeply engrained it is in human thought and action. At the same time, there is no denying that there were opposing tendencies in Nazi society anchored in a *"völkisch"* (populist, racialist, nationalist) ideology that rejected the value of individuality and that also influenced how people behaved during this period. The aspect of human dignity, along with the question of the potency of the social structural characteristics of class and gender as well as other differentiation criteria used by the prisoners, must be examined closely so that in the following empirical section (part III) we can see whether these differentiation characteristics are accorded significance and what importance they have in the accounts of Holocaust survivors.

This fairly extended introduction to my topic, which appears under the heading of "Sociological Avenues of Inquiry," must not be construed to mean that I am taking an intellectual-historical approach to these issues. Instead, I must explore the "basic concepts" of society and humanity so that, in the empirical section of this work, I can show that these ideas could only remain effective in the Nazi concentration camps because they existed as convictions in the minds of real, physical human beings. We must reconstruct the "basic concepts" so that we can sociologically analyze their power to shape human behavior, as this work aims to do.

While the first avenue of approach to my topic serves to develop a theoretical argument that can illuminate the various facets of my questions relating to a prisoner society, the second avenue of approach focuses solely on the empirical material. With the help of autobiographical accounts and literature of memory, I will reconstruct both the diverse micro-social levels of camp life and the key elements of the social structure of the prisoner society. My analysis, which is influenced heavily by Bourdieu's sociological theories, will reveal the extent to which individual perspectives depend on one's position in the social space and how deeply the symbiosis of body and mind is embedded in human social behavior. The empirical material shows that there was a great deal of social differentiation in the Nazi concentration camps. However, it is also apparent that the fundamental distinguishing characteristics of social identity – regardless of how they are actually materialized based on one's social position – can be boiled down to a few equally fundamental aspects, some of the most important of which are *gender*, *class*, and the *belief in "ethnic" affiliation*.

In the final section (part IV), I review the concepts and means used to constitute a social identity – and thus human dignity – in the Nazi concentration camps on the basis of the theoretical and empirical material. The "basic concepts" of society that have been identified and the special "rules of behavior" in the concentration camps will be examined in light of the questions formulated earlier, and I will consider the extent to which looking through the "window" of the Holocaust can enable us to draw conclusions about the social reach of these "basic concepts."

2

The "Third Reich" and the Nazi Concentration Camps

If one asks how Hitler was possible, one cannot help concluding that the spread of socially sanctioned models of violence and of social inequality are among the prerequisites of his advent.

Norbert Elias (1996: 19)

To lay the groundwork for a theoretically supported view of the social world of the Nazi concentration camps, we first need to examine the social reality of the time. To this end, I will present a historical-sociological overview of the situation – one which strives to depict not the full historical picture but rather an outline of the social dimensions and proportions of this National Socialist experiment.[1] I follow Zygmunt Bauman's argument that

the Holocaust [. . .] should be looked upon as, so to speak, a sociological "laboratory". The Holocaust has exposed and examined such attributes of our society as are not revealed, and hence are not empirically accessible, in "non-laboratory" conditions. [. . .] *I propose to treat the Holocaust as a rare, yet significant and reliable, test of the hidden possibilities of modern society.* (Bauman 1989: 12; emphasis in original)

To use Bauman's terms, we first need to describe the historical "laboratory" so that we can observe the "experiment" more closely and analyze what happens when people are subjected to such horrific trials.

To this end, I will present the historical, social, and legal background to the establishment of the concentration camp system (2.1) and discuss what it meant to the society of the "Third Reich" (2.2). I will supplement this sociological sketch with a description of the organizational structure of the concentration camps (2.3), and I will also take a closer look at the SS personnel who worked in the camps (2.4).

This historical, organizational, and social overview should reveal the constraints and automatisms to which both the normal population and those persecuted by the Nazi regime were subjected. It will also show how the persecution and surveillance strategies used against opponents of the regime and other victims of persecution were accepted by society. Furthermore, it will reveal the weaknesses in the system that, as will be seen later, made it possible for the prisoners to defend certain "territories of the self" (Suderland 2004) and thus their own humanity.

In depicting this situation, I will focus not only on ruptures and radicalization but also on the continuities that made such radicalization possible in the first place and that therefore have a bearing on the sociological questions to be explored here. These continuities not only constituted the conditions for the existence of the Nazi concentration camps, they were also the foundation of the common threads running through the hidden social world of the concentration camp prisoners – common threads that could not be eliminated despite the best efforts of the SS and that are the particular focus of this work.

2.1 The establishment of the Nazi concentration camps: Historical, social, and legal background

For German society, the end of World War I in 1918 was an upheaval that shook the "social space"[2] to the core and resulted in aftershocks felt long afterwards. First and foremost, the defeat meant a bitter loss of international prestige that pained not only the German aristocracy and traditional ruling elite but also large swathes of the patriotically inclined population. The end of the war also marked the loss of the central figure of the Kaiser as well as the first faltering steps toward civil democracy and the creation of a new social order.

The immense reparations demanded of Germany by the Treaty of Versailles were felt to be a humiliating disgrace, and they crippled the country economically. The massive inflation of 1922–3 and the global economic crisis that began in 1929 led to deep-seated uncertainty among the entire German population and triggered something approaching panic in the middle classes. These sections of society did not have much confidence in the young Weimar democracy, and heated debates in the cluttered party landscape did little to put them at ease (cf. Wendt 1995: 34ff.).

However, these immediate causes for concern had their roots in the late nineteenth century and the challenges posed by the capitalist industrial economy that was in the process of softening social contours which had been relatively sharply defined until then. The structural crisis of modernization had aroused widescale fears and resentments expressed in an antisemitism that was prevalent even in imperial Germany (cf. Wendt 1995: 42ff.). The repercussions of the military defeat and the two interwar crises, which caused the situation in Germany to deteriorate sharply in just a decade, led to a renewal and radicalization of the experiences and apprehensions that had plagued the labor, retail, and agricultural sectors as well as white-collar workers for some time. These apprehensions were initially expressed more through antipathy and mistrust toward Jews than through aggressive forms of repudiation (Longerich 2006: 66). However, the dark mood and propaganda of the time cleared the way for those who loudly proclaimed that they would take things into their own hands and put the world to rights once more.

> In terms of effective history, the extent to which these crises actually objectively threatened the material existence of the middle class – or certain circles within it – and drove it to the brink of extinction is largely irrelevant. The more decisive factor is that the crises were subjectively viewed as an existential threat and thus helped to create fertile social-psychological ground for right-wing radicalism. Members of the middle class in industry, retail, agriculture, and the white-collar sector saw themselves as losers and victims of the modernization process; they believed they had been declassed and that their inherited social status and bourgeois identity were threatened. (Wendt 1995: 42–3)

This progressive erosion, coupled with the rapid disintegration of the traditional social order and values, wore out those sections of the middle class mentioned above. The overall process of urbanization and rural exodus, of massification, uprooting, and proletarianization, made them feel as though they were victims of industrialization, besieged by large concerns, corporations, warehouses, and mass producers, on the one hand, and confronted by the self-organizing, socialist working class, on the other. It was therefore clear who the bogeymen were: "People became anti-capitalist and anti-socialist" (Wendt 1995: 43).

Existing antisemitic leanings, which were strengthened by propaganda, made it easy to create a suitable scapegoat: "the Jew" as the big capitalist, stock exchange speculator, warehouse king, cattle dealer – but also as the Marxist, Bolshevik, and uncultivated prole.

> What made the Jewish placement in the class war truly special was that *they had become objects of two mutually opposed and contradictory class antagonisms.* Each of the adversaries locked in the mutual class battle perceived of the Jewish mediators as sitting on the opposite side of the barricade. The metaphor of the prism, and hence the concept of a *prismatic category*, seems to convey this situation better than that of the "mobile class". Depending on the side from which the Jews were looked at, they – like all prisms – unwittingly refracted altogether different sights; one of crude, unrefined and brutal lower classes, another of ruthless and haughty social superiors. (Bauman 1989: 43; emphasis in original)

In his study of the history of antisemitism in German seaside resorts, Frank Bajohr[3] emphasizes that

> the end of World War I and the Nazi seizure of power [marked] important stages of radicalization that cannot merely be smoothed over in an undifferentiated continuity thesis. After 1918–19, there was a rise in the number of antisemitic hotels and violent attacks on Jewish guests. At the same time [. . .] social hostility toward Jews and political-ideological agitation became more closely intertwined. After 1918, "Jew-free" seaside towns were no longer just refuges for antisemites. They became models among antisemitic agitators for a "Jew-free" Germany as whole. (Bajohr 2003: 166)

These social changes can be viewed as the collective collapse of entire contingents in the social space of society. The whole structure of this social space had been unsettled by various developments such as industrialization, military defeat, and economic crisis. The working class sought a handhold in political mobilization and organization; the middle class felt threatened on two sides, looked for scapegoats for its social decline, and found its opponent in the bogeyman of the Jew and the socialist; and German Jews, who had just managed to claim a place for themselves within this social space following their social emancipation, increasingly found themselves subjected to hostility and resentment.

> From the process which brought their emancipation from the ghetto, they [the Jews] could not but emerge heavily bruised. *They were the opacity of the world fighting for clarity, the ambiguity of the world lusting for certainty.* They bestrode all the barricades and invited bullets from every side. The conceptual Jew has been, indeed, construed as the archetypal "viscosity" of the modern dream of order and clarity; as the enemy of all order: old, new, and particularly the desired one. (Bauman 1989: 56; emphasis in original)

The extreme uncertainty of large sections of society, the distrust of the Weimar party government, the lack of a "strong hand," and the concerns about dwindling economic opportunities, combined with a marked aversion to socialist and social-democratic tendencies and the traditionally antisemitic tenor of society, created a fertile breeding ground in which the pithy pronouncements and promises of someone like Adolf Hitler could flourish. The *"völkisch"* ideology propagated by him and his party, with its appeals to the *"Volksgemeinschaft"* (people's community), also prompted many of the fearful to believe that a joint effort – which would naturally demand sacrifices from everyone – could counter these threatening developments for the better (cf. Wippermann 1997). It is not terribly surprising, then, that when the Nazis seized power in 1933, Hitler and his loudly trumpeted and highly visible measures were welcomed by large sections of the population. For example, the hasty passage of the so-called

Reichstag Fire Decree in 1933 initially alarmed only the regime's political opponents; much of the rest of German society supported the arrest and imprisonment of "enemies of the state" who stood in the way of "healing the national body."

The "Decree for the Protection of the People and the State" (Reichstag Fire Decree), enacted on February 28, 1933 immediately after the burning of the Reichstag, was based on Article 48, Paragraph 2 of the Weimar Constitution and thus "key elements of the Constitution [. . .] were undermined using tools from the Constitution itself" (Hensle 2005: 78). Unlike previous emergency decrees that were limited in time and restricted to a certain region (cf. Hensle 2005: 77f.), the Reichstag Fire Decree applied to the entire German Reich for an unlimited period. "It was soon aptly referred to as the actual constitution of the Third Reich or as its 'basic law,' as it ultimately represented the decisive step toward the establishment of the Nazi dictatorship even before the Enabling Act" (Hensle 2005: 78–9).

> Sections 114, 115, 117, 118, 123, 124, and 153 of the Constitution of the German Reich are suspended until further notice. Therefore, restrictions on personal liberty, on the right of free expression of opinion, including freedom of the press, on the right of assembly and the right of association, and violations of the privacy of postal, telegraphic, and telephonic communications, warrants for house searches, orders for confiscations, as well as restrictions on property, are also permissible beyond the legal limits otherwise prescribed. (RGB1 1933 I: 35; translation from USHMM n.d.)

Criminal punishments were also made more severe. By suspending Article 114 of the Weimar Constitution (fundamental right to individual freedom) and downplaying the "restrictions on personal liberty," the Reichstag Fire Decree legitimized the imposition of *Schutzhaft* or "protective custody"[4] – that is, arrest and imprisonment as a preventive measure to protect the population from anticipated offenses – and thereby laid the legal foundation for the establishment of the Nazi concentration camps. The similarity between the wording of the Reichstag Fire Decree and that of earlier emergency decrees, the decree's deliberate targeting of the political left and republicans, and the fact that the decree was signed by Reich President Hindenburg soothed the conscience of the conservatives and swept aside their misgivings (Wendt 1995: 83). Much of the population was therefore insensitive to the monstrosities already lurking behind the establishment of the concentration camps.

"Protective custody" entailed three criteria which caused anyone arrested on such grounds to be stripped completely of their rights: the lack of a warrant, the lack of appeal, and the generally indefinite term of imprisonment in state-run concentration camps (Hensle 2005: 80).

The wave of arrests that began immediately after the passing of the Reichstag Fire Decree led to the imprisonment of a tremendous number of political opponents who were transferred to the first quickly erected and largely provisional camps (cf. Benz et al. 1997: 284ff. and 549f.; Hensle 2005; or Wendt 1995: 153ff.).

These first prisoners were confined to concentration camps on the order of the Gestapo (the secret state police). The camps were placed under the central control of the SS in 1934, and when the *Reichssicherheitshauptamt* (Reich Security Main Office or RSHA) was established in 1939 – incorporating the Gestapo – this organization became the foremost authority in charge of imprisoning people in them (Benz et al. 1997: 549f.; Schulte 2005). Of the first fifty-nine camps set up within the German Reich, most had closed again by 1934. Theodor Eicke, commandant of the Dachau camp, was assigned the task of expanding and reorganizing the entire camp system: "This foreshadowed a fundamental functional change in the concentration camps. Instead of a temporary instrument of repression necessary for the consolidation of the new regime, these camps were now to be permanent facilities for the preventive detention of anyone whom those in power might define as opponents" (Sofsky 1997: 30). In the beginning the concentration camps[5] served primarily to eliminate political opponents, but they were increasingly used for other people considered harmful or expendable as well as for minorities. This particularly applied to Jews, who in 1933 made up around half of one percent of the entire population of the German Reich[6] (Benz et al. 1997: 532), along with undesirable groups such as "anti-social elements," homosexuals, and Sinti and Roma (referred to at the time as "Gypsies"). We know now that the mass arrests of 1938 – which sent 12,000 "work shirkers" and "anti-social elements" to concentration camps (*"Aktion Arbeitsscheu Reich"*; cf. Schüler-Springorum 2005a: 157ff.) – not only served the purposes of biologistically based "crime prevention" but also heralded the start of the economic involvement of the SS in the construction and raw materials industries. Concentration camp prisoners who were "able to work" would be used to make bricks and quarry stone for redesigning Berlin and other "Führer cities" (cf. Schulte 2005: 143).

Most prisoners were sent to the seven concentration camps (and their satellite camps) that had been newly established by the start of the war. During the war, the camps evolved into huge labor pools where – following the motto of "extermination through work" – first the existing concentration camp prisoners and then Soviet POWs, citizens of defeated nations, and finally Jews from all over Europe were forced into the ranks of slave laborers living and working in inhumane conditions (for this and all following data, see Benz et al. 1997: 284ff.; Schulte 2005). The project for settling the Eastern territories (*"Ostraum"*) first gave rise to these plans, which were pursued from mid-1941 but lacked the necessary labor force. Since the Nazis needed three times the number of forced laborers than there were concentration camp prisoners at the time (Schulte 2005: 146), they decided to expand the concentration camp system and imprison people en masse. Although Himmler's ambitious Eastern settlement plans failed, they had far-reaching consequences: They "demolished all previous concepts of the scale of the concentration camps and laid the cornerstone, both psychologically and practically, for the exorbitant expansion of the concentration camp system," thereby paving the way for "industrialized mass murder" (Schulte 2005: 148).

The evolution of the concentration camp system through the systematic use of prisoners as forced laborers accelerated in 1942 when the camps were placed under the authority of the *SS-Wirtschaftsverwaltungshauptamt* (SS Economic Administration Main Office or WVHA). "The massive expansion of the concentration camp archipelago from the fall of 1942 – in terms of both the number of camps and the number of inmates [. . .] – was based almost entirely on the hiring out of concentration camp prisoners" to state-owned and private enterprises (Schulte 2005: 150–1). "This drastically changed the concentration camp system, which was no longer characterized by a few large main camps but rather by a growing number of satellite camps distributed throughout Germany and the adjacent occupied territories" (Schulte 2005: 151). By the end of the war, there were twenty-four main camps with around 1,000 satellite camps and countless outposts in the Nazis' sphere of influence (cf. Benz and Distel 2005a; Schulte 2005; Wustlich 2006).

From 1941, the systematic mass murder of Jews above all, along with Sinti and Roma, as well as (mostly Russian) POWs, was carried out in some camps. A few camps were used solely for this purpose (such as Chelmno and Sobibór) and are usually referred to not as concentration camps but as extermination camps. Auschwitz and Majdanek were exceptions in that they were both concentration and extermination camps. Regardless of this, most concentration camps had their own execution facilities and were able to carry out large-scale, organized liquidations. Buchenwald, for example, had a special facility for shooting prisoners in the back of the head (the *"Genickschussanlage"*; cf. in particular Kogon 2006). A lesser-known fact is that both the Ravensbrück concentration camp for women (cf. Benz et al. 1997: 651; Jaiser 2000) and the Stutthof concentration camp (cf. Orth 1998) had gas chambers.

2.2 Germany and its forcible detention camps

The simplest and most prevalent stance was [. . .] a flaunted indifference and passivity toward the "Jewish question" – an attitude that is not to be confused with a mere lack of interest in the persecution of the Jews, but instead must be seen as an attempt to dodge any responsibility for what was happening through ostentatious ignorance.
Peter Longerich (2006: 328)

The historical record shows that right from the start, the Nazi forcible detention camps were not hidden places constructed in secret; they were widely familiar, highly visible – though not openly discussed – places of terror directly in the middle of society (cf. Sofsky 1997: 55). The regime wanted the early camps to have a deterrent and disciplinary effect on the populace, an impact that was initially achieved in part through deliberate reports in the media about them (Königseder 2005: 31; Tuchel 2005: 44). The ultimate consequence of this was that "there was hardly anywhere in German territory without a camp that was either part of the concentration camp system or that went by the name of work education camp, special camp, police custody camp, forced labor camp, youth protection camp, or ghetto and fulfilled similar functions under the same catastrophic conditions" (Benz and Distel 2005a: 7). "Looking at the locations alone, you realize just how many people lived in the immediate vicinity of the concentration camp [system], which grew and grew" (Wustlich 2006). The Nazi regime could rest assured that the population would initially gener-ally accept its claim that these camps were being used to imprison oppo-nents of the regime who were considered social disruptors (as described above). It was possible to set up the camps without any great secrecy thanks to the population's agreement in principle, on the one hand, and the intimidation of those opposed to the measures, on the other, com-bined with the legal foundations established by the regime. People knew about the camps, and they either felt that the strong hand of the new regime was necessary to correct undesirable social developments, or they dared not express their misgivings in public and instead opted to remain inconspicuous and compliant to avoid putting themselves at risk.

In his study of the complicity of the German population, Peter Longerich refers to an "atomization effect" in society

> that can be attributed to the regime's monopolization of the public exchange of opinion. [. . .] "German society" – which was actually atomized into individuals, families, neighborhood associations, cliques, and the remains of communities – no longer had sufficient communication channels and discursive mechanisms to form its own demonstrable opinion, which was "publicly" and visibly manifested, independent of the regime. (Longerich 2006: 27)

In the early days of the "Third Reich," public opinion – as influenced by media propaganda – ranged from indifferent acceptance to enthusiastic agreement with the claim that the people sent to concentration camps had, in a way, brought their fate upon themselves.

Recurring waves of antisemitic propaganda in the years leading up to World War II, in conjunction with anti-Jewish rallies organized by the Nazi Party and portrayed in the media as spontaneous public actions (cf. Longerich 2006), facilitated the internalization of the propagated fear of the machinations of "world Jewry" and the dangers of "race mixing." This internalization, together with legal measures such as the so-called

"Nuremberg Laws,"[7] gave rise to an everyday antisemitic reality that ensured there would be no public indignation at the obvious repressive measures being taken against Jews and opponents of the Nazi regime.

Concentration camp prisoners who managed to escape could therefore not count on the population to show them any solidarity or help them hide and go underground. In a country where a board game like "JUDEN RAUS!" ("Get the Jews Out!")[8] was widely distributed (cf. Rogasky 1988: 24), "the boundaries of the camp did not end at the physical barrier and the barbed wire" (Sofsky 1997: 58). Ruth Klüger, who was imprisoned in Theresienstadt, Auschwitz-Birkenau, and a satellite camp of Groß-Rosen as a child, describes her impressions as follows:

> [I]n the few years that I had lived as a conscious person, my rights had been removed piece by piece, so that Auschwitz had a kind of logic to it. It was as if I had invaded a stranger's property and was told that my presence there was undesirable. As my presence had been undesirable in Aryan stores a couple of years earlier, according to the clearly marked signs in windows. Now the wheel had turned one further cog, and the soil on which you stood wanted you to disappear. (Klüger 2001: 95)

The establishment of the concentration camps can be seen as a violent intervention in the existing social order, an order which had been destabilized by crises and was to be bolstered by removing certain elements of the population and shunting them off to specially constructed *outposts*. These segregated groups consisted of those who, according to the prevailing Nazi ideology and its underlying values, occupied the lower levels of the social hierarchy: racially, politically, and socially "inferior" people. All of this was instigated by political will and legal writs from above, but it took place with the assent of those who had lost their social orientation through dynamic processes of change and who hoped that the political measures would establish a new order within which they could reclaim their secure and rightful place (cf. Suderland 2004).

Conditions were ripe for the propaganda departments of the Nazi regime to mold "popular opinion" in order to create a basis for the public acceptance of Nazi policy. There was therefore a widespread consensus that it was necessary for the Nazis to violently pursue their goals against the declared opponents of the regime – the dictatorship was bringing its opponents to their knees. Social insecurity combined with traditional resentments meant that the bulk of the German population was receptive to the promises of the regime and believed in the efficacy of the solutions being touted.

> In spite of the coercive, dictatorial character of the Nazi regime, the Nazis listened to "popular opinion." The Nazi government was not a pure dictatorship from top to bottom, it was a *social practice* in which the German

population participated in a variety of ways. Regarding the attitude of German society toward the Jewish minority, it is telling that strong tendencies toward exclusion and isolation had emerged long before 1933 [. . .] which gradually reduced the opportunities for social contact between Jews and non-Jews. This promoted the development of a fundamental attitude toward the Jewish minority, without which the Nazis' policy of exclusion would not have been so successful. (Bajohr 2003: 167–8; emphasis added)

To the prisoners themselves, the camps appeared to be self-contained, hermetically sealed spaces with a social topography that the inmates first needed to familiarize themselves with if they were to survive. The visible barriers between themselves and the outside world were nearly impenetrable, so the prisoners were utterly in thrall to the totality of this new environment. Nevertheless, many concentration camps did have contact with the outside world either on account of the camp's location or because its prisoners worked outside the camp premises in road construction or private companies, for example. Many of the smaller camps in particular were on the outskirts or even right in the middle of a town[9] or had been set up in factories; some were directly adjacent to railway lines or walking paths, so train passengers or people out for a Sunday stroll could see what was happening in the camp[10] and vice versa (cf. Gyulai 2001; Semprún 1990). There was also direct interaction between prisoners and civilian laborers working at the same factories (cf. Antelme 1998; Levi 1995). And when work details guarded by SS personnel had to pass through towns, the inhabitants could watch the bedraggled, emaciated prisoners marching by each day (cf. Borowski 1992; Delbo 1995). The impression left by these pitiful creatures was undoubtedly often tempered by the thought that these *"Volksschädlinge"* (public pests) and *"Untermenschen"* (subhumans) were best off being punished and guarded (cf. Delbo 1995).

> Though former neighbors of the camps insist otherwise, it was certainly not the case that those in the vicinity of a concentration camp had no idea what was happening inside it; in fact, there was a diverse network of relationships between "inside" and "outside," though the prisoners could only indirectly participate in it. Regardless of the impression of many prisoners that they were in a hermetically sealed place beyond all established norms, documents [. . .] show how closely intertwined a concentration camp was with its surroundings in its day-to-day operations. From bidding on construction contracts to food deliveries and the search for escaped prisoners, those living near a concentration camp played a role in the activities there – usually as observers, not seldom as beneficiaries, and sometimes as perpetrators. (Matthäus 2005: 370)

2.3 The organizational structure of the concentration camps

As described earlier, the first concentration camps were established in the territory of the German Reich immediately after the Nazis seized power. In the bureaucratic jargon of the Nazis, the word *Konzentrationslager* (concentration camp) was shortened to KL, not KZ as is common in German today. The Nazis gradually introduced other types of camps as well. While some of these had different forms of organization, the effect they had on their inmates was largely the same. Therefore, in this section, the well-documented organizational structure of what were officially called concentration camps will stand for all types of forcible detention camps and will serve to illustrate the degree of violence, constant surveillance, contradictory orders, and physical depletion to which the prisoners were subjected.

A standard organizational and administrative structure began to evolve with the establishment of the first large Nazi concentration camps. When the existing camps were reorganized in 1936 by Theodor Eicke, a formal structure emerged which largely remained in effect until the end of the "Third Reich" (cf. Morsch 2005: 58).

The concentration camps were overseen by the *Inspektion der Konzentrationslager* (Concentration Camps Inspectorate or IKL), which was first under the authority of the Waffen-SS and then, from March 1942, the SS Economic Administration Main Office or WVHA. The so-called *Amtsgruppe D – Konzentrationslager* (Office Group D – Concentration Camps) of the WVHA was divided into four offices: the Central Office, Prisoner Work Deployment, Medical Services, and Camp Administration (cf. Pohl 2003: 138).

The concentration camps themselves were each divided into five departments based on functions and responsibilities (cf. Kammer and Bartsch 2002: 134ff.; Paczuła 1995; Sofsky 1997: 106ff.):

- The *commandant's office* (Department I) with the camp commandant and his staff. The guidelines issued by the SS gave the commandant the power of control over the camp.
- The *political department* (Department II) with the records office. This department was a "hybrid" (Morsch 2005: 65) in that it was under the authority of both the Gestapo and the camp commandant. The political department was responsible for the dreaded prisoner interrogations as well as the entire registration system. It also usually controlled the camp prison ("cell building") and the crematoria (ibid.: 67).
- The so-called *"protective custody camp"* (Department III), which was the prisoner compound surrounded by barbed wire. It was ruled over by the SS guard squads known as the *SS-Totenkopfverbände* (Death's Head Units), who were trained and organized in a paramilitary fashion, along with the prisoner functionaries to whom the guards sometimes

entrusted wide-ranging tasks. The guard squads were under the authority of both the camp commandant and a specially appointed SS supervisor who was not part of the commandant's office.[11]

- The *administrative department* (Department IV), which managed both the prisoners' personal effects and the camp's own equipment and facilities.
- The *medical services department* (Department V), which was under the authority of the camp physician and was responsible for providing medical services to the prisoners and SS personnel.

Even as the camp system grew and countless satellite camps were set up, this administrative structure remained largely unchanged. Only external work details located very far from a main camp would sometimes have their own parallel sub-structure, such as medical services supervised by the camp physician at the main camp, or a satellite camp commander who reported to the main camp commandant (cf. Morsch 2005: 60).

Each camp had at its head a camp commandant, appointed by Himmler at Eicke's recommendation, who had considerable authority. The Concentration Camps Inspectorate issued orders to the camp commandants, who, in turn, issued written commandant, garrison, and personnel orders that regulated daily operations and "[exploited] every disciplinary opportunity to maintain the appearance of soldierly order and discipline and to ensure that the deadening and disinhibiting effect of the daily terror did not influence the behavior of the SS men toward each other or the German population" (Morsch 2005: 61). The camp commandants independently decided which punishments to mete out to prisoners and which disciplinary measures would be taken with respect to their subordinate SS personnel. To support their disciplinary authority, the commandants were assigned so-called *Gerichtsführer* (legal officers) after the war started. These officers initiated investigations in cases of suspected fraud, theft between comrades, or bribery, and they also investigated all "unnatural deaths" in which SS members were in any way involved.

> The job of the legal officers largely consisted of the obstruction of justice. Internally, they were tools used by the commandant to maintain the desired balance between wanton, random acts of violence perpetrated by the SS against the prisoners and the containment of this violence for pragmatic reasons. Externally, it was the job of the legal officer to ward off interference by other Nazi authorities. (Ibid.: 65)

The camp commandants also independently promoted or transferred low- to mid-ranking personnel in the Death's Head Units. "It was through personnel policy above all that the commandant could make decisive changes. Depending on where he transferred ruthless and cruel SS men and what position he assigned them to, he could influence the living and working conditions of the prisoners in entire sections of a concentration camp" (ibid.: 62). Within the organizational and administrative structure of the concentration camps, the adjutant to the camp commandant was also very important since he usually had the full confidence of the commandant and either laid the groundwork for all major decisions or actually made these decisions himself on behalf of his superior (cf. ibid.: 63).

The prisoners were generally familiar with the camp commandant by sight at best, while his adjutant tended to work entirely in the background. The political department, however, was the first administrative office that the prisoners would get to know – and usually fear. Details on each prisoner in a camp were meticulously recorded in the camp registry office.[12] The head and staff of the political department were generally directly delegated by the Gestapo (and sometimes the criminal investigation department of the police) and were subordinate to the Reich Security Main Office. The members of the camp Gestapo wore civilian clothing and were considered not just administrative experts but above all prisoner interrogation specialists. "An order from the camp administration to report to the political department always struck terror into the hearts of the prisoners because they knew that the 'aggravated interrogation methods' used during questioning caused many prisoners to return to the camp with severe injuries, if they returned at all" (ibid.: 66). However, in their own way, the camp SS were equally afraid of the Gestapo officials, who were under orders from the Reich Security Main Office to "[keep] local tabs on" the camp commandant's office (Sofsky 1997: 106). The political department also supervised the registry offices set up in each camp, which were primarily engaged in systematically covering up the causes of prisoner deaths as well as recording births and marriages.[13]

The "protective custody camp" that held the prisoners was overseen by a commander appointed by the concentration camp's commandant. This commander was also the commandant's deputy, and the largest department in the commandant's office was under his authority. "The main job of the commander was to organize the daily acts of terror perpetrated against the prisoners" (Morsch 2005: 67). Although the basic rights set out in the Weimar Constitution had been long suspended by the Reichstag Fire Decree, in the early days it was not always possible to prevent individual public prosecutors from investigating the terror and random murders carried out by the SS in the camps. "The SS responded by using the camp regulations to create a normative framework for a permanent state of emergency" (ibid.: 64) so that prisoners could be punished lawfully if they violated the regulations. These regulations, which were nearly identical for all of the camps, dictated every detail of how the prisoners were to behave. But this overregulation made it practically impossible for the prisoners to follow all of the rules simultaneously without breaking any and thus created a basis for terror through punishment.

The disciplinary code based on the camp regulations defined how prisoners were to be punished if they broke the rules; the list of punishments ranged from standing for long periods of time, to flogging, to the death penalty, which the camp commandant was authorized to impose.[14] The camp regulations were enforced by the block leaders, SS non-commissioned officers who were each responsible for two to three prisoner blocks and who were especially feared by the inmates for their unrestrained brutality. They would turn up unannounced all over the camp and were kept extremely well informed of irregularities, usually by their snitches. The block leaders were largely autocratic in their decisions to mete out punishments summarily or follow the chain of command (cf. Szalet 2006).[15]

In the women's camps, these functions were carried out by female guards who, as women, were not allowed to join the SS Death's Head Units. The women were employees of the Reich who had service contracts first with the WVHA and later directly with the respective camp commandants, and they were obliged to render services for the Waffen-SS (Distel 2005: 204; Schwarz 1998: 805). They went about their jobs with corresponding vigor. Historical sources and reports from survivors show that they were no less cruel or brutal than their male colleagues in performing their "duties" (cf. Distel 2005; Duesterberg 2002; Schwarz 1998).

In the "protective custody camp," a second prisoner index was kept parallel to the files in the political department to record all changes affecting the prisoners. The SS reporting and work deployment officers who were entrusted with these tasks received support from a large number of prisoners who dealt with this work each day in the orderly rooms.

The administrative department handled all issues concerning housing, food, and clothing for the prisoners and SS personnel. It also oversaw the camp's own workshops and factories and supervised the technical sub-department responsible for the maintenance and operation of the facilities in the concentration camps. This department was additionally in charge of managing the prisoners' money and personal effects. The administrative department was thus "located at the fount of all camp wealth" (Sofsky 1997: 107), giving its employees relatively uncontrolled access to immense assets and making it a center of graft and corruption. These misdoings rarely resulted in disciplinary action, however, because too many individuals and entire networks profited from them and therefore had no interest in bringing them to a stop (cf. Orth 1998). The administrative department was largely responsible for the malnutrition of the prisoners, the catastrophic hygienic conditions, and the preferential treatment given to particularly obliging prisoner functionaries (cf. Morsch 2005: 68).

The medical services department of each concentration camp was overseen by the respective SS camp physician, who was able to work relatively autonomously and independent of the overarching medical services department of the Concentration Camps Inspectorate. Each camp medical services department was responsible for the health of the prisoners, the

SS personnel, and the guard squads. Based on its size, each camp had a number of SS physicians who were assisted by prisoner doctors, along with SS medics who received support from prisoner functionaries. The medical services department had authority over the camp pharmacies, which were involved in procuring and managing poisons, among other things, and over the camp dentists, who were also responsible for managing the gold taken from the teeth of prisoners. The brothels set up in some camps were also under the supervision of the medical services department.

Prisoner medical services were a very contradictory affair. On the one hand, the medical services department was expected to provide a minimum level of care and ensure that sick prisoners were able to return to work – even though it did not have access to sufficient resources for doing so. On the other hand, it was under orders to rid the camp of prisoners who were "dead weight" ("*Ballastexistenzen*"; ibid.: 68) by selecting them for death by phenol injection or gas (cf. "SS 'Medical Services' in KL Auschwitz" 1995: 79). Sometimes, in order for them not to be selected, prisoners who had contracted one of the rampant epidemic diseases were pointedly denied treatment and kept in an isolation ward as a "therapeutic measure" to prevent the disease from spreading to the SS personnel or neighboring civilian population.

Their professional qualifications gave the SS physicians a special status among the SS officers in the camp (Langbein 1995: 61). Additionally, since the infirmaries were hermetically sealed areas with their own offices, the camp doctors were relatively free to do as they pleased. This meant that they could engage in their own personal medical research. The most infamous example of this was SS doctor Josef Mengele in Auschwitz-Birkenau, who carried out or authorized wide-ranging experiments and even deliberately killed prisoners, primarily in connection with his research on twins (cf. Langbein 1995; Nyiszli 1993).

In some camps, widescale medical experiments were carried out on prisoners in the interests of the military. This included research into the prevention of diseases such as typhus and malaria, the effects of exposure to extreme situations like toxic gas or freezing temperatures, and combat surgery issues such as sepsis and bone transplantation. There were also racially motivated experiments and research which usually ended with the murder of the test subjects, as well as experiments motivated by the Nazis' population policy, including mass sterilization and hormone treatments for homosexuals (cf. Pohl 2003: 143; Winau 2005).

The SS physicians assigned to the concentration camps were generally dedicated Nazis who used their autonomy in the medical departments to enthusiastically pursue the regime's goals of "healing the national body." SS physicians were therefore particularly heavily involved in the Nazi crimes committed in the concentration camps.

Their crossing of boundaries can be attributed in part to Nazi medical policy, which made the individual subordinate to the group. The Reich Physicians' Ordinance of 1935 had made doctors responsible for the health not just of the individual but of the people. The concepts of *Volk* [people] and race had been given precedence over the individual. [. . .] But something else contributed to the heedless use of people as test subjects: the scientification of medicine, which had turned people into objects in the field of medicine long before 1933. (Winau 2005: 176–7)

Since the nineteenth century it had been proposed that "imposing rules on scientific research would bring it to a halt; without human trials, it would be impossible to test therapies so that medical discoveries could be made for the benefit of humankind" (ibid.: 166).[16] This postulate supported the legitimacy and necessity of medical experiments in the Nazi concentration camps – especially since such experiments were only being carried out on creatures considered to be "sub-humans of little worth."

The organizational structure of the concentration camps was flexible because many of the departments were substantially autonomous. However, it was also often "unpredictable" in that, "[f]ormally, it was functionally structured. Actually, however, it was constantly involved with a host of improvisations, corrections, and rivalries" (Sofsky 1997: 108). In particular, the principle of dual subordination found in many of the departments and units led to forms of overregulation that were countered in practice by deregulation and arbitrariness. This omnipresent arbitrariness resulted in a total and life-threatening degree of uncertainty among the prisoners. The camp SS reacted to their own uncertainties by training the guard squads in a way that generated a type of "mental standardization" (ibid.: 110) to ensure they always acted in accordance with Nazi ideology.

2.4 The concentration camp SS and guards

We are to do our duty decently, but without going soft. Hard – just – devastating when need be. This is our rallying cry.
Karl Otto Koch (commandant of several concentration camps, in Commandant's Order No. 8 from Buchenwald concentration camp on August 30, 1937; quoted in Orth 1998: 774)

While it may be tempting at first glance to view those who were not victims but rather perpetrators in the concentration camps as a homogeneous group, a closer look reveals greater differentiation. The perpetrators actually consisted of heterogeneous conglomerates made up of people from a variety of backgrounds. A more detailed examination of the SS personnel who had different formal functions and positions in the camps is also important because while the organizational structure was tight, this heterogeneity played a role in the hidden social practices of the prisoners in Nazi concentration camps.

One defining characteristic of the staff structure in the concentration camps was the social network of SS members shaped by the principle of "personnel rotation" (Orth 1998: 756) which spread through every single camp. A "finely woven network of official and functional relationships" emerged early on – with marriage sometimes lending a kinship dimension to it – and this network played an essential role in the personnel policy of the camps in later years (cf. ibid.: 765ff.).

The commandants were the center of the camp SS. Of the forty-six SS officers who served as camp commandants during the twelve years of the Nazi regime, only seventeen held this position continuously over a longer period of time. These especially successful commandants were younger on average than the others, had better organizational and administrative skills, and had experienced much more extensive official socialization within the SS leadership (ibid.: 756).

When the concentration camps passed under the authority of the WVHA in 1942, their personnel policy was overhauled. Oswald Pohl, head of the WVHA, felt that the existing commandants were not up to the task of managing the camps as labor pools for the war effort. Some of the commandants were also too heavily involved in corruption or were alcoholics, so it seemed advisable to Pohl to remove them from office. A transfer did not necessarily entail demotion for these SS members since most of them were simply assigned to another post. It was only in exceptional situations – when the incriminated commandants had been blatantly remiss in their duties by pursuing their own personal interests – that the offenses were investigated and the respective officers punished, sometimes by being dismissed from the SS[17] (ibid.: 758ff.).

If we expand our view to include the commandants' staff – and thus the entire SS leadership responsible for the crimes in the concentration camps – then the following picture emerges: Only a vanishingly small proportion of the SS members who made up the commandants' staff were officers; around 90 percent of them were merely of enlisted rank. From 1933 to 1945, the top level of the camp hierarchy consisted of only around 320 people who could be considered the "elite troop of terror" (Orth 2005: 130f.).

Most of the camp SS belonged to the generation who had not actually fought in World War I but who grew up with the myths surrounding it. They were influenced as much by their fascination with what masses of people and technology could achieve in a modern war (cf. Winkler 2006: 339) as they were by the talk of the "war guilt lie" and the "stab in the back legend" (*"Dolchstoßlegende,"* ibid.: 360). These myths were instrumental in shaping the identity of the generation that grew up during the war, and it led the members of this generation to be attracted to *"völkisch* right-wing radicals" (Orth 2005: 131).

Most of the camp SS came from middle-class backgrounds in the skilled trade or commerce sectors, so they had felt particularly insecure and threatened by a loss of social status on account of the crises of the Weimar Republic (see chapter 2.1). A number of them had been temporarily unemployed during the Weimar period and had joined the Nazi Party, SA, or SS at a young age (ibid.: 131). After the Nazis seized power in 1933, many of these SS members were given full-time positions which enabled them to turn their private dedication to the Nazi cause into a source of income and to escape their uncertain employment situation. Since their uniforms and soldierly trappings were outward evidence of orderliness and respectability, the paramilitary organization of the SS also enjoyed social recognition. For those who felt their previous social position had been precarious, joining the camp SS was a sign of social advancement.

If members of the camp SS turned out to be overqualified to serve in the guard squads – where all of them trained to begin with – or if they had connections to the people empowered to make decisions on promotions, they usually managed to move quickly into the commandant's staff.

> The integral components of this intricate social network included personal friendships and sometimes quarrels, a social context oriented on the ideologeme of the "SS kinship community" and a special linguistic code. [. . .] At its heart, however, the network was held intact by the crimes its members committed together: through official socialization and the execution of duties, through forms of collective violence. The perpetration of crimes based on a division of labor shaped the group and bonded it together. (Ibid.: 132)

The relationships between these SS elites were not restricted to their official work, however. The SS officers were housed with their families – wives and children – in SS housing developments that were part of the camps, so they frequently spent much of their free time together as well. Since they viewed themselves as an "SS kinship community," group trips to the cinema or theater were as much a part of their social program as regular evening get-togethers. The SS members went to dances, swimming pools, and local inns and restaurants together, which meant that they were also integrated into the civilian population. These activities laid the groundwork for friendships and even marriages. Such leisure activities – which suggested normality – and the family lives of the SS leadership served as a source of the personal stability that it was thought these SS members needed in order to carry out the tasks that were so indispensable to the German "people's community" (ibid.: 133).

Their world-view also contributed to the different ways in which they dealt with different groups of prisoners.[18] The main targets of terror and violence in the camps were Jewish prisoners, who suffered much higher death rates than other groups of prisoners right from the start. Attempts made in the second half of the war to turn the concentration camps into slave labor pools for the armaments industry and private enterprises failed in part because of the long-established practice among the camp SS of terrorizing and exterminating Jewish prisoners instead of keeping them fit to work through more "measured treatment" (ibid.: 135ff.).

The historical sources offer scant insight into what prompted these people to dedicate their lives to "murderous violence" (ibid.: 138). Though the backgrounds and life stories of many of these SS leaders are relatively well documented, we can do little more than speculate on their reasons and motivation. Karin Orth points out that

> what seems at first glance to be a problem with the historical sources available to us [. . .] leads us, upon closer inspection, to the heart of what drove these men. The people in question were not intellectuals or academics, they were not members of the (educated) bourgeoisie for whom it was natural to reflect upon their own lives, trace the roots of their own motives and, ultimately, write everything down. It is not just that no subjective sources which could reveal an insight into the motives of the camp SS have been passed down to us – it is that such documents never existed in the first place. [. . .] The actions of the SS members in the concentration camps were driven largely by the intricate social network to which they owed their social advancement. (Ibid.: 138f.)

Within this community, they had learned what to consider "common sense" (ibid.: 139), which comprised a racist and antisemitic consensus as well as the unquestioning use of violence against the "internal enemy" (Sofsky 1997: 103) within the "*Volksgemeinschaft.*"

SS doctors held a special position within the ranks of the SS leadership. Not only were they academics whose formal training was entirely different from that of their SS colleagues in other departments, they were also viewed suspiciously by their non-academic comrades within the "SS kinship community" because of their reputation as intellectuals (cf. Langbein 1995: 61). They themselves often saw their work in the Nazi concentration camps as a career springboard since it offered them undreamt-of opportunities to carry out their own research, through which they hoped to achieve recognition in the field of medical science. Many of them had close relationships with scientific research institutions, including the infamous Josef Mengele, who was in constant contact with his doctoral advisor Professor Freiherr von Verschuer, head of the Kaiser Wilhelm Institute for Anthropology in Berlin, to whom he sent specimens from the test subjects he murdered in Auschwitz for further investigation (ibid.: 65).

The relatively small number of camp commandants and SS personnel

in leading positions throughout the Nazi period should not disguise
the very high number of rank-and-file SS men in the guard squads and
in administrative roles in the camps – all of whom were in a position to
commit acts of violence against the prisoners.[19] When World War II began
in September 1939, there were around 21,000 concentration camp prisoners guarded by about 24,000 members of the SS Death's Head Units.
"Thus, at least theoretically, at this point there was more than one guard
for every prisoner" (Sofsky 1997: 101). Confrontation with the "internal
enemy" was part of the training regime for the Waffen-SS, so serving as
a guard in the concentration camps was an integral aspect of SS instruc-
tion. Only a small number of the Death's Head Units were permanently
involved in the daily operation of the camps. Nonetheless, "even a restrictive estimate suggests that at least 55,000 SS men and women did service
in the camps" (ibid.: 102).

Various factors influenced the character of the camp SS personnel.
Formal specialization was one aspect, but personal relationships and
networks were equally important in determining what an SS man would
be assigned to do. A clear organizational hierarchy governed the power
of command and delegation and resulted in a great deal of paperwork.
This was countered by the tremendously significant "practical and mental
standardization" (ibid.: 103) that could be achieved on the basis of personal relations and by following the example of others.

The status framework of the SS followed a military hierarchy of rank,
but it was one in which personal authority played just as weighty a role as
camaraderie – an aspect characterized in particular by each member's willingness to be an accomplice for the group (ibid.: 103f.). In addition to the
soldierly hierarchy, all ranks of the camp SS were subject to an actively promoted precept of equality that aimed to strengthen individual integration
into the community of SS comrades. Extensive delegation was the reward
for total allegiance. "Just as each superior was supposed to present a personal example, every individual SS member was expected to demonstrate
personal initiative" (ibid.: 105). Correspondingly, the SS men delegated
to carry out tasks frequently expressed their total identification with the
ideological goals and commands of their superiors as well as their own personal initiative through the arbitrary use of violence against the prisoners.

> [The SS man] proved he belonged by doing *more* than was demanded in
> a specific instance [. . .] – by anticipating orders and carrying them out in
> advance, even before they were given. [. . .] When a subordinate is told
> that he must demonstrate his social affiliation by personal commitment
> and engagement, arbitrary action becomes the proof of obedience. (Ibid.;
> emphasis added)

But who were these people, where did they come from, and what did they
hope to gain by serving in the SS Death's Head Units? First of all, it must

be noted that the guard formations in the concentration camps were very heterogeneous.

> We find men and women, veteran soldiers and those in the prime of youth, Germans and non-Germans, SS members [. . .], rank-and-file sentries and highly decorated high-ranking SS leaders, Christians and deists, committed adherents to the Nazi world-view and forcibly recruited members of the Wehrmacht, people who had served as concentration camp guards only for a few weeks and those who had served for twelve years, sadistic mass murderers and those who treated the prisoners comparatively humanely. We know a relatively large amount about some of these groups of perpetrators, but nearly nothing about others. (Orth 2005: 126)

Guard duties in the concentration camps were governed by a uniform principle that primarily distinguished between "internal" and "external" security through the "guard squads" and the "commandant's office" (ibid.: 127). To this day, there is scant information available regarding the social composition of the guard formations (cf. ibid.: 127ff.). It is worth bearing in mind that in addition to the members of the SS Death's Head Units who served as guards, so many additional guards were needed when the camp system was expanded in later years that other – non-voluntary – recruiting tactics were used as well. With the outbreak of the war, the SS Death's Head Units were militarized to become the "the nation's second weapon-bearer" and the core of the Waffen-SS (ibid.: 127). They also continued to make up the permanent basis of the concentration camp guard formations who would have to cope with the "rise in 'enemy elements'" (ibid.) expected after the start of the war and the resulting increase in concentration camp prisoners. One of the first measures introduced to meet this elevated demand for guards was the calling up of older SS reservists to strengthen the Death's Head Units (ibid.: 128), which began to erode the previously applicable "recruitment ideal"[20] (Sofsky 1997: 110).

By the outbreak of the war at the latest, a variety of paths could lead to service in the guard squads of the concentration camps, and many of them were based largely on chance; fervent adherence to the Nazi world-view did not always play a decisive role. Wehrmacht soldiers who had become temporarily unfit to fight on the front were sometimes forcibly recruited for duty in the camps, and so-called "*Volksdeutsche*" (ethnic Germans) were also called up to serve as camp SS personnel in the territories occupied by Germany.

Labor offices recruited women for the women's departments or camps, sometimes by giving them false information or downplaying the reality in the camps. In January 1943, a decree was issued on the recruitment of female factory workers as guards in the concentration camps. These women were usually assigned to guard prisoners who were being forced to work in private factories (Distel 2005: 203f.; Orth 2005: 126).

With the exception of a core group of permanent staff who were frequently assigned to leading positions at outposts and satellite camps when the camp system expanded (Sofsky 1997: 102), the guard formations were "a third-class force, [. . .] neither physically fit nor especially motivated, neither ideologically schooled nor disciplined militarily – a motley crew, anything but an elite" (ibid.: 110).

Just as the various routes leading to the guard squads differed in terms of Party and SS membership as well as the recruitment channels themselves, there were differences between the perpetrators with respect to their backgrounds and life trajectories. However, there is not enough precise data on this for a social statistical analysis. "The troop of concentration camp guards as a whole as well as the guard squads in each concentration camp were extremely socially heterogeneous as regards nearly every parameter one could use to carry out a social structural analysis. The only key factors mentioned are age, sex, nationality, and affiliation with a Nazi organization" (Orth 2005: 129). The motives for voluntarily joining the Death's Head Units varied widely and often had little to do with an extreme Nazi ethos. The opportunity for social advancement without the need for formal training was just one possible motive. A secure income and the ability to establish a livelihood may have prompted others – particularly younger men – to take this route. Admission into the male community of the Death's Head Units, the paramilitary organization of the units, and the chance to wear a uniform that garnered respect were probably enticing prospects for others (Sofsky 1997: 99).

Like the prisoners, the guards were part of a "total institution" (Goffman 1961) and had the principles of obedience and loyalty drilled into them. The bullying and degradation that the guards experienced during their training could be channeled into violence against the prisoners. This was all the easier because violence against prisoners was established by the camp regulations and disciplinary code as an approved means of expressing power relations in the camps. Though their standing orders prohibited the guards from abusing or harassing the prisoners (Sofsky 1997: 112), it was generally extremely difficult if not impossible to monitor this, so the guards in the camps had a great deal of freedom (ibid.: 113). "The concentration camp had been deliberately constructed as a double total institution. On one side were the inmates of the military formation, who were at the same time the personnel of the prisoner camp; on the other stood the prisoners. Feelings of revenge and hatred among the staff could be redirected toward them" (ibid.: 114). It was up to the individual guards to choose how or whether they would maltreat prisoners. The cruelty of the guards was rooted not so much in the characteristics of a particular social background or life trajectory as in the total communal indoctrination into a generally desired brutal approach to dealing with "internal enemies," compliance with which was rewarded by loyal camaraderie and association with a respected community. "One source of terror lay in this anxiety among the personnel – their fear of the prisoners, and of transgressing against the loyalty and conformity of the group" (ibid.: 110). The guards, both male and female (cf. Distel 2005: 206), learned to treat the prisoners with inhumane brutality through a communal practice based not just on explicit orders but on the opportunity to demonstrate unconditional loyalty to shared goals: fighting the prisoners who were "internal enemies" and maintaining the conformity of the group to which one was proud to belong (cf. Sofsky 1997: 110).

It is apparent that neither the elite SS leadership nor the guard squads can be dismissed as homogeneous groups. While certain shared experiences and sensitivities in the interwar period could have had a unifying effect and created favorable conditions for an ideology oriented on the interests of the *"Volksgemeinschaft,"* it is important to emphasize that socialization within the SS – ranging from particular initiation rites, through companionable drinking sprees, to participation in bloodbaths among the prisoners – played an instrumental role. Wearing the black Death's Head uniform and following military standards of conduct were the signs that one belonged to the group, and they promoted the group's homogeneous outward appearance.

The feeling of belonging to a racial and ideological elite was stronger among the SS leadership than among the rank-and-file sentries, who were themselves heavily subjected to all of the harassment of military drills. For these guards, using brutal violence against defenseless prisoners was a way of venting their frustration within a tolerated framework. The camp system functioned on the basis of ideological reasoning which decreed that such excessive violence was not only justified but desirable and would therefore go unpunished. Regardless of this, the people employed in the concentration camps had been primed to a certain extent by their different life trajectories and backgrounds. This meant that they brought with them an indeterminate potential that allowed for different ways of treating the inmates. Such potential was also partially responsible for whether they would classify the prisoners – or certain prisoners – as "internal enemies" (Sofsky 1997) and take every opportunity to commit acts of violence against them. However, the widespread antisemitic consensus among them meant that, in any case, Jewish prisoners had the worst prospects for escaping abuse.

Whether they had joined the Death's Head Units voluntarily out of ideological conviction or whether they had landed among the camp SS via other recruitment channels, we can assume that they felt like a part of the SS community. They carried out tasks "important to the Reich" on different levels of the hierarchy, and the "SS kinship community" gave them a basis for identification.

2.5 Summary: A complex interrelationship

The preceding summary of the historical situation should go some way toward clarifying the way the camp system functioned, and it should place the Nazi concentration camps within a historical context. This overview has revealed that historical circumstances which were viewed by the majority of the German population as a political and social crisis paved the way for the Nazi concept of the concentration camps. Widespread frustration with the difficulties of the first German parliamentary democracy and the prevalence of a somewhat tempered antisemitism in German society created the conditions for establishing a terror regime which a substantial portion of the population initially hoped would be the solution to its problems. The various measures that promised to bring order to the confusion of the Weimar period – a confusion felt to be extremely threatening in some circles – were supported by a legal framework that made it easier for society to accept them. Legal formulations initially obscured the fact that these laws and decrees were only apparently directed solely at enemies of the state, or Jews if need be. Only the subsequent imprisonment practices made it clear that the floodgates had been opened to the wanton use of state power.

Although political decisions handed down from above had a significant influence on the establishment of the camps, a closer look shows the extent to which social developments and effects were responsible for the continued existence of these "total institutions." Despite any claims to the contrary, these camps were not hermetically sealed facilities structured exclusively by political decisions and the power of command. A certain social consensus regarding the justification for the camps, together with deliberate propaganda on the part of the regime, created the basis for widespread public knowledge that generally went far beyond merely realizing that the camps existed (Longerich 2006). The organization and management of the concentration camps linked them to the civilian environment (Benz and Distel 2005a). And the drastic rise in the number of satellite camps and outposts in the second half of the war, along with the use of prisoners as slave laborers in private companies, meant that the concentration camp system was closely intertwined with German society as a whole.

The organizational structure of the camps resulted in fierce rivalries regarding the exact jurisdiction of certain departments or offices, and dual subordination was put into practice as well. This lack of clarity encouraged the proliferation of arbitrary measures and decisions within the camps.

After being admitted to the Death's Head Units, the SS personnel and guard squads were "brought into line" by means of shared murderous practices. Both the leadership cadre and the rank-and-file enlisted personnel underwent an initiation that made them part of the "SS kinship community" into which they were literally sworn. Variations in educational level and social background were partially leveled by this second socialization, but such variations were also the reason that even the camp SS personnel were not all the same and took different approaches to the use of arbitrariness and violence.

However, this discussion of a camp system must not obscure the fact that the system was run by people, individuals who put the system into action and gave it a character which must be understood in a social context. The fact that SS members were recruited from the heart of German society and that, over the years, a large number of people were assigned to guard the prisoners shows just how much normal society was involved in the murderous practices in the camps.

Part II

Sociological Avenues of Inquiry

3

Introductory Comments on the Disciplinary Context and Methods

3.1 Empirical material and methodological approach

Now that I have introduced the issues addressed in this work and outlined their historical context, I want to explain my approach and methodology.

It is one thing to experience social practices directly but quite another to analyze them from a theoretical standpoint, even if the results approximate each other because they refer to the same social reality. In any case, credence must be given to the people who relate their real experiences and share their view of things with us – though we must then face the fact that there are always different ways of viewing the same thing depending on one's perspective. All that sociologists can do is reconstruct this complex multitude of perspectives without judging, simplifying, or taking a "scholastic point of view" which would lead them to disregard the ambivalences, "partial contradictions," and, above all, conditions influencing the agents and situations (cf. Bourdieu 1998: 127ff.) – because "[t]he simple [. . .] is never anything but the simplified" (Bourdieu 1994: 139). Therefore, in this study I have also attempted to develop a method for dealing appropriately with the ambivalences, "partial contradictions," and conditions affecting the agents.

After much consideration, I rejected my initial plan to find answers to my questions by interviewing Holocaust survivors myself. There were several reasons for this:

- First, survivors of the Holocaust are now scattered across the entire globe and are at a very advanced age, so it is difficult to track down suitable interviewees.
- Second, many of them have already had to tell their story numerous times and it has never brought them the slightest relief. Anyone who has spoken with these survivors knows just how many sleepless nights and nightmares precede and follow such interviews.
- Third, their experiences have been well documented in a wealth of

autobiographies, oral history projects, and other historical and socio-logical studies, so there is enough material available for me to pursue my research without conducting my own interviews.

• And finally, in oral interviews, the interviewer generally places certain expectations on the interviewees. Though it is not always the case, this can prompt interviewees to tailor their responses to the sus-pected research interests of the interviewer. This is precisely the effect that must be avoided at all costs, however, if the aim is to discover and depict how the interviewees (and not the interviewer) construct meaning.

All of these factors led me to seek answers to my questions in the ample autobiographical material that is already available. In my extensive reading of Holocaust literature, I discovered that such material does indeed hold the answers. In their accounts, Holocaust survivors reveal how they construct meaning, and their shrewd analysis of the social world in the Nazi concentration camps often illustrates very clearly what they believe to be the "basic concepts" of humanity and society. The dif-ficulty lay not in finding answers to my questions but in choosing which materials to use. There is such a vast body of Holocaust literature that it was absolutely necessary for me to limit the materials to analyze for this study. Since the purpose of this work is to produce exploratory findings rather than representative ones – that is, it aims at a qualitative descrip-tion and analysis of the society in the camps – the source material had to be kept to a manageable amount. To avoid the effect of temporal distor-tion that is so frequently alleged (see 3.2), I have primarily focused on accounts written not long after the former prisoners were liberated from the concentration camps. I have also looked at transcripts and videos of interviews carried out in the context of oral history projects. Many of the works now available to us were written early on but not in German (such as Antelme 1998; Borowski 1992; Delbo 1995; Levi 1995; Neurath 2005; Tillion 1975; and Vogel 2002). In these cases, I have had to rely on the German translations that were often not published until much later.

Since the questions at the heart of this work are historical in nature but my methodology involves analyzing autobiographical literature, among other things, I would like to say a few words about the disciplinary context of the study to clarify how my research fits into the field of sociol-ogy. First I will discuss some of the methodological aspects of my work that set it apart from literary or historical studies. I will look at the extent to which literature is a suitable material for analysis in sociology, as well as the particular problems posed by so-called "Holocaust literature" (3.2), and I will also formulate some thoughts about the relationship between historical scholarship and sociology to help place my work in a discipli-nary context (3.3).

In the empirical section of this book (part III), I will use the personal accounts of Holocaust survivors to identify the "basic concepts" of society that were prevalent among the prisoners in Nazi concentration camps. But prior to this, in chapter 4, I will examine the historical and social situation from a theoretical perspective using a variety of ideas stemming from Pierre Bourdieu's sociological concepts in order to develop a theoretical tool for investigating the question of society in the camps. This chapter culminates in a theoretical blueprint that should make it possible to discern the complex conflicts between various "basic concepts" of society both outside and inside the Nazi concentration camps. This blueprint will also be used as a tool to argue from a theoretical standpoint that the aspects of camp life depicted in the empirical section of the book (part III) do actually have the hallmarks of what could be called a prisoner society.

3.2 The impossibility of representing reality and the special characteristics of Holocaust literature

Today, I am not sure that what I wrote is true. I am certain it is truthful.
Charlotte Delbo (1995: 1)

The spectrum of potential objects of sociological research is broad, and the range of data that can be collected or consulted is equally large. Decisions have to be made on a case-by-case basis regarding which data are most suited to answering the questions that have been posed. First, the nature of the question must be clear: Is it a question of quantitative distribution or qualitative characteristics? In the former case, a researcher will use quantitative data collection methods and draw on selected data sources that are representative of a particular population. When it comes to qualitative characteristics, however, other methods must be employed that provide a deeper insight into the type, disposition, or consistency of the research object in question. My study clearly falls into the latter category, so qualitative methods must be used.

The questions that then arise are whether literature is an appropriate source of data for answering qualitative sociological questions and how the literary depiction of reality actually corresponds to social reality. It is also necessary to ask whether so-called Holocaust literature, usually comprising autobiographies and memoirs, can provide any information on the "basic concepts" of society and the special "rules of behavior" in the Nazi concentration camps that are the focus of this work (which thus deals with the nature of ideas and patterns of behavior). I would like to look at both of these aspects in more detail in the following.

Sociologists like Norbert Elias, Erving Goffman, and Pierre Bourdieu, to name just a few, have always drawn on literary sources to illustrate their research findings. Nonetheless, the scientific admissibility of such an approach continues to be a matter of debate in sociological circles. The key question here is whether literature is capable of making "true" statements about social reality. This brings us to the fundamental difficulty of representing reality, a difficulty that even applies to scientific findings. The problem is that reality can only ever be depicted in a mediated fashion – that is, the only way to recount findings and assessments is to use tools that evoke the intended notion of reality. This applies to literary depictions as well as other attempts to document reality, either in visual form through photographs or art, or with the help of sound, or in terms of numbers, as is usually the case in sociology. All types of data reflect specific perspectives and can only illuminate particular facets of reality; as a consequence, such data must not be mistaken for social reality itself.[1]

Unlike the study of art or literature, however, sociology is emphatically concerned with the question of the reality behind the data – regardless of the specific nature of those data – because sociologists want to be able to say something about real social relations. Whatever the methodology, attempts to explain such relations from a sociological viewpoint are always constructivist and synthesizing undertakings in that they draw connections between apparently disparate elements (Kuzmics and Mozetič 2003: 298). All scientific approximations of reality are generated using specific categories, experiential filters, and relevance criteria (ibid.: 119) which constitute theoretically charged selection models. We also must not be deceived by mathematically quantifiable results, because even in a purely quantitative survey the underlying questions and design of the study will have been shaped by presuppositions that assume certain connections exist between elements.

The study at hand draws on historical scholarship based on source material analysis, which conveys relatively assured facts, but it also makes use of a large number of memoirs and autobiographical accounts, some of which have strong literary leanings. In light of this, some consideration needs to be given to the applicability of literary materials in sociological research.

The sociology of literature is of little help to us here, as this field is concerned primarily with literary production – that is, the market, the methods of production and reception, and the authors' social origins and environment. Within this field, literature itself is viewed as a symptom of social developments and serves as the basis for social analyses (cf. ibid.: 35ff.).

In their 2003 study entitled *Literatur als Soziologie* (Literature as Sociology), Helmut Kuzmics und Gerald Mozetič systematically examine the suitability of literature as a source of data for sociological research – and they argue fervently in favor of its use. They mention three sociologically relevant functions of literature (ibid.: 26ff.):

- as an illustration of findings obtained by other means, where concrete, vivid literary depictions serve to describe what has already been proven sociologically;
- as a source of evidence for how the social sphere permeates the private sphere and as an indication of values and attitudes;
- as an analytic description and interpretation of the social world using literary means.

The illustrative function needs no further examination in this context, but the function of literature as a source material and analytical tool must be explained in more detail.

The value of literature as a source material (ibid.: 29ff.) is all the greater when there are few original, contemporary sources available; this seems to be the case most often when it comes to emotions and subjective evaluations (cf. ibid.: 30). "Those who take a fundamentally positive view of the sociological quality of literature as a source material seem to agree that psychological processes above all – a person's world-view, their experiences and feelings – are often described very precisely in literature" (ibid.: 31). While historical sources supply detailed information about specific events ("*Who* did *what* to *whom, when,* and *where*?"), literary treatments of the same events can provide a deeper insight into personal evaluations of the facts and into individual or socially prevalent attitudes. In order to assess such information sociologically, "it is evident that other sources must be consulted as well, [. . .] including sources that contrast factual knowledge with novelistic fiction" (ibid.: 117). "Acknowledging the constructivist character of every observation" – even scientific observations – "[. . .] does not imply arbitrariness because observations can always be subjected to an intersubjectivity test" (ibid.: 110).

Consequently, in a sociological analysis, the facts must be ascertained so that the information gleaned from literature about the world-view, experiences, feelings, values, and attitudes of individuals can be placed in a social context. Literature can therefore be a helpful supplemental tool when sociologists have difficulty finding the corresponding information by other means. By revealing how actualities affect everyday life, literature opens up important perspectives to sociology that would otherwise be difficult to detect (ibid.: 121). This makes it possible to take a synthesizing, sociological approach to explaining coexistent aspects that are apparently disparate and unconnected (ibid.: 298) even though they are extremely significant to the social agents involved.

However, literary texts can only contribute to sociological findings if they are analyzed with a sociological eye (ibid.: 293), because the discovery of an "analytically valuable description and treatment of social life" in literature "depends [. . .] ultimately on the current state of knowledge in sociology" (ibid.: 27).

Literature can also be a significant source of sociological data in terms of the analytical descriptions and interpretations of social life contained within it (ibid.: 32ff.). Even fiction can provide a deep and convincing insight into mindsets and emotional states through the analytical description of constraints and plights, for example (ibid.: 288). "Fiction can [. . .] claim *narrative* verisimilitude [. . .]. Even the most fantastic tales suggest finely wrought judgments of the relations between the individual and the collectivity" (Régnier-Bohler 1988: 313; emphasis in original). While sociology is responsible for constructing theoretical concepts, literature can certainly contain theoretically rich descriptions that counteract mainstream sociology's "decontextualization" and "quantifying operationalization" – and the accompanying "disregard for conditions" (Kuzmics and Mozetič 2003: 290) and "academic desiccation of reality" (Elias 1996: 45). "Sociology does not have a monopoly on sharp views of the social world or reflective competence" (Kuzmics and Mozetič 2003: 34), and even overstatement and exaggeration can sometimes be acceptable ways of conveying a situation. "In visual terms, if a face is painted particularly luridly or is lit 'unnaturally' brightly, this draws attention to certain features that would otherwise be lost in the pallor of endless facts and figures" (ibid.: 290). Kuzmics and Mozetič emphasize "the opportunities offered by a holistic, synthesizing interpretation of literary works when such works deal with typical aspects of society in much the same way that sociology itself does" (ibid.: 297). To take advantage of these opportunities, however, the works must be "interpreted contextually and interrelated with other sources, data and interpretations" (ibid.: 293).

> The strength [of literature] is that it illustrates the things that scientific works generally only refer to in terms of concepts or numbers which give no indication of their significance in everyday life. [. . .] At the least, it should be acknowledged that literature has a dual cognitive function. First, literature is a valuable aid in cases where sociology has access to or can produce only little or no data. [. . .] Second, literary works often feature ideal-typical models that can be useful for a differentiated analysis of social constellations. (Ibid.: 120–1)

In terms of Bourdieu's theoretical concepts, which will be explained in more detail later, this means that even fictional literature can contain detailed descriptions of the implicit "conditions of possibility" (Bourdieu 1991a: 1) that actually exist for the types of people depicted.

At this point it is necessary to say a few words about the special nature of autobiographical works, which are clearly not pieces of fiction but rather texts that are attempting to reconstruct reality.[2] Does what was said earlier about the informative value of literary works in general also apply to the reality depicted in autobiographical works? Fiction is replaced by construction in autobiographical literature, meaning that actual events are filtered through personal perceptions and experiences, and the connections that are made in this way have both an individual slant – resulting from one's social position – and a societal one. There is therefore a social distortion factor that affects one's view of events and influences the written depiction of these events by encouraging the use of a particular narrative strategy. This narrative strategy, in turn, incorporates "culturally composed and socially acquired rules" for recounting events (Jureit 1998: 28). The task of the work at hand is thus to identify these "socially and historically motivated concepts of the social world" (Christin 2005: 205) in the former prisoners' autobiographies in order to find out something about the inmates' world of meaning.

The elapsed time between having an experience and writing about it is often viewed as another problematic distortion factor when it comes to the authenticity of autobiographical works. However, memory research has shown that "temporal proximity to a recounted event is not as decisive a factor as the individual's powers of perception at the time of the event and the significance that is attributed to one's personal experiences" (Jureit 1998: 6). The autobiographical construction of meaning therefore entails truths that are "personally authentic but not factually accurate in the conventional sense" (ibid.: 17). But the approach to fictional literature described earlier can also be applied to this personal construction of meaning: A witness, who is a real person with a concrete social position, develops a social perspective that intrinsically encompasses the implicit "conditions of possibility" (Bourdieu 1991a: 1) of the real world. Because "a person's reservoir of experience [. . .] is both individual and collective, conscious and unconscious" (Jureit 1998: 20), an individual will reproduce values and attitudes that actually exist in society. The analytical descriptions in autobiographical literature can therefore also be consulted as reflexive analyses of the social world in the way that Kuzmics and Mozetič propose (2003: 120f.).

So-called Holocaust literature is a special genre in that it is classified according to its particular subject matter – the Holocaust[3] – and not according to literary criteria. In the following, the term Holocaust literature will be used to describe works that address the experience of Nazi persecution in the form of diaries, date books, memoirs, and prose or poems. For the purposes of my study, this includes the first systematic scholarly analyses by former concentration camp prisoners, such as Paul Martin Neurath's 1943 dissertation (2005) or the report by Eugen Kogon[4] that was written in 1945 and published in 1946 (Kogon 2006). What it does not include, however, are the numerous academic and scholarly publications by third parties – that is, people who did not experience the Holocaust "first hand." There is no question that this latter type of scholarly literature from various disciplines is essential for presenting the current state of research, but it cannot claim the same type of authenticity as the former texts.

The problem of depicting reality takes on new dimensions in view of the crimes committed by the Nazis, which generally surpass our ability to comprehend them. Although many of these crimes have been exposed and reconstructed through historical research, they still seem beyond belief in a way. It is no surprise that doubts are often expressed about whether such a terrible reality can be depicted at all, and Holocaust survivors in particular frequently begin their accounts by saying that the horror is actually "unspeakable" (Pollak 1988). This acknowledgment of the inadequacy of language is all the more understandable considering the radical and singular nature of these crimes. In essence, though, this relates back to the problem addressed earlier in this section – but considering the abysmal depths of human thought and action that are associated with the subject, it seems inappropriate to let this laconic remark stand without further explanation. I therefore want to look at the particular problems of Holocaust literature in more detail, especially in terms of the justified question of whether this genre of literature can or should be used as a source of data and object of analysis like the other types of literature mentioned earlier.

In the wake of the Holocaust – and, to a certain extent, even in the midst of it – so much literature was produced that it is now impossible to maintain an overview of it. "The extent of the persistent effort on the part of so many to articulate the Holocaust itself testifies to the magnitude of the event and emphasizes our common need to bring it under whatever control continued reflection may afford" (Rosenfeld 1980: 4), and "more than a dozen books by Elie Wiesel alone have now told us that the Holocaust demands speech even as it threatens to impose silence" (ibid.: 14).

Holocaust literature occupies an area of tension between the apparent inadequacy of language for expressing such events and experiences and the inescapable need to tell as much as possible and to bear witness. The crimes of the Nazis, which were of such a scale and severity that many accounts and studies classify them as "breaches of civilization" and a "return to barbarism," are responsible for "fundamental changes in our modes of perception and expression" (ibid.: 12).

But these previously unthinkable acts of violence were first made possible by civilization's progress and achievements, which gave rise to the means and opportunities for simplifying and accelerating the systematic process of extermination. The realization that civilization's innovations could be turned against humans and humanity was not entirely new, as "wars of expulsion and extermination aimed at systematically destroying the very foundations of enemy societies were first experienced during the colonial adventures in the early years of the German Empire" (Wüllenkemper 2007). The destructive potential of modern thought and civilizational expansion had therefore reached the European continent long before, when the "cultural potential for violence was taken from the colonial empires to European battlefields" (ibid.) in a world war involving the latest technologies.

Nonetheless, the extent and specific quality of the cruelties meted out by the Nazis made them appear, to those who suffered under them, to be the very end of humanity. "If one can talk about such a thing as a phenomenology of Holocaust literature, it would have to be in terms of this contradiction between the impossibility but also the necessity of writing about the death of the idea of man in order to sustain that idea" (Rosenfeld 1980: 8). The authors of all of these accounts and memoirs thus face the problem of finding ways to express the contradiction between, on the one hand, feeling completely stripped of humanity and debased and, on the other, simultaneously documenting that, despite everything, "the idea of man" could never really be destroyed. The authors therefore try to portray their own internal "diminishment" in this terrible situation and express the "silencing power" (ibid.: 11) in words. Writing is often viewed as "a last-ditch means of approximating and preserving the human in the face of a viciousness poised to destroy it" (ibid.: 13). "Concentration camp experiences are boundary experiences in a dual sense: experiences on the boundary of what is possible and thus on the boundary of what is speakable" (Pollak 1988: 89). When one has lived through this terrible reality, a type of language is needed that can equally express both the real events and the subjective experience of them as well as the psychological deterioration and torpor in the face of such boundless horror. In this conflict of needs, the metaphor of "unspeakability" appears to be a suitable tool for at least hinting at a suffering that is difficult to comprehend but was actually experienced.

"Every statement about the concentration camps is influenced by the recollection of facts as well as by one's own self-concept" (Pollak 1988: 89), though this self-concept was under severe attack in the camps and was therefore subject to negotiation. It is precisely this subjective depiction of an experience that provides an insight into the former prisoners' world of meaning. To use Neurath's terminology, the "basic concepts" of society apparently continued to play a rudimentary role within this world of meaning and should therefore be discernible through systematic analysis. A few special features of this genre of literature must be taken into account, however, if we want to develop "the kind of practical criticism that will allow us to read, interpret, and evaluate Holocaust literature with any precision or confidence" (Rosenfeld 1980: 19). One of the peculiarities of Holocaust literature is that the authors often introduce analogies only to expose their inadequacy and reject them (ibid.:21). Furthermore, linguistic devices used to depict events are generally not meant metaphorically but instead describe exactly what they refer to. "This, we are told, is what happened. It has no symbolic dimensions, carries no allegorical weight, possesses no apparent or covert meaning" (ibid.: 24). The only meaning behind the words is that this actually happened *in this way*. To portray the abysmal emotional depths that they felt in the face of this reality, however, the authors often draw on literary models and allusions that they assume their readers will be familiar with, understand, and relate to emotionally (ibid.: 29ff.). In his book *A Double Dying* (1980), Alvin Rosenfeld mentions the images of hell (ibid.: 29) that are frequently used to evoke visions of horror without the need for further explanation. Another type of example is Chaim Kaplan's use of Psalm 121, which reads "he that keeps Israel shall neither slumber nor sleep," but which Kaplan modifies to read "the enemy of Israel neither sleeps nor slumbers" (quoted in ibid.: 30), a change which, in a single blow, turns the certainty of divine protection in the original line into its exact opposite.

So while analogies are introduced in Holocaust literature just to be rejected, familiar literary models are generally used to express the reverse of what was originally intended. "Christianity's distinctive contribution" (ibid.: 29), however, appears to be limited to providing images of hell.

Holocaust literature is very clear on another point as well:

> No one touched by the Holocaust is ever whole again [. . .]. The Holocaust has worked on its authors in a double way, then, simultaneously disabling them and enlarging their vision, so that they see with an almost prophetic exactness. Holocaust writers, in short, are one-eyed seers, men possessed of a double knowledge: cursed into knowing how perverse the human being can be to create such barbarism and blessed by knowing how strong he can be to survive it. (Ibid.: 32)

Though many examples of this literature may appear to be "records of despair," such writing can serve, "at its best, to discover reflexes of assertiveness" (ibid.: 187). And the "sharpened senses," the heightened individual powers of perception at the time of the experience (Jureit 1998: 6), make the written recollections of Holocaust survivors an important source of data for my analysis.

Rosenfeld also comes to the conclusion that works of Holocaust literature are representative expressions of a collective fate and that we should therefore turn our attention to the "collective voices rather than to more isolated instances of expressive genius" (Rosenfeld 1980: 34).

To supplement the facts established by historians, Holocaust literature reveals something about values and attitudes through its "ideal-typical models" (Kuzmics and Mozetič 2003: 120). Analytical descriptions and interpretations of the social reality in the Nazi concentration camps can give us an insight into the viewpoints of the people imprisoned there. But to gain this insight, we have to take the observations and shrewd analyses of the authors very seriously (ibid.: 300), because their reflexivity is an integral and indispensable component of the sociological study of camp society that is the focus of the work at hand.

With its clear descriptions and analyses of the social world in the camps and its illumination of the values and attitudes (cf. ibid.) of the prisoners held there, Holocaust literature can provide answers to the questions of the "basic concepts" of society and the special "rules of behavior" in the Nazi concentration camps – answers that would otherwise be unobtainable today, over sixty years after the end of the Nazis' reign of terror.

3.3 The relationship between historical scholarship and sociology

Sociologists and historians each see the mote in their neighbour's eye. Unfortunately, each group tends to perceive the other in terms of a rather crude stereotype.

Peter Burke (2005: 2)

My study of what the "basic concepts" of society meant to the prisoners in Nazi concentration camps is concerned with matters of recent history. It thus seems reasonable to ask whether this is "actually" a historical study and not a sociological one. It is especially important to address this issue explicitly because the relationship between history and sociology has been a matter of ongoing debate and continues to be conflicted, even though the fields have converged on similar objects of research (cf. Burke 2005: 16). The contrast between the two disciplines is often painted in broad strokes, so in the following I will attempt to briefly explain my own position, which focuses more on disciplinary nuances within a shared scholarly interest in the same object of research.

British historian Peter Burke sums up the smoldering animosity between historians and sociologists as follows:

[Some] historians still regard sociologists as people who state the obvious in a barbarous and abstract jargon, lack any sense of place and time, squeeze individuals without mercy into rigid categories, and, to cap it all, describe these activities as "scientific". Sociologists, for their part, have traditionally viewed historians as amateurish, myopic fact-collectors without system, method or theory, the imprecision of their "data base" matched only by their incapacity to analyse it. [. . .] Their conversation [between historians and sociologists], as the French historian Fernand Braudel [. . .] once put it, has often been "a dialogue of the deaf". (Burke 2005: 2–3)

French sociologist Pierre Bourdieu also remarked on the disciplinary differences between history and sociology a number of times (cf. Bourdieu 2004). For instance, he says: "Historians have always paid the utmost attention to the distinctiveness of historical events and harbored an active distrust of generalization, not least on account of the danger of anachronism, which includes the unforeseen transference of words and concepts from their source area" (ibid.: 119). However, Bourdieu believes the roots of the "deep" discrepancies between historians and sociologists can be found in the differences between the "tradition" and "composition" of the two disciplines (ibid.: 194). "The *social* barriers between the disciplines appear to be very strong, as does the need for historians and sociologists to distance themselves from one another, even though the list of shared research methods, tools and problems is long enough to form the basis for more intensive interaction" (ibid.: 99; emphasis added). The different ways in which the fields approach the use of sources and theories lies at the heart of these "social barriers." From the perspective of historiography, sources are the "core" of all scholarly work (Freytag and Piereth 2004: 45; cf. also Beaufaÿs 2003: 128f.) and are considered to be the very "foundation of historical knowledge" (Wolbring 2006). In a frequently cited essay, historian Reinhart Koselleck (1977: 45) called for source materials to be granted a "veto right" ("*Vetorecht,*" quoted in Freytag and Piereth 2004: 104) that would prevent historians from making false statements. The sociological counterargument is that the notion of a "'veto right' on the strength of the source materials" conveys the impression that

> sources speak for themselves and incorporate their own instruction manuals. [. . .] You cannot avoid anachronism simply by clinging to the captivating discourse of the historical agents themselves and acting as if you believe they are telling the truth about the world they lived in, while at the same time forgoing the conceptual tools which could illuminate the classification struggles of which they are a product. (Christin 2005: 201)

So while historians view "relics" and "traditions" as their main sources of data and strive to reconstruct the past (Faber and Geiss 1992: 82), sociologists usually generate their own data by conducting surveys. When sociologists address a historical subject, they generally do not draw on the primary sources considered by historians to be "authentic" (ibid.: 84) but instead use the research of historians as their empirical basis (Schützeichel 2004: 14). Viewed from this perspective, sociology would appear to be a "second-tier science" (Simmel quoted in ibid.: 14). While historical scholarship has the universally and socially recognized function of bearing responsibility for what has been (Bourdieu 2004: 76), sociology faces the accusation that "the singularity, specificity and empirical wealth of historical subjects are lost when they are put through the sociological wringer" (Schützeichel 2004: 14).

From a sociological standpoint, by contrast, the "social barrier" (Bourdieu 2004: 99) is rooted in differing approaches to theory, because sociologists "feel more compelled than historians to produce concepts and theories" (ibid.: 105). "Sociology accuses history of theoretical abstinence and source material positivism. Historical scholarship is said to rely on theories imported from sociology and is considered theoretically inferior" (Schützeichel 2004: 14). Most historians are characterized has having a "nearly atavistic distrust of theory" (cf. Daniele Roche and Christophe Charle quoted in Christin 2005: 196, footnote 3).

The ferocity of the debate between representatives of these two academic disciplines reveals that the argument is about much more than just methodology – it is clearly about the position and significance of the disciplines in the field of social sciences, within which history and sociology fight for social influence. History and sociology are supposedly in contradiction because history believes itself to be hermeneutical in that it engages in inductive, source-driven empiricism aimed at an event-oriented, diachronic perspective, while sociology engages in the theory-driven, synchronous analysis of structures with the aim of a deductive-explanatory depiction of the general or typical based on data (cf. ibid.: 196; Schützeichel 2004: 13). However, these alleged contradictions are called into doubt by the wealth of historical and sociological research which makes use of methods and perspectives attributed to the other side.

> The story of the relationship between history and sociology is one of trials and tribulations. Prominent representatives of both sides stress that, despite what the "guardians" on either side say about the apparent opposition of the two fields, there is no methodological or theoretical basis for separating the disciplines. But in academic practice itself, different styles of scholarship have emerged which mean that the disciplines rarely speak the same language.[5] (Schützeichel 2004: 19)

In my opinion, a scholarly work should be attributed to one of these two academic disciplines not on the basis of its object of research, but on the basis of its style of research and presentation. Beyond such unedifying disciplinary declarations of position, the works of Max Weber – a scholar held in equally high esteem on both sides – can "at least teach historians the art of asking 'universal' questions in light of individual objects (and constructing their object accordingly), while sociologists – who are more ambitious and arrogant on account of their position – can learn to ask their universal questions in light of concrete case studies" (Bourdieu 2004: 23). As just such a "concrete case study," the work at hand draws on literary sources to examine a historical subject – but in the types of questions it poses and the way it attempts to answer them, it pursues interests that are generally considered sociological. Class, gender and "ethnicity" are taken to be elemental social structural characteristics in the field of sociology, so asking what these "basic concepts" of society meant to the prisoners in Nazi concentration camps can be viewed as a genuine sociological undertaking. By the same token, investigating how these social differentiation concepts shape society – in other words, identifying the complex and far-reaching effects of values and attitudes – can also be considered a traditionally sociological pursuit.

4

Sociological Orientations

It may surprise you to know that I consider myself an eclectic author, but also a reflective eclectic. Drawing on a variety of sources is not incompatible with the demand for theoretical coherence within a field. [. . .] "Eclectic" does not just mean adopting things randomly; as the word itself suggests, it involves choosing, adopting, but in a selective way.

Pierre Bourdieu (2004: 138)

The question of what the "basic concepts" of society entailed in the special case of the concentration camps appears straightforward, but it harbors a complex set of problems that demand a nuanced approach. Since my research question combines the topics of *concentration camps* and *society*, there are also multiple dimensions to the sociological orientation required here. Several conceptual tools will be needed to do justice to the complexity of the subject at hand and to examine individual aspects – particularly those relating to the specific characteristics of the concentration camps – in more detail than would be possible with a single theoretical concept. However, it does not seem sensible to employ numerous sweeping theories in parallel, and I believe that the key question of the "basic concepts" of society should be the guiding factor in choosing a dominant theoretical concept. In the following, therefore, I will explain why I have opted for the sociological concepts of Pierre Bourdieu (4.1) and which other theoretical tools I will use to explore the "basic concepts" of society (4.2) and the situation in the Nazi concentration camps (4.3). At the end of this chapter and thus the introductory portion of this work, I will pull these individual aspects together to present a theoretical perspective on the society of the "Third Reich" and the Nazi concentration camps (4.4).

4.1 Preliminary remarks: The sociology of Pierre Bourdieu and the use of other central theoretical ideas

[I]s it really all or nothing? Do you have to choose between Bourdieu and everyone else? Is that compatible with Foucault, etc.? This question is almost insulting. I am an eclectic and I demand that my work be used in an eclectic way – which is not to say that I would be satisfied for someone to take what I do and make something arbitrary out of it.

Pierre Bourdieu (2004: 140)

Pierre Bourdieu[1] developed a set of theoretical analytical tools for the field of sociology that enable us to examine how society functions in special circumstances and to compare "'realities' that are very different on a phenomenal level" (Bourdieu 2004: 117). "The social space has always been diversified" (ibid.: 87), so his conceptual constructs make it possible to "increase the explanatory power" of an analysis "without losing any of the historical singularity of the objects being examined" (ibid.: 118). This means that despite the terrible reality in the Nazi concentration camps, the study at hand can identify general characteristics by analyzing a specific situation – as Zygmunt Bauman argues (1989: 12) – and thus lend support to the view that the attempts by the SS to dehumanize the concentration camp prisoners ultimately failed (cf. Suderland 2004).

For Bourdieu, "concepts, ideas and patterns of thought [. . .] [were] – often practical – principles of scientific activity. Those that [Bourdieu] attempted to coin himself – even in the case of the apparently most abstract concepts like habitus, field and cultural capital – are synthetic and synoptic expressions for condensing research programs and scientific orientations" (Bourdieu 2004: 135). Concepts, to Bourdieu, are "simply tools for drawing out the questions that one might otherwise fail to ask, they are tools for the construction of the object" (ibid.: 141). With regard to the issues addressed in this study, Bourdieu's tools are what make it *possible* to ask whether there is a correspondence between the "basic concepts" of society outside and inside the concentration camps, even though many historical facts would prompt us to view the world of the camps entirely differently – namely, as more of a counterworld in which social rules no longer seem to apply.

Bourdieu always insisted that society exists in two forms: "It exists as objectivity, in the form of social structures and mechanisms [. . .] and it also exists in the minds, in the individuals, it exists in an individual, incorporated state. The socialized biological individual is the individual social entity" (Bourdieu 2004: 78). This creed of social complexity is also reflected in Bourdieu's socio-theoretical concepts: On the one hand, the different types of capital are a representation of social differentiation in practice, but, on the other, they are also tools for analyzing the "social space." They are linked to individuals in the form of "economic," "cultural," and "social capital," and can sometimes – but not always, and often only by means of hidden strategies – be passed on to others or converted into other types of capital (cf. Bourdieu 1984, 1986, 1998). On the level of action, the types of capital act as symbolic distinction criteria in the social "space of lifestyles" (cf. Bourdieu 1984, 1998) and are therefore also known as "symbolic capital" (cf. Bourdieu 1985, 1998). Functionally defined segments of the social space where individuals compete for positions (of power) are referred to as "social fields" (cf. Bourdieu 1993a; Bourdieu and Wacquant 1992). These social fields are shaped by institutions that are, in turn, countered by the "habitus" of the agents, which, as "the social made body" (Bourdieu in Bourdieu and Wacquant 1992: 127), influences the individuals' strategies for action (cf. Bourdieu 1998, 2000d). Cognitive structures are thus incorporated in individuals and adapted to the structures of the world. At the same time, however, individuals influence the real world through their own actions and thus shape the world's structures (cf. Bourdieu 2004).

This mutual conditionality found throughout Bourdieu's work is an attempt to move beyond the traditional dichotomies of conventional sociological concepts. It aims to reveal the "logic of practice" (cf. Bourdieu 1990, 2000b), which is a practical logic of the agents that pursues its own "economy" and "strategy" – with no regard for the "scholastic" efforts of sociological thinkers who want to impose the logic of their own analytical, scientific viewpoint on the real-life agents (cf. Bourdieu 2004). "Sociology has to include a sociology of the perception of the social world, that is, a sociology of the construction of the *world-views* which themselves contribute to the construction of this world" (Bourdieu 1994: 130; emphasis added). To answer the question of whether the "basic concepts" of society remained in effect in the Nazi concentration camps, it will be necessary to show that the "social space" of the concentration camps was shaped by structures that roughly corresponded to those of the "social space" of society at the time, and that the prisoners themselves – through their incorporation of the social, their "habitus" – were agents who reproduced their view of the "basic concepts" of society in this social space by adjusting their behavior to the special conditions in the concentration camps.

Bourdieu himself emphasizes that it is necessary to "try to implement the conceptual integration characteristic of any advanced science" (Bourdieu 2004: 139). This further encourages me to implement theoretical concepts from other sources alongside Bourdieu's concepts in order to identify certain social structures that are important to the research question at hand and to gain a more precise understanding of the special characteristics of the concentration camps.[2]

Bourdieu's tools supply the bulk of what is necessary to investigate the "basic concepts" of society. The mutual conditionality between individuals and society as well as social differentiation based on class and gender can both be analyzed using Bourdieu's concepts. There is a limit, however. To the best of my knowledge, Bourdieu never specifically dealt with the special question of how racism and antisemitism work.[3] The unique aspects of this cannot be explained using the concept of the "social space" or of "social fields," and differentiation based on class and gender also fails to touch on the distinctiveness of the type of biologistic, racist thought and action that were prevalent in the "Third Reich." We therefore lack a suitable conceptual tool for analyzing this. But the special treatment of Jews and "Gypsies"[4] played an important and unique role in the society of the "Third Reich" and its "*völkisch*" ideology as well as inside the concentration camps, so one can surmise that the "basic concepts" of society include an additional type of differentiation beyond class and gender that covers this aspect. At first glance, the term "ethnic group" would seem apt for representing the special way in which Jews and "Gypsies" were treated.[5] However, this term unacceptably reproduces racist Nazi ideas that imply a shared genetic heritage, and it thus cannot be used here without further reflection. Furthermore, on the basis of their racist ideology, the Nazis took very different approaches to dealing with different "races," with Jews and "Gypsies" occupying their own special position among the "races" considered to be "inferior."[6] To address this particular issue, I will explain some of the problems with the concept of "ethnic groups" and then turn to the work of Max Weber, who dealt with precisely this phenomenon – though in a somewhat incidental manner – by introducing the concept of caste (Weber 1978).

Irrespective of Bourdieu's concepts, which can help to show how individuals and society mutually constitute each other, perspectives on the relationship between the individual and society have changed over time. As will be explained in more detail later, within the Nazi dictatorship – and thus within German society under the Nazis – there were historically based, opposing views of the ideal relationship between the individual and society which had massive and conflicting effects on people's real lives. Bourdieu argues that reconstructing the world-views shaped by the perception of the social world is essential to reflexive sociology, and this must be taken into account in the study at hand if we want to discern the tremendous potential for conflict within the society of the "Third Reich." In order to incorporate this aspect into my study, I will turn to the writings of Louis Dumont (1992), who has taken an ideal-typical approach to the examination of how views of the relationship between the individual and society have changed throughout history.

Bourdieu's concepts, particularly that of the habitus, can be used above all to show that the social is deeply embedded in both the human mind (cognitive) and body (incorporated), so people always contribute individually to the creation of society through their thoughts and actions – and this even applies to the special situation in the concentration camps.

However, it is difficult to account for the special characteristics of concentration camps, in all of their lethality, using concepts from a generalized and wide-ranging theory of society. What are these special characteristics? First, there is the omnipresent violence resulting from the excessive and public use of torture. The theories of Michel Foucault (1995) provide the basis for considering this aspect in more detail. Then there is the fact that the people in the camps were held there under duress and were forced to live together under the constant threat of violence. Erving Goffman thoroughly explores this issue in his book *Asylums* (1961), in which he introduces the term "total institutions." And finally, there is the often fierce will to survive on the part of the prisoners, a will which was frequently expressed in the face of this constant danger by means of cultural practices (Suderland 2004). Zygmunt Bauman's concept of culture (1992) opens up a perspective on this special dimension of cultural activity.

In the following, I will first introduce the main points of the "basic concepts" of society from Bourdieu's perspective, supplemented with ideas from other sociologists where necessary (4.2). The subsequent section (4.3) will focus on the special theoretical approach to examining the unique characteristics of the concentration camps.

4.2 The "basic concepts" of society

Every society we know of has fundamentally similar criteria for social differentiation. There is vertical differentiation, or social ranking, which can be expressed in different ways – through notions of class or caste, for example – depending on the part of the world and the period of history, and there is also gender differentiation, where physical, biological characteristics are the determining factor for social classification.[7] These two social determinants – rank and gender – largely inform the internal structure of every known society, regardless of whether the social framework is simple or complex, egalitarian or hierarchical. In societies without a complex division of labor, structures are cemented by clearly defined institutions, and social affiliations are explicit and made apparent to those who belong to them by means of symbolic identifiers. In complex societies, by contrast, the structures and affiliations are not always so easy to recognize or explain. Distinctions are more likely to be discerned on the basis of hidden modes of action; there may be something like social mobility, and social relations may have lost some of their unambiguousness. Even in apparently egalitarian social systems, the social reality falls far short of equality, and social positions endowed with more or less power will be valued differently.

The two types of social differentiation mentioned above – gender and class – therefore play a formative and effective role in all societies, even when their symbolic encoding lacks the obvious, clearly declared identifying character found in traditional societies, and even when the society's propagated ideology assumes that all individuals are equal.

Most societies also feature birth-related differentiation criteria, such as affiliation based on the idea of genetic encoding or kinship, which are important for establishing external boundaries, identifying outsiders, and defining what constitutes a "people," "clan," "race," "ethnicity," or sometimes even a "nation."[8]

Regardless of what form the social ranking or gender-related assignment of tasks takes in a particular society, both structural characteristics are also used in modern Westernized societies to define the relationship between each member and the whole – that is, between the individual and society[9] – because these individual designations are also viewed as social duties.

These "basic concepts" of society, which influence how people *perceive* their social world, manifest themselves as concrete individual viewpoints and help determine whether certain behaviors or attributes are considered to be appropriate to each person's social position. They heavily influence one's perception of oneself and others. In Bourdieu's terms, these structural characteristics are incorporated in such a way that they preconsciously shape a person's thoughts and actions and thus appear almost natural. Therefore, it is not very surprising that in the recollections of Holocaust survivors, these social structural characteristics play a key role in fostering a sense of identity when it comes to the subject of human dignity. The concepts of social position and clear gender affiliation are viewed as genuinely human attributes, and the Nazis' attempt to rob certain individuals of these attributes for ideological reasons using various means is rejected as an inhumane act by the individuals in question. While these structural features are not usually addressed in an analytical way in the recollections of Holocaust survivors as they would be in a scientific study, they are, by their nature, always present and form the bedrock of the arguments found in these writings.

In the following, I will attempt to paint a picture of the fundamental ideas about the relationship between the individual and society and the meaning of class and gender against the backdrop of the "Third Reich" and the Nazi concentration camps. A discussion of the term *caste* will help to explain the way in which Jews and "Gypsies" were commonly dealt with in society at the time. In the empirical section of this study (part III), it should then be possible to discern these structural features in the thoughts and actions of the concentration camp prisoners and explore the role they played in maintaining human dignity.

4.2.1 Individuals and society: Views of a complex relationship

"[T]he world encompasses me but I understand it." Social reality exists, so to speak, twice, [. . .] outside and inside of agents.
        Pierre Bourdieu (in Bourdieu and Wacquant 1992: 127)

Sociology has traditionally taken the view that the concepts of the individual and of society must be analyzed separately and that a certain antagonism has to be revealed between the two forces. For example, role theory looks at this apparent conflict from the worm's-eye view of the individual, while system theory takes a bird's-eye view – or the "church-steeple perspective," as Norbert Elias calls it (cf. Elias 2000: 467) – in its analysis of key social relations. In both cases, the objects of the analysis are viewed as static entities instead of processes. One problem with this is that the physical agents get theoretically lost and mutate into "disembodied spirits" (cf. Krais 2004: 193) representing the idea of autonomous individuals – though there is no empirical basis for this in actual social practice.

In the postscript to the revised edition of his book *The Civilizing Process* (Elias 2000: 449ff.), Norbert Elias thoroughly criticizes what he believes are ideologically influenced perspectives on individuals and society which view either "the free individual" or "society as a whole, the nation," as "the highest value" (ibid.: 469). "This split in the ideals, this contradiction in the ethos by which people are brought up" (ibid.), finds its way into sociological theories, leads to blind spots, and makes it difficult to view people from a dual perspective (cf. ibid.: 468).

> It can be stated with great certainty that the relation between what is referred to conceptually as the "individual" and as "society" will remain incomprehensible so long as these concepts are used as if they represented two *separate* bodies, and (above all) bodies normally at rest, which only come into contact with one another afterwards as it were. (Ibid.: 455–6; emphasis added)

In the Western world, the view of the individual as an autonomous being can be traced back to Descartes, among others, whose realization *"cogito ergo sum"* in the first half of the seventeenth century laid the cornerstone for the self-certitude of human thought.

According to Louis Dumont, the idea of individualism actually has its roots in the foundation of the Protestant faith, in which "the Christian is an 'individual-in-relation-to-God'" (Dumont 1992: 30) and is therefore self-sufficient (cf. ibid.: 59). This "inworldly individual" no longer needs the church as an "institute of salvation" (ibid.) because he or she is in a continual direct dialog with his or her God.

If the Reformation paved the way for a type of "introverted individualism" (ibid.: 153), the more recent manifestation of this view of humanity can ultimately be attributed to the Enlightenment, which formulated the ideal of freedom from state paternalism and led to "extraverted individualism" (ibid.). However, in connection with this, Jean-Claude Kaufmann points out the significance of state paternalism, which he views as a prime motivator in the construction of identity. The emergence of the concept of the individual and the individual's release from conventional ties resulted in tighter social controls by the state (Kaufmann 2005: 64). Kaufmann therefore concludes "that identity [. . .] results from a very precise, clearly delimited [. . .] process that can be exactly historically dated" (ibid.: 12–13). The need to more carefully control and precisely identify people who had been freed from previously existent social ties – particularly migrant workers, the poorest of the poor – led to the creation of employment records in France in 1781, the precursor to identification cards. These were a prerequisite for being hired by a company; like passports, they held the official visas that were required if someone moved from one town to another; and debts were also recorded in them (ibid.: 21f.). These measures, together with the right to life and liberty that was legally accorded to each person (Taylor 1992: 12), create the perception of an individual who is always in a position to make decisions autonomously. Objectively there seems to be a choice between different options, even though some of these options are more likely to be chosen than others. "From the standpoint of the individual making the choice, what counts is not the objective feasibility of an identity but rather the individual's own notion of what is feasible" (Kaufmann 2005: 102). The dissolution of conventional social structures in the wake of the French Revolution, the effects of which eventually spread beyond Europe to the entire world, made it necessary to search for new types of social affiliations (ibid.: 28f.). The invention of individual identity can be understood as a reaction to the liberation of individuals from relations that had seemed firmly set – a type of liberation which enabled ongoing intervention by the authorities while also giving individuals the impression that they could choose their affiliations freely. The necessary sense of "identity is a permanent invention forged from non-invented materials" (ibid.: 106).

The ideal of the autonomous individual is therefore closely coupled with the idea of individual identity, something which is extremely important in the context of the issues explored in this study. Because the concentration camp prisoners perceived themselves to be fundamentally autonomous individuals with a multi-faceted personal identity, they found it unbearable to be reduced to nothing more than a number. This self-perception was therefore the social impulse behind their defensive strategies. "The conception of the individual as *homo clausus*, a little world in himself who ultimately exists quite independently of the great world outside, determines the image of human beings in general" (Elias 2000: 472). And "[w]hat the concept of society refers to appears again and again as something existing outside and beyond individuals" (ibid.). Norbert Elias disputes the empirical content of this analytical separation of the individual and society. Even though our sense of society and individual is shaped by this viewpoint – because it is deeply rooted in modern thought – Elias shows us that the idea is ideologically tainted, and he demands a thorough sociological investigation of the nature of "the invisible wall" (ibid.: 472) that has led this supposed split to remain largely unquestioned. Elias argues that because people create societies, the individual cannot be separated from the social. He also points out that, on account of their actions, individuals – and thus societies – are always in a process of change, so there can never be a static and totally clear image of a society. Individuals' perceptions of themselves and society will be shaped by the prevailing notions surrounding them; a sociological analysis must not adopt this perspective without further reflection, however, but should instead investigate its formative power and its influence on individual social action[10] (cf. ibid.: 472ff.).

This is important to the study at hand in two respects: First, it explains how individuality could be a matter of life and death to the concentration camp prisoners; and, second, we must acknowledge that this viewpoint is a deeply rooted modern ideology if we want to explain why, despite the assumed antagonistic split between the individual and society, it was inevitable that the prisoners themselves would bring fundamental aspects of society with them into the hermetically sealed world of the Nazi concentration camps.

Bourdieu's work represents a sociological-theoretical construct that attempts to render the symbiosis of the individual and society in manageable concepts. His theoretical ideas – particularly the concept of habitus – make it possible to reconcile the individual and society. Social structures are by no means absent from such an analysis; they continue to exist in the form of objectivities that are reflected in the social agents' schemes of perception, appreciation, and action (cf. Bourdieu 1984: 100 and *passim*). Preferences, inclinations, and viewpoints that have been acquired under the objective conditions of each person's social position are absorbed – incorporated – to become the habitus that unconsciously influences their behavior and perception as agents. People living under similar social conditions accordingly have similar views of the world; they feel an elective affinity and affiliation with one another on account of their shared preferences, inclinations, and viewpoints and ultimately establish their social identity through them.

According to this argument, individuals are born into and shaped by social structures, but through their actions they also contribute to the perpetuation or modification of these structures. The habitus acquired through one's social situation, which is incorporated and deeply anchored in each individual, makes the agents (often involuntary) accomplices to structures that have long existed and which they are probably outraged by and would rather abolish. Bourdieu was criticized for this idea of the dual existence of society – in structures and in individuals – and thus the complicity of the individual, in part because it calls into question the idea of the autonomous individual, but probably also because it is especially painful for intellectuals to realize that even they contribute to social conditions they would rationally prefer to eliminate. Bourdieu was and is also accused of social determinism – unjustly, I believe, because throughout his work he explicitly describes how "the knowledge of determinisms" is "a path to freedom" (Bourdieu 2004: 145; cf. also Rieger-Ladich 2005). This also entails understanding the inertia of the habitus, which explains the tremendous difficulties that must be overcome when one tries to make changes.

Dumont says there are two basic types of society: The first is the premodern, holistic, strictly hierarchical society in which the community, the nation, the whole, is the highest value. The individual's social duties are not freely chosen but are assigned; free choice is not even an option in these societies. The individual is expected to submit to this social order, and most people in such premodern societies have no rights of their own because they are essentially the property of the land that they populate and cultivate. In return, they are protected by a ruler, liege, or someone similar.

Modern, individualistic societies, by contrast, are based on the ideal of *égalité* or the equality of all people who are granted the natural right to life and liberty. This also entails personal responsibility to God and the world, so individual freedom of choice is balanced by internalized values that take the form of an individual's conscience or internal arbitrator (cf. also Dumont 1992: 25, 279f.).

This analytical distinction between two basic social configurations can help identify the prevailing values of a society, but we must not forget that social practices as a process are never as clear as the ideologically shaped categories proposed by Dumont. In connection with totalitarianism – and specifically the "Third Reich" – Dumont shows that, in the modern age, "individualism is all-powerful on the one hand and, on the other, is perpetually and irremediably haunted by its opposite" (ibid.: 17). The survival of premodern elements in various areas of social practice in modern societies leads modern values to blend with their opposites, resulting in an extremely complex social framework (ibid.). "[T]he remarkable and engrossing fact is that the combination of heterogeneous elements [. . .] results in an intensification, a rise in the ideological power of the corresponding representations. This is the ground on which totalitarianism grows as an involuntary, unconscious, and hypertensive combination of individualism and holism" (ibid.: 18). In his essay entitled "The Totalitarian Disease: Individualism and Racism in Adolf Hitler's Representations" (Dumont 1992: 149ff.), Dumont points out the significance of the German version of individualism – the "German ideology" – which was primarily a cultural-educational ideal (cf. also Cahnman 2005). The goal of self-cultivation and internal freedom was coupled with a strong sense of community here, making this ideology a "combination of individualism and holism" (Dumont 1992: 153). Dissatisfaction with the rise of capitalistic economic thought and the development of the bourgeoisie, which were viewed as signs of "Westernization" and "denaturing," triggered a type of "holistic protest" (ibid.: 154) that was expressed in a variety of social movements. Different currents of thought all crystallized around the widespread certainty that things should not be allowed to continue as they were. Celebration of community was the trend of the time and it was cultivated in a wide range of movements, like the nearly paramilitary gymnastics movement founded very early on by "Pater" Jahn (cf. ibid.: 153) as well as the *Lebensreformbewegung* (life reform movement),[11] which called for a "return to nature," and youth movements such as the *Wandervogel* (Wandering Bird).[12] Even in the Zionist movement, the term *yishuv*, representing the "Jewish community," played an important role in the development of the social utopia in Palestine (cf. Barnavi 1992: 197), and members of the socialist and communist labor movement also swore oaths to the community of their comrades. These diverse movements ranged from the far left to the far right along the political spectrum, and they included mystical and spiritual groups as well. "Community [. . .] was the 'idol of this age'" (Wildt 2007: 353).

In this context, the National Socialist movement was part of a so-called "conservative revolution"; as an "antithetical copy of the Marxist and Bolshevik movement," it turned the class struggle into a "race struggle" (Dumont 1992: 150). This movement found adherents particularly among the people who felt cast adrift during the war-torn Weimar period (see also chapter 2.1). One of the central ideological postulates of National Socialism was the idea of the *"Volksgemeinschaft"* or "people's community." This term did not originate with the Nazis, however, as it had already appeared in the early nineteenth century (cf. Münkel 2004: 161; Wildt 2007: 26ff.). At the start of the twentieth century, it was picked up again by the youth movement to describe its ideal of "German community" (Münkel 2004: 161). In the initial enthusiasm at the start of World War I, the term *"Volksgemeinschaft"* acquired new overtones when it became associated with the pursuit of civic and national reformation. The term peaked for the first time in this period,

> when the objective was to bring the Germans together under the Reich war flag. When Wilhelm II declared that he no longer recognized parties, only Germans, he crudely but effectively expressed both the political necessity of mobilizing the entire population for the war and the need for inclusion and integration in the whole, something that was demanded by social democrats and German Jews as well. The fact that social class divisions soon broke open again in the war society and old antisemitic resentments began to circulate once more may have harmed the *"Volksgemeinschaft"* as a concept of reality, but this did not cause it to lose any of its magic as a promise for the future based on the myth of a past actually experienced. (Wildt 2007: 352)

In the Weimar Republic, conservatives, liberals, social democrats, and union leaders all appropriated the term *"Volksgemeinschaft"* to invoke the feeling of a shared world of experience and to create a sense of community. "Nearly all parties propagated the idea of the people's community as a political program – with both gradual and fundamental differences" (ibid.: 353).

> Even parties loyal to the Constitution propagated the *Volksgemeinschaft* idea, and in doing so they gave terminological ammunition to a destructive adversary – because the populist-integrative appeal for unity and community, and against "fraternal strife" and "party bickering," not only undermined a republican political culture that demanded discussion and compromise, it disavowed a civic society characterized by disputes and debate. (Ibid.: 354)

For Michael Wildt, the idea of the *"Volksgemeinschaft"* was the reason that democracy failed in the Weimar Republic, because the "homogeneity phantasm" (cf. also Bielefeld 2001: 142) that was so prevalent at the time hindered the kind of heated but fruitful discussion of political developments that is essential to democracy.

The basic difference in the way the term *"Volksgemeinschaft"* was used by various groups consisted of the emphasis placed on the generally *inclusive* or *exclusive* character of the community[13] (cf. Wildt 2007: 352ff.). The Nazis quickly adopted the word, imbued it with *"völkisch"*-racist elements, and highlighted its exclusionary character above all: "The German community of the people [. . .] encompasses all those who by virtue of ancestry, language and culture are part of the German community of the people [*sic*] [. . .] a Jew, therefore, cannot be a member of the German people" (Fritz Reinhardt 1937 quoted in Münkel 2004: 161). Even political opponents who were considered to be corrosive elements in this community could be effortlessly excluded, because "anyone who spoke of or called for a class war abnegated the *'Volksgemeinschaft'* and thus an essential foundation of the Nazi state" (Münkel 2004: 161–2).

Dumont calls Nazism a "pseudo-holism" (Dumont 1992: 158) primarily because the driving forces behind it consisted of the ideal of the *"Volksgemeinschaft"* as well as the social Darwinist idea of the "struggle of all against all – and hence individualism" (ibid.: 174). In Nazism this mutated into a race struggle, where the notion of a material, physical homogeneity resulting in an identical way of thinking and feeling was attributed to race (ibid.: 175). Holism is therefore restricted to one's own race in Nazism; Jews are accused of being associated with the type of extroverted individualism that is to be rejected, and only "Aryans" are considered part of the holistic *"Volksgemeinschaft."*

This racist fundamental ideology was accompanied by a selective return to premodernity that was expressed both in the Führer cult (cf. Kershaw 1997) and in the idea of "continuing the 'German drive toward the east' that was halted in the Middle Ages" in order to acquire

Lebensraum or "living space" (Wippermann 1997). As early as 1923, Adolf Hitler wrote in *Mein Kampf*:

> If new territory were to be acquired in Europe it must have been mainly at Russia's cost, and once again the new German Empire should have set out on its march along the same road as was formerly trodden by the Teutonic Knights, this time to acquire soil for the German plough by means of the German sword and thus provide the nation with its daily bread. (Hitler 2009: 87 quoted in Wippermann 1997: 15)

The Führer cult of the "Third Reich," which began and was nurtured by means of propaganda even before the Nazis seized power, took on positively archaic forms, and as a result the authority of the Führer rapidly replaced the authority of the state and became the lynchpin of the Nazi movement:

> It became its organizational principle, integration mechanism and central driving force. [. . .] According to [Max Weber], charismatic authority is the opposite of bureaucratic authority based on rules, regulations and routine. The personalized, arbitrary and unruly exercise of charismatic authority cannot replace the impersonal functionalism of bureaucratic authority in a modern state, it can only be superimposed on it. (Kershaw 1997: 23; translated from the German)

As a consequence, the structures of an orderly government were undermined and the institutional governmental framework was subjected to an ongoing process of disintegration (cf. ibid.).

The oath of allegiance that was to be sworn to Hitler personally from 1934[14] is one facet of this Führer cult; another is the nationalist-romantic idea of Hitler as the heroic leader of the people, towards whom each of his followers was obliged to work (cf. ibid.: 24). In conjunction with the idea of the "Aryan community of the people" that was supposedly chosen and qualified to rule the world, this rather vague concept had an integrative effect on everyone who felt that it applied to them.

> The establishment of a unified and racially homogeneous community of the people, the restoration of national strength and greatness, the creation of an expanded Greater Germany – all of these goals corresponded to the hopes of millions of people. [. . .] Ultimately, the authority of the Führer [. . .] was important as an entity for authorizing and sanctioning even the most radical and inhuman initiatives that were undertaken by others and that fell under the generalized and indeterminate ideological precept of promoting the goals of the Führer. (Ibid.: 32; translated from the German)

The "pseudo-holism" of the "Third Reich" effortlessly exploited deep-seated individualistic categories of thought to successfully propagate the racist idea of a superior "Aryan race." At the same time, it took advantage of the widespread frustration with the Fatherland's loss of strength and honor after World War I and with capitalistic economic behavior by evoking the *"Volksgemeinschaft"* that each person was expected to submit to and that was supposed to lead directly to the resolution of – and thus deliverance from – the problems of the age. The Führer cult, which took on a religious character, had an integrative function above all and facilitated a form of leadership that had premodern traits in many respects.

This mixture of modern elements and seemingly archaic relics of a past and "better" age was reflected in the social life of the time. Through social practices, it found its way into the minds of those who gave no intellectual consideration to the problems of the period but who instead were able to soothe their fears and uncertainties by celebrating a *"Volksgemeinschaft"* that apparently protectively encompassed them. Fostered by the tradition of a "German ideology," a tremendous propaganda machine was able to make the idea of a "people's community" into a perceived reality for the population. In an essay entitled "'Volksgenossen' und 'Volksgemeinschaft'. Anspruch und Wirklichkeit" ("'National Comrades' and 'People's Community': Pretensions and Reality"), Daniela Münkel shows how the "propagandistic staging of the idea of a people's community" was "flanked by real measures" and was thus able to become a reality (Münkel 2004: 163). Radio broadcasts played an important part in this, as did the annual cycle of holidays. Through the distribution of low-cost radios known as *"Volksempfänger"* (people's receivers) and the psychologically orchestrated presentation of the Führer and "his people's community," the pseudo-holistic idea of a German people insinuated itself into the living rooms of the population. Major events held throughout the year on a pompously massive scale, which were broadcast and discussed on the radio, together with decentralized, regionally organized festivities, strengthened the bonds both with one's real local community and with the idea of a "people's community" [15] (cf. ibid.: 164f.). The wearing of traditional regional costumes also implied that Nazism was rooted in German history and tradition, and it supposedly symbolized the diversity of the "German tribes" (cf. ibid.: 167). The speeches given regularly at such events by Nazi leaders always emphasized the importance of the "farming community" for Germany and strengthened "the image of a retrogressive, agrarian society" (ibid.).

In his impressive, extensively researched book *Volksgemeinschaft als Selbstermächtigung* (*Volksgemeinschaft* as Self-Empowerment), Michael Wildt shows how the exclusionary element of violent antisemitism in particular was essential to the establishment of the *"Volksgemeinschaft"* as a political order independent of the nation state whose boundaries were drawn – not theoretically but in actuality – through violence (cf. Wildt 2007: 355). Medieval-style "processions of shame" (ibid.: 366) played an important role in this, as did the violent discharge of "the wrath of the people" through antisemitic pogroms which, as Wildt documents in nightmarish detail, took place throughout the German Reich, in cities but particularly in the countryside, on a growing scale until reaching their apex in November 1938.[16] The *"Volksgemeinschaft"* was brought into being through the actual violent exclusion of those who were not supposed to be part of it. This process was abetted by highlighting the attractive aspects of this community in the media and at public festivities while at the same time making a public show of excluding all those who did not belong by means of assaults and brutal violence. "In this sense, *Volksgemeinschaft* is the promise of a meta-modern regime of racial inequality, within which the body of people that creates and preserves its state of homogeneity gains political sovereignty" (ibid.: 361). It should be noted that this mixture of individualistic and holistic ideas of society was like a doctrine of salvation for the people of the time and had a massive impact on their real lives. People from the heart of this society helped bring this new idea of the *"Volksgemeinschaft"* into being. The society of the "Third Reich" was just as complex as the individuals who comprised it. These included staunch Nazis, naïve hangers-on who were infected by Nazi enthusiasm, and regime opponents of every stripe. "In spite of the coercive, dictatorial character of the Nazi regime [. . .] [t]he Nazi government was not simply a dictatorship from top to bottom, it was a social practice in which the German population was involved in a variety of ways" (Bajohr 2003: 167). The society of the "Third Reich" projected the image of a unified "people's community," and those who did not belong to it were denounced, exposed, beaten, persecuted, imprisoned, or killed. In this way, unwelcome forces in this society were separated and isolated; they did not really disappear, however, but were transferred to the Nazi concentration camps to be domesticated. It is no surprise, then, that the majority of those who were left to live "freely" in this society really did believe that the concentration camp prisoners were the corrosive "scum" on the *"Volksgemeinschaft"* as defined according to the Nazis' *"völkisch"* concept. Above all, the prisoners were visibly identified as this "scum" through the physical violence and inhuman living conditions to which they were subjected.

In fact, there was a conflict here between two "basic concepts" of society, namely, between those who (still) clung to the progressive idea of individualism and those who adhered to the pseudo-holism of the conservative revolution, a conglomeration of historicized glorification of the "racial *Volksgemeinschaft*" and supposedly modern aggressive individualism of the social Darwinist variety. This was a no-holds-barred fight, and the stronger side was undoubtedly the one that knew it had the national power monopoly at its back, meaning that it could commit boundless violence against the subordinate side and would be applauded by the general public for doing so.

The Nazis focused their attack on civic law, which was seen as an expression of a "French-progressive and liberal-materialistic ethos, particularly in its incorporation of foreign, Roman-Jewish legal principles." Nazi legal theory formulated an entirely different source of law: It called on an unwritten right of the people that stood above the law. [. . .]

The "people's law" practiced by the local Nazi Party groups in their campaigns against Jewish citizens mimicked the traditional popular courts of honor that always had existed alongside the law of the state. But in its actual content, this law aimed not to restore a traditional system of order but to establish a new system in the form of a racist, antisemitic people's community. (Wildt 2007: 368–9)

But the fact that, in the modern age, "individualism is all-powerful on the one hand and, on the other, is perpetually and irremediably haunted by its opposite" (Dumont 1992: 17) shows that the individuals who made up the society of the "Third Reich" adhered to very different and sometimes diametrically opposed "basic concepts" of society. "[T]he remarkable and engrossing fact is that the combination of heterogeneous elements [. . .] results in an intensification, a rise in the ideological power of the corresponding representations" (ibid.: 18).

Following Bourdieu's line of argumentation, even if we take into account the structural differences between premodern-holistic, modern-individualistic, and pseudo-holistic totalitarian societies (cf. ibid.), the fact remains that society is constituted exclusively through the actions of its individual members – even when those members are not viewed as autonomous individuals, as in holistic societies. The individuals are the social agents who knowingly or unknowingly create the structure of society in the first place. Because values and attitudes are incorporated, their effective form is usually not questioned. The idea of the *"Volksgemeinschaft"* illustrates how incorporated values can also be used to bring about change, as this idea was already firmly established in a broader sense among large sections of the German population and was therefore a suitable vehicle for promoting the Nazi radicalization of society.

Bourdieu shows us that people are driven by "socially constituted interests" which are rooted in their concepts of themselves and their world (cf. Bourdieu 1998: 79). These "basic concepts," which are also the very personal impetus behind individual action, "only exist in relation to a social space in which certain things are important and others don't matter and for socialized agents who are constituted in such a way as to make distinctions corresponding to the objective differences in that space" (ibid.: 79).

Having explored the fundamentals of the complex relationship between individuals and society and looked more closely at the concrete attitudes to this in the society of the "Third Reich," we have been able to take our *first theoretical step* toward validating Neurath's claim that the "basic concepts" of society within the Nazi concentration camps were essentially the same as those outside the camps (cf. Neurath 2005: 261). Although the exceptional cruelty and terrible conditions in the concentration camps may distort our ability to see this, Bourdieu's arguments show that it is unthinkable that the "basic concepts" of society stopped at the gates of the Nazi concentration camps as long as these camps were populated by people in whom such concepts were deeply rooted in the form of their habitus.

The dual existence of society – in structures and in individuals – and thus the aspect of individual complicity (cf. Bourdieu 2004: 78 and *passim*), demands that we take a dual view of people as individuals and as a part of the whole to which they contribute (cf. Elias 2000: 468). As the agents of what constitutes a society, both the camps' staff and their inmates brought the existing, effective social contradictions of their time into the society of the camps. In the empirical section of this work (part III), I will show that prisoners with a more holistic orientation – such as those from socialist or communist movements or with backgrounds in organized religion, such as Jehovah's Witnesses and Christian clergymen – had fundamentally different concepts and behaviors oriented on this holistic ideal than those – such as intellectuals and artists – who adhered to individualistic ideas.

4.2.2 Classes and ways of life: Social differentiation

The social space is indeed the first and last reality, since it still commands the representations that the social agents can have of it.

Pierre Bourdieu (1998: 13)

An economically based concept of class is firmly established in European societies. This class concept originated with the social-statistical analyses carried out by Friedrich Engels primarily among laborers in England in the first half of the nineteenth century. The definition of class was narrowed by Karl Marx to focus on the acquisition of the means of production, but in common usage the term has since distanced itself from its origins and it now refers to different – and thus differentiable – economic circumstances, with individuals in comparable situations being viewed as a single class. "What [. . .] poses problems is the fact that wealth – whether measured against the amount of money one currently possesses or some future assured income – remains an abstraction, while class is a concrete, living concept in human consciousness, a very human concept, and it cannot be reduced to a list of numbers" (Halbwachs 2001: 31). In his works published at the start of the twentieth century, French sociologist Maurice Halbwachs[17] stressed that classes are "a matter of social beliefs" (ibid.: 31) even when they are not categorized on the basis of "their respective economic institutions" (ibid.). Halbwachs developed four criteria for analyzing social classes: first, wages and lifestyle; second, the type of occupation and activity carried out and the resulting relationship with the material; third, social action; and, fourth, history and memory, with the latter serving primarily to legitimize hierarchical social positions. At the forefront of all four aspects is a person's social awareness of their own situation, which acts as a practical tool for the basic classification of living situations (cf. de Montlibert 2003: 34). It is not so much the quantifiable amount of available income that indicates a person's social affiliations; similar ways of life are what make people appear to have an affiliation with one another, and these lifestyles can vary widely even when the amount of available money is the same, as Halbwachs empirically demonstrates with the help of income and consumption data (cf. Halbwachs 2001).[18]

Just as Norbert Elias did in the 1930s in his work *The Civilizing Process* (Elias 2000), Maurice Halbwachs emphasizes right at the dawn of the twentieth century that society exists in two logics: in its structures and in the minds of its members. As a result, inequalities are (re)produced, on the one hand, and, at the same time, mentally represented in the perceptions of individuals, on the other. Halbwachs's theories make it possible to critique the legitimation strategies of the ruling classes (cf. de Montlibert 2003: 43f.) while also showing that individuals contribute to the perpetuation of inequality through their socially influenced ways of life.

> In fact, many needs which are primarily social in nature develop only as the result of a lengthy education. They require continual contact with the society, a knowledge of its highest forms of expression, the development of a sense of and taste for the advantages it offers to those who benefit from it. [. . .] In every human society, certain value judgments emerge which determine the priority of whatever commodities are most desirable. The closer one gets to the deeper, more primordial aspects of human society,[19] the clearer and more imperative these general judgments become, and they are reflected in the priority and relative importance of various expenditures. In general, different social groups satisfy their needs in a very wide variety of ways [. . .]. (Halbwachs 2001: 54)

Halbwachs addresses two important aspects here: first, that social practices lead to differentiation and thus to an awareness of differences; and, second, that these differences are not neutral but are instead loaded with values, so differing ways of life are subject to a hierarchical classification that is not externally imposed but is produced by the actions of individuals themselves as members of a society.

Although not all aspects of this view of classes and society are elaborated upon in Halbwachs's work as they are in Bourdieu's sociological constructs, it is difficult to overlook the fact that there is a certain connection between the ideas of the two thinkers. Bourdieu's social space is an analytical model of society comprising a space of differences, but it is actually created in real life through different lifestyles, as can be empirically shown. The works of Halbwachs demonstrate that such ideas had already been proposed in the first half of the twentieth century and were also empirically founded. The theories of both Halbwachs and Bourdieu reveal that distinctions can only continue to exist if the social agents themselves make them and that such distinctions are not attributable solely to one's economic situation. Halbwachs's *The Psychology of Social Class* (1958 [1938]) takes a direction similar to that of Bourdieu's habitus concept in that his approach takes account of the social aspect of the individual,[20] although the physical aspect is not initially explored in any depth by Halbwachs.

While Bourdieu himself frequently postulated the universal and constant applicability of his theoretical construct of the social space (cf., e.g., Bourdieu 1998: 3; 2004: 87), Halbwachs's writings give me additional encouragement to apply Bourdieu's concepts to the questions at issue in my own work, since as early as the first decades of the twentieth century – the time period relevant to this study – Halbwachs was reaching the same conclusions that Bourdieu would subsequently reach much later. Halbwachs's fundamentally similar sociological propositions relating to classes and ways of life (Halbwachs 2001) support the idea that people living in the "Third Reich" did in fact make distinctions in precisely this way – even if they were imprisoned in a concentration camp.[21]

Both Halbwachs and Bourdieu repeatedly use the term *class* to describe these hierarchically differentiated, social, and often merely potential formations. In my study, I use the term as a type of shorthand to represent the complex social relations always implied by Bourdieu – relations that will be explained in more detail in the following and placed in the context of the subject at hand.

Bourdieu's model of the social space is an attempt to represent the complex, reciprocal social relations between social agents. The spatial imagery illustrates how a concrete social position is always tied to a particular perspective – Bourdieu frequently uses the term "world-views" (Bourdieu 1994: 130) to describe this – and thus how reality is perceived in a relational way (cf. Bourdieu 1998: 3ff.). The main thinking here is "that to exist within a social space, to occupy a point or to be an individual within a social space, is to differ, to be different [. . .] 'to be distinctive, to be significant, is the same thing,' significant being opposed to insignificant" (ibid.: 9).

The world-view that is the source of the agents' respective dispositions is incorporated as "habitus," and the agents are only partially conscious of it. Any decisions that have to be made by individuals are subject to the individuals' dispositions and world-views, so freely made decisions usually serve to perpetuate existing social relations (cf. Bourdieu 1998: 6).

While Halbwachs speaks generally of "social consciousness," Bourdieu is more concrete in that he describes habitus as incorporated schemes of perception, appreciation, and action (cf. Bourdieu 1984: 100 and *passim*). The relational integration of social agents on the basis of their concrete position in the social space leads individuals to have different preferences, inclinations, and tastes. These are both cognitive and physical, and they are expressed in the individuals' mental as well as physical bearing. This argument emphasizes that cognitive, reflexive aspects are not the sole driving force behind social action; instead, habitus must be viewed as a sense rooted deep in the body, a "practical sense" that steers the actions and judgments of individuals.

> But the essential point is that, when perceived through these social categories of perception, these principles of vision and division, the differences in practices, in the goods possessed, or in the opinions expressed become *symbolic differences* and constitute a veritable *language*. Differences associated with different positions, that is, goods, practices, and especially *manners*, function, in each society, in the same way as differences which constitute symbolic systems, [. . .] that is, as distinctive signs. [. . .] Difference becomes a sign and a sign of distinction (or vulgarity) only if a principle of vision and division is applied to it which, being the product of the incorporation of the structure of objective differences [. . .], is present among all the agents [. . .] and structures [their] perceptions. (Bourdieu 1998: 8–9; emphasis in original)

In this context, Bourdieu also refers to classes of habitus or taste (ibid.: 7) to describe the individual conditioning resulting from one's real position in the social space which enables the mutual knowledge and recognition of social similarity or difference. "The habitus is this generative and unifying principle which retranslates the intrinsic and relational characteristics of a position into a unitary lifestyle, that is, a unitary set of choices of persons, goods, practices. [. . .] Habitus are generative principles of distinct and distinctive practices" (ibid.: 8). The resultant extremely selective "logic of classes" (ibid.: 10) must not lead us to believe, however, that individuals who are similar to each other in this way, even if they themselves sense this similarity, will necessarily form "real classes, real groups, that are constituted as such in reality" (ibid.). Proximity in the social space and the accompanying similarity in lifestyle and habitus only indicate a "potentiality of unity" and thus primarily constitute a "probable class" (ibid.: 11).

The practices and associated characteristics of the agents in a social space are largely influenced by two criteria: access to economic capital and access to cultural capital. Cultural capital encompasses not only tangible cultural goods but also education and taste, which, in turn, influence how one deals with economic capital (this is where Halbwachs's concept of class comes in) and determine the opportunities for acquiring it. Education and taste are necessary to appreciate economically acquired cultural goods, but they are also a prerequisite for assuming the type of professional positions that enable the acquisition and propagation of economic capital (cf. Bourdieu 1986). "The position occupied in social space, that is, in the structure of the distribution of different kinds of capital, which are also weapons, commands the representations of this space and the position-takings in the struggles to conserve or transform it" (Bourdieu 1998a: 12). It is clear that, according to Bourdieu, social action can never be value-neutral because social conditioning leads the agents themselves to consider any such action to be symbolic of certain values. This lends credence to the notion that, because social actions are so highly charged with meaning, agents act with the underlying intention of expressing their own social position. In this sense, "disinterested acts" (ibid.: 75ff.) are unthinkable. The "cognition" and "recognition" (ibid.: 85) of the socially charged nature of human action and the understanding of the social space as a "symbolic space" (ibid.: 1) point to a "relationship of infraconscious, infralinguistic complicity" between "agents and the social world" (ibid.: 79). Such complicity also implies complicity with the dominant relations, and thus power relations, and it is not just cognitive but actually incorporated and therefore habitually deeply rooted in the individual. The indication here is that people are equipped with a socialized, structured body "which has incorporated the immanent structures of a world or of a particular sector of that world [. . .] and which structures the perception of that world as well as action in that world" (ibid.: 81). Bourdieu also refers to the resulting "socially constituted interests" (ibid.: 79) as "social libido" (cf. chapter 1, note 6) because they represent an urge for social action which works pre-consciously and pre-linguistically like an "impulse" (ibid.). The consequence of this "social impulse" is that "social agents have 'strategies' which only rarely have a true strategic intention as a principle" (ibid.: 81).

In the first step of my argument in the preceding section (4.2.1), the close integration of individual and social action was clearly illustrated to support Neurath's assertion that the society within the concentration camps was not significantly different from that outside of them. My examination of the socially prevalent concept of class in this section has shown that human action is never perceived as value-neutral by social agents. Instead, such action is shaped by an individual's social perspective, and perceived differences are viewed as being symbolic of social differences. In this respect, the class concept stands not so much for a direct link with economically quantifiable circumstances as for a differentiated social perception which is categorizing and based on a widespread social consensus.

In my second theoretically oriented step of argumentation, I have used Bourdieu's theories to corroborate the claim that not only is individual action always social action, it is also categorizing and evaluative and thus contributes to the construction of social hierarchies. The social positions derived from individual actions are therefore not neutral but hierarchical, and they are made discernible to everyone involved by means of taste and lifestyle. The empirical results of Halbwachs's research into *classes and ways of life* (cf. Halbwachs 2001) prove that this conclusion was reached even prior to the time period that forms the historical backdrop to my study.

The theoretical view that has emerged so far – that individuals and their actions always have a social, categorizing aspect – makes it even more likely that Neurath was correct to think the "basic concepts" of society continued to hold sway in the Nazi concentration camps. If it is true that the individual is always social as well, and that agents are conditioned by a habitus that leads them to pre-consciously incorporate schemes of perception, appreciation, and action, then we can assume that even when people are violently confined behind electrified fences under terrible conditions, this "social made body" (Bourdieu in Bourdieu and Wacquant 1992: 127) does not suddenly evaporate. On the contrary, we must assume that any attempt to interfere violently with these social constants will be vehemently opposed, not just reflexively but by means of a social reflex as well. The focus on the individual – which has been highly valued by most people in the modern Western world but which is also subject to a consensual social classification through which one is identified and one identifies oneself – appears to be one last opportunity to transform the concentration camps into a social space in which social continuities are maintained. The concentration camps thus became literal *outposts of the social space* because they were populated by people who came from a society and who had incorporated that society's effective schemes of perception, appreciation, and action and brought them into the camps with them. The SS only partially succeeded in imposing a fundamentally different structure on these concentration camps and turning them into a counterworld. The limits of the effectiveness of their attempts were determined by the inmates, whose habitus was dependent on the real social world outside of the camps.

4.2.3 Gender: Physical characteristics and their symbolic significance for social differentiation

Gender is a fundamental dimension of the habitus which, like the sharps and clefs in music, modifies all of the social qualities associated with the fundamental social factors.

Pierre Bourdieu (1997b: 222)

Of all the forms of social distinction, gender differentiation appears to be the most fundamental way in which people distinguish themselves from one another. In ancient, premodern, and modern complex societies alike – regardless of whether they aspire to egalitarian ideals or are obviously hierarchically structured – gender differentiation exists as an apparently unquestioned effective force because it would appear to be based on seemingly unalterable, physical, biological characteristics. Even though the social nature of gender differentiation has been at least partially acknowledged in most modern societies, the justification for this type of distinction is still attributed largely to allegedly genetic physical and hormonal factors.[22]

This first and most important social classification takes effect at the moment of birth when an obstetrician determines whether a baby is a boy or a girl, thus setting the child's social course for the future on the basis of primary physical characteristics (cf. also Martschukat and Stieglitz 2005). "Thus, in the course of the socialization process every agent inevitably acquires a gendered habitus, an identity which has incorporated the existing division of labor between the genders" (Krais 1993: 170). This gender classification will also influence one's body from the moment one is born. "[T]he differentiation of male and female shapes the body, the *hexis*, and the habits of the body; guides perception of one's own body and of others' bodies; and determines the agent's relation to his or her body [. . .] and therefore determines identity in a very fundamental, 'bodily' sense" (ibid.: 161). This distinction is much more closely bound in human consciousness to the physical state of being in the world than any other social distinction; it therefore expresses itself more directly as such a distinction, and it also means that gender is present in every social situation.

The key point is that the construct of gender – unlike other social classifications in modern societies – has an antagonistic structure wherein the genders exist in relation to each other in the form of a binary code which does not allow for nuances or for anything to exist in between. According to Bourdieu, gender identity is a fixed component of the habitus, which thus always has both a gendered and a gendering dimension. The habitus generates "imperatives of social order" (Bourdieu 1997a: 168) that are also "insidious injunctions" (Bourdieu 2000d: 141) to the body and are very deeply rooted in individuals. With reference to gender identity, this means that the early social identification of being male or female is nearly irreversible or can only be overcome with tremendous effort. Bourdieu talks about the "somatization" of social relations in this context (Bourdieu 1997a: 166).

> The most serious social injunctions are addressed not to the intellect but to the body, treated as a "memory pad." The essential part of the learning of masculinity and femininity tends to inscribe the difference between the sexes in bodies (especially through clothing), in the form of ways of walking, talking, standing, looking, sitting, etc. (Bourdieu 2000d: 141)

While the basic classification of male or female is an either/or proposition, we must bear in mind that the classification in itself is meaningless without reference to the other gender. Its meaning is derived solely from the contrast that stems above all from the biological division of labor in reproduction. While the male makes a single, inconspicuous contribution to reproduction, the female is visibly associated for a longer period of time with the expectant mother. This clearly asymmetric relation has been reframed socially: conception as a male act, the potential for conception as male virility, the family as male property and a visible sign of the acceptance of responsibility, something which the man must protect – all of these notions take the biological asymmetry and flip it around on a social level (cf. Bourdieu 1997a, 2001a; Krais 1993; O'Brien 1983). "[T]he visible differences between the female body and the male body [. . .] become the most perfectly indisputable guarantee of meanings and values. [...T]his worldview [... considers] the difference between biological bodies as objective foundations of the difference between the sexes, in the sense of genders constructed as two hierarchized social essences" (Bourdieu 2001a: 22–3). In gender research, the concept of "genus groups" has been introduced to describe the gender classification that accompanies the usual social classification and thus represents another factor leading to inequality (cf. Dölling 1999: 19).

Gender differentiation therefore manifests itself as a hierarchical relationship in which greater value is ascribed to the masculine than to the feminine. "Many of these antagonisms associated with gender difference relate ultimately to the antagonism between discontinuity and continuity" (Bourdieu 2001b: 14), and they can be found in all areas of society. The "short but spectacular and ostentatious appearances" are reserved for men (ibid.: 13), while women are assigned the arduous, tedious, small tasks that are considered to be of less value.

By associating social inequality with the differences in the "biological reality" (Bourdieu 2001a: 11) of the body – this reality being an externally visible dissimilarity that can apparently be unequivocally discerned – the relationship between the genders is made to look like a natural power relationship, and the "comprehensive acts of social construction" (Bourdieu 1997a: 175) that produce this relationship are obscured. Gender is thus a social structural category that affects "all social fields and relations as an accepted and dominant structural principle" and "a social usher" (Krais 2001a: 333) and is therefore inescapable.

The social world [. . .] carries out a coup against each of its subjects in that it imprints their bodies with what amounts to a program for perception, appreciation and action [. . .]. In its gendered and gendering dimension, as well as all other dimensions, this program acts like a (second, cultivated) nature, that is, with the commanding and (apparently) blind force of the (socially constituted) impulse [. . .]. (Bourdieu 1997a: 168)

The somatization of gender relations is thus the somatization of a power relationship (ibid.: 166). Regardless of one's position in the social space – within which individuals are assigned to regions that tend either to dominate or be dominated (cf. Bourdieu 1985) – the position of women is always a position of being dominated (cf. Bourdieu 1997b: 221ff.).

> Masculine domination, which constitutes women as symbolic objects whose being (*esse*) is a being-perceived (*percipi*), has the effect of keeping them in a permanent state of bodily insecurity, or more precisely of symbolic dependence. They exist first through and for the gaze of others, that is, as welcoming, attractive and available *objects*. [. . .] As a consequence, dependence on others (and not only men) tends to become constitutive of their being. (Bourdieu 2001a: 66; emphasis in original)

Bourdieu argues that women must therefore "always be viewed in the context of this dual relation: in relation to men in the same position and in relation to women in other positions" (Bourdieu 1997b: 223). As the ones who are dominated, women have a different habitus from men, who are raised to be dominant – even if only over their own wives. The habitus of the dominated, according to Bourdieu, fundamentally differs from that of the dominant because the dominated always "see more than they themselves are seen" (Bourdieu 1997a: 163, footnote 13). They adopt the viewpoint of the dominant and turn this gaze upon themselves so that they can do what is expected of them. The "clear-sightedness of the dominated," which is commonly referred to in women as "feminine wiles" or "feminine intuition" (cf. ibid.: 163), makes women complicit in "masculine domination" (Bourdieu 1997a, 2001a). Because they are forced to utilize existing structures or search for ways of circumventing them, these structures remain uncontested (cf. Bourdieu 1997a: 178).

> This [. . .] often forces them to resort to the weapons of the weak, which confirm the stereotypes – an outburst that is inevitably seen as an unjustified whim or as an exhibition that is immediately defined as hysterical; or seduction, which, inasmuch as it is based on a form of recognition of domination, tends to reinforce the established relation of symbolic domination. (Bourdieu 2001a: 59)

Despite occupying a position that tends to be dominant, even men are subject to an ethical code governing their masculinity. Aside from the expectation that the male body should be self-controlled and superior, masculinity ("virility") is linked to the "principle of the conservation and increase of honor" (cf. ibid.: 12ff.). Demonstrations of masculinity follow "the logic of prowess, the exploit, which confers honor" (ibid.: 19), while an "indirect challenge to [. . .] masculinity" is taken as a challenge to this male honor (ibid.). A "man of honor" therefore owes it to himself to disregard fields and activities assigned to women (ibid.: 30) and "to disencumber [himself] of all the behaviors incompatible with [his] dignity" (ibid.: 33). The hierarchical division of genders "gives men the monopoly of all official, public activities, of representation, and in particular of all exchanges of honor – exchanges of words [. . .], exchanges of challenges and murders (of which the limiting case is war)" (Bourdieu 2001a: 47). The "sense of honor, virility, 'manliness' [. . .] is the undisputed principle of all the duties towards oneself, the motor or motive of all that a man 'owes to himself' [. . .] in order to live up, in his own eyes, to a certain idea of manhood" (ibid.: 48). This is the only way to explain why, "like nobility, honor [. . .] *governs* the man of honor, without the need for any external constraint" (ibid.: 49–50; emphasis in original).

Masculinity and femininity can therefore be viewed as extremely dominant, formative principles of social differentiation that are deeply inscribed in the body and mind, that structure individual identity, and that influence a person's "world-views" (Bourdieu 1994: 130). We must consider men and women alike to be governed by this formative force, from which they cannot simply free themselves.

If we go back to the initial question posed in this work and ask what significance gender differentiation has in terms of the "basic concepts" of society and whether these structures are reflected in the ideas and behavior of the concentration camp prisoners, the answer should be clear from the analysis above.

In the first step of the preceding argument, it became apparent that the idea of individuality plays an essential role in the identity of people in modern societies, even though the individual contributes to the constitution of the social and thus always has a social element as well. The second step showed the extent to which social action is always categorizing and how individuals play a part in their own social positioning by symbolically communicating their affiliations through their respective lifestyles.

This section has demonstrated that this social positioning is additionally governed by the binary code of gender, which, like other social forms of social placement, is incorporated in the habitus, is anchored in the mind and body, and continually influences social action. The third theoretically oriented step of my argument supports the idea that gender identity, as another facet of social identity and a fundamental principle of social differentiation, must have continued to be of immense importance to the prisoners in Nazi concentration camps in its role as one of the "basic concepts" of society. Neither the SS nor the inmates – regardless of where they came from – could have escaped this formative influence, so the concentration camps must be viewed as *gendered and gendering outposts of the social space* in which the "perception of the social world" (ibid.: 130) was always guided by this fundamental binary encoding (along with other social influences) which affects how men and women view other men and women.

Bourdieu's perspective on gender differentiation gives us multiple criteria which can be useful for analyzing the significance of class and gender as basic social structural characteristics in the Nazi concentration camps. First of all, it is apparent "that 'gender' does not refer to a particular field of the social world [. . .] but instead is a concept which addresses a *dimension* of the social world that plays an important, normative, and structuring role in the generation of social realities by means of the actions of agents" (Dölling 1999: 22–3; emphasis added). With respect to the study at hand, the question to ask is "how and in which figurations, in relation to which other factors [in the Nazi concentration camps] is 'gender' the basis of inequality – or, in more general terms, when does it contribute to the structuring of social fields and processes in its role as a powerful, hierarchizing mode?" (ibid.: 23).

Second, social differentiation according to gender is based on physical traits that symbolize social values. This makes the body more of an object of sociological inquiry than is usual.[23] In the context of the work at hand, we must ask what it meant for the concentration camp prisoners when illness and deprivation caused these physical traits to become invisible – that is, to disappear as visible symbols. Does the dominance of this binary code disappear as well, or is the opposite true?

Third, differentiation according to gender is incorporated as habitus in a way that leads agents to unconsciously accept it as natural and irreversible. Therefore, we must analyze whether this incorporated aspect can still dominate male or female perception and behavior, particularly with regard to the "insidious injunctions," even when normal living conditions no longer apply and the traits considered to be masculine or feminine are no longer obvious. What significance is accorded to mimesis, performance, and ritual (cf. Wulf 2005) as the enactment and reaffirmation of gender classification?

And finally, as described above, women are always dominated within the hierarchical social space; even if they hold a dominant social position, they are subordinate to men in the same position. We must therefore consider how important it was for women – who are dominated in any case – to have access to the "weapons of the weak" in the concentration camps, as well as how men coped with being in the position of the totally dominated. Were their usual respective strategies useful or harmful when it came to preserving their own dignity in the inhuman situation in the camps? And how important was it for men at the lower end of the scale in the social space to already have routines which were adapted to the position of being dominated?

4.2.4 "Ethnic group" and caste: The belief in genetic kinship and the notion of social inescapability

Some accuse me of being a Jew, others forgive me for being a Jew, still others praise me for it, but all of them reflect on it.
                    Ludwig Boerne (1832, quoted in Cahnman 1989b: 25)

In light of the specific situation of certain members of society during the Nazi dictatorship – namely, those who were considered foreign (*fremdartig*) and therefore alien (*artfremd*)[24] and not part of the "people's community" – the question arises as to whether the "basic concepts" of this society can be sufficiently described to show that ideas regarding the relationship between the individual and society diverged and that social differentiation according to class and gender was prevalent here, as in all societies. Even concepts like "race" and "ethnicity" are not enough to fully explain why Jews and "Gypsies" were treated as they were within the group of those who were considered "alien."

In his seminal text entitled "The Social Space and the Genesis of Groups," Bourdieu admits that the social space can be shaped by entirely different characteristics besides class affiliation and lifestyle, such as the idea of "ethnic" affiliation. He says there is something akin to a "space of ethnic groups" (Bourdieu 1985: 743, footnote 4) that is hierarchically structured according to a ranking of "ethnic groups" – but he does not delve very deep into this concept:

> In some social universes, the principles of division that, like volume and structure of capital, determine the structure of the social space, are reinforced by principles of division relatively independent of economic or cultural properties, such as ethnic or religious affiliation. In such cases, the distribution of the agents appears as the product of the intersection of two spaces that are partially independent: an ethnic group situated in a lower position in the space of the ethnic groups may occupy positions in all the fields [of the social space], including the highest, but with rates of representation inferior to those of an ethnic group situated in a higher position [in the space of ethnic groups]. Each ethnic group may thus be characterized by the social positions of its members [in the social space], by the rate of dispersion of these positions, and by its degree of social integration despite this dispersion. (Ethnic solidarity may have the effect of ensuring a form of collective mobility.) (Ibid.: 743, footnote 4; full quote)

For the topic at hand, however, this is not terribly helpful since Bourdieu does not really clarify what the term "ethnic group" encompasses, and we must know what is meant by it in order to determine its dispersion in the social space or its position in the "space of ethnic groups."

In the context of my study, there are two problems associated with the concepts of "race" and "ethnic group."

The first basic problem with the concept of "ethnic group," which prevents me from applying the underlying thinking to the question of the "basic concepts" of society, is that it conveys preconceptions and tacit assumptions. It is important to remember that the act of naming is an "act of symbolic imposition" and a form of "symbolic violence" (Bourdieu 1985: 732), because things are brought into being with the help of words (Bourdieu 1994: 138). With respect to the subject at hand, this means that, just as with the concepts of gender and class, we must investigate the thinking behind the concepts of "race" and "ethnic group," because "the objectivist break with pre-notions, ideologies, spontaneous sociology, and 'folk theories,' is an inevitable and necessary moment of the scientific procedure – you cannot do without it [. . .] without exposing yourself to grave mistakes" (ibid.: 130). In politically correct German usage today, the term *Rasse* (race) is generally no longer used in connection with people.[25] The preferred term has instead become *Ethnie* (ethnic group), though I believe this term aims to describe the same thing as "race." The thinking here is that "social groups" can be viewed as "ethnic groups" when they "have their own language, history, culture, their own institutions, a specific area of settlement, possibly also a shared religion, and they are aware of their unity and affiliation" and they "form a cultural, social, historical and genetic unit and are otherwise known as 'tribes' or 'peoples'" (*Meyers Großes Taschenlexikon* 2006: "Ethnie," "Ethnische Konflikte," 1999f.).

The first part of the cited definition shows that the material basis for the term "ethnic group" is still quite vague and could be easily applied to a variety of social groupings that would not otherwise be viewed as such (such as Catholics or Bavarians). The second part of the definition shows that the term actually relates to notions of similarities that are not explicitly mentioned but rather tacitly assumed and are simultaneously used as a principle of differentiation for describing oneself or others – that is, for social practice. But even Max Weber points out that "[a]lmost any kind of similarity or contrast of physical type and of habits can induce the belief that affinity or disaffinity exists between groups that attract or repel each other" (Weber 1978: 388). Bourdieu might annotate Weber's argument as follows: "[A]s a constellation [. . .] begins to exist only when it is selected and designated as such, a group, class, 'gender,' region, or nation" – or "ethnic group" one might add – "begins to exist as such, for those who are part of it and for others too, only when it is distinguished, according to one principle or another, from other groups, that is, via cognition and recognition" (Bourdieu 1994: 138).

The unquestioning adoption of the notions associated with the concept of "ethnic group" is of dubious epistemic value from a scientific point of view because it disguises the fact that this concept is a social classification based on a belief in the material foundation of "ethnicity." Unlike the concepts of class and gender – where there is a material basis for social differentiation in the form of one's lifestyle as expressed through expenditure and goods, on the one hand, and in the "biological reality" of the body (Bourdieu 2001a: 11), on the other – this unifying materiality is lacking for the category of "ethnicity" and is replaced by nothing more than the belief in such a materiality. In social practice, this manifests itself in the prevalent idea of "ethnic membership," which, however, does not necessarily have to lead to "concrete social action" (Weber 1978: 389). Even if "social action" does take place on the basis of the belief in blood affinity which is commonly referred to as "ethnic," the term is not suitable for a sociological analysis:

> All in all, the notion of "ethnically" determined social action subsumes phenomena that a rigorous sociological analysis [. . .] would have to distinguish carefully: the actual subjective effect of those customs conditioned by heredity and those determined by tradition; the differential impact of the varying content of custom; the influence of common language, religion and political action, past and present, upon the formation of customs; the extent to which such factors create attraction and repulsion, and especially the belief in affinity or disaffinity of blood; the consequences of this belief for social action in general, and specifically for action on the basis of shared custom or blood relationship, for diverse sexual relations, etc. – all of this would have to be studied in detail. It is certain that in this process the collective term "ethnic" would be abandoned, for it is unsuitable for a really rigorous analysis. (Ibid.: 394–5)

Therefore, "[i]f sociologists are not to make social science merely a way of pursuing politics by other means, they must take as their object the intention of assigning others to classes and of telling them thereby what they are and what they have to be [. . .]"[26] (Bourdieu 1985: 735).

The second problem with the term "ethnic group" has to do with the subject at hand, because merely referring to the "ethnicity" of Jews and "Gypsies" does not adequately explain the diverging ways in which different "inferior races" (from a Nazi perspective) were treated. According to the Nazis' race biology theories, under certain circumstances some of the so-called "inferior races" could be "racially improved" (*"aufgeartet"*) or "nordicized." In the eastern territories, for example, "those capable of being 'Germanized,' among them thousands of children who were taken from their parents and brought to German families or *Lebensborn* homes" (Kammer and Bartsch 2002: 94), were to be re-educated to become German.[27] This measure was intended to advance the "Germanization" of the world. While it was claimed that those "capable of being Germanized" could be "racially" improved through the mixing in of German blood,[28] Jews and "Gypsies" were explicitly excluded from this as it was assumed that, in their case, "race-mixing" would not lead to an improvement but would instead strengthen the supposedly inferior traits of their respective races.[29]

The plans for *"Judenmischlinge"* ("persons of mixed blood") as set out in the protocol of the Wannsee Conference[30] on the "final solution to the Jewish question" reveal that "persons of mixed blood of the first degree" were to be treated as "full Jews" and therefore deported and murdered in the same way as Jews. Only after "voluntary" sterilization might they be granted "compassionate leave to remain in the Reich" (cf. Pätzold/Schwarz 1992: 109ff.). In the official follow-ups to the Wannsee Conference, however, this solution was bluntly rejected as unsatisfactory since the "mixed-blood problem" was "not exclusively a race biology problem" (cf. ibid.: 117). The issue appears to have been that, according to the views of the time, the "Jewishness" of such individuals made itself apparent in all social situations – it was not, as Bourdieu assumes, restricted to "some social universes" (cf. Bourdieu 1985: 743, footnote 4) but was instead an indelible mark.

The apparent indelibility of negative traits also applied to those persecuted as "Gypsies," though the argumentation behind this must have followed a somewhat different logic in Nazi ideology. "Gypsies" are historically thought to have originated in India primarily on account of the similarity between the Romany language and Sanskrit,[31] so from a Nazi point of view this would have made them "Aryans." Nazi race researchers, however, followed a line of thinking that had been popular for some time, namely, that they were members of India's pariah caste and thus would have been viewed as inferior outsiders even within Indian society (cf. Zimmermann 1996: 135). Most of the population was already convinced that this minority posed a "social danger," and the danger was thought to have been all the greater on account of the "race-mixing" that had taken place with other "inferior peoples" on the long migration from India to central Europe. According to the pseudo-scientific race research of the time, 90 percent of all "Gypsies" were considered to be dangerous "persons of mixed blood" (cf. Pohl 2003: 111f.; Zimmermann 1996).

So-called "sub-humans" were categorized as either people who could "remain available as leaderless laborers and furnish Germany each year with migrant workers for special tasks" (Himmler, quoted in Kammer and Bartsch 2002: 84) or people who ostensibly had to be liquidated, according to the Nazis, for the purposes of the "final solution of the Jewish question" and of "combatting the Gypsy nuisance" (cf. Kwiet 1997: 50). However, this categorization still requires some explanation and apparently followed a logic that was older than Nazism itself. The construction of a "space of ethnic groups," as Bourdieu suggests, would account for the fundamental distinction made between "ethnic groups" and "races" that were apparently capable of being re-educated and genetically improved and those for whom this was not an option.

While Nazi ideology certainly had a formative influence on the way society treated these minorities, we must also look at how such groups were treated throughout history. If we accept Bourdieu's habitus concept, for example, we must assume that "ethnic" distinctions like these are also incorporated as schemes of perception, appreciation, and action (cf. Bourdieu 1984: 100 and *passim*) and become natural-seeming categories of division that are embodied and "so forgotten as history" (Bourdieu 1990: 56). The racist ideology of the Nazis undoubtedly intensified such pre-existing dispositions, but this alone does not explain the tremendous social power that these distinctions had in the real social actions of people of the time. And without the habitus concept, there is no plausible explanation for why these particular distinctions were made even by those persecuted by the Nazi regime, who were imprisoned in the concentration camps together as persons more or less "alien to the German race" and were all subjected to the violence of this system. Despite this, the inmates used the same principles of differentiation in their social practices with one another as were used by society outside the camps, which is why there is ample evidence that antisemitism and antiziganism were prevalent within the society of concentration camp prisoners as well.[32]

In this context, the already vague concept of "ethnic groups" reaches its limits and fails to account for the prevailing schemes of perception, appreciation, and action in the society of the time. For one thing, it masquerades as a pseudo-neutral concept by invoking a list of any number of traits, as we saw in the definition cited above – "their own language, history, culture, their own institutions, a specific area of settlement, possibly also a shared religion," etc. – and subtly using them to construct "a cultural, social, historical, and genetic unit" (cf. *Meyers Großes Taschenlexikon* 2006).

> One of the greatest difficulties with scientific writing arises from the fact that the contemporary terms we borrow from the object of our study are almost always approaches to social struggles. For example, this is the case with words that refer to groups and that are frequently used in conflicts regarding the boundaries of these groups, that is, the conditions for belonging to a group or being excluded from it. (Bourdieu 2004: 114)

Special vigilance is called for here because "[t]he preconstructed is everywhere" (Bourdieu in Bourdieu and Wacquant 1992: 235). "The force of the preconstructed resides in the fact that, being inscribed both in things and in minds, it presents itself under the cloak of the self-evident which goes unnoticed because it is by definition taken for granted" (ibid.: 251).

Regarding the study at hand, we must also analyze what notions about the specific characteristics of Jews and "Gypsies" were prevalent in society at the time – and probably remain so in today's society – and how these notions led to them being considered special groups among all "alien" peoples: that is, we must determine which principle of differentiation beyond "ethnicity" was actually at work here.[33] If it is true that Jews and "Gypsies" were treated differently from other groups who were excluded from the "people's community" – and there is historical evidence that this was in fact the case for the "society outside and that inside the camp" (Neurath 2005: 261) – then we are clearly dealing with a principle that must be considered a "basic concept" of society.

Therefore, if we used the term "ethnic group" in this analysis of the "basic concepts" of society, we would unwittingly make the mistake of implicitly accepting the material similarity and unity of the people so described without revealing the acts of social construction behind the concept. We would also be overlooking the fact that, when it came to dealing with Jews and "Gypsies," a special principle of differentiation beyond "ethnic group" was at work. In the following, I will try to explain this other principle of differentiation, one which would have such fatal consequences for the Jews and "Gypsies" in Nazi Germany and which, in my opinion, is still widely in effect as a classification principle today.

Looking at the history of antisemitism and antiziganism, we can see that there was indeed a special aspect to the treatment of these two groups of people – who were certainly viewed as "ethnic groups" in real life – which did not apply in the same way to other "ethnic minorities." Evidence of this can be found not only in the recurring pogroms against Jews or the drastic punitive measures taken against "Gypsies," which sometimes had the character of a spectacle (cf. Willems 1996; Zimmermann 1996) and which differed considerably from the official treatment of other minorities,[34] but also in the everyday relationship between Jews and "Gypsies" and the rest of society (cf. Herzig 1996). This history is probably the reason why the Nazis were able to act as radically as they did without being held at bay by the majority of the population, as most people had long been convinced of the material basis for this seemingly natural attitude of fierce resentment. To understand the social mechanisms at work here, it is particularly enlightening to look at the historical genesis and consolidation of antisemitic and antiziganistic patterns of thought and behavior because, on the basis of Bourdieu's theories, we can assume that these patterns entered the population's habitus as forgotten history and were thus able to remain in effect long after the historical circumstances that gave rise to them had passed.

If we attempt to sum up precisely where the reservations toward Jews and "Gypsies" lay, we can see that various processes were at work on different levels of society throughout history, and these processes interacted and ultimately amplified each other in relation to the minorities in question.

First of all, complex changes in the early modern period led to the emergence of such attitudes on a political level. Both the crystallization of the modern territorial state and the Reformation completely rearranged the existing structures of people's lives. The Reformation splintered Christianity into "competing denominations whose demarcation strategies led to considerable aggression which also affected minorities" (ibid.: 29). Ultimately, the Reformation served the purposes of the territorial state: Sovereigns were granted unlimited authority over their subjects, even acting as the supreme bishop in their territories (*"summus episcopus"*; ibid.),[35] and they usually had extensive access to church funds (ibid.: 31). In return, they supported the Lutheran and Calvinist Reformations instead of other competing spiritual movements which questioned the power of the authorities (ibid.: 29f.)

> The important aspect of this process is the emergence of a unified territorial state with clearly defined borders, unlike the states of the Middle Ages. This entailed the elimination of independent or competing powers in each territory, such as the imperial knights, as well as the estates that claimed the right of co-regency for themselves. It also involved the creation of a unitary, though hierarchically structured, group of subjects. (Ibid.: 30)

Some of these states were tiny,[36] and their isolation from the outside world influenced the prevalent concept of "foreigners" and "strangers" as people who were the subjects of a different sovereign. This antipathy was all the stronger toward those who were not the subjects of *any* sovereign and were thus actually lordless, like Jews and "Gypsies" (cf. ibid.: 30ff.).

We have already seen that, in terms of the notions of the individual and society, the Reformation strongly influenced people's perceptions and how they thought about their relationship with God and the world. But it is also clear that the Reformation had a strong influence on the development of the political system and its sociocultural effects, since it served the purposes of this system.[37] The process triggered by this had far-reaching consequences:

> The homogenization of the members of the state – as initially expressed in the concept of the subject in relation to the sovereignty of the monarch, and later in the concept of the community of citizens – and the homogenization of the state territory are two sides of the same coin. They serve to foster a sense of identity internally and are, at the same time, forms of community-building aggression that draw boundaries and exclude people externally. Contrary to the national historical narrative, we must remember that the attempt to integrate and unify the population of a delimited country by means of similar language and cultural tradition is a type of sovereign violence – a document of civilization and simultaneously of barbarism. The social construction of the subject (in the precise sense of the word)[38] takes the shape of a multiple subjugation: to the constraints of territorial limitation, cultural integration, and social adaptation. This push toward modernization is the actual drama that the subject needs to come to terms with. Through the hatred of the "lordless," the "rabble of Gypsies" who apparently submit to no ruler, the subject expresses his rebellion against his confinement in the rigid shell of a new type of bondage. (Maciejewski 1996: 17)

This "territorial homogenization" was in fact accompanied by the standardization of the image of who constituted an enemy (cf. ibid.: 18). By
means of this process, "Gypsies" became "against their will [. . .] representatives of the lost world of the premodern, a world of yesterday" (ibid.:
20) and thus embodied the exact opposite of what the Jews represented in
their role as the supposed enemy: "the colonizers of progress, representatives of urban, bourgeois, and ultimately industrial conditions" (cf. ibid.:
27, footnote 37).

"Gypsies," like Jews, were excluded from subjecthood on account of
their minority status – just as they could not be members of guilds – so
their options actually were limited. On the other hand, they were not
subject to the same restrictions as guild members, for example, and could
therefore sometimes respond to economic requirements in a much more
agile, innovative way (cf. Battenberg 2001: 107ff.). It was thus not unheard
of for them to be given certain privileges by a sovereign if this ruler
hoped to gain an advantage in the expansion of his state by exploiting
their commercial or economic expertise (cf. ibid.; Herzig 1996: 31). This
was more often the case for Jews, some of whom were able to join courtly
society as court factors or so-called Court Jews[39] and who were expected
to apply their skills and knowledge – and, in particular, their often geo-
graphically extensive social and commercial networks – to the acquisition
of goods and money for the benefit of territorial lords (cf. Herzig 1996:
41f.). Although Jewish court factors accounted for a minute fraction of
the already marginal Jewish community, they attracted the attention of
people in and around the court, who were usually not entirely well disposed toward them (cf. ibid.: 42). "Gypsies," by contrast, might at best
be allowed by the authorities to work in a medical capacity on account
of their traditional knowledge of particular treatments or in the military
owing to their special skills in handling horses.[40] As a result, they were
more likely to be objects of contempt rather than envy (cf. ibid.: 38).

Another aspect of the political ruptures of the time, one which also
began with the Reformation, was the burgeoning rejection of poverty,
which was seen as an indicator of "disorder" and "an attack on the fabric
of society" (cf. Maciejewski 1996: 14f.), an attitude which had far-reaching
consequences for public poor relief as well. The Protestant ethic viewed
beggars not as venerable figures to be supported in accordance with
God's will but as idlers trying to shirk their responsibility to God and the
world. "Gypsies" did not appear to hold down regular jobs and could
still benefit from their beggar status in the premodern period (cf. ibid.),
as could the many Jews who had been impoverished primarily through
taxation policies requiring them to pay extra duties to their respective territorial princes and who therefore wandered the countryside as beggars,[41]
sometimes in criminal gangs. Other sections of the population also grew
increasingly poor following the overthrow of the feudal economic system,
and in conjunction with the strengthening of the Protestant attitude

toward "useless beggars" (Herzig 1996: 34), this led "Gypsies" and Jews to be declared enemies of society.

In terms of population numbers, these two minorities always represented a vanishingly small proportion of society as a whole.[42] Both groups also generally lived somewhat apart from the social majority on account of centuries-old traditions as well as legal regulations, although there were numerous opportunities for social contact, particularly in the economic sphere. Jews were either required by law to live in ghettos or – at least in the cities and larger towns – lived in the same residential areas for the ease of practicing their religious rituals together. In the case of "Gypsies," it was assumed that most of them traditionally lived in itinerant communities and were not resident in any one place.[43] This special status manifested itself again in different ways as a result of political developments in the modern territorial state and led to worry and resentment on the side of the "subjects" – feelings which were amplified by the effects of the Reformation.

These developments probably also contributed to the myths about these two minorities that had been circulating for hundreds of years, providing a pseudo-plausible explanation in public discourse for the wandering lifestyle of both groups, a lifestyle which was generally viewed with suspicion. The myths associated with both groups are based on the idea of an irredeemable guilt relating to the life of Christ in the New Testament, and they reveal yet another link between the political and legal situation of Jews and "Gypsies" and religious motivation. In reference to the Jews, a myth was told about a Jewish shoemaker named Ahasver, the Eternal Jew, who was doomed by Jesus to wander until Judgment Day because he had refused to allow Christ to rest at his house as he made his way to Golgotha (cf. Baleanu 1992).[44] "Gypsies" were also associated with a myth relating to a refusal to provide shelter (cf. Herzig 1996; Köhler-Zülch 1996; Maciejewski 1996; Zimmermann 1996) which supposedly explained the "Gypsy's accursed impulse to wander" (Maciejewski 1996: 26, footnote 26): "The pilgrims from Little Egypt [. . .] were on a journey of atonement *because* their forebears had refused to provide shelter to the Holy Family fleeing from Herod. They were therefore damned to wander the earth restlessly and homelessly" (Maciejewski 1996: 15; emphasis in original). Both minorities were also repeatedly accused of stealing children and subjecting them to (ritual) abuse. A striking parallel to the traditionally anti-Jewish accusation of deicide based on Jewish guilt can be found in the myth that a "Gypsy" made the nails for the cross (cf. ibid.: 26, footnote 26).

So while the political upheaval and all of the new uncertainties it brought with it were accompanied by negative myths about Jews and "Gypsies" on the level of discourse, the privileges occasionally granted to these minorities on the level of social practice were envied, as was their greater (usually enforced) mobility owing to their special status.

This mobility was primarily expressed through itinerant trade on the part of Jews, while it was simply assumed to be a genuine way of life for "Gypsies." Jews were rumored to profiteer from their lawlessness and pose stiff competition to stationary traders, while "Gypsies" embodied the lost freedom of state subjects because, as a traveling people, they were bound to no particular place and thus no particular ruler. The itinerant trades that they traditionally practiced, such as repairing pots and grinding knives, also put them in competition with stationary traders, who came under additional pressure later in the course of industrialization.

To sum up, we can say that the political and religious upheavals in the early modern period changed people's lives in a way that unleashed insecurities and caused some people to experience actual social decline. In terms of both discourse and social practice, this led to the emergence and strengthening of resentment toward those who were apparently not bound by the same constraints as the subjects of the newly created territories: Jews and "Gypsies." The fact that these minorities were actually subject to more drastic constraints and disciplinary measures and also had fewer rights does not seem to have played a significant role in how they were perceived.

At this point it is necessary to take a closer look at the solidifying social barriers that hindered easy social relations on all sides. The aspects of social practice mentioned thus far largely belong to the realm of economics. However, social interaction was additionally impacted by the fact that both minorities had different marriage rules from the social majority, and they restricted and regulated their communal meals as well. Their religious – or, more generally, ritual – purity requirements also differed from the prevailing Christian concepts. Although the majority of "Gypsies" were Catholic, their unconventional way of life led them to be accused not just of idling but also of godlessness and impiety. Different types of misgivings were expressed toward each of the minorities, but what the two groups had in common was that they were separate communities isolated within the larger society. Their cultures diverged from that of the majority and were sometimes cultivated with a certain pride, so the tendency toward separation came from both sides.

Both minorities were traditionally associated with specific occupations as well; there were different reasons for this, most of them stemming from the rules of the social majority. For instance, "Jewish usury"[45] was the product of the Christian ban on lending money, which meant that this forbidden and therefore "sinful" activity had to be carried out by those who were not bound by this law, while "Gypsies" collected junk and rags because certain dirty, impure tasks were disallowed in Christian society. The numerous other occupational bans placed on Jews and "Gypsies" led to specific job profiles for each minority which ultimately took on the appearance of a hereditary division of labor.

Though the two minorities were integrated to a limited degree in the

majority society[46] and this society was happy to take advantage of the services they provided,[47] they held an inferior social position, meaning that
they actually had inferior rights and were situated very low in the social
hierarchy. It is also worth noting that the two minorities were considered
to be related in popular and pseudo-scientific thinking, as "Gypsies" were
thought to be a group that had splintered off from the Jews. If nothing
else, their supposed mutual Asian origins were viewed as the shared
reason for their idiosyncrasies.[48]

If we focus on the level of *social practice* relating to these three
characteristics – separation, hereditary division of labor, and assignment
to a strictly defined position within the social hierarchy with different
(and, in this case, inferior) rights – we can see that these are the traits commonly considered to be the three pillars of the caste system. Basic notions
of purity and impurity are also fundamental differentiation criteria in the
caste system (cf. Dumont 1980; Skoda 2003); here, too, they are the basis
for separation, hereditary division of labor, and positioning in the social
hierarchy,[49] and they result in fears of contact, avoidance strategies, and,
ultimately, legal sanctions.

Having drawn an analogy between the traditional social treatment of
Jews and "Gypsies" and the fundamental criteria of the caste system, we
have to ask whether a long-established social mechanism similar to a caste
system is prevalent even in central European, Western society. If this is
the case, it would explain why something like a stigma or notion of impurity has always clung to these two minorities, even though the historical
situation has changed and even when the social separation and division
of labor no longer apply, so that, for example, the knowledge (or even just
suspicion) alone that someone is Jewish is enough to cause that person to
be viewed – and consequently treated – in a fundamentally different way.
I first want to briefly outline how the separation, hereditary division of
labor, and low social position of Jews and "Gypsies" have evolved since
the Enlightenment – an evolution that has been very different for each of
the minorities, though a stigma has remained attached to both – before
turning my attention to the nature of social castes.

Even the dawn of the Enlightenment in the eighteenth century did not
bring about a greater tolerance of others; the aim instead was to level out
differences. The more "subcutaneous" misgivings (Herzig 1996: 44) still
remained, however, and with the burgeoning nationalism of the nineteenth century they coalesced to form strengthened social barriers.

A closer look at this historical process reveals that the basic disposition of society developed very differently with respect to Jews and to
"Gypsies." The emancipation of the Jews[50] gave them legal equality as
citizens, at least officially. But despite the popular romanticization of
traveling people, who became the subject of opera libretti and romantic tales, stricter legislation was introduced for "Gypsies" and a system
was established for keeping records on them – one involving measures

that later proved to be suitable for use on Jews in the "Third Reich" (cf. Zimmermann 1996).

These legal foundations notwithstanding, the majority society never took a neutral approach to dealing with these minorities. Even with the so-called assimilation of a large number of Jews – many of whom no longer followed their religion, lived separately from the rest of society, or pursued the occupations traditionally associated with them – there was still a pronounced attitude of antisemitism that meant the "Jewishness" of these people was never forgotten. This antisemitism intensified particularly after the devastating defeat of World War I, for which many people felt "the Jews" were responsible (cf. Wildt 2007). The pan-European processes of political and demographic dissolution and displacement triggered by this war also resulted in many Jews moving from the former Austro-Hungarian territories in Eastern and Southern Europe[51] to Germany and Austria,[52] supposedly bringing both their "Jewishness" and their "alien" culture with them. Even the so-called assimilated Jews in Germany and Austria felt alienated by this stream of Eastern European Jews[53] and behaved "antisemitically" toward them (cf. also ibid.).

Modern antisemitism[54] may have been controversial and hotly debated in certain social circles – for example, whether the rumored shrewdness and subtlety of "the Jews" might not be advantageous to society, an attitude which is no less prejudicial in itself than rejecting these supposed traits as dangerous. But the romantic image of the "Gypsies" did nothing to counter the widespread agreement regarding their apparent criminal tendencies and social unsuitability and the resulting antiziganist consensus that this minority had to be marginalized and controlled.

What is clear from all this is that, independent of the different social practices directed at these two minorities, both Jews and "Gypsies" always bore the stigma of being minorities and thus being different. With this in mind, I want to return to the principles of the caste system and weigh up whether, first, it is acceptable to introduce the caste concept in the context of the topic at hand, and, second, whether this concept could help explain the unique aspects of the social practices being analyzed here.

To the best of my knowledge, Max Weber was the first sociologist to use the caste concept outside of the context of the Indian caste system. In his 1922 essay on "Class, Status, Party," he writes that distinct status groups in the social order can have aspects of a "closed caste" (Weber 1978: 933) when

> [s]tatus distinctions are [. . .] guaranteed not merely by conventions and laws, but also by religious sanctions. This occurs in such a way that every physical contact with a member of any caste that is considered to be lower by the members of a higher caste is considered as making for a ritualistic impurity and a stigma which must be expiated by a religious act. In addition, individual castes develop quite distinct cults and gods. In general,

however, the status structure reaches such extreme consequences only where there are underlying differences which are held to be "ethnic." The caste is, indeed, the normal form in which ethnic communities that believe in blood relationship and exclude exogamous marriage and social intercourse usually associate with one another. [...S]uch a caste situation is part of the phenomenon of pariah peoples and is found all over the world. These people form communities, acquire specific occupational traditions of handicrafts or of other arts, and cultivate a belief in their ethnic community. They live in a diaspora strictly segregated from all personal intercourse, except that of an unavoidable sort, and their situation is legally precarious. Yet, by virtue of their economic indispensability, they are tolerated, indeed frequently privileged, and they live interspersed in the political communities. The Jews are the most impressive historical example. A status segregation grown into a caste differs in its structure from a mere ethnic segregation: the caste structure transforms the horizontal and unconnected coexistences of ethnically segregated groups into a vertical social system of super- and subordination. (Ibid.: 933–4)

[T]he development of status groups from ethnic segregations is by no means the normal phenomenon. On the contrary. Since objective "racial differences" are by no means behind every subjective sentiment of an ethnic community, the question of an ultimately racial foundation of status structure is rightly a question of the concrete individual case. (Ibid.: 935)

What strikes me about Weber's argument is that he views "ethnic" differentiation not as something real and material but rather as a question of belief, that is, a social agreement that these "ethnic" differences actually exist. In recognizing that this can become a matter of caste if a social hierarchy is associated with "ethnic segregation" and citing Jews as an example of such a caste, he is referring explicitly to historical developments and thus to a historical situation in which the differentiation of this minority from the majority is guaranteed "by conventions and laws" but also has a ritual dimension.

It therefore appears that while the formal emancipation of the Jews eliminated the legal basis for differentiation, it did not eliminate its conventional and ritual aspects. In fact, it is clear that owing to the tenacity of the habitus, social intercourse with Jews only changed in certain sections of society and in liberal circles and, despite the altered legal status of Jews, there were still widely accepted attitudes toward and ways of interacting with this minority. I believe Weber's allusion to *contamination* through interaction with "lower" castes is very important in this context because this aspect can be seen as the source of the stigma that continued to cling to both Jews and "Gypsies."

Louis Dumont, who intensively studied Indian society (cf. Dumont 1980), strongly criticized Weber for applying the caste concept elsewhere (cf. ibid.: 249f.). He argues that for the concept of caste to be applicable, "the entire society must without remainder be made up of a set of castes" (ibid.: 215).[55] More recent caste research has distanced itself from this type of theoretical fundamentalism, just as sociology now critically questions the concept of societies as intrinsically coherent systems. Upon closer examination we find that different patterns of interpretation coexist in complex societies, so the concept of caste is valid here because – as Weber describes it – it can in fact be applied to special selected social groups without having to categorize the entire society in this way. In my view, reducing a society to an intrinsically coherent system is an unacceptable oversimplification that can cause us to lose sight of special phenomena.

In general, I do not think enough attention has been paid to the idea that the formulation of the caste system in India is actually European in origin, and that the caste concept had a tremendous influence on policies and administration in the Indian colonies. It was colonial administrative policy that sharpened the distinctions between and strictly divided the existing social groups in Indian society. The term "caste" comes from the Portuguese word *casto*, meaning pure or chaste, and was intended to describe the "phenomenon of the separation and hierarchical organiza-tion of groups particularly in relation to marriage" (Skoda 2003) – so the word itself is a product of the conceptual world of the invaders. What's more, the term *casto* was simultaneously applied to two different (though, in our eyes, seemingly similar) Indian social categories, namely *jati* and *varna* – meaning roughly "type" and "color" – which are "multiple and context-dependent hierarchies" (ibid.) that have been empirically shown to be not nearly as closed as our pedestrian understanding of the Indian caste system would lead us to believe.[56] Therefore, several factors seem to indicate that the idea of resolutely immutable caste affiliation is rooted more in European thought than in traditional Indian thinking. In an essay entitled "Unberührbar heißt rechtlos" ("Untouchable Means without Rights"), Melitta Waligora (2006) points explicitly to this situation and goes so far as to refer to the caste system as "an invention of the modern colonial era." While the idea of castes as an ideal form of status-based society certainly already existed in India, even in the eighteenth and nineteenth centuries there were large groups of people who stood outside of what we would today call the caste system (cf. ibid.).[57] According to Waligora, the normative closure of the Indian castes can be traced back to the colonial powers, who, particularly in the second half of the nineteenth century, thought that they could simplify a society that was otherwise complex and relatively inscrutable to Europeans by forcing the local peoples to assign themselves to a caste in social statistical surveys – surveys that demanded an unambiguousness which was as new as it was incomprehensible and difficult to comply with for the people surveyed. Nevertheless, cooperation with the colonial powers was necessary here because unambiguous classification had concrete consequences in terms of whether a person would be admitted to the military or to an administrative career, for example, or the jurisdiction applicable to each caste (cf. Waligora 2006).[58]

Let us return to the opening question in this chapter, the aim of which was to identify socially prevalent principles of differentiation that cannot be sufficiently explained using everyday, untheoretical concepts like "race" or "ethnic group" but which nonetheless are clearly the basis for social action in some cases. In light of the inadequacy of differentiation according to "race" or "ethnic group" – a differentiation which is frequently found even in sociology – I felt it necessary to explore the caste concept, as this describes ways of thinking and acting based on categories of purity and impurity that were (and are) increasingly potent even in central Europe in the wake of specific historical events and that emphasize the presumed impurity of certain social groups.

As for whether it is acceptable to introduce a concept that seems to spring from an entirely different cultural space, I think that, in light of the actual origins of this type of thinking, the answer is yes. The caste concept and discussions of "contamination" can be found in a number of twentieth-century sources, so it seems reasonable to apply this concept to the social attitude toward certain minorities in German society in the twentieth century.[59] Caste also seems to be a suitable term because it describes a social force that requires no material – and thus rational – basis. The belief alone that there is such a material basis is enough to act as a "logic of practice" (Bourdieu 1990) which has concrete effects on the schemes of perception, appreciation, and action (Bourdieu 1984: 100 and *passim*) of the social agents. The fourth step of my argument has therefore shown that in addition to differentiation according to individuality, class, and gender, a social mechanism closely related to caste must have been prevalent as a non-negotiable differentiation principle in the Nazi concentration camps, because the prisoners would have been familiar with it from their previous lives and would have incorporated it as social normality. The fact that this social mechanism had tremendous potency and range can be seen not just in the popularity and actual success of the Nazis' racial ideas but also in the differentiation principles used by the prisoners themselves in the society inside the camps which will be the focus of part III of this work.

4.2.5. *Summary: Habitus and society*

The idea of society is a powerful image. It is potent in its own right to control or to stir men to action. This image has form; it has external boundaries, margins, internal structure. Its outlines contain power to reward conformity and repulse attack. There is energy in its margins and unstructured areas.

Mary Douglas (2002: 141)

The preceding arguments lead me to the conclusion that the "basic concepts" of society include particular *principles of differentiation* that have a universal validity to a certain extent, even though their substance and forms can vary greatly depending on the time and location. It is evidently important to social agents that these differentiation principles appear to be based on material foundations that can be placed in relation to each other in an evaluative way and thus have far-reaching social consequences.

A closer analysis, however, reveals that the material basis for differentiation can have very different qualities. The concept of the *individual* – as the word itself indicates in its definition of "that which cannot be divided" – is oriented first and foremost on this *material* basis. Depending on the prevailing ideological understanding of the relationship between the individual and society, individuals may either be viewed in terms of their function as the smallest building blocks of society, or they may be imbued with idealized characteristics arising from the notion of absolute independence and autonomy, a viewpoint which places individuals in continual opposition to society. The society of the "Third Reich" was torn between these two opposing viewpoints, which led the Nazi regime – as the representative of a pseudo-holistic world-view – to exercise the utmost thoroughness and brutality in taking real, violent action against representatives both of the holistic view (such as communists) and of individualistic ideology (such as intellectuals and artists). On the level of individuals themselves, the underlying scheme of evaluation that has been incorporated by the social agents influences their perceptions and actions in such a way that their respective viewpoint appears to be an unquestioned *logic of practice* (cf. Bourdieu 1990) that also shapes their *identity* (cf. Kaufmann 2005). If the material basis of the individual is completely unequivocal, then the relationship that is assumed to exist between the individual and society is essential to the respective "idea of society" (Douglas 2002: 141). In comparison, the material basis of the concept of *class* is considerably more fragile, above all because it is expressed solely through lifestyles that ultimately become symbolically loaded signifiers of particular affiliations. The persons, goods, and practices that social agents choose to surround themselves with (cf. Bourdieu 1998: 8) serve as substantial symbols of social differentiation and are associated with value judgments on the level of perception. This means that lifestyle differentiation is strictly *relational* in the social space of a society. Concrete ensembles of persons and goods as well as certain practices are consensually evaluated as belonging to a specific class on the levels of perception and action. The social agents incorporate the resulting *hierarchy of social positions* and associate it with specific ideas of *honor* which are shaped by *habitus*. In an environment like the Nazi concentration camps, the original material basis for class sensibility would seem to have been entirely abolished. However, through the agents' habitus, a logic of practice shaped by the agents' class sensibility from their former lives could continue to operate even when this logic was dissociated from material circumstances.

In the case of *gender*, on the other hand, the material basis for the binary classification of male or female can be found in the *"biological reality" of the body* (Bourdieu 2001a: 11). The gender relationship based on this is not only antagonistic, it is also hierarchically classifying and is therefore a *power relationship*. Like class affiliation, gender identity is associated with a specific notion of *honor* that must be preserved and defended. With gender differentiation, the body is the superficial focus of the logic of practice, and the social dimension of gender is disguised almost beyond recognition. This focus on the body makes gender differentiation one of the most fundamental forms of social differentiation – even more than the other differentiation principles – and thus gives it *universal validity*. As a consequence, there can be universal agreement regarding this differentiation principle, since its material basis – the "biological reality" of the body – applies to all people, meaning that gender distinctions can apparently be made and understood easily regardless of one's language or culture. Gender has been so fundamentally incorporated in human thought, feeling, and action – in the habitus – that it appears to be a natural category and is therefore present as a primary trait in all social situations and constellations, making its social dimension easy to overlook.[60] The *sense of honor* associated with gender affiliation is therefore often the primary driving force behind social action, as such action can establish clarity and restore wounded honor.

Differentiation according to *"ethnic" criteria* is undoubtedly prevalent in society, but it is also extremely complex because its apparent material basis is *genetic kinship*, which, upon closer inspection, is revealed to be a *social construction*. The characteristics that supposedly indicate genetic kinship may be material in nature, but they are influenced by "tradition" and "customs" in a way that explains "attraction and repulsion" and supports the "belief in affinity or disaffinity of blood" (Weber 1978: 394f.). Kinship may certainly be established through marriage on this social basis, but it is not the cause of it. The belief in blood affinity has tremendous social potency and is often the reason for social demarcation and conflict. Nonetheless, history has shown that in addition to processes of social closure, there have always been movements toward a social opening which permits the mingling of groups that were originally separated. In certain cases, however, the belief in "ethnic" similarity is so strong and *heightened* that the attributes associated with an "ethnic group" take on a finality and become an inescapable social, hierarchical classification. With this form of social differentiation, notions of otherness are accompanied by ideas of *purity* and *impurity*, so the opening of social boundaries is avoided at all costs and transgressions are severely penalized out of fear of contamination. This special principle of social differentiation is put into practice in Indian society, where it is known as the *caste* system. The strictness of this differentiation in India can be attributed largely to Western influence, however, so we can assume that this kind of differentiation principle is prevalent in Western societies as well. The history of the treatment of *Jews* and *"Gypsies"* in Western socie-ties supports the idea that such structures did (and do) exist here as well.[61] This differentiation principle has also been incorporated in the habitus and "so forgotten as history" (Bourdieu 1990: 56), and it influences the social agents' schemes of perception, appreciation, and action. Unlike the social differentiation principles mentioned earlier, this principle is nearly entirely devoid of a material basis. Instead, it is rooted exclusively in the alleged knowledge of one's respective "ethnic" affiliation and it seems to be almost non-negotiable, which is why the term *caste* appears to be very well suited to describing this social mechanism.[62]

These views of the individual and his or her relationship with the rest of society, the firm belief in the social import of gender, the significance of class, and certain heightened notions of "ethnic" affiliation can there-fore be considered "basic concepts" of society (Neurath 2005). Based on either actual, empirically demonstrable or merely assumed materiality, they are *the* essential criteria for social differentiation, and they appear to the social agents to be so self-evident and natural that their charac-teristics do not need to be questioned, at least not in everyday social interactions. *Quasi-natural lines of demarcation* with immense social reach form around these criteria. They are incorporated in the mind and body on an individual level, they form the basis for one's social identity, they give direction to and guide social actions, and there is a widespread social consensus regarding their credibility. Pierre Bourdieu describes this amalgamation of the individual and the social as follows: "[T]he world encompasses me [. . .] but I comprehend it [. . .] precisely *because* it comprises me. It is because this world has produced me, because it has produced the categories of thought that I apply to it, that it appears to me as self-evident" (Bourdieu in Bourdieu and Wacquant 1992: 128; emphasis in original). This self-evidence has two effects, however: first, we are never aware of the obviousness because everything is as we expect it to be; and, second, it is only in the face of severe, unexpected deviations from the familiar that we feel compelled to make adjustments that will bring us back to trusted and therefore seemingly essential path-ways. If, as described above, the self-evident use of certain "principles of vision and division" (Bourdieu 1998: 8) is a fundamental characteristic of society, then, following Bourdieu's argument, we must assume that these principles are incorporated and influence social agents so that this self-evidence is never considered or questioned. But in a situation where suddenly nothing appears to be as it was before, in a "topsy-turvy world," these incorporated principles of differentiation can be particu-larly potent. Because they are not just *cognitive concepts in the mind* but also *habits of the body*, they manifest themselves – much like the physical desire for food or sleep – in the form of a *self-evident demand for differentiation* along familiar lines of demarcation and for *the preservation of one's specific notion of honor*. Bourdieu describes this desire as "social libido," a "social impulse" which "only exist[s] in relation to a social space in which certain things are important and others don't matter and for socialized agents who are constituted in such a way as to make distinctions corresponding to the objective differences in that space" (Bourdieu 1998: 79).

Based on the arguments in the preceding sections, I propose that even the prisoners in Nazi concentration camps (contrary to the intentions of their tormentors) constituted social spaces because the social world had "produced" them and was thus "encompasse[d]" in them as habitus (Bourdieu in Bourdieu and Wacquant 1992: 128), so we can assume that these incorporated criteria and "principles of division" were the only ones available to the prisoners. In the empirical section of this work (part III), I will use the theoretical perspectives developed here to search for evidence of how concepts of the individual, gender, class, and a kind of caste thinking continued to be essential "principles of division" influencing the "world-views" (Bourdieu 1994: 130) of the concentration camp prisoners in their accounts and how important these concepts were in the context of the camps.

4.3 Concentration camps

Thus far, we have introduced and discussed aspects of social differentiation as "basic concepts" of society. But in the context of the social world of the Nazi concentration camps, it is necessary to examine the peculiarities of this situation for the prisoners, as otherwise it will not be possible to understand how they adapted their behavior to the life-threatening conditions in which they found themselves. The situation in the camps was roughly outlined earlier in the historical overview, so in the following I want to focus on three aspects in particular that had a formative influence on the life of the prisoners in Nazi concentration camps: first, the continuous presence of violence and public torture; second, the hermetically sealed environment and meticulous control exercised over every aspect of the prisoners' lives; and, third, the tormentors' clear goal of preventing any form of self-determined cultural activity on the part of the prisoners and dispossessing them of their cultural roots through coercion and derision. As we delve deeper into the questions at the heart of this study, sociological theories from Michel Foucault, Erving Goffman, and Zygmunt Bauman will provide orientation and shed more light on the special aspects of the social world in the Nazi concentration camps.

4.3.1 The significance of physical torture: Michel Foucault's restoration of sovereignty through "the vengeance of the sovereign" and the "dissymmetry of forces"

Everyday life in the Nazi concentration camps was characterized by hunger, illness, heavy labor, and a wide range of physical and psychological deprivations. Death and dying were omnipresent in the camps, so the prisoners did not ask themselves whether they would die, but rather how; death was a certainty for them, but the act of dying itself left room for speculation and fear (cf. Améry 1980a: 17f.; Levi 1989: 148). Sickness, starvation, and exhaustion threatened the lives of the inmates, as did the prospect of faceless, industrialized death. And hovering over everything was the constant danger of corporal punishment and torture with fatal consequences. Public punishment in front of all the inmates of a camp – an involuntary audience that sometimes numbered in the tens of thousands – was a recurrent ritual on the part of the camp SS. In the memoirs of former concentration camp prisoners, these horrific incidents always play a significant role and are reflected upon in detail.

This public ritualized cruelty is one reason that Nazism is often referred to as a "relapse into barbarism" (cf. Adorno 1971, for example), as such unbridled violence runs contrary to the principles of human dignity and recalls the more lawless epochs in human history. Barbarism represents "brutalization and dehumanization" as well as a type of "decivilization" (Elias 1996: 196) which employs violence to destroy anything in its path. With the help of Michel Foucault's perceptive analyses,[63] however, we can see that this apparently untamed and uncontrolled excess of violence had another facet as well, because a specific aspect of the Nazi system can be found within it – namely, a remaining premodern element that, together with the Führer myth, made up a premodern component of this pseudo-holistic regime.

In his widely received work on *The Birth of the Prison* (Foucault 1995), Foucault traces the historical development of punishment, in the course of which its function has evolved from a punitive measure intended to restore "sovereignty" (ibid.: 48ff.), which is described as a political ritual of the premodern period, to a corrective measure intended to improve the delinquents of the modern age (ibid.: 8). With the birth of the Enlightenment, it was possible to see even in the worst "criminal" a man whose dignity must be acknowledged despite his disgraceful deeds: "In the worst of murderers, there is one thing, at least, to be respected when one punishes: his 'humanity'" (ibid.: 74).

Foucault views this development as a fundamental change in the objective of punishment. In the premodern period, the objective was to torture the body of the criminal, who was subjected to disgrace by means of a ritual public display of "corporal punishment" (ibid.: 33f.), in order to restore the sovereignty insulted by his transgression before the eyes of the public (ibid.: 48). At the start of the modern period, we still find a "trace of torture" in the mechanisms of criminal justice, but the focus now is on the soul of the offender, who is to be viewed as an individual and whose "heart," "thoughts," "will," and "inclinations" are to be reformed (ibid.: 16).

However, the idea of correction to reform the delinquent led to a boom in disciplinary measures, and the body of the offender became the focus of attention in a new way. "The body now serves as an instrument or intermediary: if one intervenes upon it to imprison it, or to make it work, it is in order to deprive the individual of a liberty that is regarded both as a right and as property" (ibid.: 11). At the end of the eighteenth century, prisons evolved into laboratories for testing the "micro-physics of power" (ibid.: 160) in which the training of the body served the purposes of the rational exploitation of the prisoners' labor, on the one hand, and led to their "increased domination," on the other (ibid.: 138). From this point on, discipline and surveillance go hand in hand, ultimately prompting prisoners to internalize the discipline demanded of them and turn the controlling gaze onto themselves in order to preempt much worse forms of punishment (cf. ibid.: 201ff.; Gehring 2004: 91; Traverso 2003: 27ff.).

In this sense, the Nazi concentration camps are undoubtedly modern institutions that could only have existed from the twentieth century onward. Historically tested approaches to total discipline were put to use in them, and technical developments were effortlessly integrated at the same time, without which it would have been impossible to implement the camps' underlying goals on such an industrial scale: namely, the demonstration of power and absolute sovereignty through subjugation, forced labor, and annihilation. Just as the prisons of the late eighteenth century had "something more alarming" about them because Enlightenment philosophy had converged with economic calculation and "an ancient cruelty that now took on new, more rational forms" (Traverso 2003: 30), the Nazi concentration camps were "a *unique synthesis* of a vast range of modes of domination and extermination" (ibid.: 151; emphasis in original) that had already been trialed over the course of history. As explained in more detail above, Nazi ideology borrowed its concept of the "people's community" and similar notions from the premodern period (see section 4.2.1; cf. Wildt 2007) and applied them to the image of the modern German state. A similar phenomenon was at work in the concentration camps, as these were certainly not correctional facilities – or, to be more precise, they may only have served such a purpose in the early phase of the "Third Reich" when the regime wanted to send a quick, clear signal to its opponents and thus set up the camps as a warning to others. Very soon, however, the camps were no longer facilities for rehabilitating supposed reprobates; they were institutions for eliminating unwelcome elements (see also chapter 2.1). "Annihilation through labor" played an increasingly important role here, as did industrialized death. Furthermore, acts of staged and ritualized torture took place in the camps right from the beginning. This was utterly incompatible with the Enlightenment idea of reform; on the contrary, the use of violence in the concentration camps bears a striking resemblance to Foucault's descriptions of torture[64] in the premodern age (Foucault 1995: 3–69).

"[T]he fusion of historical experiences and models of reference, some openly acknowledged, some subconscious or even unconscious," is what makes Nazism so "radically and terribly new, to the point of being unimaginable and incomprehensible to many of its contemporaries" (Traverso 2003: 151–2). With respect to the question of the "basic concepts" of society, we need to analyze and evaluate individual factors if we want to understand these contradictory social forces during the Nazi era. To this end, I will first take a closer look at Foucault's analysis of torture before attempting to draw parallels which will cast a new light on the glorified idealization of premodern ideas in the "Third Reich" and what actually took place in the Nazi concentration camps.

Foucault's book begins with a detailed description, based on contemporary sources, of a scene of torture in Paris in 1757 (Foucault 1995: 3ff.), the barbarity of which does not differ very much from the scenes of torture in Nazi concentration camps as described in Holocaust literature. To name just one example, I would like to mention an incident described by David Faber (2001). The scene takes place not in one of the infamous large concentration camps but in the Szebnie forced labor camp near Kraków. Faber reports that he and his young friend Sammy were forced to dig deep holes in the ground to anchor fence posts. As they were digging, the handle of his friend's shovel broke. When the guard saw the broken shovel, he had the boy hung from a tall pole by his hands, which were tied behind him, in the middle of the roll call square.[65] Screaming in pain, the boy hung there from nine in the morning for the entire day, within the visual range and earshot of the other prisoners who had to continue working in the grounds. His hands soon turned black, followed by his entire body, at which point the boy begged for someone to kill him and release him from his agony. The evening roll call took place in view of this scene of torture, though by that point Sammy had apparently lost consciousness and fallen silent. The announcement by the camp commandant, *Hauptsturmführer* Grzymek, to the prisoners standing at roll call ended with the following words: "You're still going against *my* rules! I'll show you what happens when you sabotage German property!" (Faber 2001: 123; emphasis added). Then he shot the "delinquent" in the face. When even this did not finish Sammy off, Grzymek put a bullet in his brain. His friend David Faber and two other prisoners were forced to carry the body back to their hut (cf. ibid.).

Foucault identifies two key criteria of premodern torture: First, the ritual and public act of punishment is targeted at the body of the delinquent, by means of which, second, the injured sovereignty of the ruler is restored in the eyes of the public. Torture is therefore also a political ritual which reconstitutes "a momentarily injured sovereignty" through a "direct reply to the person who has offended [the sovereign]" (Foucault 1995: 48).

> Its aim is [. . .] to bring into play, as its extreme point, the dissymmetry between the subject who has dared to violate the law and the all-powerful sovereign who displays his strength. [. . .] [I]n this liturgy of punishment, there must be an emphatic affirmation of power and of its intrinsic superiority. And this superiority is not simply that of right, but that of the physical strength of the sovereign beating down upon the body of his adversary and mastering it. (Ibid., 48–9)

"[Torture] made the body of the condemned man the place where the vengeance of the sovereign was applied, the anchoring point for a manifestation of power, an opportunity of affirming the dissymmetry of forces" (ibid.: 55), and thus a demonstration of the impotence of the condemned (ibid.: 50). Viewed from this perspective, there is "in the least criminal a potential regicide" (ibid.: 53–4). If there is a lack of "continual supervision," the sovereign's claim to power must be renewed through "the spectacle of its individual manifestations" (ibid.: 57). It is essential for this ceremony of punishment to have military characteristics to demonstrate the armed justice of the sovereign (ibid.: 50). Particularly if the delinquent has come from among the people, it is necessary for the common people to play a role in his punishment as spectators (ibid.: 59).

Returning to the situation in the "Third Reich" – a dictatorship under a "Führer" to whom not only his followers but every single regular soldier had to swear personal allegiance, a state and a society in which public ritual played an important role in strengthening the "people's community" – we find that, despite its sundry modern aspects, there were countless parallels with premodern societies even outside of its penal practices (cf. Wildt 2007; see also section 4.2.1). In terms of "penal style" (Foucault 1995: 7), the ritualized public torture carried out in the concentration camps is a logical extension of both the pillorying and "processions of shame" that had boomed in popularity since the mid-1930s (cf. Wildt 2007) and the forced labor that took place openly in public. These highly visible "traces of torture" (Foucault 1995: 16) mimicked premodern forms of law which had never entirely disappeared and continued to have currency in the form of folk traditions (cf. Wildt 2007: 366f.). However, this practice of mimicry spoke a clear language and was a tangible demonstration of the inequality and asymmetry of this society. The torture scene from the Szebnie camp recounted above reveals the "dissymmetry of forces" (Foucault 1995: 55), the "vengeance of the sovereign" (ibid.), and the impotence of the masses. This premodern demonstration of power through punishment was apparently effortlessly integrated into the modern form of discipline in the concentration camps. Foucault himself points out that "the practice of the public execution haunted our penal system for a long time and still haunts it today" (ibid.: 15). The crimes and violence of the Nazis sprang from "common bases of Western culture" (Traverso 2003:150); their singularity lies in the Nazis' "capacity to find a way to *synthesize* the West's various forms of violence" (ibid.; emphasis in original) and implement them in completely conflicting modern ideas. The "clues" pointing to a past thought to be long gone are so "blindingly visible" (ibid.: 149) that they are easy to overlook.[66] It is critical for us to find these "clues," however, because they can help to show how two completely contradictory ideas and their adherents grappled with each other in the Nazi concentration camps: on one side, a relic of premodernity, the idea of a society of non-equals and a "sovereign" who wants to preserve the "dissymmetry of forces" at any cost and who, in the absence of "continual supervision," must defend his sovereignty against all "potential regicides" by means of "spectacle"; and on the other side, the prisoners who view themselves as individuals in an enlightened society and who, for their part, try to defend their human dignity. This grappling took place in a literal sense, meaning that such struggles were actually carried out between real agents in the concentration camps, even though the abstract ideas behind these struggles may not have been consciously perceived by everyone. The "Führer" was represented by his henchmen who were assigned to defend the dignity of Adolf Hitler against the "internal enemy" (Sofsky 1997: 103), while the prisoners risked their own lives fighting for a different idea of society based on the concept of the fundamental dignity of all human beings. This asymmetry of power and the impotence of the prisoners was a daily reality in the Nazi concentration camps, and the hidden strategies of the prisoners were an attempt to counter it.

In the section above, I have explained the strategies employed in the concentration camps to demonstrate the unlimited power of the Nazi regime in light of Foucault's theories on torture. In the following, I will turn to the strategies of the inmates who tried to defend their human dignity – their very "self," as Erving Goffman says.

4.3.2 *"Total institutions" and the possibility of surviving one: Erving Goffman's "secondary adjustments"*

In the 1950s, the American sociologist Erving Goffman[67] carried out research in psychiatric institutions and developed a theory of "total institutions" on the basis of this work (cf. Goffman 1961). According to Goffman, all institutions have "encompassing tendencies," but some are encompassing to a "discontinuously greater" degree than others: "Their encompassing or total character is symbolized by the barrier to social intercourse with the outside and to departure that is often built right into the physical plant, such as locked doors, high walls, barbed wire [. . .]" (ibid.: 4). Goffman distinguishes between five sub-categories of total institution: (1) care homes for those considered incapable of caring for themselves, such as orphanages or homes for the elderly; (2) care homes for those considered incapable and also a danger to the community, such as "TB sanitaria" or "mental hospitals"; (3) institutions that are designed to protect the community from danger but make few or no concessions to the welfare of their inmates, such as prisons, POW camps, and concentration camps; (4) institutions that accommodate people carrying out work together, such as army barracks, ships, and so on; and finally (5) places of retreat from the world, such as cloisters, convents, and so on (cf. ibid.: 4f.).

All of these types of institutions share a few basic characteristics:

> First, all aspects of life are conducted in the same place and under the same single authority. Second, each phase of the member's daily activity is carried on in the immediate company of a large batch of others [. . .]. Third, all phases of the day's activities are tightly scheduled, [. . .] the whole sequence of activities being imposed from above by a system of explicit formal rulings and a body of officials. Finally, the various enforced activities are brought together in a single rational plan purportedly designed to fulfill the official aims of the institution. (Ibid.: 6)

Total institutions thus stand in stark contrast to life in modern individualistic societies (cf. Dumont 1992), in which the private sphere is generally clearly separated from the sphere of work and the individual's life in no way follows a "single rational plan" (Goffman 1961: 6; cf. also Duby 1992).

Goffman believes total institutions are extremely interesting for sociological research: "In our society, they are the forcing houses for changing persons; each is a natural experiment on what can be done to the self" (Goffman 1961: 12). By implication, this means that a sociological analysis of such institutions can be used to find out what *cannot* be done to the self – that is, to find the limits of the experiment. This brings us back to the subject of the study at hand.

The strategies used by the inmates of "total institutions" to assert their sense of self are particularly interesting in respect to the questions posed in this work. In connection with this, Goffman proposes the concept of "secondary adjustments," which he defines as "practices that do not directly challenge staff but allow inmates to obtain forbidden satisfactions or to obtain permitted ones by forbidden means" (ibid.: 54). "Secondary adjustments provide the inmate with important evidence that he is still his own man, with some control of his environment; sometimes a secondary adjustment becomes almost a kind of lodgment for the self, a *churinga* in which the soul is felt to reside" (ibid.: 55; italics in original). Goffman makes a distinction between disruptive practices aimed at radically changing or abolishing the institution (ibid.: 199) and more moderate forms which aim to make optimal use of the institution's structures for the benefit of the inmates (ibid.). Just like the "underworld" of a city, these secondary adjustments represent the "underlife of the institution" (ibid.).

With respect to the focus of my work, the inmates' strategies are particularly important because their success depends on social networks that must facilitate the creation of positions of power and of dependencies within the inmate society while at the same time enabling solidarity. The "counter-mores" (ibid.: 56) that thus emerge are frequently characterized by a reversal of values which "permits the inmate to reject his rejectors rather than himself" (McCorkle and Korn quoted in ibid.: 58). "Secondary adjustments" may also be expressed through collective action, where the staff cannot determine the source of the disruption and therefore the infractions cannot be punished on an individual basis (ibid.). Differentiated bond formation may also take place, but within a very limited circle of persons and usually in a physically delimited area such as a barracks (ibid.: 59).

The emergence of new social relations in the form of dependencies, power relations, and sometimes groups united in solidarity, all of which have holistic traits, must not blind us to the fact that these adjustment strategies are often viewed as individual opportunities to carve out niches in a system of oppression and reconnect with one's previously cultivated world-views in order to retreat from the immediate hardship of the situation. Goffman mentions four types of behavior in connection with this: first, "situation withdrawal" or complete encapsulation (ibid.: 61); second, the "intransigent line" in which a "high individual morale" leads to a total refusal to cooperate, though this is usually just an initial reaction to the situation in a "total institution" (ibid.: 62); third, "colonization," a particular alignment on the part of the inmate whereby he views the world of the institution as the entire world so that it is possible for him to make a "home" there (ibid.: 62f.); and, finally, "conversion," in which the inmate strives to be perfect and copies his superiors (ibid.: 63f.).

Both "secondary adjustments" and the other four strategies described above play a prominent role in the social world of the concentration camps, as we will see later on. With the exception of the withdrawal strategy, which usually ends in complete apathy, all of the other strategies offer the opportunity to (individually or collectively) make use of various networks, either those that already exist or those that are yet to be established. This can take place in the form of activities undertaken alone or with other prisoners that either destroy the structure of the camp or exploit the situation for the benefit of the prisoners. However, it can also take place virtually, in a sense, either alone or in conversation with others, when the inmates lose themselves in their imagination or in mental exercises, where the concepts of the social world applicable outside the "total institution" result in a feeling of having done something to oppose the oppressors and to preserve something of oneself. The most important sociological question that arises from all of this is: Under which social conditions can these strategies be introduced and sustained? (Cf. Ibid.: 199.)

The specific ways in which these strategies were employed by the prisoners in Nazi concentration camps will be the subject of the empirical section of this work and, above all, the concluding discussion (parts III and IV). But at this point, we can already say that from Goffman's point of view, too, the inmates of a "total institution" are agents who adjust their strategies to the opportunities available to them and to the particular situation and, in doing so, play a part in shaping their social world as best they can despite their plight. Ideas play just as important a role as actions here, meaning that both cognitive and embodied aspects of the social world influence the strategies of the inmates equally. This makes it possible to view the inmates' behavioral and adjustment tactics as habitus strategies (Bourdieu) that are adapted to the specific conditions in total institutions.

One special aspect of the "underlife" (ibid.) in the Nazi concentration camps applies to cultural activities, so in the following I will explore the significance of such activities from Zygmunt Bauman's point of view.

4.3.3 Suppressing the "odors" of death: Zygmunt Bauman's concept of culture

In showing us the image of a human being as a "collective individual" or a "collective individuated by the fact of embodying objective structures" (Bourdieu 2005: 84), Bourdieu clearly illustrates how individual action is always simultaneously social action. Goffman's notion of "secondary adjustments" in total institutions also cannot be adequately explained without taking account of how individuals have incorporated the social significance of their actions. In their memoirs, Holocaust survivors frequently describe the importance of cultural activities as a secret survival strategy. In light of this, we can assume that the goals pursued through secondary adjustments comprised not just the acquisition of food or clothing but also the creation of opportunities for cultural activity.

In his book *Mortality, Immortality and Other Life Strategies* (1992),[68] Zygmunt Bauman[69] formulates theories of culture that are directly connected to death and dying. Specifically, he views culture as a life strategy.

Bauman's concept of culture is particularly relevant to the Nazi concentration camps and the omnipresence of death there. Even in his book *Culture as Praxis* (Bauman 1999), which was first published in 1973, Bauman grappled with various theories of culture and tried to systematically organize diverse views of the concept. The three main sections of this book are entitled "Culture as Concept" (ibid.: 1ff.), "Culture as

Structure" (ibid.: 47ff.), and "Culture as Praxis" (ibid.: 87ff.). His own position is formulated in the third of these sections: Culture is a genuine human practice that plays a role in identity formation and thus holds a critical potential relative to the constraints of reality. "Culture, which is synonymous with the specifically human existence, is a daring dash for freedom *from* necessity and freedom *to* create. It is a blunt refusal to the offer of a secure animal life. It is [. . .] a knife with its sharp edge pressed continuously against the future" (ibid.: 136; emphasis in original). "[T]he most important of all attributes of all culture [is] its critical capacity, based on its assumed and struggled-for supremacy over the real. [. . .] The culture may exist only as an intellectual and practical critique of the existing social reality" (ibid.: 137). "Culture is [. . .] the natural enemy of alienation. It constantly questions the self-appointed wisdom, serenity and authority of the Real" (ibid.: 139).

In *Mortality, Immortality and Other Life Strategies*, which was written nearly twenty years later, Bauman goes much further: He reveals culture to be an omnipresent engine of life (and survival). According to Bauman, "the absence of a solution [to the problem of death] is the ultimate source of horror" (Bauman 1992: 17). In his earlier work he speaks of culture's supremacy over reality, but in this later work he is more specific: This inevitable and final reality is death, and culture is the product of the ceaseless struggle with mortality.

> Once learned, knowledge that death may not be escaped cannot be forgotten – it can only not be thought about for a while, with attention shifting to other concerns. Knowledge has, so to speak, an olfactory rather than a visual or audial quality; odors, like knowledge, cannot be undone, they can be only "made unfelt" by being suppressed by yet stronger odors.
>
> One can say that culture, another "human only" quality, has been from the start *a device for such a suppression*. This is not to imply that all the creative drive of human culture stems from the conspiracy "to forget death" – indeed, once set in motion, cultural inventiveness acquired its own momentum and like most other parts or aspects of culture "develops because it develops." But this is to imply that, were there no need to make life worth living while it is known that, in Schopenhauer's words, life is but a short-term loan from death, there hardly would be any culture. [...C]ulture is after that permanence and durability which life, by itself, so sorely misses. But death (more exactly, awareness of mortality) is the ultimate condition of cultural creativity as such. It makes permanence into a task, into an urgent task, into a paramount task – a fount and a measure of all tasks – and so it makes culture, that huge and never stopping factory of permanence. (Ibid.: 3–4; emphasis added)
>
> Mortality is ours without asking – but immortality is something we must build ourselves. Immortality is not a mere absence of death; it is defiance and denial of death. (Ibid.: 7)

I have quoted Bauman at length here because the metaphor he employs immediately brings to mind the situation in the Nazi concentration camps. The "odors" of death, a phrase that Bauman uses figuratively, can be found in the literal sense in the accounts of concentration camp survivors: the smoke continuously billowing from the chimneys of the crematoria (which existed not only in Auschwitz but in nearly all concentration camps), the smell of burnt human flesh – the omnipresent knowledge of the inevitability of one's own impending death. The image of a "never stopping factory of permanence" also seems to be a metaphorical response to the relentless factories of death mentioned so often in Holocaust literature.[70]

At the same time, these passages go to the heart of Bauman's deliberations on theory and culture. His two main theses are as follows:

- First, culture is a matter of striving for "survival" by distracting us from the fact that we have to die (ibid.: 5), since "[i]nstinctively, we feel the danger in searching for the human limits at too low a level . . . at a point at which existence appears – through the suffering, misery and frustration – so denuded of 'value' that death finds itself rehabilitated and the violence justified" (Blanchot 1969: 269–70, quoted in Bauman 1992: 6).
- And second, culture serves the purposes of "immortality," that is, the effort to counter transience with something permanent, as culture offers the opportunity of "surviving, so to speak, beyond death, denying the moment of death its final say, and thus taking off some of its sinister and horrifying significance" (Bauman 1992: 6).

Life's lack of value takes on a special nuance in the face of the Nazis' machinery of annihilation. Culture is about "transcendence, about going beyond what is given and found" (ibid.: 4). This is the precise aim of the secret cultural activities described by numerous Holocaust survivors: not letting death, and thus the Nazis, have the final say in the camps. In the pressure cooker of the concentration camps, where the destructive heat of National Socialist ideas was unleashed upon all "potential regicides," cultural activity was not just a way of opposing the given situation, and thus death, it was a weapon in the fight for a different idea, namely, the idea of the inextinguishable dignity of the human being.

4.4 A theoretical perspective: The complex society of the "Third Reich" and social reality in the forcible detention camps

Having wrestled to find a suitable sociological perspective on the "topsy-turvy world" of the Nazi concentration camps and how the "basic concepts" of society influenced the prisoners in these camps, I would like to combine the foregoing considerations to formulate a *single* theoretical perspective on the issues at hand. Several different aspects need to be addressed to answer the questions of how influential the "basic concepts" of society were among the prisoners in the Nazi concentration camps and how these prisoners adjusted their strategies to cope with their situation.

The sociological theories of Pierre Bourdieu, particularly his *habitus concept*, can help explain how it is possible for something that we would call society to come into being in the first place and how individual actions contribute to it. People are always born into social situations, and they absorb and internalize – or incorporate – the respective "principles of vision and division" (Bourdieu 1998: 8) of those situations. The body acts as a type of "memory pad" here (Bourdieu 2000d: 141) in that it transports the "basic concepts" of society both cognitively and as physical habits, so these concepts are embedded in thought and in the body and thus influence social behavior. As a result of this incorporation, an individual's schemes of perception, appreciation, and action appear completely self-evident and, in the form of habitus, create a largely stable foundation for an individual's intrinsic motivation to preserve the order of the world that they are most familiar with. On the level of individuals, the social world is not just received, it is also produced, and a certain inertia of the habitus causes its structures to be perpetuated, at least in broad strokes, so that while change is not impossible, it is certainly an effort.

Viewed from this perspective, the individual and society are not in opposition to each other; instead, one cannot exist without the other. This does not mean, however, that society is a homogeneous structure, because different groups within a society may pursue opposing interests and strategies at the expense of other groups in the social space. In the modern age, the social space is generally extremely complex, and conflicts within it tend to take place along the boundaries between classes and between genders, and sometimes between communities considered to be "ethnic groups" or even castes (cf. Weber 1978). Social lines of demarcation are drawn at the edges of these interest groups – groups that by no means need to act as communities but that, through their habitus, have command of different and often symbolically loaded strategies of exercising power which they use to defend and maintain their borders. The *social space* thus generated by all social agents and conveyed via their lifestyles is a *symbolic, hierarchically structured space*, a space of *differences* and *similarities* that are viewed as signs of social affiliations. Because individuals are all categorized (and they categorize themselves) according to their gender and class affiliation as well as their apparent "ethnic" affiliation depending on the social context, then, following Bourdieu's arguments, we must view the social space as a space of real possibilities for the social agents, a space characterized by a *complex web of invisible and overlapping boundaries*. Individuals incorporate principles of differentiation, and these induce them to maintain and heed, and thus contribute to the continued existence of, these boundaries.

Based on Bourdieu's habitus concept, we can assume that the essential principles of social differentiation are, on account of their incorporation, so evident that they will continue to have an impact even in physically and psychologically extreme situations like those found in a concentration camp, where everything is designed to level out all differences between the inmates. Even if the material basis that could symbolize one's usual position in the social space is torn away with the intent of leveling differences, the prisoners' habitus will ensure that their perceptions, evaluations, and (within a very restricted scope) behavior are still influenced by the structures they had previously experienced. As the *last remaining constant* from their former lives, the habitus of the prisoners – at least as it relates to their notions of "right" and "wrong" or "important" and "unimportant" – can help them preserve the *unchanging constituents of the social order* and the concept of their own *identity*. It is in the "nature" of society, which shapes individuals differently depending on their position in the social space, that the content and form of these concepts will not be congruent for all prisoners. Based on this *concept of social space*, the concentration camps must be viewed as *outposts of the social space* in which the conflicts of normal society continue to be played out. We can also assume that "ethnic" conflicts would play an even larger role here because the prisoner society usually comprised individuals from all over the world and was therefore a random jumble of languages and cultures, causing otherwise subliminal reservations toward different "ethnic groups" to have an especially strong effect, particularly under the immediate pressure of this unique situation.

In view of the special conditions in these camps, where the prisoners were trapped and faced the constant threat of death from hunger, illness, or violence – first and foremost because they were subject to a *"total institution"* – it is probable that the inmates had to shift their priorities and adjust their behavior to the circumstances. In this respect, the social space in the camps must have been a distorted image of normal social reality rather than an exact reflection of it. We would therefore expect that some differences would be leveled out in the face of these grave circumstances, while others – the ones the prisoners considered most fundamental – would become more sharply defined. Bourdieu's theories therefore provide the sociological foundation for Zygmunt Bauman's claim that the *Holocaust is a "significant test"* (Bauman 1989: 12), since the "basic concepts" of society were very clearly expressed by the prisoners themselves in the Nazi concentration camps, while the less fundamental concepts became insignificant.

The regular public *acts of violence* carried out by those in power in the "Third Reich" were demonstrations of a complete *dissymmetry of forces* (Foucault 1995). Such acts staged both inside and outside the camps helped restore the *"sovereignty"* (ibid.) of the "Führer" that had been *injured* through opposition and hammered home the absolute subjugation of those who opposed the regime and were persecuted by it. In the society outside of the camps, these acts took the form of "processions of shame" (Wildt 2007), pogroms, public mass arrests, boycotts, and other types of "performative discourse" (Bourdieu 1994: 137) that were documented in writing, photographs, and film and made public. In the society of the "Third Reich," the opponents of the regime struggled as best they could – though with little success – to disrupt and destroy this total asymmetry of power. Within the camps, however, the strategies employed in this struggle had to be adjusted to the particular situation in a "total institution." In order to preserve their *self-image as human beings bestowed with dignity*, the concentration camp prisoners had to make "*secondary adjustments*" (Goffman 1961). Driven by their habitus, and with the help of these "secondary adjustments," they could pursue either their individualistic or holistic (Dumont 1992) "basic concepts" and "socially constituted interests" (Bourdieu 1998: 79) and thereby remain true to their respective "world-views" (Bourdieu 1994: 130). In doing so, they presented to themselves – and potentially to others – an image of themselves as human beings and members of a human community "in which certain things are important and others don't matter" (Bourdieu 1998: 79). The conflicts that surfaced in the course of this – which took place between the SS and the prisoners in the concentration camps as well as within the prisoner society itself – corresponded to the ideological conflicts of the age, where fierce battles were fought between individualistic, holistic, and pseudo-holistic viewpoints. These were "*struggles for the power to produce and to impose a vision of the legitimate world*" (Bourdieu 1994: 134); the prisoners were subordinate to the SS in these struggles, but the battles remained undecided within the prisoner society itself. Both the public violence and torture carried out by the SS against the prisoners and the secret individual or collective activities carried out underground by the prisoners can be viewed as acts of "*performative discourse*" (ibid.: 152) in which no punches were pulled in the fight to enforce one's interests.

Independent of any specific world-view, Zygmunt Bauman's theory (1992) plausibly explains how, in the omnipresence of death, *cultural activities* in particular could help the prisoners briefly reclaim their feeling of human dignity and *suppress the "odors" of death*. "Secondary adjustments" were therefore made not only so that the prisoners could hold on to their former "world-view" but also so that they could at least temporarily block out the constant threat of death whenever possible. Cultural activities were very frequently the objective of these "secondary adjustments," and they therefore play an especially prominent role in the recollections of former prisoners.

In view of all this, we can expect the prisoner society in the concentration camps to be a *distorted image of the social space* of society outside the camps, with *the same lines of conflict* found in any other society. Given the circumstances, however, some of these conflicts were exacerbated while the intensity of others was reduced. The most essential criteria for this are *principles of differentiation* which make it possible to identify important differences and similarities even in this "topsy-turvy world." The "basic concepts" at work here must be so *universally conveyable* that their potency and fundamental importance could be maintained in such a motley, multilingual, and multicultural involuntary community. Because their material basis still seemed to exist in the camps, we would expect the concepts of the *individual* and of *gender* to have had the highest priority when prisoners interacted with each other. Differentiation according to *class* and lifestyle, on the other hand, relies on a material basis that continued to exist only in the prisoners' memories, so it is likely that these distinctions became less important in the prisoner society. The new, unequal material relations in the forced society of the concentration camps led to unfamiliar experiences that were probably an adequate basis for a new class order applicable to the time of imprisonment which merged with the prisoners' existing habitus. We can assume that the prisoners socially positioned themselves according to those experiences which were thought to be better. Because differentiation according to *"ethnic"* criteria lacks all material basis anyway, this "principle of vision and division" (Bourdieu 1998: 8) seems particularly likely to have caused strife in the prisoner society. Under the precarious conditions in the concentration camps, confrontations between people from different countries and cultures were bound to entail conflict, and it was difficult to come to terms with the "plurality of world-views" (Bourdieu 1994: 134). This is probably why incomprehension of the other was so easily expressed in terms of "ethnic" or even *caste* distinctions (Weber 1978) which were familiar constants of social differentiation and therefore did not further unsettle the *existing world-view* of the prisoners but instead *confirmed* it.

Part III

The Social World of the Nazi Concentration Camps

The SS who view us all as one and the same cannot induce us to see ourselves that way. They cannot prevent us from choosing. On the contrary: here the need to choose is constant and immeasurably greater. The more transformed we become, the farther we retreat from back home, the more the SS believe us reduced to the indistinctness and the irresponsibility whereof we do certainly present the appearance – the more distinctions our community does in fact contain, and the stricter those distinctions are. The inhabitant of the camps is not the abolition of these differences; on the contrary, he is their effective realization.

Robert Antelme (1998: 88)

While we have found preliminary theoretical answers to the question of the potency of the "basic concepts" of society in the Nazi concentration camps, this by no means obviates the need to examine the empirical material itself. The opposite is true, in fact, because these answers were found using theories established at very different times and based on sociological questions and empirical data which are, in some cases, far removed from the social reality in the camps. There is no question that these theoretical answers require empirical backing which will make it possible to say something about the actual situation of the camps' prisoners. This empirical analysis should test the reach of the theories introduced here as well as Zygmunt Bauman's claim that the Holocaust can be viewed "as a rare, yet significant and reliable, test of the hidden possibilities of modern society" (Bauman 1989: 12) which shines a new light on the objects of our sociological research today.

Furthermore, an empirical basis is essential because the question of what impact the "basic concepts" of society had among concentration camp prisoners first arose in my mind in response to the emphatic autobiographical accounts of former prisoners which present a multifaceted view of how important these concepts were to the inmates' survival and their perception of themselves. If I had not been confronted with this generally very personal view of the social reality in the camps – a reality depicted both as an extreme contrast to the prisoners' former lives and as a desperate attempt to maintain continuities – I probably never would have thought to ask the question in the first place.

I believe that the quality of a sociological theory stems solely from whether it can help us understand and describe the complexity of social reality without robbing this reality of any of its opposing tendencies and contradictions. But the only real authorities on actual social practice are the *social agents themselves,* who are essentially the experts on their respective position in the social space and their corresponding view of the world and who are familiar enough with their own apparently logical practices and "strategies" (Bourdieu 1998: 81) that they can describe and explain them. Even when the narratives of former prisoners appear to exceed the limits of our comprehension, we have no choice but to engage with them and give consideration to their sometimes extremely divergent perspectives if we want to learn something about the social world of the concentration camps. At the end of his book *The Human Race*, Robert Antelme[1] bitterly warns that the unimaginability of the horror he experienced must not be used as a "shield"[2] (Antelme 1998: 290) to distance ourselves from all of this. Turning this around, I would say that the accounts and recollections of the people who actually experienced and suffered these horrors themselves are the only thing that can help us imagine them. Moreover, I see no cause to take the supposed impossibility of depicting or imagining these events as a reason for questioning the survivors' accounts of them, as the survivors are the only true experts here, and only they can tell us what their experiences were.

In the following, I will use empirical material[3] as the basis for examining the social aspects of the everyday life of the prisoners. My first step will be to explain the structure of everyday camp life, which comprised different levels of sociality (chapter 5). Then I will describe the prisoner society, with all of its diverse social structural features, and turn my attention to the prisoners as individuals who were both part of their societies of origin and members of the newly created society of prisoners (chapter 6). Finally, based on the empirical material that has been presented, I will analyze in part IV the extent to which the prisoners can be viewed as active agents and which concepts and means they had at their disposal in the terrible reality of the camps to secretly counter the challenges to their social identity and their human dignity (chapter 7).

5

Camp Life

[H]e has a body – a body that has been exploited to the utmost: with a number tattooed on it to save on dog tags, with just enough sleep at night to work during the day, and just enough time to eat. And just enough food so it will not die wastefully. As for actual living, there is only one place for it – a piece of the bunk. The rest belongs to the camp, the Fatherland. But not even this small space, nor the shirt you wear, nor the spade you work with are your own.

Tadeusz Borowski (1992: 131)

Without knowing what everyday life was like for the prisoners in the concentration camps, it is impossible to understand their recollections and narratives. On the one hand, an extremely strict daily regime meant that there was almost never a time when the prisoners had nothing to do. On the other hand, there were many contradictions within this regime which seem irrational and can only be explained by taking into consideration both the disparities and "dual subordination" within the camp SS (see chapter 2.3) as well as the contradictions and oppositions within the prisoner society itself.

As an introduction to camp life, I will first describe the prisoners' transition into the world of the concentration camps (5.1). Then I will briefly outline the usual daily routine of the prisoners, which was very similar in all concentration camps (5.2), in order to finally make an analytical distinction between the three levels of sociality that were characteristic of the contradictory reality in the camps (5.3).

5.1 Arrival and registration of the prisoners at the camp or: How the "practical logic" of the camp gradually revealed itself to the prisoners

When a newcomer first enters a concentration camp, it looks completely different to him from what he had imagined it would be. He may have thought of it as a sort of super-prison, with thick stone walls and a great number of dark cells [. . .]. What he actually finds is a sort of military camp. [. . .] He discovers that life can be made unbearable by regulations and conditions which lack the romanticism that the free world is accustomed to ascribe to the sufferings of its heroes. [. . .] In the beginning, however, each new experience is an isolated incident, and his new world looks like an amazing kaleidoscope, changing shape and color every minute. The only part of the picture that is stable is its frame – the concrete wall and the barbed wire.

Paul Martin Neurath (2005: 11–12)

The first impression that prisoners usually had of a concentration camp was the camp gate. Many survivors recall their horror at the sight of this gate and the unmistakable premonition they had of what was to come (cf., e.g., Steinberg 2001: 42). The gate dwarfed all other buildings in the camp and – depending on which side of it you stood – was a highly visible sign of either enclosure or exclusion. There was usually an aphorism on the gate, such as *"Arbeit macht frei"* (Work sets you free) in Dachau and the main camp at Auschwitz, or *"Jedem das Seine"* (To each his own) in Buchenwald. "The gate marked the transition between two zones. Ahead of it stretched the domain of the SS; behind it lay the barracks settlement of the prisoners. At the same time, it symbolized the code of terror. It did not open up a path to freedom, but marked its end" (Sofsky 1997: 59). Jorge Semprún recounts how, upon seeing the gate at the end of his *long voyage*[1] to the Buchenwald concentration camp, the phrase "leave the world of the living [. . .] [whirled] dizzily in the deep recesses of his brain" (Semprún 1990: 236).

Once the newcomers had passed through this gate, they encountered the social space of the camp, whose principles they would soon have to figure out if they wanted to survive. But they first had to endure a variety of initiation rituals before they could become part of this space. The primary purpose of these rituals was to accustom the newcomers "step by step [. . .] to a terrible and immense horror" (Frankl[2] 1985: 27–8) and to rid them of their former societal attributes. "Driven by constant bullying and blows, [the prisoner] is rushed through a well-organized routine" (Neurath[3] 2005: 12). There was a "coercion of nudity" in the camp (Levi[4] 1989: 113). On the one hand this was literal, as "[o]ne entered the Lager [i.e., the camp] naked [. . .], deprived not only of clothing and shoes (which were confiscated) but of one's head of hair and all other hair" (ibid.). But nudity was also highly symbolic because it hammered home the utter defenselessness and worthlessness of the prisoners who were stripped bare. "Now a naked and barefoot man feels that all his nerves and tendons are severed: he is helpless prey" (ibid.). This coercion of nudity entailed an additional humiliating component for women and girls, who were essentially sized up by the men and subjected to mockery and lewd remarks. Emilie Neu, who was twenty-three at the time of her imprisonment, remembers: "We had to undress and shower, and the

SS came in and watched us. It was awful for us young girls. We stood there, and the men came in and watched us. We had to put up with it" (in Walz 2005b: 115). Urzula Wińska, a Polish woman who was thirty-nine when she was imprisoned in Ravensbrück, recalls in an interview: "We marched [naked] past two Gestapo men who sat on a table and hit the breasts of the young girls with a cane and kicked the older women in the buttocks . . . – and we circled past them. They assessed our ability to work" (in Walz 2005a: 15':38''ff.).

> They turned us into numbers. They took away anything that indicated our social, cultural position. They robbed us of everything. We were given these striped prisoner uniforms; they didn't fit. They would be knee-length on one person and they'd hang to the floor on another. We looked like scarecrows. The younger girls burst into laughter because the elegant women from an hour ago had been turned into ridiculous caricatures. (Ibid.: 16':44''ff.)

The theft of all of one's social – and thus human – attributes and this state of literal and symbolic exposure culminated in the assignment of a number that replaced the prisoner's name from that point on. These numbers were visibly sewn onto the prisoners' tattered clothing in every concentration camp; only in Auschwitz were the numbers additionally tattooed on the inmates' forearms. Ruth Elias[5] reports: "We had to hold out our left forearms, and each of us was tattooed with a number. At first we did not understand why, but gradually it dawned on us: They no longer considered us to be human beings" (Elias 1999: 109).

After being forced to leave their possessions and regular lives back home, the prisoners often had to endure an extremely arduous, inhumane journey of many days to reach the camp. They were either crammed together in goods cars, which some of them did not survive, or transported to the camp in buses with darkened windows or on the backs of trucks. Very few were taken to the camp on a regular passenger train. Upon arrival, their scanty luggage was taken away from them and they were separated from their family members, if this had not already happened prior to the transport. They were forced to remove all their clothes, they were stripped of their last personal possessions (like their wedding rings), they were completely shaved, and they were robbed of their name. "To be dispossessed of one's own name is among the most far-reaching and profound mutilations of the self" (Sofsky 1997: 84), so this was usually one of the first personal low points for newcomers to the camp. "The [admission] ritual did not assure the continuity of time; rather, it was a radical rupture. It did not regulate biographical transition; it destroyed the cohesion of personal history" (ibid.: 83). In his essay "The Biographical Illusion," Bourdieu emphasizes the importance of one's own name: "As an institution, the proper name is independent of time and space and the variations according to time and place; in that way it offers to the designated individual, beyond all biological or social changes, the nominal constant, the identity in the sense of self-identity, *constantia sibi*, required by the social order"[6] (Bourdieu 2000a: 300). And vice versa: As long as you have your own name, you have the remainder of an identity and biographical constancy. If someone wants to rob you of your dignity and express their intention of ending your life, then this name must be taken away from you. Primo Levi, who was imprisoned in Auschwitz, says:

> The operation [of receiving the tattoo] was not very painful and lasted no more than a minute, but it was traumatic. Its symbolic meaning was clear to everyone: this is an indelible mark, you will never leave here; this is the mark with which slaves are branded and cattle sent to the slaughter, and that is what you have become. You no longer have a name; this is your new name. (Levi 1989: 119)

Jewish prisoners were additionally affected by the fact that tattoos and other lasting marks on the skin are forbidden by the Torah,[7] so it is likely that, for devout Jews, this compulsory tattooing entailed a sense of humiliation even beyond that described by Primo Levi.

There is no question that the purpose of this admission ritual was to impress upon the *"Zugang"*[8] or *"newcomer"* (Levi 1989: 39) that the principles from his or her previous life no longer applied. Individuals were thrust into this new form of existence *"more than naked"* (ibid.: 113): Their possessions had been left at home, confiscated, or involuntarily sold for a ludicrous price.[9] Even academic titles were no longer of interest to anyone – on the contrary, it was smarter not to reveal such a title because the notoriously anti-intellectual SS would take it as a disastrous provocation (cf. Améry[10] 1980a: 3f.).

Before the prisoners were assigned to a hut and a work detail, they had to be classified (for details on this see Eberle 2005). Colored triangles with the point facing down were sewn onto the prisoners' clothing as a highly visible symbol of a prisoner's category;[11] these categories also represented the *"Nazis'* categorization of their 'opponents'" (ibid.: 91).[12] The colors were as follows: *green* for criminals, *red* for political opponents, *purple* for International Bible Students,[13] *blue* for emigrants, *black* for so-called *"anti-social elements,"* *brown* for "Gypsies," *pink* for homosexuals,[14] and, finally, *yellow* for Jews.

Jews received a second triangle for more precise identification. This second triangle was sewn, point upward, onto the inverted yellow triangle to form a six-pointed star resembling the Star of David, so Jews were specially identified by this star within the camp society just as they had been in their previous lives[15] (cf. also Kogon 1946, 2006).

Prisoners were often assigned to categories very randomly.[16] For example, Jews were frequently given a red triangle in addition to their yellow one because they were considered intrinsic enemies of the state. Black triangles representing "anti-social elements" were also regularly issued on no specific basis. A letter in the center of the triangle indicated the prisoner's country of origin, for example "F" for France or "P" for Poland[17] (cf. Eberle 2005: 102ff. and Kogon 2006: 36[18]).

The triangle classification system determined the prisoners' position within the structure of the prisoner society – and not just from the perspective of the SS. A prisoner's category comprised a specific class taxonomy combined with a geographic or national code, and it was the indicator of the prisoner's degree of political and social deviation. Although a prisoner's classification often said very little about his or her actual former life, the triangles were visible signifiers of the social classes in the camp (cf. Sofsky 1997: 118ff.). The color coding was also used as a communication shorthand within the prisoner society, as every prisoner quickly learned what was meant by a "green" or a "red." This classification system was an attempt by the SS to fragment the prisoners, but it also served as the basis of the prisoners' own internal strategies of dissociation – and sometimes of community-building.[19] "The identities that groups of prisoners formed to dissociate themselves from other triangle categories and nationality identifiers were often based on the prisoners' social, political, and cultural backgrounds and the misgivings rooted in them" (Eberle 2005: 101).

Once the prisoners had endured these deeply symbolic rituals of dehumanization and had been assigned to a prisoner category, they were admitted to the camp. The physical structure of the camp reflected the outward uniformity of the social mass of inmates: The huts were usually built to a standard size, and they were lined up in identical rows, stretching as far as the eye could see in the large camps. They were generally situated either parallel or at right angles to each other. The wide camp streets were dead straight. The arrangement of the huts and the quality of the living quarters corresponded to the prisoner hierarchy: that is, the higher up you were in this hierarchy, the closer you were to the center of power and the better your quarters would be (cf. Sofsky 1997: 52f. and 67f.). It goes without saying that "quality" was extremely relative here; the differences might consist of whether two or five people had to share a bunk, or whether the hut was heated by a stove or not.

The physical compaction of the prisoners was accompanied by the abrogation of time. The permanent overcrowding in the quarters and the impossibility of being alone for even a moment were agonizing enough for the prisoners. On top of this, each day in the camp followed the same pattern: reveille in the dark of night, hours spent standing at roll call, hard labor to the point of utter exhaustion, another roll call, a brief period of sleep bordering on unconsciousness – and all while the prisoners were in a state of permanent hunger, tormented by lice and pests, and in extremely bad physical health. Taken together, this seemed to suspend the normal flow of time. In connection with this, Viktor Frankl writes:

"[I]n time, it was the limitlessness of the term of imprisonment which was most acutely felt; in space, the narrow limits of the prison" (Frankl 1985: 92).

The shock that newcomers felt at the finality of the physical overcrowding and negation of time was compounded by another phenomenon which was as surprising as it was incomprehensible: the so-called prisoner functionaries.[20] These were prisoners whom the SS had appointed to enforce their orders and harass fellow prisoners in the interests of keeping order in the camp:

> [T]he greater part of the memories [. . .] of those who came back begin with the collision with the concentrationary reality and, simultaneously, the unforeseen and uncomprehended aggression on the part of a new and strange enemy, the functionary-prisoner, who instead of taking you by the hand, reassuring you, teaching you the way, throws himself at you, screaming in a language you do not understand, and strikes you in the face. He wants to tame you, extinguish any spark of dignity that he has lost and you perhaps still preserve. (Levi 1989: 41)

Newcomers were also immediately confronted with the workings of the official camp hierarchy established by the SS and the tacit hierarchy among the prisoners themselves. For example, Ruth Klüger[21] says: "I learned the hierarchy of the numbers: those with the lower numbers were socially above those with the higher ones, because they had had to live for more days, weeks, and months in a place where no one wanted to live. A topsy-turvy world" (Klüger 2001: 96). The comments of both Primo Levi and Ruth Klüger indicate that social mechanisms were at work in the camps which could also be found in the society outside (cf. Suderland 2004). Social inequality, a familiar component in every society, seems to be so essential to personal inner equilibrium that criteria for differentiation will be generated in any situation, even if the criterion is simply having spent "*more days, weeks, and months* in a place where no one wanted to live."

Let us take another look at the process of transitioning from the outside world to the society of the concentration camp:

> New arrivals usually knew nothing about the conditions at the camp. Those who had come back from other camps were obliged to keep silent, and from some camps no one had returned. On entering camp a change took place in the minds of the men. With the end of uncertainty there came the uncertainty of the end. It was impossible to foresee whether or when, if at all, this form of existence would end. (Frankl 1985: 91)

When Viktor Frankl uses the term "uncertainty" here, he clearly does not mean the daily minor uncertainties that are continually encountered in normal life and that are dealt with practically using the repertoire of the habitus. The "hysteresis" (Bourdieu 2005: 86; cf. also Suderland 2009b) or inertia of the habitus had to be overcome under the life-threatening conditions in the concentration camps. Newcomers' initial experiences triggered a feeling of shock which quickly made them all realize that they were dealing with a matter of life and death and that the utmost vigilance would be needed to cope with this completely unfamiliar situation (cf. Frankl 1985). The inmates had to internalize the new necessities of this camp society immediately if they were to have any sort of influence over their situation.

> After a few weeks or months the prisoner is completely adapted to life in the concentration camp. This means, in some cases, that he has regained his spirit as a political fighter, in other cases, that he has regained his private personality. In still other cases it may mean that he has restricted his intellectual life to the petty camp gossip about food, mistreatment, and release, and has limited his personal life to close contact with only one or two men. But no matter what form the adaptation takes, the new man becomes part of the community of prisoners. He learns to think and evaluate in the same ways that the others do and acquires the distorted logic of the camp. (Neurath 2005: 14)

5.2 Prisoner life: Recurring processes

You'd like to know
ask questions
but you don't know what questions [. . .]
and we don't know how to answer [. . .]
so you ask simpler things:
tell us for example
how a day was spent
a day goes by so slowly
you'd run out of patience listening
but if we gave you an answer
you still don't know how a day was spent
and assume we don't know how to answer.

Charlotte Delbo (1995: 275)

While there were certainly variations in particular camps on account of local circumstances or special prisoner work details, the daily routine[22] was largely the same in all Nazi concentration camps, and it was characterized by features which were fundamentally contradictory. On the one hand, there was the extreme uniformity of the days, which began long before dawn and were filled until lights out with continually recurring activities – usually consisting of periods of heavy physical labor alternating with hours of standing at roll call. On the other hand, this uniformity was permeated with a permanent sense of uncertainty regarding potential attacks by the guards or even other prisoners. This uncertainty demanded that the prisoners be alert at all times, despite the monotony and exhaustion, and keep their wits about them so that they could react to unexpected situations quickly and correctly. The only time this cycle was broken was on Sundays, when either no work was carried out or the only work that took place was within the grounds of the camp. But this was not a liberating, relaxing, or pleasant change of pace for the prisoners because they knew that the SS particularly liked to spring "surprises" on them on such days. "On Sunday roll call was not so early. Not so long before dawn. On Sunday, the columns did not step out of the camp. We worked inside the camp. Sunday was the day everyone feared the most" (Delbo[23] 1995: 90).

Though reveille was at different times in different camps, in all of the camps[24] the prisoners were woken before dawn, usually after having spent the night crammed into a bunk with several other people. They then had to make up their beds (cf. Améry 1980a) and wash themselves as fast as they could. As the sanitary facilities were completely inadequate, both quantitatively and qualitatively, and the conditions were extremely unhygienic, these morning ablutions were usually more an act of self-preservation than an opportunity for the thorough cleaning the prisoners so desperately needed. They had to quickly gulp down their coffee substitute, usually a lukewarm liquid of a nondescript brown color. If, despite their hunger, the prisoners had managed to save a piece of bread from the evening before, they might be able to rush through a (nutritionally very poor) breakfast before having to stand at roll call. Once both the living prisoners and those who had died during the night had been accounted for in a correct and orderly fashion, the various work details were assembled. Recalling the time he spent in the Dachau concentration camp, Paul Martin Neurath describes how the prisoners departed for work each morning:

> Next order: "Working groups gather!" The rigid lines disperse, and for a few minutes the camp looks like a disturbed anthill. Everyone runs as quickly as he can to his working group. Officers scurry around and shout and beat and kick those who are not fast enough. Finally the working groups are formed. Group after group passes the officer in charge [. . .]. The capo[25] (that is, the prisoner in charge) reports the number, the officer checks it, the necessary SS men are detached. They take their rifles from their shoulders, form alongside the column of prisoners, and the group moves through the "door" with the iron promise, "Work makes one free." (Neurath 2005: 25–6)

In many camps, the camp orchestra would play as the columns of prisoners marched out to work (cf., e.g., Fénelon 1997; Lasker-Wallfisch 1996; Neurath 2005). Their places of work were sometimes very far away and difficult to reach, and while the prisoners marched to them – often wearing only primitive wooden clogs – they had to sing in unison on command. The repertoire here ranged from popular German folk tunes and ballads to hiking songs from the German youth movement and marching songs. "As the men march on, the guards begin to scold them for not keeping step, not singing loud enough, or for speaking to their neighbors. Occasionally, they hit them, but not too often, for that might bring disorder into the ranks" (ibid.: 26). The work itself varied widely depending on the camp and the time of imprisonment: "We work beneath the earth and above it, under a roof and in the rain, with the spade, the pickaxe and the crowbar. We carry huge sacks of cement, lay bricks, put down rails, spread gravel, trample the earth... We are laying the foundation for some new, monstrous civilization" (Borowski[26] 1992: 131). The prisoners went to work in all kinds of conditions, without adequate protection from the cold, wet, or heat:

> The prisoners go to work, no matter what the weather may be. We worked when men died like flies from sunstroke, and we worked when men dropped dead from the cold. We worked in snowstorms when we could not see each other and in fog so dense that we could not see our own hands. We worked in hail and thunderstorms and endless pouring rains. The prisoner goes to bed in his wet shirt and dries it with the heat of his body, but the rest of his clothing is still wet in the morning. (Neurath 2005: 26)

If the prisoners had not yet been assigned to a work detail or the weather conditions delayed work on certain projects,[27] the guards tormented them and kept them occupied with useless busywork.

> The women of Ravensbrück tell about interminable days during the quarantine period (before their incorporation in the factory work squads) spent shoveling the sand of the dunes: in a circle, under the July sun, each deportee had to move the sand of her pile onto that of her neighbor on the right in a pointless and endless merry-go-round, because the sand ended up back where it came from. (Levi 1989: 121)

The work often had to be done on the double, and the prisoners were pushed to continue working without pause. The SS set dogs on the defenseless prisoners and randomly beat and shot them as well. During their short lunch break they were usually given watery soup with little nutritional value and no appreciable amount of vegetables or meat, which therefore did not satiate the prisoners but merely filled their bellies. This liquid diet caused the prisoners to have to pass water frequently, and their malnutrition also led many of them to suffer from permanent diarrhea which accelerated their physical deterioration and also meant that they constantly had to visit the latrines or soiled themselves (cf. Levi and De Benedetti 2006).[28]

Prisoners who were assigned to work indoors considered themselves lucky since at least they were not exposed to extreme weather conditions and were usually supervised by civilians. But the work itself was often no easier in the factories than it was outdoors in the quarries and gravel pits (cf., e.g., Gyulai[29] 2001). Additionally, in the factories – most of which were armaments plants or other operations critical to the war effort – the prisoners had to work night shifts, and it was much more difficult to get the rest they needed in the camp during the day than during the night (cf. ibid.). The working day was typically no shorter than twelve hours (cf. Kammer and Bartsch 2002: 140) and this, together with the insufficient provisions, the lack of breaks, the terribly unhygienic conditions, and the permanent psychological pressure, was a burden that the prisoners could generally only withstand for a few months before they broke down physically and mentally and succumbed to sickness and death.

The prisoners also carried out all of the work that had to be done in the concentration camps themselves. This included activities in the kitchens, infirmaries, and various camp workshops as well as transportation and messenger duties and work in the SS administrative offices.

When the work details returned to the camp in the evening, the prisoners had to carry any dead or severely injured inmates with them so that the number of prisoners at the morning roll call corresponded to the number at the evening roll call before supper (cf. Distel in Benz and Distel 2007: 101). If there were discrepancies – which very often arose owing to a simple miscount but which were sometimes caused by prisoners who had hidden or escaped – then the already lengthy roll call process would stretch to hours, until either the mistake was clarified or any prisoners who had fled were found (cf. ibid.). Sentences that had been passed during the day, such as an hour hanging from a post or twenty-five lashes, were also carried out at roll call in the presence of the entire prisoner population (see also chapter 4.3.1). "Often the 10,000 have to sing lusty songs while the sentence takes its course" (Neurath 2005: 32).

After the evening roll call, the prisoners were given their meager ration of a small piece of bread and another liter of insubstantial soup. The bread, which "indisputably contained a very large quantity of dross, amongst which sawdust was much in evidence" (Levi and De Benedetti 2006: 44), had to be portioned by each prisoner so that they would have a piece left for breakfast the next morning. This was extremely difficult because the prisoners were starving and struggled to find the willpower to divide their already tiny portion of bread instead of just eating it all at once. There was also always the risk that a fellow prisoner might steal the bread during the night, so the ration that had been so painstakingly put aside would not be available in the morning.

Prior to lights out, the nightly lice checks were carried out; these were even more thorough on Saturday afternoons, when the prisoners' heads and beards were shaved again. Primo Levi reports from Auschwitz:

Every prisoner had to strip and subject his garments to a meticulous examination by the specially appointed inspectors, and if even a single louse was found on a deportee's shirt, all the personal clothing of every inmate of the dormitory was immediately despatched to be disinfected, and the men were subjected to a shower, preceded by a rub-down with Lysol.[30] They then had to spend the entire night naked, until their clothes were brought back from the disinfection hut in the early hours of the morning, soaking wet. (Ibid.: 43)

Lights out was usually at nine o'clock in the evening; after this time, the prisoners were no longer allowed to leave their huts. Anyone who did ran the risk of being "shot without warning 'on attempt to escape'" (cf. Neurath 2005: 32). But there was no chance of undisturbed rest for the prisoners in the concentration camps. Not only were the bunks overcrowded, the inmates plagued by pests, and the blankets completely inadequate, everyone also had to visit the "pail" several times during the night to relieve themselves. There was thus no end to the disruptions at night. Furthermore, the block leaders often amused themselves by storming into the huts and bullying the prisoners into engaging in military drills or gymnastic exercises – or even torturing and killing them if they felt like it (cf., e.g., Szalet[31] 1945, 2006).

After a night of rest like this – which was anything but and actually represented ongoing torture in the form of sleep deprivation[32] – the prisoners were woken before dawn to face another day of monotony and continual danger.

Most prisoners soon fell ill under these conditions, but they were not given any opportunity to recuperate. Some of these illnesses could have very banal origins, such as shoes that didn't fit. In an interview, Primo Levi says:

They shoved a pair of shoes at us; no, not even a pair, just two different shoes, one with a heel, one without. You almost had to be an athlete to learn to walk in them. One was too tight, the other too loose, you had to negotiate complex deals, and if you were lucky, you managed to find two shoes that went together reasonably well. In any case, all the shoes hurt your feet; and anyone with delicate feet ended up with infections. I know from experience, I still have the scars. [. . .] But if you were prone to infections you died "from shoes," from infected foot-wounds which never healed. Your feet swelled up and the more they swelled the more they rubbed up against the shoes; you might end up in the hospital, but swollen feet were not sufficient an illness to get you admitted to the hospital. They were too common a complaint [in Auschwitz-Monowitz], so if you had swollen feet you were sent to the gas chambers. (Levi 2001: 213)

Only the worst cases were sent to the infirmary – the so-called sick bay – where the patients were left to lie on the makeshift beds in a stupor, unquarantined and in the most unhygienic conditions, without receiving any special medical treatment because the facilities were so primitive and inadequate. As a result, the risk of infection was particularly high in the sick bays and the prisoners avoided being sent to them whenever possible. Because they were so undernourished, the prisoners were seldom able to heal, so all sicknesses tended to become chronic and the onset of an illness was like a death sentence. If sick prisoners did start to get better, they were sent back to their huts and work details before they were fully recovered (cf. Levi and De Benedetti 2006: 71).

Everyday life in the camps was thus characterized by extreme uniformity, where the prisoners' constant state of exhaustion and malnutrition could send them into a trancelike state. But the inmates had to be exceptionally vigilant at the same time in order to avoid making a mistake that would attract the attention of the guards and give them a pretext for drastic punitive measures. Therefore, in addition to their exhaustion and debilitation, the prisoners felt a permanent tension that never entirely disappeared. This applied even to the prisoners with "lower numbers" (Klüger 2001: 96), although these inmates had a special understanding of both the camp and the guards which enabled them to devise routines that helped them to survive.

There were few opportunities for the type of self-determined action that corresponded to the inmates' perception of themselves as autonomous individuals, and the opportunities that did arise were dependent on chance, demanded special skills, and always entailed dire risks to life and limb. But the memoirs of former concentration camp prisoners tell us that, above all, it was this concept of being an autonomous individual that drove the prisoners to search almost ceaselessly for such opportunities, as trivial as they may have seemed. These opportunities varied depending on the prisoners' location and tasks in the camp, both of which were also associated with different forms of sociality.

In the following section, I will analyze three such forms of sociality to explain when and how opportunities arose for the prisoners to conquer or defend their "territories of the self" (cf. Goffman 1971; Suderland 2004).

5.3 Three levels of sociality

Wherever a large number of people are thrown together, no matter under what circumstances and to what purpose, they will soon work out a system of routine and cooperation, to smooth friction and to perform whatever tasks the situation may require. If they are together long enough, a more or less structured society will develop, based on the social background and concepts which its members bring with them from their previous surroundings. The prisoners in a concentration camp are no exception to this rule.

Paul Martin Neurath (2005: 131)

Although the Nazi concentration camps took on forms that were historically unique in both qualitative and quantitative terms, and social practices emerged here that were difficult for outsiders or newcomers to comprehend in many respects, external models can be found for every aspect of social life in the camps. This applies first and foremost to the organization of the camps, which was based heavily on military practices and was, as Primo Levi remarks, "an inglorious copy of the army proper – or, more accurately, its caricature" (Levi 1989: 116). Many camps developed both a lively economy and a cultural life that were able to take root in the shadow zone between the flouting of regulations and the toleration of this by the SS. And finally, a hidden social life was able to flourish in secret despite its latency. The prisoners had to employ imaginative new practices in order for this latent camp life to emerge, but their ultimate aim was to reproduce familiar activities that were extremely important to them because they represented continuity with their previous existences.

The *military organization* of camp life was the *first level of sociality*, and it displayed what are perhaps the most obvious parallels with familiar practices from normal existence. Most prisoners probably had very little concept of such an organization before they were sent to a concentration camp, but nonetheless they were able to quickly identify the military nature of camp life. As Paul Martin Neurath notes in the opening epigraph to this chapter: "When a newcomer first enters a concentration camp, it looks completely different to him from what he had imagined it would be. He may have thought of it as a sort of super-prison [. . .]. What he actually finds is a sort of military camp" (Neurath 2005: 11). Military practice largely comprises the requirement to wear a uniform, a code of honor with specific forms of salute and salutation, a strictly regimented daily regime, and regular physical exercises. It is additionally characterized by the notion of reliable comrades and shared duties and suffering. This military mimesis was clearly an important element of self-valorization and identity for the SS, even though the SS committed acts in the camps – individually and as a group – that ran counter to the concept of real military honor. The prisoner society, in turn, also represented a distorted image of the military – the "inglorious copy" or "caricature" of the army to which Levi referred above. But even German society as a whole imitated the military in many aspects at the time, so the concentration camps were not quite the total counterimage of normal life that they are often made out to be. Levi recognizes that this emulation of military organization was in no way restricted to the concentration camps: "Within much more extended limits, one gains the impression that throughout all of Hitlerian Germany the barracks code and etiquette replaced those which were traditional and 'bourgeois'" (Levi 1989: 118).

There is also a passage in Jean Améry's book *Örtlichkeiten* (Localities) that illustrates how everyday life at the time already held a potential that merely needed to be instrumentalized by the Nazis for their own purposes. In the passage in question, Améry describes his impressions of the German population in Cologne, which he passed through at the end of 1938 as he fled from Vienna to Belgium:

> Almost all of the women wear ankle-length dresses and coats and those soft men's felt hats tilted at a slant that will define their silhouette for years to come, until the end of the war. All of the men have athletic shoulders thanks to the shoulder pads sewn into their jackets. Both men and women have something distinctly military about their appearance. Is this the Third Reich look? The traveler [i.e., Améry] interprets the fashion in this way – and will only find out much later that Madame Schiaparelli in Paris was actually to blame for the small misdeed, and not the Führer at all [. . .]. (Améry 1980b: 33–4)

Améry's observations are confirmed by none other than Heinrich Himmler himself: "In my view we have a much too strong masculinization of our whole life, which goes so far that we militarize impossible things and – if I may here speak openly – see the *height of perfection* in lining people up and organizing them and getting haversacks packed" (Himmler in a speech to SS generals in 1937,[33] quoted in Schoppmann 1995: 11; emphasis added). I believe this shows that neither political terror nor orders from above were needed to lay the groundwork for what happened in the concentration camps; everyday life in Nazi Germany had begun to change long before in a way that minimized society's horror of such camps – because the mechanics of them were familiar. Or, as Zygmunt Bauman says: "'The Holocaust did not just, mysteriously, avoid clash [*sic*] with the social norms and institutions of modernity. It was these norms and institutions that made the Holocaust feasible" (Bauman 1989: 87). The military nature of daily life at the time was literally reflected in the practices of the concentration camps. In this respect, at least, the "topsy-turvy world" of the camps actually corresponded to the reality of many people's lives.

Additionally, the concepts of military order and organization were so prevalent in society that the concentration camp prisoners themselves are likely to have recognized them right away. Hans Reichmann[34] remembers: "Suddenly someone shouts 'Attention!' I haven't heard that military command in twenty years. Nearly all of us had been soldiers, many of us officers. We snap to attention" (Reichmann 1998: 155). The only way to debase these "internal enemies" (Sofsky 1997: 103) – particularly the resistance fighters from the political left, who were usually organized in a strict paramilitary fashion, as well as veteran soldiers, some of whom, notably, were German nationalist Jews – was to lampoon the familiar and generally respected military order which had become second nature to them and thus expose the prisoners to ridicule. Primo Levi describes this as follows:

An army has a uniform: the soldier's uniform clean, honored, and covered with insignia, while that of the *Häftling* [i.e, prisoner] is filthy, dull, and gray[35] – but both must have five buttons, or else there was trouble. An army marches by in military step, in close order, to the sound of a band; so too there must be a band in the Lager, and the march-past must be a march-past by the book, with "eyes left" before the reviewing stand and to the sound of music. [. . .]

A barracks heritage also was the ritual of "making the beds." Of course, this locution is largely euphemistic; where there were bunk beds, each berth comprised a thin mattress filled with wood shavings, two blankets, and a straw pillow. [... A]ll beds had to be put in order within a minute or two [. . .]. Those were frantic moments: the atmosphere filled with dust to the point of becoming opaque, with nervous tension and curses exchanged in all languages, because "making beds" (*Bettenbauen*, the technical term) was a sacral operation to be performed in accordance with iron rules. The mattress, fetid with mold and strewn with suspect stains, had to be fluffed up: for that purpose there existed two slits in the lining, through which one could insert the hands. One of the two blankets was supposed to be turned under the mattress and the other spread out over the pillow in such a way as to form a neat step, with sharp edges. When the operation was finished, the ensemble must look like a rectangular parallelepiped with well-smoothed edges, on which was placed the smaller parallelepiped of the pillow.

For the SS in the camp, and consequently for all barracks heads, *Bettenbauen* had a prime and indecipherable importance: perhaps it was a symbol of order and discipline. Anyone who did not make his bed properly, or forgot to make it, was punished publicly and savagely. Furthermore, in every barracks there existed a pair of functionaries, the *Bettnachzieher* ("bed after-pullers," a term that I believe does not exist in normal German and that Goethe certainly would not have understood), whose task it was to check every single bed and then take care of its transversal alignment. For this purpose, they were equipped with a string the length of the hut: they stretched it over the made-up beds, and rectified down to the centimeter any possible deviations. Rather than a cause of torment this maniacal order seemed absurd and grotesque: in fact, the mattress leveled out with so much care had no consistency whatever, and in the evening, under the body's weight, it immediately flattened down to the slats that supported it. In point of fact, one slept on wood. (Levi 1989: 116–18)

The most spectacular displays of military imitation in the Nazi concentration camps were the prisoner roll calls which took place twice a day. The number of prisoners varied greatly depending on the size of the camp, so these morning and evening assemblies were spectacles of different scales – but their focus was always the unmistakable demonstration of power on the part of the representatives of the regime and the public display of the prisoners' complete lack of identity and helplessness. The torturous sentences carried out during these roll calls emphasized the asymmetry of power and humiliated even those who were not being punished themselves but who were turned into an impotent audience (cf. also chapter 4.3.1).

Regardless of whether it was hundreds or thousands of debased people having to stand motionless for hours, these roll calls were recurrent scenes of terror during which the inmates always feared the worst. Anyone who weakened and fainted, or moved perceptibly, or talked to his or her neighbors was likely to be the target of a whipping by the guards or a bite by their dogs, as was anyone who stood at the edges or in the first row of the formation.

This type of military drill not only made it easier to monitor and manage the mass of prisoners, it also revealed the full impotence and pitifulness of the inwardly and outwardly decrepit inmates, it exposed them to ridicule and therefore made them the objects of the deep contempt of their tormentors.

However, the memoirs of former prisoners recount not only the terror of these roll calls but also the strategies the prisoners used to pursue their own goals. Charlotte Delbo, who was first imprisoned in Auschwitz and later in the Ravensbrück women's concentration camp, describes how the women warmed each other's hands in the freezing cold: "[E]ach places her hands under the arms of the one in front of her. Since they cannot do it in the first row, we rotate. Backs to chests, we stand pressed against each other, yet, as we establish a single circulatory system, we remain frozen through and through" (Delbo 1995: 63). After she had fainted on one occasion and the women around her had caught her and roused her back to consciousness, she returned to her original position. "I am surrounded by my comrades. I take my place once more in the poor communal warmth created by our contact, and since we must return completely, I return to the roll call and think: It's the morning roll call [. . .]" (ibid.: 65). As the female members of the so-called "SS retinue" who were counting the prisoners approached with their fiercely barking dogs, everyone quickly arranged themselves in an orderly fashion. "The cold nips our hands emerging from below our comrades' arms. Fifteen thousand women stand at attention" (ibid.: 66). "When they [the SS women] have passed by, each one of us places her hands back in another woman's armpits. Coughs repressed until then burst forth and the blockhovas [i.e., block leaders] shout 'Quiet!' at the coughs in their impossible languages" (ibid.). Elsewhere, Delbo describes a selection during which the women were forced to file past the SS and show their legs. "Quickly the young ones make their way to the outside edge of the ranks, shielding the older women, who walk in the center" (ibid.: 190).

Ruth Klüger, who was deported with her mother to Theresienstadt and later to Auschwitz-Birkenau and Christianstadt, describes an entirely different strategy that she used to make it through the seemingly endless roll calls: She recited poems and ballads – silently, of course, in her mind, so she would not attract attention (Klüger 1999: 123ff.):

> In some cases, where the goal is simply to make it through something, less profound verses are perhaps more suitable than those that blow the roof off the house. Incidentally, even in my normal life there had been situations – such as dentist visits – when I couldn't enjoy the time but instead just had to pass it with the help of something like the "The Cranes of Ibycus." Schiller's ballads became my roll call poems as well. Thanks to them I could stand for hours in the sun without falling over, because there was always another line to recite, and if you couldn't remember a line, you could spend time thinking about it instead of thinking about your own weakness. By then the roll call would probably be over and you could turn off the gramophone record in your head [. . .]. (Ibid.: 124)

Even as a young girl, Klüger had spent a great deal of time reading and reciting poems – because, being Jewish, she was no longer allowed to go to school and she had lost her friends (cf. Klüger 2001: 19ff.) – so these silent recitations were a comfort to her. They enabled her to remain herself and continue doing something she had done for years in order to cope with a world that was incomprehensible to her. They also distracted her from her mortal fear. At the same time, the silent recitations were like an act of "sabotage" (Klüger 1999: 151) in that they strengthened her power of resistance in situations she might otherwise not have survived. She later wrote about her poems:

> They're childish poems, their regularity a counterweight to the chaos, a poetic and therapeutic attempt to counter this senseless, destructive circus in which we were foundering with something linguistically whole and rhyming; the oldest aesthetic concern of all, really. The poems had to have several verses as a sign of mastery, of the ability to organize and objectivize. I was [. . .] well read, my head was full of six years' worth of classics, Romantic literature and sentimental nineteenth-century poetry. (Klüger 1999: 126–7)

The very different cases described here illustrate how, despite the enforced military order and the torment and abasement that went along with it, the prisoners had some scope – however minimal – to thwart the intentions of their tormentors and remind themselves that not everything could be entirely controlled by the SS. Or, as Robert Antelme puts it, the SS were "made to feel utterly certain they [had] been cheated" (Antelme 1998: 74) because they could not succeed in gaining total control. "The more our condition as men is contested by the SS, the more likely our chances of being confirmed as such" (ibid.: 96). Tadeusz Borowski puts it this way: "And even if nothing is left to us but our bodies [. . .], we shall still have our memories and our feelings. [And I believe the dignity of man is rooted in his memories and feelings]" (Borowski 1992: 134; new translation from the German text in Borowski 2008: 60–1 in brackets). These examples also depict different aspects of the scope for action available to the prisoners: Charlotte Delbo describes activities of solidarity, while Ruth Klüger's recitation of poems represents individuality.

Solidarity strategies are mentioned in many prisoner memoirs, particularly in relation to the hours-long roll calls and work detail marches. Despite their profound debasement, the inmates had not abandoned the idea that they were all in the same boat and dependent on one another and therefore had an obligation to use these strategies as skillfully as possible, as described by Charlotte Delbo above.

> [I]t was important not be separated from one's group. We had to leave together or remain together. Each one of us had experienced fully the fact that an isolated individual is defenseless, that you cannot survive without the others. By "the others" we meant those members of our group who hold you up, or carry you when you can no longer walk, those who help you hold fast when you're at the end of your rope. (Delbo 1995: 193)

What Ruth Klüger describes, by contrast, is not only an individual strategy that helped her withstand the endless roll calls, it was a strategy based on her personal experiences and habits and therefore strengthened her own perception of herself. In connection with this, Robert Antelme writes:

> We are being transformed. Our faces and bodies are going downhill, there's no more telling the handsome from the ugly. In three months' time we'll be more different still, we'll be even less distinguishable from one another. Yet each of us will continue, in a vague way, to maintain the idea of his own singularity. (Antelme 1998: 87)

Loden Vogel,[36] who kept a diary while he was imprisoned in Bergen-Belsen, says: "I'm dead tired, hungry and perplexed – but somewhere there is still a part of my self, the most important part, calm and unscathed. [. . .] Some part of us always stays the same" (Vogel 2002: 95). While I think there is no question that these thoughts are based partially on an illusion – as the prisoners actually changed drastically in certain respects under these exceptionally oppressive circumstances – Vogel's words underscore how important the perception of the continuity of individuality was.

The military organization of the camps was not solely an adaptation of a familiar practice which took certain aspects of the outside world to the extreme, it also conveyed to the prisoners that the SS viewed them all as equally worthless and meaningless, while at the same time demonstrating the opposite – namely, that solidarity and individuality could not really be eradicated in this way. Even martial forms of "disciplinary training" (Bourdieu 2000b: 145) like the prisoner roll calls, which were supposed to constitute the literal subjugation of the individual, could not entirely prevent the prisoners from finding ways and means of expressing solidarity and individuality and thus expressing themselves as human beings.[37]

The *second level of sociality* in the Nazi concentration camps was a kind of *shadow zone* between the prisoners' flouting of the strictest camp regulations and the occasional tacit toleration of these transgressions by the SS. Paul Martin Neurath uses the term "forgotten rules" to describe this (cf. Neurath 2005: 97f.):

> In this classification belong rules forbidding the production and trading of a great number of articles such as wooden clogs, "flatirons" for making beds, sandpaper for cleaning the closet, steel wool for polishing dishes, breadbags, and so forth. Production is illegal, as it is done at work, from stolen material. Trade is illegal, as all trade is forbidden. Usually transporting the articles from the place of production to the camp is also illegal, but possession is usually considered legal. Nobody can do without these articles. The officers see them thousands of times. But occasionally a corruption scandal involving one of these articles is brought to light, and without warning, men are punished for having produced, smuggled, sold, or bought it. (Neurath 2005: 98)

The hidden economy of the camp was actually essential if the prisoners were to meet all of the explicit demands of the SS. For example, the prisoners were always expected to have a full set of buttons on their jackets – but if they lost a button, there was no regular way to get a replacement without the risk of punishment (cf. Améry 1980a: 10). These and other situations, as well as the fact that the prisoners lacked such essential goods as food and medicine, led to a lively barter system operating outside the official camp organization which followed economic rules and, in some cases, even involved SS members or civilians.

In the chapter entitled "This Side of Good and Evil" in Primo Levi's first book, *Survival in Auschwitz* (Levi 1995: 77ff.), Levi provides a breathtaking depiction of the camp economy. He describes how the camp market fluctuated in response to certain rumors or events, and I quote him here at length to offer a deeper insight in the functioning of this economy:

> The Market is always very active. Although every exchange (in fact, every form of possession) is explicitly forbidden, and although frequent swoops of Kapos or *Blockälteste* [i.e., block seniors] sent merchants, customers and the curious periodically flying, nevertheless, the north-east corner of the Lager (significantly the corner furthest from the SS huts) is permanently occupied by a tumultuous throng, in the open during the summer, in a wash-room during the winter, as soon as the squads return from work.

Here scores of prisoners driven desperate by hunger prowl around, with lips half-open and eyes gleaming, lured by a deceptive instinct to where the merchandise shown makes the gnawing of their stomachs more acute and their salivation more assiduous. In the best cases they possess a miserable half-ration of bread which, with painful effort, they have saved since the morning, in the senseless hope of a chance to make an advantageous bargain with some ingenuous person, unaware of the prices of the moment. Some of these, with savage patience, acquire with their half-ration two pints of soup which, once in their possession, they subject to a methodical examination with a view to extracting the few pieces of potato lying at the bottom; this done, they exchange it for bread, and the bread for another two pints to denaturalize, and so on until their nerves are exhausted, or until some victim, catching them in the act, inflicts on them a severe lesson, exposing them to public derision. [. . .]

At the Market you can find specialists in kitchen thefts, their jackets swollen with strange bulges. While there is a virtually stable price for soup (half a ration of bread for two pints), the quotations for turnips, carrots, potatoes are extremely variable and depend greatly, among other factors, on the diligence and the corruptibility of the guards at the stores.

Mahorca[38] is sold. Mahorca is a third-rate tobacco, crude and wooden, which is officially on sale at the canteen in one and a half ounce packets, in exchange for the prize-coupons that the Buna[39] ought to distribute to the best workers. Such a distribution occurs irregularly, with great parsimony and open injustice, so that the greatest number of the coupons end up, either legitimately or through abuse of authority, in the hands of the Kapos and of the Prominents;[40] nevertheless, the prize-coupons still circulate on the market in the form of money, and their value changes in strict obedience to the laws of classical economics.

There have been periods in which the prize-coupon was worth one ration of bread, then one and a quarter, even one and a third; one day it was quoted at one and a half ration, but then the supply of Mahorca to the canteen failed, so that, lacking a coverage, the money collapsed at once to a quarter of a ration. Another boom period occurred for a singular reason: the arrival of a fresh contingent of robust Polish girls in place of the old inmates of the Frauenblock. In fact, as the prize-coupon is valid for entry to the Frauenblock[41] (for the criminals and the politicals; not for the Jews [. . .]), those interested actively and rapidly cornered the market: hence the revaluation, which, in any case, did not last long.

Among the ordinary Häftlinge there are not many who search for Mahorca to smoke it personally; for the most part it leaves the camp and ends in the hands of the civilian workers of the Buna. The traffic is an instance of a kind of "kombinacja" frequently practiced: the Häftling, somehow saving a ration of bread, invests it in Mahorca; he cautiously gets in touch with a civilian addict who acquires the Mahorca, paying in cash with a portion of bread greater than that initially invested. The Häftling eats the surplus, and puts back on the market the remaining ration. Speculations of this kind establish a tie between the internal economy of the Lager and the economic life of the outside world [. . .]. (Levi 1995: 78–80)

I have quoted Levi extensively here because I suspect it is difficult for us to imagine how a black market like this could arise out of nothing – out of nothing because the prisoners possessed nothing. And yet references to this type of economy can be found in nearly all memoirs of former prisoners, though a detailed market analysis like Levi's is rare.[42] This suggests it is almost like a natural law that wherever people come together, under whatever circumstances, a market like this can emerge.

Whether or not civilians took part in this market activity depended on the specific conditions in the camp. The Buna plants in Auschwitz employed many civilian laborers alongside thousands of concentration camp prisoners. In other camps, too, there was contact with the outside world – suppliers often worked with smaller camps, for example, which could not produce all of their necessities internally – and with extreme caution, civilians could be included in the prisoners' economy. As the tobacco example shows, civilian workers could also benefit from such transactions. But there were also borderline cases in which personal advantages were probably just one motivation among many for participating in such trade – another motivation perhaps being the chance to help the prisoners. Roman Frister[43] recounts the case of a civilian laborer in the Starachowice camp, where he was imprisoned with his father as a boy and forced to work in a steel mill. This civilian worker at the same plant passed letters between Frister's father and the Fristers' former neighbors, who were holding onto money and valuables for the family. Frister's father wrote to the neighbors and asked them to send money to the civilian worker, who was to keep half and use the other half to regularly buy fresh food for Frister. Although this transaction involved a high degree of personal risk for the civilian himself, he honored the agreement and kept father and son supplied with secret deliveries of milk and bread daily (cf. Frister 2001: 31f.)

One important prerequisite for almost any type of hidden economy was the ability to acquire – or "organize," in the camp jargon – suitable materials for producing the coveted items that would otherwise have to be stolen. Someone on an external work detail might try to secretly cut birch twigs for a broom that could be traded quickly (Borowski 1992: 74) or steal something that could be turned into something else useful. For example, Primo Levi says that while working in the Chemical Kommando, he stole several small iron-cerium rods which, secretly, at night, under the blankets, he and his friend Alberto scraped down into flints for the cigarette lighters produced by other prisoners. The secrecy of their activities was necessary not only to avoid severe punishment but also to prevent competitors from bringing similar articles to the market.

The finished products were exchanged for bread which kept Levi alive until the arrival of the Red Army (cf. Levi 2000: 118–22).

Bargaining with goods like this not only helped ensure survival (at least for a short time), it also gave rise to opportunities for corruption. Bribes were aimed above all at those who had some influence over who would be assigned to which work detail or who would be selected for deportation or execution, as well as those responsible for managing materials or food. Most of the corrupt individuals were so-called prisoner functionaries[44] who worked in these areas and had a certain amount of leeway they could take advantage of (cf. Neurath 2005: 152f.). However, in some cases it was possible for prisoners to bribe SS officers as well, or at least engage in business with them. For example, Borowski describes how a guard sold drinking water to a prisoner at a horrendous price on a hot summer day as the prisoner was waiting for the arrival of a transport on the infamous ramp at Auschwitz. On this particular day, Borowski was part of the ramp commando that had to collect and sort the possessions of new arrivals while these individuals lined up for selection. This sorting job was desirable because it was relatively easy for the prisoners to secretly acquire clothing, food, money, and occasionally jewelry or gold which they could later trade for something else or make use of themselves (cf. Zywulska[45] 2004). The SS guard offered to sell water that the prisoner would have to buy at the end of the day using money acquired in this way:

> "Hey you, fatso!" His boot lightly touches Henri's shoulder. *"Pass mal auf,* want a drink?"
>
> "Sure, but I haven't got any marks," replies the Frenchman with a professional air.
>
> *"Schade,* too bad."
>
> "Come, come, Herr Posten, isn't my word good enough any more? Haven't we done business before? How much?"
>
> "One hundred. *Gemacht?"*
>
> *"Gemacht."*
>
> We drink the water, lukewarm and tasteless. It will be paid for by the people who have not yet arrived. (Borowski 1992: 34)

Paul Martin Neurath describes widespread rackets that would have been unthinkable without the assistance and active participation of the SS and civilians. These were responsible for bringing a huge amount of money and luxury goods into the camp: "tea, coffee, [. . .] liquor, [. . .] fruit, fat, chocolate, and smoking material [. . .]" (Neurath 2005: 212).

> The risks that went with this kind of traffic, particularly for SS men and civilians, were so tremendous that the prices asked went way beyond what an ordinary "rich" man in the camp [. . .] could possibly pay. Thus the goods

were kept within the small circle of those who made big money from the various rackets. The rest of the camp knew about this only by hearsay, but details were quickly broadcast every time the administration uncovered a case and a civilian or an SS man landed in the camp for it. (Ibid.: 213)

In his shockingly laconic story "This Way for the Gas, Ladies and Gentlemen" (Borowski 1992: 29–49), Tadeusz Borowski explains how the prohibited plundering of new arrivals in Auschwitz became part of the prisoners' normal daily lives:

> It is almost over. The dead are being cleared off the ramp and piled into the last truck. [The clothes have been unloaded.] The Canada men,[46] weighed down under a load of bread, marmalade and sugar, and smelling of perfume and fresh linen, line up to go. [The Kapo has stuffed gold, silks and black coffee into the tea kettle. It's for the guards at the gate, so they let the commando through without inspection.] For several days the entire camp will live off this transport. [Eat ham and sausages, jam and fruit, drink its schnapps and liqueurs, wear its clothes, do business with its gold and goods. The civilians will take much of it out of the camp, to Silesia, Krakow and elsewhere. In return, they'll bring cigarettes, eggs, schnapps and letters from home.] For several days the entire camp will talk about "Sosnowiec-Bedzin." "Sosnowiec-Bedzin" was a good, rich transport. (Borowski 1992: 49; new translation from the German text in Borowski 2008: 220 in brackets)

When Borowksi says here that "the camp" will live off the riches from this transport in the coming days, he clearly does *not* mean that the entire camp and all of its inmates will enjoy these advantages, but rather only those who were part of the right networks and in a position to engage in trade. The amenities and privileges came at the personal price of having to participate in the macabre activities on the ramp.

The prisoners developed a subtlety born of desperate need which they put to use alongside skills many of them had acquired in their previous lives. But the camp economy was also based on the courage of desperation. Without the cooperation of civilians and the SS, the entire economy would have been impossible. First, it required the tacit – and sometimes purchased – tolerance of the guards who only occasionally intervened, or the indifference of guards who simply might not have felt like carrying out a thorough inspection on a particular day and knew full well that they could make up for it by catching somebody the next time the opportunity arose. But the camp economy also needed this external support because it kept money and goods flowing into and out of the camp, which was the only way the market could flourish.

This complex cooperation between a wide variety of agents can only be partially explained by a shared ideology. We can assume that the prisoners shared a variously motivated opposition to the Nazi regime which could have formed a limited basis[47] for such conspiratorial activity, but the strongest driving force for participating in the camp economy was probably the opportunity to improve the situation in the camp (for oneself). The spectrum here ranged from satisfying simple, basic needs to maximizing profits in the hope of lasting betterment, both material and social.

The civilians, who generally had very bad living conditions themselves, probably also took part in the economy despite the threat of punishment by the SS in order to better their own miserable material situation. A certain degree of sympathy for the prisoners may have also played a role here (cf. Frister 2001). In rare instances, the sole intention may have been to help individual prisoners, an exceptional situation described by Primo Levi, for example (Levi 1995: 119ff.).

The situation was much more complicated in the case of the SS, as their ideological indoctrination would have made them extremely reluctant to engage in conspiratorial activity with the prisoners they were supposed to view as "sub-humans." According to the accounts of survivors, however, such cooperation was the order of the day in all of the camps, so we must assume that forces other than ideology were at work here. This is especially apparent in an entirely different area also couched in this shadow zone, namely, the wide-scale cultural activities of the prisoners, which will be discussed in more detail later.

Though in light of scenes like those described by Borowski above it is somewhat difficult to see similarities between the world inside and the normal world outside the camps, it is certainly clear that when it came to the camp economy, all three groups of people involved in it followed the general rules of economics in which supply and demand are closely intertwined. The market was kept going by black-marketeering and corruption, two activities which follow not just the laws of economics but also social "laws," because they are based on networks and trust and are associated with the formation of elite groups to a certain extent. Although economic activities strengthened the prisoners' self-image as autonomously thinking and acting individuals, they could also expose the inmates to the scorn of the guards if they were discovered bartering for the odds and ends critical to their survival and the SS or guards felt like punishing them for it at that particular moment. Inept transactions could additionally harm an inmate's standing within the prisoner society and open him or her up to "public derision" (Levi 1995: 78). Aside from the fact that the economic sphere was banished to a shadow zone in the concentration camps – like black markets always are – I think it is just as impossible to separate the economic sphere from the social sphere here as it would be in normal, "free" life outside the walls of the camp.

Let us now turn to the second area in the social shadow zone of the camps: cultural activities, which took place on a scale that was impossible for the SS to overlook if they were monitoring the prisoners closely enough.[48] The most famous examples of such activities come from the

Theresienstadt camp, but cultural activities actually took place in *all* camps, including Auschwitz. Unlike the hidden camp economy, these cultural activities did not serve the purposes of immediate physical survival – at least not at first glance. But besides their hunger and thirst, the prisoners did feel an urgent need for cultural pursuits, so many inmates took part in them whenever various types of secret performances were planned. The SS could usurp these prisoner activities at any time, and SS members were as arbitrary in their punishments as they were in their rewards. This meant that the opportunities for action on the prisoners' part could bolster their sense of identity (if they remained undiscovered or unpunished), but they could also damage it (if they were abused or punished by the SS) (cf. Daxelmüller 1998 or Elias 1999).

Much has been written on the topic of culture in the concentration camps,[49] and the focus is usually on the cultural activities that were coerced from the prisoners or tolerated in the camps. The discussion of "culture in the concentration camps" often rouses very conflicting emotions. On the one hand, it seems unimaginable that there could have been orchestras, theatrical performances, or cabaret evenings in these camps described as hell on earth. The fact that the SS sometimes demanded such events for their own entertainment appears to stand in stark contrast to their racist *Übermensch* ideology which led them to view the performers as "sub-humans." And yet, "even in the Auschwitz-Birkenau camp [. . .] in early 1944 there was a cultural performance in family camp B IIb – for the entertainment of the SS. Not long after, 3,800 inmates of B IIb were murdered in the gas chambers along with the performers" (Kolmer 2002). The SS also demanded cultural performances from the prisoners in order to humiliate the inmates and subject them to ridicule (cf. Daxelmüller 1998: 998). This was the case with the orchestras found in most camps, which were forced to play while the columns of prisoners marched in and out of the compound (cf., e.g., Delbo 1995: 106f.; Fénelon 1997; Lasker-Wallfisch 1996).

In this context, it is also worth mentioning *Der Führer schenkt den Juden eine Stadt* (The Führer Gives a City to the Jews),[50] a film that was devised to deceive the international public about the true conditions in Theresienstadt. This film was intended to depict the "lively activities of the inhabitants of the Theresienstadt Ghetto," and it was made with the coerced participation of many prisoners of the camp, most of whom were only passing through on their way to an extermination camp.[51] Façades and cafés were built and concerts and lectures with prominent individuals[52] were staged for the film in order to give the impression that this camp was actually an acceptable, pleasurable place to live (cf. Margry 1992). The film itself naturally gives no indication that, before it was even completed, both the involuntary writer and director, Kurt Gerron,[53] as well as most of the cast and crew were sent to Auschwitz to suffer the fate that the Nazis had planned for them all along (cf. Wlaschek 2001).

Unfortunately, even today, the cultural activities in the concentration camps that are often described in great detail by survivors and that are so important to personal remembrance run the risk of being completely misinterpreted by the never-tiring Holocaust deniers and relativists: "The concentration camp as a carefree rest and relaxation spot for bored, work-shy individuals with no intention of doing anything but making music, writing poems, painting [. . .] and celebrating holidays throughout the year at the expense of the war-stricken Germans" (Daxelmüller 1998: 992).

My study naturally takes a completely different view of the cultural activities of the concentration camp prisoners. The purpose is not to question the suffering of the inmates but, on the contrary, to show that it was precisely this suffering that made it necessary for the prisoners to develop cultural strategies so that they could continue to feel like human beings. It seems that a piece of bread was as important to survival as the certainty that one was still capable of cultural activity. Because the world of the camps was so completely absurd and "topsy-turvy," these cultural activities were especially important as a symbol of continuity with one's previous life. And just like the hidden camp economy, the secret cultural life in the Nazi concentration camps would have been impossible without the participation of many different people. Complex cooperative relationships were necessary here, and they could often only arise through the tacit tolerance of the SS.

Charlotte Delbo reports that as soon as their complete physical exhaustion had abated thanks to the somewhat improved conditions in a "privileged commando" (Delbo 1995: 167), the prisoners began to plan such cultural activities:

> One of us recounted plays to the others, who managed to work close to her, digging with their spades or hoeing. They'd ask: "What are we going to see today?" Each telling was repeated several times. Each one wanted to hear it in turn, and the audience could never exceed five or six. However, the repertory was beginning to be used up. Soon we started considering "putting on a play." Nothing less than that. Without texts, without the means to get some, with nothing. And above all, with so little free time.
> [. . .] Imagination is the first luxury of a body [. . .]. And suddenly, in the small camp, we were coming back to life, and everything was coming back to us. (Delbo 1995: 167–8)

The French women imprisoned together with Delbo hatched a plan to stage Molière's *Le Malade Imaginaire* (The Imaginary Invalid) – and not solely out of a need for cultural and mental stimulation:

> Personal pride and the spirit of rivalry also played their part. We wanted to show our Polish companions, who sang so well, what we were capable of.
> [. . .]

Claudette, who worked in the laboratory where she had a table, pencil and paper, undertook to reconstruct from memory *Le Malade Imaginaire*. No sooner was the first act completed than rehearsals began. I write this as though it were simple. You may think you've got a play down pat, that you see and hear all the characters, but it's no easy task for someone who's just recovered from typhus and is constantly hungry. Those who were able to do so helped out. Recapturing a line was often the victory of an entire day's quest. And the rehearsals... They took place after work, after supper – supper was two hundred grams of dry bread and seven grams of margarine – at the time when, in a dark, freezing hut, you experience more keenly than ever a profound weariness. Persuading and bullying, calling on the spirit of camaraderie, managing flattery and insults, such were the means resorted to on a daily basis by our camp volunteer theater director. [. . .] Every evening, stamping our feet and waving our arms – it was in December – we went on rehearsing. [. . .] The day set for the show – the Sunday after Christmas – was drawing near. However, it was impossible to set things up ahead of time because of the supervisor, an SS female officer, whose only virtue was that, utterly absorbed by her love affairs, she gave us some breathing space. Eva, the draftswoman, was making a poster to be placed on the hut's inner door on Saturday, after the last round of the SS. Why a poster when everyone was informed of our plans? Because we were at last living our illusion. A colored poster, on which one could read: *"Le Malade Imaginaire*, after Molière, by Claudette. Costumes by Cecile. Directed by Charlotte. Set and props by Carmen." [. . .] Our play, however, was only in four acts. We had not succeeded in re-creating Molière's structure, scene by scene. Yet, as I recall, nothing had been left out. (Ibid.: 168–9)

Delbo describes in detail the ingenuity that went into the stage and costumes. Since the women worked in an agricultural experimental station, they had been able to "organize" various materials for their play: "A yellow-green powder whose composition I didn't know (it must have been an insecticide) was used to good effect for the doctor's wonderfully bilious makeup" (ibid.: 170). Then the performance began:

The traditional three knocks were heard. The curtain went up (no, opened). The Polish women were in the audience. Most of them understood French. [. . .] It's magnificent. [. . .] It was magnificent because for the space of two hours, while the smokestacks never stopped belching their smoke of human flesh, for two whole hours we believed in what we were doing. (Ibid.: 171)

We can read several things in Delbo's account. First, there exists a state of deprivation and exhaustion so profound that it is impossible to think of anything other than food and rest. But once this lower limit of physical existence has been overcome – "Imagination is the first luxury of a body" (ibid.: 168) – it seems that a need arises for human engagement in the form of cultural activities which offer an opportunity to connect with one's personal – and communal – past. The self-appointed task is not the only challenge; there is also the challenge of building a community (in this case, among the French women) and distinguishing oneself from others (in this case, in the form of friendly antagonism with the Polish women). But without the calculable negligence of the SS guard who did not bother checking on the prisoners too carefully because she was occupied with her own affairs, the entire undertaking would have been impossible. We can assume that the SS woman took this into account, as she certainly would have had no reason to believe that the prisoners would continue to follow the rules if they were being supervised carelessly or not at all. Although the performance had to be carried out with the utmost secrecy, the indirect participation of the guards was necessary to make it possible in the first place. The success of their secrecy also played a part in the triumph felt by the prisoners, who had identified and taken advantage of weaknesses on the side of their opponents and managed to trick the SS woman. They thus fought against a despised system by identifying and exploiting the social contexts of their subjugators – who not only had been ideologically indoctrinated but who also had their own predilections and weaknesses, some of them acquired in their previous lives.

In her memoirs, Ruth Elias discusses a similar cooperative cultural event in the Taucha concentration camp near Leipzig: a New Year's Eve celebration among the female inmates in 1944 (cf. Elias 1999: 180ff.). Once the prisoners had provided for their "physical nourishment" on the evening through the clever "organization" of food and coal for heating, Elias put together an entertainment program (ibid.: 180). The imprisoned women from different countries "were asked to present something that was typical of their homeland," and a stolen red pencil was used as lipstick and stage makeup by the "performing artists" (ibid.).

On the evening of New Year's Eve, the women waited until they heard singing and noise from the German quarters, at which point they thought they were safe from the guards and SS officers, who would be distracted by their own New Year's festivities. After the room warmed up and the women shared a meal, the evening's entertainment began, featuring songs and poems in Hungarian, Slovakian, Czech, Polish, and French. Elias performed a song from a German operetta, but she adapted the lyrics to fit the situation in the camp. While she was singing, the camp commandant entered the hut. Though she was startled and terribly frightened, Elias gathered her courage and asked him if he had liked the song and whether he wanted to hear another. Instead of answering her, he ordered her to report to him at ten o'clock the next morning (cf. ibid.: 180ff.).

Afraid of what punishment she might face, she went to the commandant the following morning and, to her astonishment, was ordered to put together a cabaret show for the SS within ten days. If she refused, she would be locked up in the bunker – one of the punishments most dreaded by the prisoners.

Although Elias had taken classical piano lessons and played accordion in a dance band (cf. ibid.: 48f.), she had no experience with organizing a cabaret evening and felt that she faced an insurmountable task. She had no choice but to follow this order, however. After consulting anxiously with the other prisoners, she had the idea of asking "the Gypsies" (ibid.: 182) for help. She had become acquainted with these women by secretly taking food to them, and she was familiar with their good humor and lively singing and dancing. The women immediately agreed to cooperate,[54] and all of the prisoners worked together to assemble a program of songs, sketches, and dances. The performers were accompanied on the piano by "a Polish prisoner, a woman who in her former life had played for silent films" (ibid.: 183). "As paradoxical as it may sound, this marked the beginning of ten wonderful days. All our spare time was taken up with rehearsals. It was a demonstration of the friendship and comradeship that bound us together" (ibid.). Elias was part of a work detail that had contact with the outside world, so she was always able to smuggle food – especially bread – into the camp, and therefore,

> [n]obody wanted Ruth of the Leipzig detail to be locked up in the bunker – perhaps because that would have meant a loss of bread for everybody – so the women and girls did their utmost to make things work. [. . .]
>
> On the day of the performance we walked into the dining room and found it filled with SS people and Wehrmacht soldiers. [. . .] The show went off without a hitch. Each of us did her best so that no one would be punished. The costumes were everyday prison garb, and there was no scenery, but the piano was given a place of honor at the front of the stage. And then, at the conclusion of the first number, a miracle: The Germans began to applaud – faintly at first, then the applause grew stronger, louder. Soldiers and SS men and women were clapping for political prisoners and Jews and Gypsies. And they were aware whom they were applauding. Listen, you supermen, I thought, we have managed to show you that we're human beings, and that despite your rule of terror we still have our pride. And now you are applauding us. Thank you for giving us the chance to show you that you haven't succeeded in breaking our spirit. (Ibid.: 183–4)

The camp commandant was so pleased with the performance that he asked Elias to put together more evenings like this. She was even able to convince him that men were essential to the show so she could arrange joint rehearsals and performances with male prisoners. In addition to practicing the program together with the men, these rehearsals were an opportunity to share information between prisoners held in different parts of the camp[55] (cf. ibid.: 184ff.).

There were many such incidents of art being commissioned from the prisoners by the SS in the concentration camps, as Stefanie Endlich describes in her essay "Kunst im Konzentrationslager" (Art in the Concentration Camp) (2005). In addition to entertainment programs, many visual artworks were commissioned as well. Although visual artistic depictions always reflect a personal, interpreted perception of the world and thus represent the artist's individuality – in terms of both individual skills and an individual viewpoint – the SS officers do not seem to have considered it an insurmountable contradiction to request portraits from concentration camp prisoners, for example, even though they had long sought to strip all traces of individuality from these prisoners through physical and symbolic violence. Dina Gottliebova (later Dina Babbitt), for instance, was forced by the infamous and feared Auschwitz physician Josef Mengele to paint signed portraits not only of "Gypsies" – supposedly for "scientific purposes" – but also of Mengele himself (cf. Klüver 2007). Mengele apparently always treated the trained Jewish painter courteously and politely, even offering her pastries sometimes (cf. ibid.).

To sum up: There were various facets to the shadow zone in which it was possible for the concentration camp prisoners to participate in communal, wide-scale cultural activities. Ruth Elias describes a different shadow zone than Charlotte Delbo. While Delbo talks about taking calculated advantage of a guard's negligence to engage in secret cultural activities, Elias writes of a falsely assumed negligence on the part of the guards which suddenly forced her into the position of having to officially entertain the SS if she wanted to avoid severe punishment. "It is only hypothetically possible to make precise distinctions between the [. . .] levels. In actuality, the boundaries were often blurred, there were reciprocal actions, structural connections, and personal identities on the side of the artists" (Endlich 2005: 276). In contrast to Delbo's account, where the French women were driven by a "sense of rivalry" and "pride" and the Polish women took on the role of the audience (cf. Delbo 1995: 168ff.), Elias's example highlights how the communal relationship between women of various national and cultural backgrounds played an important part in the success of a secretly planned evening of entertainment. Even in the case of the cabaret performance carried out to prevent punishment, this communal relationship became an essential force which bound the participants together in their opposition to the "rule of terror."

In light of the threatened punishment, it is understandable that everyone would strive to do their best in the performance. What may surprise us, however, is that the preparations for the cabaret evening would take place over "ten wonderful days" (Elias 1999: 183) full of eager effort on the part of the performers, and that this coerced performance in front of the despised Germans would become something of a triumph for the prisoners. There were probably several reasons for this. Elias herself mentions one of them at the end of the passage quoted above: It was an opportunity to show the SS that the inmates' spirits remained unbroken and that they had access to vital resources which enabled them to be creative and artistic, despite everything. Another seemingly banal reason was that these activities were a diversion from the otherwise strenuous and bleak camp life, and they gave the prisoners the chance to see something through from beginning to end with (relative) autonomy. Even if they did this on the order of the SS, the inmates were apparently able to disregard the degrading aspects of this order and draw strength from the situation by focusing on the resources they still had within them and what they were able to achieve together.

It is more difficult to determine what motivated the SS to play this macabre game, because we only have the reports of former prisoners to go on. It seems, however, that when it came to cultural activities by the prisoners – as was the case with the economic activities described earlier, in which the SS actively participated or at least enabled by more or less deliberately looking the other way – the guards' ideologically influenced view of the prisoners as "inferior" and "sub-human" was apparently overlaid with viewpoints and habits stemming from a less extreme, more conventional life before the camps. It was not always possible for the SS to completely suppress this more "humane" view of the prisoners as individuals, so they occasionally acted on their own needs, even if this went against their ideological outlook. After all, the camp guards and SS members originally came from the *same social world* as the prisoners (see also chapter 2.4), a world in which they held many different social positions and whose influence could not be switched off on command – particularly when it came to something as genuinely human as gaining an economic or material advantage or enjoying a cultural diversion.

The shadow zone of social activity in the Nazi concentration camps therefore owed its existence not solely to the habitus of the inmates, which transported concepts and routines into the camp and enabled this kind of hidden economy and cultural scene; it was also a product of the habitus of the SS guards, who occasionally asserted themselves against their ideological indoctrination and almost unintentionally dealt with the "sub-humans" on equal terms for brief moments.

Both groups of social agents in the concentration camps displayed what Bourdieu calls a "divided" or "torn habitus" which can arise from "discordances" (cf. Bourdieu in Bourdieu and Wacquant 1992: 127; cf. also Bourdieu 2007: 100). This is a habitus shaped by contradictory influences which enabled the prisoners to take satisfaction in the success of their activities even when they were acting on the command of the SS, and which prompted the SS, in turn, to take pleasure in economic transactions with or successful cultural performances by the inmates even though their deepest convictions led them to despise these same prisoners.

The social existence of the prisoners in the Nazi concentration camps was not determined solely by the all-dominating military order and occasional spectacular cultural events, however. There was a *third, always-present level of sociality* consisting of a *minutely organized, latent social life* in which the prisoners – somewhat like micro-organisms – lived their own lives and thought or did their own things while going largely unnoticed by the SS. There was very little scope for them to do so, but nonetheless, the strategies employed by the prisoners here were as varied as the people themselves and could be both *individual* and – on a small scale – *communal* in nature. Some prisoners were absolutely determined to stick as closely as possible to familiar habits. Former Auschwitz prisoner Alojzy Fros recalls:

> I never gave up my seemingly banal habits and tried to bring order to this micro-world in which I was forced to live. To illustrate what I mean, I just want to point out that when I ate meals in my bunk in the camp, I used a box covered with a napkin as a table, on which I spread out the prepared, more or less humble "victuals." (Alojzy Fros in Jagoda et al. 1987a: 30)

Others prisoners sought creative and innovative ways to express their impressions, thoughts, and feelings, and they wound up doing things that they had never done before but that they understood how to do based on their horizon of experience. This included writing poems, which became a way for many inmates to express both their desperation and their hopes.

A tremendous variety of experiences are recounted in the memoirs of former prisoners, so I would like to focus on just a few selected examples. These should provide at least a cursory insight into the broad range of activities on this level of sociality while also illustrating how these activities were very personal, were influenced by the prisoners' respective social backgrounds, and gave the inmates a feeling of autonomy and a sense of their own position in society. This latent social life of the prisoners always entailed doing something forbidden as an act of self-assertion. But this self-assertion was as complex and nuanced as the individuals themselves; it had to be in order to express the differences between all of these people, as it was self-assertion that restored a sense of individuality to the prisoners who had been forcibly "leveled" by the SS. In addition to distracting the prisoners from the misery surrounding them, this latent camp life was a vehicle for the manifestation of *differences* and *similarities*, something which was very important to the preservation and expression of their human dignity.

There are numerous accounts of all types of distracting activities that often took place among small groups of prisoners and that were based on the prisoners' past experience and skills. For example, Ruth Elias describes how they "cooked imaginary meals" in the Taucha camp near Leipzig by describing the preparation and consumption of dishes in detail[56] until they were "satisfied" (Elias 1999: 174). They also "discussed school subjects, books, music, and sports" (ibid.). Pelagia Lewińska-Tepicht recalls similar secret activities in Auschwitz: "Conversations with women I was close to and the recounting of films, books and experiences were a good distraction from the situation" (Pelagia Lewińska-Tepicht in Jagoda et al. 1987a: 29). Stefan Kępa says something similar:

> In the evenings, our comrade Stanisław Kubiński would recount various literary works to distract the prisoners from the problems of the camp and lead them to freedom. He had an extraordinary memory and the ability to depict these works vividly; he even recited some parts from memory. Long after the narration had ended, you would still have forgotten the difficulties of camp life, and you would look forward to listening to comrade Kubiński again in the evening. (Stefan Kępa in ibid.)

Adam Kuffel writes that "various forms of mental support were no less important than material aid. From jokes which – as frivolous as they might have been – lightened the oppressive atmosphere, [. . .] to performances of serious or entertaining music, even Holy Masses and the sacraments – you could find all of it in Auschwitz" (Adam Kuffel in ibid: 41).

The range of intellectual activities was always informed by the individual experiences of those performing for or sharing with others. Borowski mentions a Kapo who was in the sick bay with him:

> He showed little enthusiasm for the stories of vulgar novels, adventure films, or of any kind of play. He hated all extravagant tales on the themes of romantic literature. But he would abandon himself with passion to any ridiculous, sentimental plot as long as I managed to convince him it was taken from my own life. (Borowski 1992: 158)

It is easy to imagine that recounted films and books were a welcome distraction, but they would certainly not have been to everyone's taste or on everyone's "cultural level." Social differences therefore manifested themselves along the lines of these hidden practices, and although everyone was in the same situation and there were hardly any material differences between the prisoners, this contributed to the preservation of fine "distinctions" (Bourdieu 1984) between different social positions.

For example, many former prisoners talk about secret religious practices in the concentration camps.[57] While some admit that their previously self-evident religious beliefs were closed off to them as a means of self-preservation or construction of meaning in light of the horrors they experienced in the camps and they began to doubt the existence of God (cf. Rahe 1998), others – even those who had not been particularly religious before – developed a deep religiosity in the camps which gave them the strength to believe that they would survive. "Never, neither before nor after (unfortunately!), did I pray as fervently as I did [. . .] in the camp. As it happens, we usually prayed together [. . .]" (Helena Dunicz-Niwińska in Jagoda et al. 1987a: 24). In some ways, the decisive factor was not the prisoner's denomination[58] but whether he or she had familiar rituals to fall back on. "I prayed a lot [. . .] I had proper conversations with God, I talked with Him in my own way" (Alfred Skrabania in ibid.). Leon Szalet also describes how prayer gave him a feeling of calm and strength, particularly on important Jewish holidays: "Our souls hungered for the comfort of the words with which we had grown up" (Szalet 1945: 68). In this religious context, Orthodox Jews had the option of *not* doing things as well. For example, a number of sources report that, despite their starvation rations and malnourishment, some Orthodox Jews still fasted on Yom Kippur because it meant that they were making an independent decision to observe a religious commandment (cf. Rahe 1998: 1016). Those who opposed any type of religious world-view, such as communists, disdained these secret religious practices, mocked their fellow prisoners because of them, and called on them to engage in political activity instead (cf. Szalet 1945: 92f.).

There are many accounts of prisoners starting to write poems even if they had no previous interest in such things. Poems would have been a part of their culture of origin in any case, so the prisoners usually had a clear – though sometimes rudimentary – concept of what form a poem should take, namely, that it should have rhythm and rhyme. Writing poems proved to be a relatively easy strategy to implement in the camps because it required nothing more than (one's own) language and a notion of the formal structure of a poem in order to express one's thoughts and feelings. Self-penned poems, which were sometimes read aloud to small groups of others and even memorized by fellow prisoners so that they would be preserved, thus represented the preservation of individuality as well as shared culture and traditions (cf., e.g., Jaiser 2000; Klüger 2001; Suderland 2004). The framework of a shared culture still left room for differentiation and spanned a "realm of possibilities" (Bourdieu 2000a: 302); these could take very different forms depending on one's individual and social experiences and they therefore actualized social differences. Concentration camp prisoners wrote everything from prayer-like verses (cf. Jaiser 2000) to expressionist poems (cf. Vogel 2002) in accordance with their previous relationship with such works.

The visual arts were difficult to engage in secretly.[59] Materials had to be acquired first – an almost insurmountable obstacle in many cases because paper, pencils, canvas, and so on, were difficult to stash away. The prisoners were very inventive, however, and used other materials as well, such as tea or charcoal tablets (cf. Endlich 2005: 279f.). Another problem was finding the time and space to immerse oneself in the surreptitious activity without being discovered or disturbed. It was usually also not easy to find a good place to hide a finished work in order to protect it from the SS. For this reason, most of the pictures produced in the camps were very small. Some artists destroyed their own secret works themselves from fear of being discovered and reconstructed them after their liberation (cf. Endlich

2005: 279). Alfred Kantor, who was deported at the age of eighteen and survived three concentration camps, says:

> [O]nce drawn, these scenes could never be erased from mind. [...M]ost of the sketches I destroyed to avoid being caught. The few Schwarzheide drawings that actually survived did so though the bravery of a friend who smuggled them out. When I was free again, the rescued material – and the lost sketches that I had committed to memory – made it possible to put together my diary. (Kantor 1971: [8])

Some sketches were hidden in canisters and buried – ultimately surviving their creators, who died in the concentration camps – only to be discovered by chance years later.

Different prisoners had very different motivations for drawing or painting pictures during their imprisonment. On one level, visual artworks were an expression of a prisoner's cultural identity and individual artistic skills and therefore represented both *individual* and *social continuity*. But these works were often not so much artistic as documentary representations of life and death in the camps; they were evidence of this life, preserved for the outside world and for posterity, transcending language. Portraits and self-portraits were the most common motifs in concentration camp art (cf. Endlich 2005: 282), and they documented both the prisoners' physical degeneration and their individual physiognomy, thus putting a face to the nameless inmates.[60] But many works deliberately rejected depictions of the camps in favor of memories of a more beautiful world. Numerous landscapes and still lifes were produced with this intention (cf. ibid.).

Playing music was yet another secret activity among the prisoners. This ranged from individual performances for the entertainment of other prisoners to the establishment of choirs and secret rehearsals by string quartets.[61] Loden Vogel, for example, mentions in his Bergen-Belsen diary that his mother sang songs for her hut leader's birthday (cf. Vogel 2002: 20). Juliane Brauer's book on music and song in the Sachsenhausen concentration camp includes examples of prisoner choirs (cf. Brauer 2009: 152f.) and a string quartet which rehearsed first in the morgue and later in the delousing hut – two places where they were unlikely to be discovered by the SS (cf. ibid.: 171ff.). The prisoners sang their own songs as a counterpoint to the songs they were continually forced to sing by the SS, a practice which was humiliating and torturous for them.

> When the torture was over, the prisoners came together in the huts and sang *their* songs, by choice and with fervor – songs they knew from the labor and youth movements or the "Wandervogel." [. . .] The SS was powerless – they were told that the songs had to be rehearsed with the newcomers for roll call. (Lammel 1995: 17–18; emphasis in original)

In her book *Music in the Holocaust* (2005), Shirli Gilbert says:

> Aside from [the] institutionalized activities, a wide range of informal and spontaneous music-making took place. The music that inmates performed ranged from popular pre-war songs to opera and operetta, folk music, standard classical repertoire, choral music, and dance melodies. In addition, a large number of new songs and pieces were created, not only in the ghettos but in the camps as well. (Gilbert 2005: 2)

Gilbert does not interpret this musical activity only as a type of mental resistance; she emphasizes that divergent cultural practices also expressed social differentiation within the prisoner society. "It explores hierarchies and other patterns of power within inmate communities, and illustrates how a variety of social and political factors affected the ways in which different groups could make use of music" (ibid.: 3). This thread of social differentiation runs through many accounts by former prisoners. For example, it is clear that Paul Martin Neurath's account was written by an intellectual, a man of science who suffered from "intellectual starvation":

> Hundreds [. . .] deal successfully with the most difficult task – intellectual survival. They resent having their minds taken up by the paltry camp gossip about food and maltreatment and release. [. . .] The whole realm of science is still open to the man who, with his companions, carries a hand-barrow full of gravel through the forest – as long as there is no SS man around.
>
> Some use brain twisters. I remember a three-day argument over the queerest subject: a mathematical theory about the disappearance of the dinosaurs. If I understood its proponent correctly, they starved to death because – while eating up the leaves of one tree, their muscles shrank so much that they could not drag themselves to the next. We argued violently over this nonsense, but we enjoyed it because it led us away from the camp and helped to keep fresh our ability to argue. [. . .] One morning in Buchenwald, I spent seven hours with a friend, dumping clay into a hole and reciting poems by Hans Christian Morgenstern. When we had dug up every line we remembered, we passed the treasure along to our friends, as an important contribution of something that did not smell of clay. For two days Morgenstern was in vogue at this working place.
>
> People less interested in intellectual training try desperately to keep their personal style. There was a man who lived by the motto, "They can force me to eat from a trough, but they can't force me to be a swine." He would spend a whole evening cleaning two herrings and cutting them into nice filets. (Neurath 2005: 133–4)

It is clear that Neurath is describing his own kind, and when he holds up an example of someone "less interested in intellectual training" (ibid.: 134), he chooses a representative of a lifestyle he still approves of.

In the case of Leon Szalet, a Polish Jew who, after Germany invaded Poland in 1939, was imprisoned for a long period of time under terrible conditions in an isolation hut in Sachsenhausen, where he was sometimes forced to spend the whole day standing in the overcrowded hut,[62] we find the following description, which includes its own analysis:

It seemed to me that the only remedy [from the hunger] was to divert our attention to some other subject. So I proposed that we hold conversation periods, to which everyone should contribute something – a talk on his field of knowledge, a story, a personal experience, an anecdote, or even a song or a poem. [. . .] The window polishers[63] undertook to watch for the block-fuehrers, and we kept the secret so well that we were not once surprised.

[Although the conversation periods could only be held irregularly, they had the effect I had expected.] These conversation periods soon became the one bright spot in our despairing existence.

Because of the varied character of our group, the most diverse problems were discussed. And everyone profited. The less educated enriched their general knowledge; the well-educated, their range of human experience. Some even learned new languages. [Since emigration was one of the most burning issues for the future, and the Anglo-Saxon countries were the most popular destination, the linguists offered to teach the basics of English to anyone who wanted to learn. From that point on, you would see small groups sitting together each day, whispering English declinations and conjugations.] [. . .]

Often when the wits among us were in good form there were moments of pure comedy which even the gloomiest could not resist. And sometimes there were moments of exultation. When suffering was gnawing most sharply at our hearts, some comrade with a few inspired words might revive our failing hopes. (Szalet 1945: 97; new translation from the German text in Szalet 2006: 141–2 in brackets)

To everyone's delight, one wit improvised a telepathic dialogue with Hitler, in which he spoke his mind to the Fuehrer with all the resources of his vocabulary, and Hitler, bursting into a frenzy, tried to answer him. This drama was acted in a whisper, of course. [But Hitler's characteristic bellow was mimicked so accurately that it was as if the frenzied Fuehrer stood before us, though in caricature.] [I]t was a masterpiece of mimicry and so amusing that for a time our troubles were forgotten. (Szalet 1945: 101; new translation from the German text in Szalet 2006: 148 in brackets)

Szalet mentions a number of different secret activities that brought the prisoners together as a community in the overcrowded hut, and he also draws an unquestioned link between his "comrades" and their backgrounds. It clearly mattered whether you were educated or not, whether you could share knowledge or experience, whether you were a comedian or were gloomy. What is merely implied in other prisoner memoirs is very explicit in Szalet's account: As a matter of course, he assigns the participants in these conversation periods to different *positions* and draws meaningful *connections* between them. In essence, Szalet paints a picture of a conventional society in which each person occupies his own position for a good reason – one has knowledge, another has experience, a third has comedic talent, each has something the others are apparently lacking. Even the body is used to convey familiar social relations in the form of parody. Everyone thrown together in this miserable situation strives to be different – they invest energy in their differences in order to distract themselves from the fact that they are all equally at risk of not surviving the terror.

5.4 Summary: A micro-sociological view of the intricacies of complex camp life or: How many realities were there?

For the deportees, entering a concentration camp represented a violent break with their previous experiences in a civilized world. Deliberately brutal and debasing initiation processes impressed upon the prisoners what their captors thought of them and what they had to face from that point on. This traumatic experience usually sent new inmates into a state of paralyzing shock, and the moment in which they entered the concentration camp became a key event in a series of previously unthinkable horrors, one which they naturally placed great emphasis on in their accounts. This extreme break with their former lives which was felt so acutely forced them to address the issue of *discontinuities* in their diaries and memoirs. "They actually want to maintain the discontinuity in their literature so that the violent nature of the trauma is preserved as a 'testimony for all time'" (Stirn 2000: 726). This makes it somewhat difficult to grasp the *relevance of the continuities that existed at the same time*, however, and it obscures the actual – though hidden – presence of various levels of familiar social interactions in the camps.

At first glance, the brutality of the SS, the dreadful hygienic conditions, the starvation and physical strain create the impression of a *counterworld* where nothing that was applicable outside the camp continued to be applicable within it, thus placing a heavy psychological burden of uncertainty on the inmates as well. These conditions were not only terrible for the prisoners, they were also symbolic of the break with their former lives. However, a closer analysis reveals that *neither the SS nor the inmates could simply shake off their social past.*

On the *first level of sociality*, there were models and analogies on the side of the SS which were reflected in the organization of the camps and the choice and execution of punishments. Camp life was structured according to a *military order* which – though it had aspects of a "caricature" (Levi

1989: 116) that exposed the inmates to ridicule – was a widely familiar model on which the prisoners could orient themselves. The continual acts of *public corporal punishment*, which were usually carried out during roll calls, were a *mimetic practice borrowed from the premodern period*, a popular form of vigilante justice that had never entirely disappeared and had become increasingly blatant since the start of the "Third Reich" (cf. Wildt 2007). In the camps, too, it had the intended effect: It was a *demonstration of the total asymmetry of power* that the prisoner society was forced to witness so that the SS could consolidate this power relationship through the visible enforcement of domination and impress upon the inmates that they were utterly impotent (cf. Foucault 1995). The dignity of the prisoners was trampled to express the idea of a *"Volksgemeinschaft"* cleansed of such unworthy creatures and to highlight the glory of the representatives of the people's community.

On the part of the prisoners, their own experience of the military – through either observation or actual participation – served as a rough guideline for the behavior expected of them. The transparent regimentation of military practice sometimes also enabled the prisoners to find and exploit loopholes for their own strategies, though they always faced the threat of discovery and punishment for doing so.

Once the prisoners had become more familiar with camp life, options opened up to them in the *shadow zone* between their flouting of the regulations and the toleration of their transgressions by the guards. Above all, this *second level of sociality* created a space for the *covert camp economy* and *cultural activities*. Both of these areas were vital to the prisoners, though in different ways, so a great deal of inventiveness was exhibited here. The principles governing these two areas were *no different* inside the camps than they were in the world outside, so these activities seem all the more preposterous and unbelievable to outsiders. But this similarity is precisely why so many prisoners were able to take part in the activities – or why they even knew how they functioned. It is also why members of the SS, despite their ideological indoctrination, could be convinced to contribute to such activities as well, either through tacit toleration or through active participation to their own advantage, even though it meant that they were cooperating with the "internal enemy" (Sofsky 1997).

The *third, most deeply hidden level of sociality* was the *latent social life of the prisoners*, the diversity of which is almost impossible to grasp. On this level, the inmates used *self-determined strategies* to distract themselves from the misery of camp life. One important task here was to bolster fellow prisoners who were particularly distressed and therefore at risk. The aspect of self-determination, which kept alive the prisoners' *memory of their individuality*, was heavily influenced by the inmates' existing skills and experiences, which documented both where they came from and where they actually belonged. This latent social life in the camps therefore served to establish hut and prisoner *communities*, on the one hand,

and to *define boundaries* and *expose social lines of demarcation*, on the other. This particularly hidden level of sociality represented a *"realm of possibilities"* (Bourdieu 2000a: 302) in two respects: The opportunities for such activities were extremely limited owing to the circumstances, and they were also determined by the prisoners' prior experiences. It was not just a matter of recognizing opportunities and seizing them; when options opened up to them, the prisoners could generally only fall back on their existing body of experience. The *interplay of the current situation and prisoners' personal past experiences* did not exclude the possibility of forging *new paths* and taking advantage of options which had not been used before, but there was still a difference between those who could call on familiar routines and those who had to first acquire knowledge of a practice in order to make use of it.

These micro-sociologically distinct levels of sociality often *overlapped* in everyday camp life, generating a *very complex social reality* in the Nazi concentration camps which was both extremely contradictory and homogeneous depending on how one looks at it. The reality of the faceless, *nameless mass* of downtrodden and degraded creatures struggling to survive was at the same time – when examined from a different perspective – a *complex society of individuals* who joined together in groups at every possible opportunity and actualized (social) differences in order to affirm their *human dignity*. On the one hand, the SS succeeded in its strategy of turning the prisoners into nameless numbers who would fight over a crust of bread; but, on the other hand, this strategy strengthened the desire of the dehumanized to assert their individuality both by expressing solidarity and by cultivating significant differences and nuances.

The strategies employed on all three levels of sociality can be considered largely "contained" forms (Goffman 1961: 199) of *"secondary adjustments"* (ibid.: 54) where existing structures must be exploited in order "to obtain forbidden satisfactions or to obtain permitted ones by forbidden means" (ibid.). If the employed strategies were not unique to individuals, the agents in the "underlife" (ibid.: 199) that consequently emerged in the concentration camps had to call on existing social networks as well as establish new ones. Some of these hidden social activities showed the traits of "colonization" (ibid.: 62f.) since normal life outside of the camp was temporarily pushed out of the prisoners' spectrum of perception and the world within the camp became their sole reference point.

Along with the economic activities in the shadow zone – which not only, but certainly very often, served to fulfill the prisoners' basic material needs – diverse cultural activities carried out on all three levels of sociality played an important role for the inmates. Zygmunt Bauman reinforces the idea that culture can be thought of as a *survival strategy* for concentration camp prisoners in that it both ties in with the past and uses innovative means to create something new, making it an expression of the "permanence and durability which life, by itself, so sorely misses" (Bauman 1992:

4). The omnipresent "odors" (ibid.: 3) of death and dying in the Nazi concentration camps could not be "undone" (ibid.) by the prisoners' cultural efforts, but they could be covered up for short periods of time.

The *habitus* of every agent involved – prisoners and SS alike – was instrumental in shaping all three levels of sociality. The possibilities and limits as well as the contradictory tendencies were rooted in the partially "forgotten history" (Bourdieu 1990) of the social agents, and the terrifying new experiences in the world of the concentration camp could lead to "divided habituses" (Bourdieu 2007) which ran counter to the rational intentions of the agents and enabled the existence of a shadow zone. For example, most prisoners still felt the ambition to perform a task well if they had fundamentally positive associations with it, even if it was being carried out at the order of the SS, just as SS officers could not suppress feelings of vanity and unadulterated pleasure if a concentration camp prisoner sketched a flattering portrait of them. As "the active presence of the whole past of which it is the product," the habitus "gives practices their *relative autonomy* with respect to external determinations of the immediate present" (Bourdieu 1990: 56; emphasis added) – that is, it makes it possible for completely contradictory tendencies to exist simultaneously.

As a result, the Nazi concentration camps were the sites of differing realities, none of which were less real than the others. The daily sight of a mass of indistinguishable and pitiable prisoners standing at roll call for hours was as much a part of this camp reality as the fact that there was "no way that you'd ever really become nobody for everybody" (Antelme 1998: 173).

The state of being somebody was determined both by *individual* aspects and by certain *social affiliations* – Neurath mentions the influence of "social background and concepts" on the individual prisoners (cf. Neurath 2005: 131) – which I will explore in more detail in the following chapter.

6

Prisoner Society

The experiences in the camp are generally paraphrased with a single word: "night-mare" or "hell." These popular designations seem very apt, and any attempt to use other terms ends in fiasco. These words underscore the inhumanity of everything that happened in the camps – and, on the other hand, a certain humanity as well. Because ultimately, even the vision of hell is the product of the human mind, and the nightmare springs from sleep and thus also from the human mind. It is not beyond the realm of possibility that someone had the nightmare of Auschwitz before it became a reality. But it's a long way from a sleeping or waking dream to realization.
Antoni Kępiński (in Brzezicki et al. 1987: 235)

The preceding chapter clearly showed that a hidden social life existed on different levels in the Nazi concentration camps and this social life bore a relation to the inmates' previous lives. The prisoners harked back to familiar ways of living either by reenacting routine practices or by adopting practices in the camps with which they were at least passively acquainted. This resulted, almost subcutaneously, in a form of social differentiation within the prisoner society in which social (class) differences were expressed by means of divergent social practices, much as in normal life outside the camps. These surreptitious activities were important not only because they distracted the concentration camp prisoners from the misery of their daily lives, but also – since they were actually prohibited – because they represented a form of resistance or at least self-assertion. One aspect of this self-assertion was that the enacted social practices – whether they involved eating the meager rations in a "cultivated" way, praying regularly, recounting films, or rehearsing with a string quartet – always actualized something that related to the prisoners' former lives and world of experience and thereby also actualized their social position.

While the SS and guard squads did not constitute a completely homogeneous group,[1] this was even more true for the prisoners. They had been taken from all corners of the world and a wide variety of social backgrounds, so they felt an affinity with sometimes wildly divergent social groups, and they had also been imprisoned in the concentration camps for many different reasons. The involuntary nature of their existence in the camps was their lowest common denominator, but this was not enough to bind them together in a homogeneous formation. Prisoners arrived at the concentration camps in a disparate and difficult to distinguish mass, and they were forced to undergo an intimidating and frightening initiation procedure which turned human beings into "numbers." This debasing process also separated them into smaller conglomerates based on the reasons for their imprisonment – a categorization which was visible even from afar – so they were easier for the camp SS to manage.

There were multiple facets to this process, however, because this categorization was also a form of social classification in the sense that both the SS and the inmates had entrenched views of the representatives of each category; even in their former lives, it had made a difference whether someone was a "criminal," a Jew, a communist, or a "Gypsy." The value judgments associated with each prisoner category therefore influenced both how the SS treated the prisoners and how the prisoners related to each other. Whether individual inmates could identify with their category, and perhaps even draw a certain strength from it, usually depended on whether such a classification had played a role in their lives outside the camp and, if so, what the connotations of this classification were.

Within this prisoner classification structure, the so-called prisoner functionaries occupied a hybrid position in that they were inmates, on the one hand, but they sometimes had considerable power of authority over their fellow prisoners, on the other. They were neither formally nor socially a part of the SS, but their privileged status also meant that they had little connection with the rest of the regular prisoners. Some prisoner functionaries viewed the tasks assigned to them by the SS as a means of achieving personal satisfaction and power, while others felt they faced an irresolvable dilemma because their decision-making authority might allow them to help a few prisoners – but not without harming others at the same time. Prisoners who had spent a long time in a camp were known as the *Lagerprominenz* (camp aristocracy, or prominents), and they enjoyed a certain prestige because others knew they could only have survived by acquiring detailed knowledge of the camp's processes and personalities and using this knowledge to their advantage. Regular prisoners deemed it worthwhile to partake of this since it could also work to their own advantage, so veteran concentration camp prisoners were treated like dignitaries.

Gender differentiation seems to have cut across all social structural differences within the prisoner society. Although men and women were usually kept strictly separated in the Nazi concentration camps,[2] basic notions about men and women on the side of both the SS and the inmates nonetheless played a differentiating role in their interactions and thus influenced life in the camps.

While the preceding chapter took a micro-sociological view of the prisoners and their clandestine activities, this chapter will take a closer look at the social structure of the prisoner society. In the following, I will first explore the social consequences of the different prisoner categories. In the context of this work, it will be particularly interesting to see who made what kinds of distinctions. Examples which reveal the views of the SS, the internal views of the prisoner society, and the self-perception of individual prisoners will all be taken into consideration (section 6.1), and these examples will show that along with the hidden social practices of the prisoners, a prisoner's "triangle category" played a significant role in how each agent was socially assessed.

To illustrate the complexity of the prisoner society, I will examine the constitution of this society from another perspective by investigating the different living situations and social positions of regular prisoners, prisoner functionaries, and the camp aristocracy and explaining how elite groups formed in the camps (6.2). Finally, I will give some thought to the importance of gender separation inside the camps, the presence of children, and the consequences of this for the society in the concentration camps (6.3).

6.1 Fragmentation, dissociation, community-building: Social processes

[T]he contemporary terms we borrow from the object of our study are almost always approaches to social struggles. For example, this is the case with words that refer to groups and that are frequently used in conflicts regarding the boundaries of these groups, that is, the conditions for belonging to a group or being excluded from it. [. . .] It therefore follows that all of these words, just like those which refer to virtues or characteristics, are objectively ambiguous.

Pierre Bourdieu (2004: 114)

Concentration camp prisoners were categorized based on the reason for their imprisonment, and the highly visible color-coded classification triangles on their clothing introduced an external criterion for differentiation into the otherwise indistinguishable involuntary community of inmates. With this classification system, the SS solidified the enemy categories that were rooted in their ideal of the *"Volksgemeinschaft."* They did so by drawing on certain notions and associated designations which already had a history and therefore served as a type of shorthand for familiar viewpoints and social experiences that the SS shared with the prisoners. Although prisoners assigned to a specific category did not necessarily actually belong to that category with respect to their worldview, nationality, "race," or any other criterion, the colored triangles were social signifiers that had an influence on the prisoner society nonetheless.

Because the categories already had social and historical weight, the prisoner classes based on them were not viewed neutrally even by the inmates themselves; instead, the classes were loaded with a significance that the prisoners could not, or sometimes did not want to, escape.

These people who were segregated from the social space of society and sent to outposts of that society – the concentration camps – were people who, according to the prevailing Nazi ideology and its underlying values, had long been situated very low in the hierarchy of the social space: namely, those who were "racially," politically, and socially "inferior." The legal decrees that regulated this represented a radicalization of conventional society, but they were fundamentally accepted by large sections of this society.[3] In this respect, the hierarchy in the camps reflected a social order which was familiar to those who had already suffered under it for a long period of time. It was a distorted reflection of this social order, however, in that the category of criminals – the "greens" – was at the top of the hierarchy because, as individuals, they could be easily exploited by the SS. In cases where a prisoner categorized as a criminal actually was a convicted felon who had ruthlessly and violently pursued his own interests with no regard for the law, the SS could generally be assured that this individual would behave in the same way inside the camps as long as it was to his personal advantage. The fact that the green triangle was also assigned to people who had been convicted of currency offenses, bankruptcy fraud, or a failure to pay alimony, however, did not lessen the triangle's effect among the prisoner society, as it was associated with a simplified, easy-to-grasp concept of the notorious, brutal, violent, self-interested offender.

In the camp hierarchy, the "greens" were followed by the political prisoners – the "reds" – who were even respected by the SS to a certain extent. The concept of the "opponent" or "enemy category" (Eberle 2005) was most applicable to inmates imprisoned for political reasons because, as opponents of the regime, they were not really "inferior" in the Nazis' biologistic view but had instead been "led astray" and otherwise showed qualities that the Nazis actually admired: They were steadfast in their world-view, they were exceptionally well organized, they fought for their community and their goals with audacity and courage, and they were prepared to go through hell for their convictions. These were all traits that, under other circumstances, the Nazis held in high esteem.

Situated in the middle of the prisoner hierarchy were the "anti-social elements," Jehovah's Witnesses, and prisoners of different nationalities, among others. Homosexuals, "Gypsies," and Jews brought up the rear in the hierarchy of the Nazi concentration camps (cf. Eberle 2005; Kogon 2006: 30ff.; Sofsky 1997: 129), a situation abetted by the fact that individuals identified in this way had traditionally been stigmatized in society already.

The triangle categories resulted in a ranking of "opponent categories" which defined the inmates' relationship with the SS. This ranking determined how close a prisoner category was to the center of power and thus what special privileges might be associated with it which could make life in the camp somewhat easier. Conversely, a prisoner's classification could also be an unalterable basis for the partial or complete denial of privileges: for example, regardless of their personal conduct on an individual level, all Jews were fundamentally forbidden from receiving packages or other mail and from reading the newspaper, a situation which made life in the camps much more difficult for them than for prisoners in other categories.

This unequal treatment, which largely harked back to distinctions made at least in part by both the prisoners and the SS, opened the floodgates to internal class struggles within the prisoner society, prevented class-transcending solidarity between the prisoners, enabled corruption, and primarily served to divide the camp society so that it was easier for the SS to control.

Unlike Kurt Pätzold, however, I do not believe that "the basic composition of the prisoner society [. . .] was in *no way* the product of arrangements that could be made by the prisoners but was instead, from the outset, the planned creation of those in power" (Pätzold 2005: 112; emphasis added). The view of society formulated by Pätzold implies that a society functions according to explicit rules which are negotiated and agreed upon by autonomous agents who have come together voluntarily. I think this view overlooks the significance of social practices in the constitution of a society and ignores what Bourdieu calls habitus. Pätzold firmly argues that the prisoners did not have the scope to influence the internal structure of this involuntary society, and he therefore considers the prisoner society to have been horizontally structured; the only sign of a vertical structure he sees is in the case of prisoner functionaries, who were granted special authority and therefore had more room to maneuver than their fellow prisoners.

Like Pätzold, Wolfgang Sofsky points out in his widely received book *The Order of Terror* that "[t]he system of classification was not the product of social inequality, but rather its most important *cause*. [. . .] The categories did not reduce inequality, but rather engendered it" (Sofsky 1997: 122; emphasis added). Even though the hierarchical classification system cemented the inequality of the prisoners in a dramatic way in the concentration camps, the prisoner categories were certainly not the reason for this inequality.

> Their ideological constructions were mutually compatible because it was possible to reach a consensus on the elements of these constructions, such as a rigid anti-humanist view of mankind; the equation of the "enemy of the state" with the "enemy of the people"; assumptions based on notions of racial hygiene and racial anthropology about genetic inferiority as the root of other behaviors; the criminalization of politically or socially deviant

behavior; and antisemitic, anti-communist and anti-democratic attitudes. (Eberle 2005: 93)

This capacity for reaching a consensus was not limited solely to groups of people thoroughly steeped in Nazi ideology, as the majority of the camp SS certainly was. Instead, as described in detail in chapter 2, it applied to large sections of the German population at the time who agreed with the Nazi world-view at least to the extent that they had largely internalized its biologistic and racist patterns of thought.

In Bourdieu's terms, the social structure within the concentration camps could be described as follows: The social space of the concentration camp was not a counterworld, as it is so often depicted, but was, on account of its prisoner classification system among other things, more of a distorted reflection of the normal social space of society outside the camps. Certain groups were not represented in this social space at all, while others – namely, those who were on the lowest rungs of the social hierarchy of the time – filled this new space and were ranked accordingly. In keeping with the social reality of the time (cf. Bajohr 2003), which the Nazis had changed drastically using a variety of measures, Jews were positioned at the very bottom of this social space, regardless of any social position they had managed to achieve previously, solely on the basis of their "being Jewish," like a caste with an indelible stigma attached to it. Even criminals were positioned higher than them. It would not have been nearly as easy to induce the prisoners themselves to acknowledge the camp hierarchy if they had not already incorporated this image of society in their previous lives (cf. Suderland 2004). Elsewhere Sofsky writes:

> Although it was forced on the prisoners by the SS, the category system was largely accepted by them. [. . .] There were several reasons for this. First, the labels used by the SS matched existing stereotypes in the social environment; the camp regime only needed to radicalize them. [. . .] Second, the rampant repression and international composition of the prisoner population often reduced communication to a series of gestures and rapid exchanges. The badges helped provide a quick orientation as to whom one was dealing with, and who could be trusted. Finally, collective powerlessness furthered the acceptance of the categories. (Sofsky 1997: 123–4)

In other words, the category system could be enforced because even the prisoners had already incorporated its fundamentals – though perhaps in a more nuanced form, with finer distinctions – so there was a latent willingness to adopt this system of crude differentiation. Everyone was familiar with how different groups (criminals, Jews, etc.) were positioned in the social space, and they knew – though they may not always have agreed with – where they themselves stood, where others stood, and what misgivings were felt toward the other groups. As a result, no one was surprised to be held in somewhat higher or lower regard than someone else.[4] We can also conclude that it was not actually the intention of the SS to establish a counterworld in the concentration camps; instead, they strove for radicalization on the basis of existing social foundations.

This perspective gives rise to a very complex picture of the prisoner society, one which is problematic and not terribly popular because it means that we can no longer view the world of the concentration camps in simple black and white. Consequently, we must face the fact that there were strong strains of antisemitism within the prisoner society; that in upholding their ideological aims, political prisoners sometimes harmed their fellow prisoners "for a good cause"; and that so-called criminals did not always fit their stereotypical image and occasionally even expressed solidarity with and supported their fellow prisoners – in brief, we must accept that our own view of the world has been shaken.

However, because this work aims to explore the social continuities that remained despite (or possibly because of) the great confusion caused by the shocking and violent "topsy-turvy world" of the camps, in the following I will look at the memoirs of former concentration camp prisoners to see how such continuities are depicted and how they were expressed. A few representative examples will show how antisemitic and antiziganist prejudices affected the prisoners' interactions with one another and what the situation was like for homosexual men. A final cursory look at other prisoner categories and the importance of national and local identities will provide an insight into the power of fundamental attitudes and stereotypes within the prisoner society.

Let us start by reviewing the situation of the concentration camp prisoners who, according to the Nuremberg Laws, were classified as *Jews* and deported to a concentration camp for this reason. These individuals were arrested usually not as a result of any action or crime on their part but solely because they were considered to be Jews and therefore members of an "inferior race" in the Nazi world-view – or, as Zygmunt Bauman puts it: "In the ultimate account, they are guilty of being accused" (Bauman 1995: 204). Even if such individuals were arrested on account of dissident resistance activities, their assignment to the "Jewish race" ultimately determined how they would be dealt with.[5] When they arrived at the camps, they were given an identifying mark that was noticeably different from that of the other prisoners: a yellow triangle that formed a Star of David when superimposed with a second triangle of a different color.[6] This was in keeping with a tradition that began in the thirteenth century and saw Jews forced to wear different special identifiers, including the pointed Jewish hat, a yellow badge on their clothing, or indeed a patch in the form of the Star of David, which was considered the symbol of Jewish identity (cf. *Encyclopaedia Judaica*[7]). Jews in Nazi-occupied Poland were forced to wear the yellow star from 1939; this law applied to entire German Reich from 1941 and then to all areas occupied by German troops from 1942 (cf. Kammer and Bartsch 2002: 118). We can assume that during this heyday of antisemitic agitation, absolutely everyone knew what the six-pointed star symbolized.

The SS was drawing on age-old traditions when it assigned this special designator to Jewish prisoners. This alone placed these prisoners in a unique position, and the double triangle identified them as being "doubly guilty," or at least "doubly accused": as both a Jew and an enemy of the state, a Jew and an "anti-social element," a Jew and an emigrant, a Jew and a "race defiler," and so on (cf. also Eberle 2005). Regardless of their national origin – namely, their language and culture – and regardless of whether they professed the Jewish faith or claimed any other sort of Jewish identity,[8] the prisoners who wore the Star of David on their clothing were considered to be a separate group in the camps. It was therefore easy for their fellow prisoners to view them as a group and to believe that they knew what characterized this group – because their own social traditions had taught them. Although the Jewish prisoners in the concentration camps represented every possible social background and came from all over the world, in the camps they were identified first and foremost as Jews[9] – but this identity did not bind them together in a social formation that pursued any common interests beyond their shared desire for the end of persecution and for liberation. "Since the Jews were such a mixed agglomeration of people, the fact that they were Jews was not an incentive to self-organization. They established their group relations on the basis of other common interests" (Neurath 2005: 70).

From the perspective of a man who primarily considered himself a Polish citizen of the Jewish faith[10] – Leon Szalet, who was imprisoned in Sachsenhausen from September 1939 to May 1940 – we find out what it was like to be viewed above all as a Jew in the camps:

> As we were digging foundations, I became acquainted with the disposi-
> tion of the so-called Sozis who made up a large portion of the punishment
> squad. The red triangle they wore on their chests was evidence of their
> socialist or communist world-view, and their assignment to the punishment
> squad indicated that they were of an especially radical disposition. But their
> actions had nothing in common with the socialist convictions for which they
> had been sent to the concentration camp. The majority of them had been
> infected with the poison of Nazi propaganda. I experienced this myself on
> the first day I worked with them. We were working in a pit that was four
> meters deep. The work squad consisted of eighteen people from the punish-
> ment squad and me, the sole Polish Jew. Even for a practiced digger, it was
> no easy task to throw earth three meters high. Since it was my first day in the
> pit and I had a bad cold, I could only work slowly. My workmates took this
> as an opportunity to curse at me. I was lazy just like every other Jew, they
> shouted. I took it easy and let others do my work for me, like Jews always
> did. Spongers like me were the reason they had been imprisoned for life.

I felt it was better not to respond to these outbursts, as any argument was doomed to failure in the face of eighteen deluded men armed with eighteen pairs of fists. But my silence only enraged them all the more, and they eventually turned to violence. One of the fellows suddenly grabbed the shovel from my hand while a second one hit me in the face, and when I hit back,[11] they all abandoned their work and set upon me. As if that weren't enough, one of them climbed up and reported me to the foreman for being a troublemaker. The foreman, another "Sozi," had me taken out of the pit and, without giving me any opportunity to defend myself, delivered such a blow to my stomach that I lost consciousness. I don't know what happened next. I didn't come to until I hit a pile of earth down in the pit into which the foreman and the blowhard had thrown me.

Since I was lucky enough to land on loose soil, I got off with no more than a fright. Once I had picked myself up and made sure I still had all my limbs, I went back to my workplace. But no sooner had I picked up my shovel than one of the fellows stood in my way and declared that they didn't want a sponger in their midst, so I had better get out of the pit. [. . .] Luckily, the signal for the noon roll call which sounded at that very moment saved me from the blind fury of my socialist work comrades, as we were ordered to a different work site in the afternoon. (Szalet 2006: 388–90)

The experience that Szalet recounts seems to have surprised him greatly since he probably assumed that the presumed opposition of the socialists and communists to what the Nazis were doing would have led to a certain sense of solidarity with Jews as well, who were also being persecuted by the Nazi regime. On the contrary, however, the comments of his fellow prisoners with the red triangle reveal two things: first, that they wanted to keep to themselves since they viewed themselves as a group with common interests – and perhaps even common conspiratorial activities and agreements; and, second, that they would never permit a "community pest" like a Jew to disrupt their close-knit group. To express this, they fell back on antisemitic stereotypes which precisely corresponded to what was published on a daily basis in the antisemitic propaganda of the time, the veracity of which they never questioned. ?

From the opposite perspective, the writings of Polish political prisoner Tadeusz Borowski paint an unambiguous picture of just how self-evident such antisemitism was in the camps. In the course of a conversation about how bad things were for him in Auschwitz, the following exchange takes place:

"Big deal," said Witek, "The Jews travel in much worse conditions, you know. So what do you have to brag about?"

Opinions were divided as to modes of travel and as to the Jews.

"Jews . . . you know what the Jews are like!" said Staszek. "Wait and see, they'll manage to run a business in any camp! Whether it's the cremo or the ghetto, every one of them will sell his own mother for a bowl of turnips!" (Borowski 1992: 127)

Elsewhere Borowski describes watching the so-called *Sonderkommando* (special work detail) march by. These were the prisoners who worked in the crematorium and were generally able to avail themselves of the possessions of those selected for the gas without being punished for it. They would therefore be well fed and loaded with goods when they returned from work and went back to their separate section of the camp:

> Small groups of people began stealing out of the barracks, rushing over to the marching column and snatching the awaited packages from their hands. The air became filled with shouts, cursing and the sound of blows. At last the *Sonder.* disappeared behind the gate leading to their quarters, which are separated from the rest of the camp by a stone wall. But it was not long before the Jews started sneaking out to trade, "organize" and visit with friends. (Ibid.: 141)

In Borowski's story "The People Who Walked On" (ibid.: 82–97), we find the following:

> And I can still see the Jew with bad teeth, standing beneath my high bunk every evening, lifting his face to me, asking insistently:
> "Any packages today? Couldn't you sell me some eggs for Mirka? I'll pay in marks. She is so fond of eggs ..." (Ibid.: 97)

Although these passages do not attest to the kind of meanness found in the account by Szalet, it is absolutely clear that a self-evident and unquestioned attitude toward Jews is being expressed here – namely, that Jews are always out to make a profit, that they will do business with anyone and everyone, and that they are utterly ruthless in doing so.

In Charlotte Delbo's memoirs, this cliché appears in a very mild form with far fewer negative connotations, but even here it is taken as a fact that all Jews are wealthy: "[S]tanding at the mouth of the crematoria men sift through ashes to find gold melted from gold teeth. All those Jews have mouths full of gold, and since there are so many of them it all adds up to tons and tons" (Delbo 1995: 8–9).

The passages from these three authors show that antisemitic attitudes took a wide variety of forms, but the antisemitic notions themselves were never questioned. Whether a Jew was accused of being a "sponger" or willing to "sell his own mother," or whether someone went so far as to say that all Jews were "rich and devious" or "wealthy and clever"[12] – these stereotypes were not invented in the camps, they were based on long-standing traditions and did not need to be confirmed by any immediate incident. They show that antisemitism was as prevalent within the prisoner society as it was in the world outside the camps.

In his dissertation on the society in the camps, Neurath explains that "the administration did not succeed in creating more anti-Semitism than some groups had brought with them from the outside" (Neurath 2005: 70). "Group relations are more subject to social prejudices following closely those prevailing outside than are relations between individuals" (ibid.: 132). These examples illustrate that different forms of antisemitism were just as prevalent in the camps as they were elsewhere, and that to be Jewish was a dominant characteristic that apparently conveyed essential information to others, leading them to believe that they knew who they were "dealing with" (Sofsky 1997: 123) if they were dealing with a Jew.

The situation was similar for the so-called *"Gypsies."* Although they had historically held a marginal social status and been associated with characteristics different from those attributed to Jews,[13] for them, too, the fact of being a "Gypsy" dominated all other aspects – such as nationality, language, or religion – and this had specific consequences in the camp society. It was usually more difficult to identify "Gypsies" in the concentration camps than it was to identify Jews, however, because the prisoner badge for "Gypsies" was not entirely standardized, so it varied from camp to camp. The guidelines and decrees[14] specifying that "Gypsies" were to be identified with a brown triangle were not followed everywhere, and in any case they were dependent on the time of arrest. The Sinti and Roma imprisoned in concentration camps prior to 1938 were usually given the black triangle for "anti-social elements" or "work-shirkers" or the green triangle for criminals according to their purported offense. These categorizations did not place them in particularly highly regarded groups, but they also did not necessarily reveal them to be "Gypsies" unless the respective individuals identified themselves as such when interacting with other prisoners.

According to the Nazis' race ideology, "Gypsies"' were especially dangerous and harmful to the community if they were not "full-blooded." There was a branch of research dedicated to studying the external "racial" characteristics of the people considered "Gypsies" by scrupulously recording every detail about them. This was easy to accomplish thanks to the long-standing, well-established tradition on the part of the police of systematically registering and monitoring traveling people. When it came to deportation and categorization in a concentration camp, however, an individual's "degree of mixed blood" no longer played a role; the authorities arrested anyone considered to be a "Gypsy," and no one in the camps cared about "racial" nuances (cf. Zimmermann 1996).

Notions of the unique "Gypsy" lifestyle influenced the popular opinion of who was thought to be a Gypsy." It was enough to have a dark or Mediterranean complexion, an itinerant profession – such as knife sharpener, basket weaver, or peddler – and perhaps to live a non-sedentary life with a family group to be considered a "Gypsy." This knowledge, which was actually more of a belief, influenced one's view of such individuals, a view which could range from romanticizing the "free life of the Gypsy around the campfire" to contempt for the "unreliable, thieving shirkers who don't lead a regular life."[15]

In Auschwitz-Birkenau, a separate "Gypsy family camp" officially known as B IIe was set up in 1943; it held around 23,000 individuals known by name who were imprisoned together in family groups. The majority of them did not survive the conditions there, which were precarious even by the standards of Auschwitz, and they died of illness, malnutrition, abuse, or gassing (cf. Bistrović 2007; Smoleń and Zimmermann 1995; Zimmermann 1996: 326ff.). Hermann Langbein,[16] a political prisoner, had the opportunity to gain an impression of the "Gypsy family camp" and describes it as follows:

A sea of huts. Roof upon roof, row upon row, as far as the eye can see. Abysmal filth. You sink up to your ankles in the street. And the sight of the Gypsies! They've been allowed to keep their civilian clothing, but they have no means of washing it. There is almost no water anywhere in the camp. They are dirty, the children are crusted with filth up to their knees. (Langbein 1979: 134)

"Gypsies" could be visually identified not only by the brown triangles issued in Auschwitz but also by their civilian clothing. The desolate conditions in which they lived additionally led them to epitomize the commonly accepted notion of "dirty Gypsies" – though it was the camps that insidiously made them this way.

There were very few opportunities in Auschwitz for the "Gypsies" to come into contact with other prisoners since the "Gypsy family camp" was completely separated from the rest of the camp. At most, there might be visual contact between section B IId, the men's camp, and the adjacent "Gypsy camp" (see the camp map in Benz and Distel 2007: 107). The prisoner functionary positions here were occupied by prisoners from other categories, so these were the only inmates to have contact with the "Gypsies" (cf. Smoleń and Zimmermann 1995).

The situation was very different in the other camps because the inmates there who were classified as "Gypsies" often – though not always – lived among the other prisoners, and if they had been categorized as "antisocial elements" or criminals it would not have been immediately apparent that they were "Gypsies" at all unless they identified themselves as such.

It is no longer possible to determine how many of the people registered as "Gypsies" in the camp administrative files lost their lives in the Nazi concentration camps.[17]

What do the memoirs of former concentration camp prisoners tell us about the relationship between "Gypsies" and the rest of the prisoner society? In more academic reports, "Gypsies" are generally only mentioned in passing when the different groups of prisoners are listed, though there is usually a short explanation of the regulations or offenses which led them to be deported; sometimes these reports also mention the number of people classified as "Gypsies" and the fact that their living conditions were especially bad in the camps (e.g., Kogon 2006, Langbein 1972, or Zámečník 2007). Former prisoners occasionally remark that the "Gypsies" were considered difficult so it was thought best to avoid close contact with them in the camps. Beyond this, the accounts of former prisoners only reveal that "Gypsies" were not popular because they apparently did not grasp the political motives behind the camps or what was actually happening in them and they were viewed as uncooperative, unpredictable, and self-serving. All of this is frequently stated as fact without any further analysis, as in the case of Neurath:

> The gypsies fitted even less than the other "blacks" into any sort of cooperative situation.[18] They hardly understood why they were in a concentration camp, and they did not care about anyone else. When they saw an advantage for themselves, they denounced others without compunction. Therefore, the others rejected the gypsies and were wary of them. (Neurath 2005: 63)

"Gypsies" play a very subordinate role in the literature of memory, and when they are mentioned – usually just as an aside – then prejudices like those explicitly named by Neurath are often voiced along with a certain disdain for or discomfort with their "savagery." We find such disdain in Borowski's brusque claim: "[. . .] I stole the stupid Gypsies' food" (Borowski 2006: 257).

Sometimes former prisoners express a kind of astonishment that, when dealt with on a personal level, "Gypsies" turned out to be friendly and cultivated people who did not really fit the cliché. In the memoirs of Josef Kohout, for example, who wrote under the pseudonym of Heinz Heger,[19] we hear about his "Gypsy friend" (Heger 1994: 66):

> He was a Hungarian Gypsy, and also well known among all the prisoners, including the seniors and even the SS, as a petty trader. He carried on regular commerce with the camp kitchen, the sick bay, and the clothing stores. You could buy from him equally a loaf of bread, a diamond ring, or a good pair of shoes. He always had more than enough money. [. . .] His hair was visibly coal black despite the prison shearing, and he had full lips and dark eyes blazing with fire when he made love, burning with hate when he was jealous [. . .]. (Ibid.: 62)

> My new friend was never short of ideas when it came to making money out of nothing. Where money was concerned he thought only of himself [. . .].

His work detachment, involved with him in alcohol smuggling, he held together by the threat that he would kill anyone who betrayed him to the SS. [. . .] This group was ruled by a combination of fear and greed; that was the bond that held it together. (Ibid.: 63)

Even if he exploited people in need such as these, he never cheated anyone. (Ibid.: 66)

The indomitability hinted at by Kohout is mentioned elsewhere as well. For example, in Charlotte Delbo's horrific account of how her dead friend's artificial leg lay in the snow for weeks (in the story "Alice's Leg," Delbo 1995: 41), Delbo remarks almost off-handedly: "We saw it [Alice's leg] a long time. One day it was not there any more. Someone must have filched it to make a fire. A gypsy woman surely, no one else would have dared" (ibid.: 41). Elsewhere Delbo writes:

The gypsies were really amazing. They walked through the camp, in the evening, after roll call [. . .] and sold all kinds of things they had filched here and there, from the checkroom, the kitchens, including cigarettes pinched from the pockets of the SS. A slightly gaping pocket and the trick was done. They approached us and, with a quick gesture, half-opened their dresses to show us what they had to offer.
[. . .] We even ran into some who were offering a piece of broiled meat. Appetizing, golden brown. However much they'd swear on their mother's head it was stolen from the SS kitchen, we never purchased it. We feared this roast originated in the crematorium. (Ibid.: 187)

The other prisoners clearly approached the courageous, wild "Gypsy" women with open skepticism. They were suspected not only of being capable of making use of an artificial leg but also of offering the flesh of dead prisoners as food – since this is the only way to interpret Delbo's reference to the crematorium. The unease and fear that these prisoners felt when dealing with the "Gypsies" was undoubtedly very real, and it is true that, particularly in the final phase of the "Third Reich," the catastrophic conditions in the camps led to isolated incidents of cannibalism (cf., e.g., Borowski 1992: 152ff.; Lasker-Wallfisch 1996: 92). However, Delbo's speculations seem to be based in some part on the atrocity stories that had circulated for centuries in reference to "Gypsies" which cast a sinister shadow over any encounter with actual individuals from this group. There is no basis – other than popular negative myths – for assuming that the "Gypsies" would sell "appetizing, golden brown" human flesh to eat, and such an assumption was made in light of the presumed uncivilized and unruly nature of the "Gypsies" and the danger lurking behind it. Furthermore, since cannibalism is absolutely taboo in civilized societies, the prisoners' fear that this taboo had been broken was associated with a fear of becoming unclean themselves through contact with the "Gypsies" (cf. Douglas 2002, 2003).

The reputed savagery of the "Gypsies" appears in a milder form in the account of Ravensbrück by Germaine Tillion,[20] who, though reflective, nonetheless falls back on clichéd formulations: she posits, for example, that the "Gypsies" were "culturally inferior" (Tillion 1975: 32) – even though, purely statistically speaking, we can assume that many of the thousands upon thousands of prisoners in the concentration camps were uncultured and uneducated. Tillion says:

> Thus I discovered two "families" of Belgian women and one old French gypsy, all bewildered and dazed by their incomprehensible misfortune. They had a basic education and decent living habits, both of which made living with the German gypsies unbearable for them. The rest (except for a few Czechs) were astonishingly barbaric – less so than certain Ukrainians, but noticeably more so than the African tribal women to whom my profession of ethnology had taken me. (Ibid.: 31–2)

Tillion's explicit reference to education and cultivation implies that the "Gypsies" described here deviated from a norm and stood out from their own kind. The others were apparently just as wild as expected, and Tillion the ethnologist tries to gauge the degree of wildness as precisely as possible by means of comparisons based on her professional experience.

The notion that such savagery went hand in hand with a rampant libido is implied by Josef Kohout when he writes: "The 'greens' and the Gypsies were most keen on the idea of a brothel, whereas the politicals were against it [. . .]" (Heger 1994: 98). An attempt to dissociate oneself from this "Gypsy savagery" can be found in the account by Eva, an anonymous interviewee in a project about sexual violence in the concentration camps (Amesberger et al. 2004) who was imprisoned in several different camps at a very young age because she was a "Gypsy." She talks about a conflict with her fellow prisoners who were also imprisoned as "Gypsies" and who envied Eva her privileged position. They accused her of sexually gratifying the SS in return for these privileges. In one such argument, Eva sets herself apart from the others with the following words: "You're wild Gypsies [. . .], you're not like we are. I didn't even grow up among Gypsy women. [. . .] And I don't want anything to do with you" (in ibid.: 212).

The legendary musical ability of the "Gypsies" is another cliché that is mentioned in several different accounts of the camps. For example, Ruth Elias recruited "Gypsies" to perform in the cabaret evening she was ordered to organize by the camp commandant because these women had always demonstrated remarkable good humor and carefree singing and dancing (cf. Elias 1999: 182; see chapter 5.3).

Other prisoners in Auschwitz-Birkenau had the impression that the inmates of the "Gypsy family camp" enjoyed better living conditions with their families, wore their own clothes, and often made music. In a report by Polish prisoners who spent some time working in the sick bay of the "Gypsy camp," we find the following:

> The Gypsies came to the camp with their families and all of their personal property, sometimes even with their caravans. Nothing was taken away from them. They wore their own clothes. Their hair wasn't cut. The German authorities treated them very differently than they did the prisoners of other nationalities. They were not sentenced to punishments like beatings, punitive roll calls, or bunker detainment. The Gypsies didn't have to carry out forced labor like the other prisoners. When they worked, it involved cleaning up in the Gypsy camp, collecting herbs for the camp soup, or carrying out administrative tasks. (Szymański et al. 1987: 200)

Most of the "facts" mentioned here are demonstrably false, but they may have corresponded to the expectations and impressions of a prisoner deployed as a prisoner functionary in a certain section of the "Gypsy camp." "Gypsies" themselves describe forced heavy labor (in the camp), brutal maltreatment, shaved heads, and so on (cf. *Memorial Book* 1993: 1495ff.).

Krystyna Zywulska, who was held in Birkenau as a Polish political prisoner and worked in the section known as "Canada" (cf. Walter 2007), where the personal possessions of Jews who had been gassed were sorted, tells of the alarmed discussion that ensued when they found out that the "Gypsy family camp" had been liquidated:

> "They're already starting to liquidate everyone!" said Bastia. How can we be sure they won't come for us in the night if they're already gassing the Gypsies? After all, the Gypsies were treated better by the camp administration than we were. Gypsy families weren't separated, while we were forbidden from even speaking to men. They didn't have their children torn from them like the Jews. (Zywulska 1980: 188)[21]

Reading between the lines, we can see that not only have the prisoners already become accustomed to the liquidation of Jews, they also sensed a certain difference in status. In this case, the difference between Jews and the other prisoners is unambiguous, but the structure of the rest of the camp society is not so clear. Somewhat later in the text, there is an explanation: "The Gypsies are being treated like Jews. They hold us in higher regard because we supposedly belong to the same race" (ibid.: 190). This apparently self-evident difference between Jews and others is even expressed by people who were themselves persecuted as "Gypsies." For example, Hildegard Lagrenne, a "Gypsy" who was born in 1921 and deported in 1940, says: "We were Catholics and Germans" (in Krausnick 1983: 33). "We didn't know what we were guilty of. We weren't communists, after all. And as far as the Jews went – what the Nazis did with *Kristallnacht* and all – we thought: Well, they were Jews, they must have been up to something" (ibid.: 36). Comments like this and the ones from the anonymous Eva (in Amesberger et al. 2004, see above) clearly illustrate that *everyone* was making some sort of effort to maintain a particular self-image. Different demarcation strategies were employed depending on the position a prisoner claimed in the social space. It is obvious, however, that the prisoner categorization system in the Nazi concentration camps served to actualize certain prevalent stereotypical attitudes toward "Gypsies," Jews, and so on – and if these stereotypes were not fulfilled in personal interactions, then the individuals in question were defined as exceptions. It is also clear that social inequality in the camps was the result of social inequality outside the camps, and the categorization measures of the SS, which were intended to unsettle the camp society, merely reinforced this inequality.

But why are "Gypsies" in particular such a minor presence in the memoirs of former prisoners compared to political prisoners, criminals, or Jews? First of all, in terms of sheer numbers they made up a relatively small proportion of all prisoners in the camps, and sometimes they were not overtly identified as "Gypsies" either. This explanation is not sufficient, however, because Jehovah's Witnesses, for example, who were imprisoned for their religious beliefs and who also made up a quantitatively small group, are referred to in numerous accounts and memoirs with a certain sense of admiration for their consistent rejection of the Nazi regime. In connection with "Gypsies," by contrast, former prisoners usually express a distance and desire for dissociation; even when someone critically analyzes the reasons behind social and cultural differences, as Germaine Tillion does (Tillion 1975: 32f.), it appears that a feeling of closeness can ultimately only arise when there seem to be no differences at all. "Gypsyhood" could explain why such people seemed to be different – and if they did not seem so different after all, then they were characterized with a "but": he was a "Gypsy" *but* he was decent nonetheless, educated nonetheless, friendly nonetheless, not devious, and so on.

In the eyes of the other prisoners, not everyone who demonstrated a lack of education, poor cultivation, unreliability, or special musical talent was automatically considered a "Gypsy" – but on account of entrenched schemes of evaluation, and even without confirmation through personal experience, "Gypsies" were immediately viewed as uneducated, uncultivated, unreliable, very musical, and sometimes even sinister as soon as their fellow prisoners knew that they were "Gypsies."

The stigma of being a "Gypsy" therefore dominated the perception of this group – as was the case for Jews. The effect that this had on the social structure of the camps will be analyzed at the end of this chapter.

Let us turn now to the male prisoners classified as *homosexual* by first taking a look at their general social situation during this period. Even prior to the "Third Reich," Germany had a long history of criminally persecuting homosexual men, though it was not until the foundation of the German Empire in 1871 that the law was standardized by means of Paragraph 175, which made "unnatural fornication" between males punishable by imprisonment (cf. Bastian 2000: 14).[22] However, precisely which sexual practices were actually considered a criminal offense was legally unclear, and individual verdicts depended largely on the interpretation of the respective judge. Regardless of this, legal practices gradually moved in the direction of punishing all "intercourse-like acts" (Grau 1995: 64).

Although ill will toward homosexual men was widespread in all parts of society, there was also an emancipation movement fronted by the sexologist Magnus Hirschfeld and institutionalized by the *Wissenschaftlich-humanitäre Komitee* (Scientific-Humanitarian Committee), which protested against the criminal persecution of homosexuals through petitions and publications. Toward the end of the German Empire, it was widely believed that homosexuality was caused by a psychological disturbance and could therefore be treated. Case law followed this thinking in that it took as a given that treatment was possible and thus accused homosexual offenders of having done nothing to counter their abnormal predispositions. As a result, the number of convictions based on Paragraph 175 rose even further.

In the Weimar Republic, the homosexual rights movement was initially bolstered by a generally more liberal climate. Berlin in particular saw a flourishing gay and lesbian subculture. With the rise of the Nazi *"völkisch"* movement, however, the situation worsened again and homosexual activities, which were considered by the proponents of this movement to be "alien" and "unnatural" – not to mention an "immediate threat to the growth of the nation" (ibid.: 4) because they supposedly squandered the potential for "Aryan" reproduction – were increasingly socially discouraged. Nazi ideology viewed homosexuality not just as a perversion but as a plague, so homosexuality came to be associated with a risk of infection that had to be prevented at all costs (cf. Dupont 2002: 190 and Grau 1995: particularly the image of the "originating centre of a homosexual epidemic," 226).

According to Günter Grau, the persecution of homosexuals in the "Third Reich" can be divided into three phases (cf. Grau 1995: 5):

- a preparatory phase between 1933 and 1935 which largely entailed the destruction of the sexual reform movement and, in the wake of the so-called Night of the Long Knives, anti-homosexual propaganda campaigns combined with individual acts of terror in the "gay scene" and the expansion of Paragraph 175 to cover all homosexual practices (not just "intercourse-like acts");
- systematic persecution between 1936 and 1939 through measures

such as the establishment of the *Reichzentrale zur Bekämpfung der Homosexualität und Abtreibung* (Reich Central Office for Combatting Homosexuality and Abortion) and a quantitative increase in criminal proceedings;

- and, from 1939–40, radicalized persecution through the legal imprisonment of homosexuals in concentration camps, the introduction of the death penalty in "'especially serious cases' (particularly among members of the SS or the police)," and increased pressure on homosexuals to submit to "voluntary" castration.

While homosexual men were under huge pressure to conform in the "Third Reich" and were forced to put tremendous effort into concealing their sexual preferences, their persecution was qualitatively different from that of people persecuted on "racial" grounds. Unlike Jews and "Gypsies," whose identity was defined by decree, homosexuals were punished for having (more or less demonstrably) engaged in specific activities, with different sentences being given to the active seducers and the passively seduced. The Gestapo's network of snitches was kept continually supplied with denunciations, which were followed by the notorious interrogations, but such processes did not always end in a conviction.

> If a homosexual man could convincingly demonstrate under Gestapo questioning that he was not homosexually active, and if proof to the contrary did not fall into the hands of the Gestapo, he would escape prosecution. The crucial point was carefully to prove that the suspect had engaged in homosexual activity, and not just that he had homosexual inclinations. [... T]he concept of extermination does not adequately describe the Nazi practice in this domain. What we see is a rather differentiated series of punishments and deterrents, whose purpose was to dissuade the "homosexual minority" from their sexual practice. (Ibid.: 6–7)

However, there is ample evidence that the Gestapo was not squeamish in its interrogations and used extremely brutal methods which significantly hampered the ability of the accused to "convincingly demonstrate" their innocence. For example, Karl Gorath says in an interview that, under interrogation at gunpoint, he confessed to "homosexual lewdness" and was consequently sent first to prison and then to a concentration camp, where he was held in "protective custody" (cf. Hutter 1998).

Female homosexuality, by contrast, was never a prosecutable offense – not even under the Nazi dictatorship – although the situation did change for lesbian women in the "Third Reich" (cf. above all Schoppmann 1991, 1995). Female homosexuality ran counter to "*völkisch*" ideology, but female sexuality was fundamentally considered to be of secondary importance, and it was assumed that women could be "cured" of their "aberrant" tendencies through pregnancy (cf. Louis 2007). Local Gestapo offices kept "lesbian files," monitored women known to the authorities, and, when they felt it appropriate, sent them to concentration camps for being "community pests" (cf. ibid.). But while homosexual women faced the threat of persecution and imprisonment in a concentration camp just like homosexual men, they did not make up a separate category of prisoners in the concentration camps; these women were usually given the black triangle of "anti-social elements," though they sometimes received a different color instead. Recent research based on prisoner accounts has revealed that there were isolated cases of female prisoners receiving a pink triangle in Ravensbrück, but this claim has not yet been fully supported by the source material (cf. ibid.). For the reasons mentioned, it is extremely difficult to systematically assess the situation of homosexual women in the concentration camps.[23] In the context of this work, therefore, representative examples of male homosexuality will be used to demonstrate how the knowledge of an inmate's homosexuality was particularly significant when it came to differentiation within the prisoner society.

Since homosexuals were subject to criminal prosecution not only long before the Nazi regime but also long after it,[24] there are very few personal testimonies from homosexuals compared to other groups of victims. The first autobiographical account of this type was written by Josef Kohout under the pseudonym Heinz Heger in 1967–8 and was published for the first time in 1972 with the title of *Die Männer mit dem Rosa Winkel* (*The Men with the Pink Triangle*) (Heger 1994; cf. also Müller 2002). In this book, Kohout strives to explain what it was like for homosexuals in the concentration camps, but he also expresses bitterness at how the suffering of homosexuals remained unacknowledged in the post-war years. This was followed in 1994 by a comparable book written in French by Pierre Seel (English: *I, Pierre Seel, Deported Homosexual*, 1995); this book describes six months spent in the Schirmeck concentration camp in Alsace (cf. Benz et al. 1997: 713f.), but it focuses more on the period of "shame" and "silence" after the end of World War II. Other than this, there are only a few written and filmed autobiographical interviews dealing with this topic (cf. Müller 2002).[25] Homosexual victims of the Nazi regime are therefore severely underrepresented in the general culture of remembrance. Even though there are many reports of homosexual practices in the camps, homosexuals have only a marginal presence in both academic and other autobiographical literature. This may be the result of a distinction made between "real" homosexuals and people who engaged in homosexual activities solely as an "emergency outlet" (Heger 1994: 23) or a form or "emergency sexuality" (Müller 2002). It seems that the decisive factor was not the activity itself but rather whether someone admitted to being homosexual or was "officially" declared homosexual by the persecuting authorities.

Based on the current state of research,[26] it is estimated that between 6,000 (Grau 1995: 6) and 15,000 (Müller 2002) men were imprisoned in

Nazi concentration camps for being homosexual, and more than half of them did not survive (cf. Grau 1995; Müller 2002: footnote 9). These men were usually identified with a pink triangle,[27] which, according to Josef Kohout, was considerably larger than the triangles of other colors (cf. Heger 1994: 32, 67), meaning others could see from a distance "whom one was dealing with" (Sofsky 1997: 123). These inmates were held in very low regard both by the camp society and by society in general. They were scorned and mocked by the SS and others, and the specific harassment of "gays" often culminated in excessive violence in which other prisoners, some of whom were camp functionaries, also participated (cf. Heger 1994).

What do we know about the treatment of homosexuals in the society of prisoners? When listing the different groups of prisoners, Neurath says that homosexuals with the pink triangle were sent to concentration camps by the criminal courts (Neurath 2005: 65). He mentions that nearly all of them were "non-Jews" and that they were housed in their own block in Dachau; only the few Jews among them were housed together in a block with other Jews – so here, too, the fact that a prisoner was Jewish appears to have been the dominant characteristic.

> Homosexuals were treated by their fellow prisoners in about the same way as they were treated outside – accepted individually but regarded in general with a certain degree of prejudice. Aside from those with a pink badge, there were, of course, prisoners who fell into other classifications and happened to be homosexual in addition. And there were others who turned homosexual under the abnormal conditions of a purely male society. (Neurath 2005: 65–6)

Neurath's comment that homosexuals were treated in fundamentally the same way inside the camps points to a phenomenon that appeared earlier in connection with "Gypsies" – namely, that individual experiences did not have to confirm existing prejudices, but such experiences also did not make the prisoners recognize these prejudices for what they were. Neurath seems certain that there were more homosexuals than there were pink-triangle prisoners in the camps because the only prisoners who wore the pink triangle were those who had been convicted of homosexuality. He does not tell us how prisoners who were homosexual but not categorized as such were treated in the camps. Who was the object of prejudice and who was accepted on an individual basis? Even reading between lines, I do not think Neurath provides an answer to this.

What follows in Neurath's account is a nearly anecdotal story about the isolation of the Jewish blocks in December 1937 in Dachau[28] (ibid.: 66) which he can only have heard about second hand because he had not yet been imprisoned at that point. In the course of this isolation period, during which many prisoners died under the dreadful conditions, a few men apparently began to engage in homosexual activities which became public knowledge when the isolation ended in January 1938. The camp administration used this as an opportunity to take action against political agitators among the prisoners in this block by accusing them of homosexual practices. Two of the accused are said to have committed suicide while six others received twenty-five blows and were subsequently handed over to a court which sentenced them to prison under Paragraph 175 – a sentence that the accused "welcomed gladly as a change from the much harder life in the concentration camp" (ibid.). However, the inmates first had to spend several months in the bunker in Dachau before they were transferred to prison.

The brevity with which Neurath recounts this story leaves many questions open. Neither the suicide of two of the prisoners nor the satisfaction of the others at having received a prison sentence is self-explanatory. Was the shame of being accused of homosexual practices so great for "real politicals" that it drove them to suicide? And were the others pleased with their prison sentence because, as "previously convicted homosexuals," they already lived with such "shame," had already experienced prison, and therefore knew that it was not as bad there as it was in the concentration camp? Beyond that, is it even conceivable that in the year 1937, Jews – since this story was about prisoners from the Jewish block, after all – would be sent from a concentration camp to face a court of law on account of homosexuality? It seems more likely to me that this was actually a rumor[29] that circulated among the prisoners for years, because the most recent literature about Dachau does not verify these events as described (cf., e.g., Zámečník[30] 2007).[31] Rumors, which were one of the few opportunities for "free thinking" in the concentration camps (Michel 2002: 64), not only served the purposes of conveying information, they also channeled emotions (cf. ibid.: 67); with the help of rumors, hopes could be kept alive and opinions could be expressed.[32] When it comes to rumors about homosexuals in the concentration camps, we must also consider that such rumors tended to involve regaling others with generalized stories about homosexuals rather than conveying facts, as this reinforced the continuity of normality in a way.

In my view, Neurath's entire one-page chapter about prisoners with the pink triangle (Neurath 2005) is full of allusions that are not easy to decipher. This chapter does not seem to actually be about the prisoners who had to wear the pink triangle, probably because Neurath was at pains to emphasize that he did not have much to say about them since he had no contact with them. Instead, the focus appears to be on those who engaged in homosexual activities in the camp even though they were not "normally" homosexual – and Neurath probably could not or did not want to discuss this openly because it might lead to the impression that he was close to such men.

The same cannot be said for Eugen Kogon, who mentions that the prisoners categorized as homosexuals were a minority who suffered particularly badly in the camps (Kogon 2006: 35).

> This group had a very heterogeneous composition. It included individuals of real value, in addition to large numbers of criminals and especially blackmailers. This made the position of the group as a whole very precarious. [. . .] The Gestapo readily took recourse to the charge of homosexuality, if it was unable to find any other pretext for proceeding against a Catholic priest or irksome critic. The mere suspicion was sufficient. [. . .] The fate of homosexuals in the concentration camps can only be described as ghastly. [. . .] If anything could save them at all, it was to enter into sordid relationships within the camp, but this was as likely to endanger their lives as to save them. Theirs was an insoluble predicament, and virtually all of them perished. (Ibid.: 35)

What he emphasizes here is that this group of prisoners was not really a group at all since it was made up of "heterogeneous" people. In this passage, Kogon seems to imply that the "individuals of real value" were the ideological opponents of the Nazi regime whom the Gestapo had deliberately falsely classified as homosexuals because no evidence could be found of their anti-government activities. The "real" homosexuals, by contrast, apparently tended to be "criminals and especially blackmailers" whom it was best to avoid. Entering into "sordid relationships" in return for life-saving privileges in the camp may have been the solution to their "insoluble predicament" for some, but reading between the lines, Kogon appears to say that the people of value would not have been capable of doing something so objectionable and thinking only of themselves. In my view, Kogon leaves no doubt in this passage as to the distance he felt toward "real" homosexuals.

Further on in this passage about the treatment of homosexuals, Kogon stresses once again that they were "consigned [. . .] to the lowest caste in the camp [. . .]. In shipments to extermination camps [. . .] they furnished the highest proportionate share, for the camp had an understandable tendency to slough off all elements considered least valuable or worthless" (ibid.). Despite the sympathy previously expressed by Kogon for the particularly bad treatment that homosexuals received in the concentration camps, his bureaucratic language has a distinct distancing effect in this passage. In saying that "the camp had an understandable tendency to slough off all elements considered least valuable or worthless" and send them to their death, Kogon glosses over the fact that, in this case, "the camp" consisted of fellow prisoners in administrative positions who were able to – and forced to – decide which "elements" were valuable and which were not. The traditional misgivings toward homosexuals, which Kogon evidently finds "understandable," led the prisoner society to share the prejudices of the SS, with the result that a very large percentage of pink-triangle prisoners were exterminated.

Hermann Langbein (2004) does not explicitly mention the category of homosexuals as such. However, in a chapter about sexuality in the concentration camp (ibid.: 402–13), he refers to the homosexual practices of fellow prisoners as an irresponsible aberration (ibid.: 405f.), with a correspondingly moralizing undertone. Above all, he accuses Kapos of sexually exploiting underage boys, called *"Pipel"* in the camp jargon, who in return received more and better food as well as other privileges, such as less dangerous or taxing work. "Abraham Matuszak reports that what functionaries in Auschwitz did with their *Pipel* cried to high heaven. If the boys were not willing, they were sent the way of all flesh" (ibid.: 405).[33]

Despite the best efforts of the Nazis to eradicate homosexuality, it remained an "open secret" (ibid.). Langbein also mentions the "voluntary" castration of Kapos who had been convicted of such practices in the camp and who were "released" (*sic*) after the procedure and got their Kapo jobs back (ibid.) – that is to say, they were not allowed to leave the concentration camp after the "voluntary" procedure but they returned from imprisonment in the bunker to the normal camp. The establishment of camp brothels can be attributed in part to the "open secret" of widespread homosexual activities among the prisoners, as the SS hoped that the opportunity to visit a brothel[34] would prevent the "German prisoners" (ibid.: 405) from making use of the "emergency outlet" of homosexuality.

In general, the authors of the accounts cited thus far heavily emphasize their distance from their fellow prisoners who were homosexual. Each author certainly knew of the existence of these prisoners – either because they knew such a prisoner category existed or because they had heard reports from others – but they themselves did not have anything to do with them personally. It is evidently very difficult for these authors to discuss their own experiences with such prisoners without falling under suspicion of having had contact with "those kind of people" and inadvertently opening themselves up to the "charge of homosexuality" (Kogon 2006: 35).

If even after the end of the "Third Reich" and in different countries (as was the case for Neurath) it was so difficult for former prisoners to say anything other than that they had distanced themselves from homosexuals in the camps, we can assume that this social mechanism was especially powerful in the camps themselves if prisoners did not want to be "suspected." When Stanislav Zámečník writes that "they [homosexuals] formed an isolated group from which even their fellow prisoners distanced themselves" (Zámečník 2007: 230), this is an indication of the fear that these "fellow prisoners" had of becoming the victims of denunciation themselves. Such statements say absolutely nothing about actual relationships with homosexuals, however. It seems that by continually repeating stereotypes about homosexuals, other prisoners could avoid "giving the wrong impression" of themselves.

But how would someone who actually wore the pink triangle and openly acknowledged his own homosexuality describe life in the prisoner society of the concentration camps? Josef Kohout, whose memoirs of Sachsenhausen and Flossenbürg are absolutely unique in this respect, describes in very direct words the double standards to which he was constantly subjected in the concentration camps. His love affair with the son of a "Nazi high-up" was his undoing and led to his denunciation in 1939, though his friend, the "second accused," was not even mentioned by name during the trial and went unpunished on the grounds of "mental confusion" (cf. Heger 1994: 24).

After six months in prison, Kohout was not released but was instead taken into "protective custody" and transferred from Vienna to the Sachsenhausen concentration camp. Even during the thirteen-day transport in cattle trucks, which were internally divided into barred cells, his two "companions" – thieves who had been sentenced to death for a murder – took a "certain grisly pride" in gloating about their crime and repeatedly sexually abused him (ibid.: 27f.), all the while insisting that they were "normal men" (ibid.: 28) and not "filthy queers" (ibid.).

In Sachsenhausen, the SS greeted him in the way they saw fit by calling him a "filthy queer" and "butt-fucker" (ibid.: 32) and beating him. Prisoners classified as homosexuals were housed in their own block in the camp and were subject to special constraints. For example, despite the bitter cold, they were ordered to sleep with their hands "outside the blankets" with the admonition: "'You queer assholes aren't going to start jerking off in here!'" (ibid.: 34). Checks were carried out throughout the night, and

> [a]nyone found with [. . .] his hands under his blanket [. . .] was taken outside and had several bowls of water poured over him before being left standing outside for a good hour. Only a few people survived this treatment. The least result was bronchitis, and it was rare for any gay person taken into the sick bay to come out alive. We who wore the pink triangle were prioritized for medical experiments, and these generally ended in death. (Ibid.: 34)

The prisoner functionaries in the homosexuals' block belonged to a different category; most of them wore the green triangle and behaved in a "brutal and merciless" way toward homosexuals (ibid.: 34). "Nor could we even speak with prisoners from other blocks, with a different-colored badge; we were told we might try to seduce them. And yet homosexuality was much more rife in the other blocks, where there were no men with the pink triangle, than it was in our own" (ibid.). In reference to his fellow prisoners in Sachsenhausen, Kohout writes the following:

> My dormitory, with 180 prisoners or more, contained the most varied collection of people. Unskilled workers and shop assistants, skilled tradesmen and independent craftsmen, musicians and artists, professors and clergy,

even aristocratic landowners. All of them, before their imprisonment in concentration camps, had been decent people in private life, many indeed highly respected citizens, who had never come up against the law, but were set apart only by their homosexual feelings. [. . .] One of my fellow prisoners, still recognizable as an intellectual despite his battered face and clay-spattered body, was a Jew as well. Beneath the pink triangle he wore the yellow triangle [. . .]. He had to suffer twice-over the chicanery of the SS and the "green" Capos, for being not only queer, but a Jew into the bargain. He was from Berlin, twenty-five years old at the time, and came from a very well-to-do family. (Ibid.: 38–9)

This list demonstrates why the prisoners with the pink triangle did not naturally form a group. Even though they all shared the same fate as homosexuals, they came to the camps from a wide variety of backgrounds. It is also worth noting the certainty with which Kohout arranges his list in a *ranking* from bottom to top according to social status, something which was undoubtedly in accord with the "normal" sense of status in the social space. The Jewish prisoner mentioned here had a special status, and not just because he suffered twice over: He was a rich Jewish intellectual whose fortune, as we are told in the account that follows, played an important role in his ultimately paying his way out of the concentration camp – though whether he was truly released is, in my view, only speculation, because all Kohout knew was that one day "he was fetched and taken away by the Gestapo" (ibid.: 40). Whether that suffices as evidence that "the deal of Jew against money had finally taken place" (ibid.) is doubtful to say the least. This may have been yet another rumor associated with the personification of the "rich Jew."

In another passage, Kohout expresses his "great respect for priests" (ibid.: 41) and recounts the story of a priest who was imprisoned as a homosexual. "[A] man some sixty years of age, tall and with distinguished features. We later discovered that he came from Sudetenland, from an aristocratic German family" (ibid.: 40). As an aristocratic clergyman, he was at the top of Kohout's ranking, so it is not surprising that Kohout expressed such reverence toward him. The SS, however, mocked the priest as a "randy old rat-bag" (ibid.: 42) and unleashed the full force of their hatred on him, which the priest bore by praying silently. Kohout goes on to say: "I felt I was witnessing the crucifixion of Christ in modern guise" (ibid.). At the next roll call, just as an SS block leader was about to hit the brutalized priest again,

from the overcast sky, a sudden ray of sunshine illuminated the priest's battered face. Out of thousands of assembled prisoners, it lit only him, and at the very moment when he was going to be beaten again. There was a remarkable silence, and all present stared fixedly at the sky, astonished by what had happened. The SS sergeant himself looked up at the clouds in wonder for a few seconds, then let his hand, raised for a beating, sink slowly to his side, and walked wordlessly away [. . .]. (Ibid.: 42)

After arriving at Sachsenhausen, prisoners with the pink triangle first had to carry out completely pointless and strenuous work – they had to "shovel up" snow with their bare hands and move it from one side of the road to the other and back again – until a new group of homosexuals entered the camp and replaced them (cf. ibid.: 35f.). Then they would be transferred to the clay pit of the Sachsenhausen brickworks and forced to work under murderous conditions which led to severe injuries and deaths every day (cf. ibid.: 37ff.). In a subsequent work detail which was assigned to build a firing range for the camp SS, Kohout and other pink-triangle prisoners had to construct earth mounds to capture bullets behind the targets (cf. ibid.: 43ff.). But the SS started target practice before the firing range was completed, while the prisoners were still loading earth in heavy barrows behind the targets, so inmates wound up being shot on a daily basis. "We soon found out that the SS far preferred to fire on us prisoners than they did at the proper targets, and had directly aimed at certain people pushing their barrows. [. . .] We had become a sitting target for the SS, who greeted each direct hit with a shout of glee" (ibid.: 44).

After Kohout had worked for two days in this death detachment, a "green" Kapo made him an explicit offer: in return for sexual favors, he would take Kohout out of the line of fire and only make him shovel dirt, which was much less dangerous.

> Quickly thinking it over, I agreed, for my will to live was now stronger than my commitment to human decency. No matter who might condemn me for it, the sight of the dead and wounded at the firing range had had too great an effect on me. I was afraid, terribly afraid. Why shouldn't I seize this opportunity to save my life, even if it was degrading? (Ibid.: 44)

In May 1940, Kohout was transferred to the Flossenbürg concentration camp. "In some ways I was sorry to go, for in the last few weeks my life had been almost bearable through this sexual relationship with my Capo. He got more for me to eat, and thanks to his help I was assigned only to easier and nondangerous work" (ibid.: 45). This experience had taught him how to behave in the new camp. Upon arriving at the Flossenbürg camp in Bavaria, the homosexuals were thoroughly inspected by "a group of eight to ten Capos" (ibid.: 47) who were "on the lookout for a possible lover among the new arrivals" (ibid.) – and Kohout accepted an offer from one of them.

> The senior whose lover I became was a professional criminal from Hamburg, very highly regarded in his milieu as a safecracker. He was much feared by the prisoners for his ruthlessness, and even by his Capo colleagues, but he

was generous and considerate to me. [. . .] He saved my life more than ten times over [. . .]. (Ibid.: 48)

When the "green" Kapo was promoted to camp senior, he was unable to continue his relationship with Kohout, but he promised that, even in his more powerful new position, he would keep an eye on him and protect him whenever necessary and possible. Kohout subsequently found himself in a number of situations in which the advocacy or dauntless intervention of his former lover saved him. "He never broke the promise he gave me when we parted. He remains in my eyes an honorable man, even if he was a safecracker and burglar by trade [. . .]" (ibid.: 61).

Kohout recounts the following about an SS block leader known for his "strictness" who punished "the slightest infringement of camp regulations" (ibid.: 49) with a beating:

Time and again I caught him looking in my direction when he thought he was unobserved. I never discussed this with any of my fellow prisoners [. . .], but I had the instinctive feeling that he was fond of me, and also "one of us," of the same sexual persuasion as we who wore the pink triangle. He concealed his feelings by rejecting any personal contact with us prisoners, and by his strictness and rigidity. For even the slightest infringement [. . .] he would order [. . .] the customary penalty. But he never watched the punishment himself, and on one occasion when he had to be present, he turned away. (Ibid.: 48–9)

When the first transports of Polish prisoners identified with the red triangle of resistance fighters arrived at the camp in the winter of 1941–2, most of the camp Kapos sought out "a young Pole as batman or 'cleaner,' though the main purpose of these lads was as bed partner" (ibid.: 59).

These dolly-boys [. . .] were generally from sixteen to twenty years old. They soon grew to be very cheeky, as they were always protected by their prominent friends, no matter how arrogantly they behaved toward their fellow prisoners. [. . .] You could soon tell easily from someone's appearance whether he had a relationship with a block senior or Capo. Being properly fed, these young Poles soon grew to be as plump as capons [. . .]. The prisoners with the pink triangle were, as always, "filthy queers" in the eyes of the other prisoners, while the very fellow prisoners who insulted and condemned us in this way were unperturbed by relationships that the block seniors and Capos had with the young Poles, and just smiled at this behavior, even if somewhat ironically. [. . .] And so the way a person was assessed by his fellows had two sides to it, as it still unfortunately does today. What in one case is accepted with a smile is completely forbidden when it is openly proclaimed or made public. Homosexual behavior between two "normal" men is considered an emergency outlet, while the same thing between two gay men, who both feel deeply for one another, is something "filthy" and repulsive. (Ibid.: 60)

Thanks to the intercession of his former lover who was now the camp senior, Kohout eventually became one of the very few pink-triangle prisoners to be promoted to Kapo himself. He took over management of the building material stores, at which point he separated from his "former Capo friend" (ibid.: 94f.).

> First of all, any sexual relation between Capos was unthinkable and would not be tolerated by the "dignitaries," while secondly, I no longer needed a relationship of convenience such as this for the sake of mere survival. [. . .] Since I now had enough to eat, I got into a relationship with another German pink-triangle prisoner – no relationship of convenience this time, but a genuine one, based on mutual understanding and trust. We got on very well together, and were as happy as anyone could be said to be in concentration camp. (Ibid.: 95)

When Kohout was ordered by the camp commander to be transferred to the Dirlewanger penal division of the SS, which was considered to be a suicide squad, Kohout says the commander sarcastically told him that "by serving at the front I might blot out the shame of my homosexuality" (ibid.: 102). However, civilian armaments workers, in whose material stores Kohout worked as a Kapo, prevented the transfer by interceding on his behalf with their head office and praising his especially careful and reliable work. A personal order from Himmler himself, which could not be countermanded, ultimately ensured that Kohout retained his position in the concentration camp (ibid.: 102).

> The camp "dignitaries" now also accepted me as a Capo equal to any other, despite my pink triangle, even the politicals no longer holding my office against me, though it was precisely the politicals who were the most vexatious opponents of their homosexual fellow prisoners. [. . .] Up till 1942, it was customary, in order to reduce the numbers of prisoners, for the various concentration camps each to dispatch a hundred or more prisoners at a time, at stipulated intervals, to the extermination camps, where they were gassed or killed by "injections." The list of those to be liquidated was left to the prisoners' office, headed by the camp senior, to draw up. If the camp senior was a political, you could be sure that, by far, the greater number of those prisoners marked down for extermination would be men with the pink triangle. (Ibid.: 103)

Kohout's memoirs provide a revealing insight into the experience of a concentration camp prisoner who was branded with the pink triangle of a homosexual and who was therefore immediately identifiable as such to his fellow prisoners. Because the pink-triangle prisoners were initially held together in their own blocks, as Kohout describes, it is possible that this – along with the special restrictions that homosexuals faced in the camp, both collectively and in their individual blocks – might have encouraged a sense of group identity which would not necessarily otherwise exist among this group of very different people. Accounts do exist of group cultural activities in the homosexual block in Sachsenhausen, where Kohout was first imprisoned: "[E]ven during this time of murder, there was solidarity among the homosexuals [in Sachsenhausen]. There are a very large number of accounts of cultural activities in Block 14 from the autumn of 1939 to the spring of 1940" (Sternweiler in Müller et al. 2002: 46).

Many accounts by survivors mention the isolation and fragmentation of homosexual inmates in the concentration camps, something which was undoubtedly a product of the fact that most pink-triangle prisoners were housed in blocks together with the other prisoners, whose reservations toward "filthy queers" (Heger 1994: 28) came to full fruition in that either they shunned the pink-triangle inmates in order to avoid being suspected of homosexuality themselves or they insulted them and subjected them to unrestrained violence.[35] There were no consistent, standardized practices for housing homosexuals in the camps, and while housing them together could encourage a sense of solidarity or group consciousness, there is no doubt that these prisoners were nonetheless isolated among the other prisoner categories.

The personal support that Kohout received from civilian workers when he was going to be transferred to a penal detachment illustrates how homosexuals always faced ambivalent attitudes. In this case, Kohout had demonstrated to the workers that he was a smart, thoughtful, and reliable foreman who was contributing to the victory of the German Fatherland through his work in an armaments factory. This was the argument the workers used when they approached the factory management to protest Kohout's transfer. This specialized task for the Fatherland outweighed the importance of "serving at the front" as cannon fodder and could also "blot out the shame of [. . .] homosexuality" (ibid.: 102) – and this seems to have been apparent even to his fellow prisoners with triangles of a different color (ibid.: 103).

On the one hand, Kohout's account tells us how he was treated as a homosexual in the camps. At the same time, however, he outlines his own perspective on social differences and relationships, painting a picture of a hierarchized social space which corresponds to that described in other accounts. His remarks about the "Gypsy Capo" (see above), the Jewish prisoner, the "green" Kapo, and the priest convey his generalizing view of "these types of people," a view that seems to remain valid for him despite the occasional personal experiences to the contrary, which he highlights in his account. The images of the "wild Gypsy," the "rich intellectual Jew," the "self-serving, ruthless criminal," and the "self-sacrificing priest" (who is ennobled before everyone's eyes by a sign from heaven) are familiar to us from many other contexts. The fact that the power-seeking "politicals" used their positions to pursue their political goals while expressing little solidarity with their "inferiors" is just as painful to Kohout as the anti-semitism of the "reds," or "Sozis," is to Leon Szalet (2006: 388f.; see above) – after all, they were all being persecuted by the Nazi regime, and they hoped that those in a position to engage in organized resistance would acknowledge and protect those who shared their fate.

Kohout also makes a clear distinction between "real" homosexuals and those who participated in homosexual relationships for "other motives." Contrary to the public discourse of the time, which was shaped by alleg-edly "scientific" arguments (cf. Grau 1995: 3), Kohout directs his contempt at "opportunistic homosexuals," most of whom he accuses of having base motives, even though he himself entered into such relationships of con-venience with Kapos for comparable reasons during his imprisonment. His need to make such a distinction may be the result of the double stand-ards to which he was subjected as a "real" homosexual – namely, that his actions were condemned as being reprehensible while similar behavior by others was excused as an "emergency outlet." There is an unmistakable note of sympathy in the passage about the SS block leader (Heger 1994: 48f.) whom Kohout suspected of also being a "real" homosexual based on his own observations of the man. Kohout may have sympathized because he knew from experience how necessary it was to keep up pretenses, and he seems to grasp that this "disguise as an SS man" was very effective. This is especially apparent in the passages in which he emphasizes, with a certain sense of emotion, that while this block leader ordered strict pun-ishments for the smallest infractions, he never carried them out himself and avoided being present at them whenever possible (cf. ibid.: 48f.).

Kohout displays an apparently infallible understanding of the hierar-chical positions within the camp society when he explains that as soon as he became a Kapo himself and thus joined the elite,[36] he had to end his relationship with another (green) Kapo because "any sexual relation between Capos was unthinkable and would not be tolerated by the 'dig-nitaries'" (ibid.: 95).

I have focused on three groups of prisoners – Jews, "Gypsies," and homosexuals – to provide *representative examples* of how stereotypi-cal attitudes that existed in the society outside the camps remained in effect inside the camps. The names and labels – or, as Bourdieu puts it, the "words that refer to groups and that are frequently used in conflicts regarding the boundaries of these groups, that is, the conditions for belonging to a group or being excluded from it" (Bourdieu 2004: 114) – as well as the colored triangles roused pre-existing resentments not only among the SS but among the prisoners as well. Resentments toward other groups also influenced the self-positioning strategies of the prisoners marginalized in some way – as Jews, "Gypsies," or homosexuals – and led to a complex network of social positions and lines of demarcation in the camps. Identifiable differences and similarities clearly played a particularly weighty role in the Nazi concentration camps because there were few opportunities to become more closely acquainted with one's fellow prisoners, and such opportunities often arose only in the utmost secrecy. The prisoners' colored triangles were a simplified form of categorization which was usually only questioned by the inmates if they themselves were affected by it and felt that their particular categorization did not fully reflect their character or was extremely unfair. Depending on what it stood for, the triangle could fragment entire categories or prompt inmates with triangles of the same color to form communities or to dissociate themselves from other individuals or categories.

Jews and homosexuals are examples of *fragmentation tendencies* because prisoners with these triangles had very little in common with each other, did not view themselves as a group, and rarely had strategies from their former lives that could be applied in the camps and that would promote a sense of solidarity. In many cases, national and cultural differences or different social positions were of greater consequence than the fact that another prisoner was also homosexual or also Jewish. While it was the intention of the SS to fragment homosexual prisoners within the prisoner society, the fragmentation of prisoners identified as Jewish was more a by-product of the circumstances. However, the fragmentation that was subjectively experienced in the situation did not prevent other prisoners from suspecting that "the gays" or "the Jews" had joined forces and were single-mindedly pursuing certain goals – for example, that the homosexuals wanted to "seduce normal men" into a same-sex relationship or that the Jews wanted to "profit from wily wheeling and dealing." Fragmentation, which did not necessarily pose a problem in normal life outside the camps, became particularly precarious within the camps because isolated inmates faced the concentrated condemnation not only of the SS but also of the majority of their fellow prisoners.

Dissociation was clearly important to all prisoners, either on an individual level, as in the case of the "Gypsy girl" Eva (see above), who vehemently insisted that she had not grown up among "Gypsies" and was therefore very different from them and not at all savage, or more generally, as in the case of the Sintisa Hildegard Lagrenne, who asserted that "Gypsies" were Catholic Germans and not Jews (see above) and, in doing so, distanced "Gypsies" as a whole from Jews. Attempts at dissociation can also be found in other remarks about "the Gypsies" or "'the Jews" which indicate that incorporated patterns of evaluation led others to suspect that these groups shared common characteristics even if there was little or no material basis for this. Even groups of prisoners who were externally viewed as having common goals and traditions employed dissociation strategies which sometimes resulted in internal divisions, as was the case with prisoners with the red triangle: Communists and social democrats played out their long-held animosities and antipathies in the camps,[37] for example, or distinctions would simply be made between the "real reds" who actually came from the resistance movement and the "nonpolitical opponents of the Nazis" (Neurath 2005: 56) who were also given the red triangle but who were not organized and had in many cases merely spoken out against the regime and been denounced for it.

Community-building in the camps usually took place among groups that had already had some affiliation outside the camps. This affiliation could be the result of notions of ethnic kinship – as was sometimes the case among "Gypsies" – which were based on shared traditions, language, culture, and concepts of honor. But even in this case, it was not inevitable that a community would form. This is illustrated by Germaine Tillion when she describes how the French and Belgian "Gypsies" – the women who came from Tillion's own cultural sphere, in other words – could not live together with the German "Gypsies" because their lifestyles were so different (see above). Community-building also took place among groups with shared world-views, such as Jehovah's Witnesses, Christian clergy, or communists, all of whom could take recourse to prior organizational and strategic experience and who already possessed a code of ethics and set of rules by which they could orient themselves in the concentration camp. The identifying characteristic of real groups with a shared world-view such as this – a characteristic which was apparently something of an advantage in the camps – is that the members of these groups were used to subordinating themselves as individuals to an idea and playing their part in the realization of this idea without complaint. As a consequence, they appeared to be more disciplined than the other members of the camp society, and they deferred to a higher goal in the prisoners' self-administrative efforts. Their behavior was therefore more in line with that demanded by the Nazis, with the result that they were sometimes more trusted by the SS, who were prone to mistake their discipline for compliance. Among the Jehovah's Witnesses and Christian clergy, who were identified with a purple triangle, there were even cases of relationships being formed across institutional barriers, relationships based on a belief in the same god, a detailed knowledge of the Bible, and the consistent rejection of the Nazi regime.

In addition to the hierarchy of prisoner categories and the ranking of social positions in the camps, the prisoner society was further differentiated on the basis of local, regional, and national factors. When inmates met fellow prisoners from their own region, this common background formed a unifying bond between themselves and their personal history and provided material for shared recollections and conversations. As Tadeusz Borowski says: "He's from Mlawa, I'm from Mlawa, you know how it is. We had palled around together and done business together – mutual confidence and trust" (Borowski 1992: 127–8).

While geographical origins could form the basis of relationships built around a shared culture, language, and customs, they could also do the opposite and signal seemingly insurmountable discrepancies. For example, Aleksander Kuliesiewicz recounts the story of a dying Goral[38] who, even in the moment of his death, felt compelled to express his disdain for his fellow Polish prisoners from the cities, whom he dismissed as "damned spoiled brats" with their "fancy talk" (cf. Daxelmüller 1998: 983f.; Suderland 2004: 128ff.). In another account, Jewish Greek women recall that they were referred to as "Grecko klepsi klepsi" in Auschwitz and Ravensbrück because of their skillful thefts in the camp – which entailed not only taking useful items from the property room but also supposedly robbing their fellow prisoners (cf. Herzog and Efrat 2005: 98f.). Other stereotypes held that Polish women were vulgar and dirty, French women were vain, Greek women were clever thieves but also clean, orderly, disciplined, and witty, Belgian women were naïve, non-Jewish Ukrainian women were cruel, Czech women were energetic, and so on (cf. ibid.: 98; see also various essays in Moller et al. 2002).

National and geographic classifications went hand in hand with a socially evaluated status that worked like a positive or negative sign in mathematics. This evaluation factor, in turn, was overlaid with the significance of a prisoner's triangle color, which represented an additional intensifying or weakening sign. In the case of Jews and "Gypsies," however, their classification was so dominant that it completely outweighed any national or cultural aspects in how they were perceived – for example, a Jewish Pole would be viewed as a Polish Jew, or a prisoner's nationality would be so negligible that he or she would be viewed and identified solely as a Jew. The same applies to "Gypsies," whose geographical origins seem to have been entirely of secondary importance, probably not least because they were suspected of being permanently rootless wanderers.

The fine distinctions in the hidden social practices of the Nazi concentration camps that were described on a micro-sociological level in chapter 5 therefore have counterparts in the social-structural distinctions within the camp society. In both scholarly literature and the literature of memory, concentration camp prisoners are often explicitly depicted as a roughly distinguished mass of people subject to forms of differentiation imposed by the Nazis. However, the social structure of the prisoner society was actually very complex, despite all attempts to simplify it. Although differentiation within this society was based less on actual social practice than on stereotypes that crystallized around proverbial attributions and coalesced into opaque conglomerates, these attributions had a history behind them, they were brought into the camps by the prisoners themselves in the form of their habitus, and they were spread and intensified by means of rumor. National origins – and thus language, culture, and the concept of ethnic affiliation – played a role here, as did a prisoner's category.

Jews and "Gypsies," however, were suspected of sharing strong commonalities which bound them together beyond all other characteristics, including national origin or any other categorization, and this purported commonality overlaid all other aspects of their identity – as if they were indelibly branded. While homosexuals were shunned and scorned within the prisoner society and undoubtedly suffered terribly in the Nazi concentration camps, it was widely thought that they could either be treated or simply not act on their homosexual disposition, and this could turn them into "nearly normal men" in the eyes of their fellow prisoners.

This type of mutual evaluation, which was independent of any concrete individual social practice, represents a second strand of social reality in the camps, one which could cause inmates to draw very contradictory conclusions about others on a personal level. This apparently did not give rise to confusion, however. If an inmate encountered an educated "Gypsy" who led a distinguished lifestyle, as described by Tillion, for example (Tillion 1975: 31f.), this did not necessarily lead the inmate to believe that their image of the "savage and uneducated Gypsy" probably did not apply to the other people in this category either.

6.2 Regular prisoners, armband wearers, camp aristocracy: The mass and the elite

In all camps, the prisoners tried to take on certain functions. We have to say openly that there were no lofty motivations behind many of these actions. It was simply the usual struggle for power, for survival, for a position, just like in the normal life of a society.

Tadeusz Hołuj (in Brzezicki et al. 1987: 237)

In the following, the term *prisoner functionary* will be used to describe those prisoners who held a position within the so-called prisoner self-administration system. The opportunities to use – or abuse – power here varied drastically from case to case. Some of these positions offered absolutely no way of influencing anything. As Primo Levi writes:

Around us, prisoners without rank, swarmed low-ranking functionaries, a picturesque fauna: sweepers, kettle washers, night watchmen, bed smoothers (who exploited to their minuscule advantage the German fixation about bunks made up flat and square), checkers of lice and scabies, messengers, interpreters, assistants' assistants. In general, they were poor devils like ourselves, who worked full time like everyone else but who for an extra half-liter of soup were willing to carry out these and other "tertiary" functions: innocuous, sometimes useful, often invented out of the whole cloth. They were rarely violent, but they tended to develop a typically corporate mentality and energetically defended their "job" against anyone from below or above who might covet it. [. . .] They were coarse and arrogant, but they were not regarded as enemies.

Judgment becomes more tentative and varied for those who occupied commanding positions: the chiefs [. . .] of the labor squads, the barracks chiefs, the clerks, all the way to the world (whose existence at that time I did not even suspect) of the prisoners who performed diverse, at times most delicate duties in the camps' administrative offices, the Political Section [. . .], the Labor Service, and the punishment cells. Some of these, thanks to skill or luck, had access to the most secret information [. . .]. One does not know whether to admire more their personal courage or their cunning, which enabled them to help their companions in many concrete ways [. . .].

The functionaries described were not at all, or were only apparently, collaborators, but on the contrary camouflaged opponents. Not so the greater part of the other persons with positions of command, human specimens who ranged from the mediocre to the execrable. Rather than wearing one down, power corrupts [. . .]. (Levi 1989: 44–6)

A remark by Aloiz Oskar Kleta, a former clerk in Auschwitz, clearly shows that the prisoner society made a very definite distinction between low-ranking and more influential positions, even if the room to maneuver was sometimes overestimated: "The prisoners, including kapos, greatly respected the inmates who worked in the Politische Abteilung (political department) and were even afraid of them. They believed that we could somehow help or harm them. I never tried to dispel this error" (Aloiz Oskar Kleta in Shelley 1986: 285).

The *Stubenälteste* (dormitory seniors) were responsible for distributing food, meaning that they could influence the basic diet of the regular inmates, which was very meager in any case, but they could also abuse their position in the worst way by trading some of the rations in return for luxury goods they kept for themselves. A prisoner at the mercy of a dormitory senior like this would continually face even greater hunger than that intended by the SS. Prisoners with armbands[39] who worked in the sick bays could save lives by giving dead prisoners the identity of living ones and vice versa in order to ward off punishments, transfers, death sentences, and so on, because the inmate facing the respective measure would then be officially documented as having died. Endangered prisoners could also usually be hidden quite easily in the sick bays, which the SS rarely inspected very closely because of their fear of contagion. But here, too, armband wearers might hawk bandages and medications for their own personal advantage instead of using them to treat sick prisoners. Prisoner functionaries who worked in the administrative offices of the SS and camp Gestapo – in the so-called political department (see chapter 2.3) – often had access to information on the whereabouts of other prisoners and on upcoming transports or liquidations and could sometimes secretly pass on this information as the first step toward a possible rescue effort.

However, these conspiratorial attempts to influence events frequently meant that *other* prisoners would suffer the fate originally intended for the prisoners who had been saved. Eugen Kogon's reference to the "understandable tendency to slough off all elements considered least valuable or worthless" (Kogon 2006: 35; see also chapter 6.1) indicates that some prisoner functionaries occasionally had the scope to make decisions about the life or death of their fellow prisoners. In light of this, it is not surprising that an armband-wearing prisoner functionary was not viewed as one among equals by the other prisoners, regardless of whether the functionary actually had such scope and, if so, whether he or she really used it. Libusé Nachtmanová, who worked in the sick bay at Ravensbrück as a translator for the head SS physician Treite, reflects on the balancing act between opportunities, dangers, and temptations that she faced in her position:

> I don't know if the prisoner functionaries were generally popular in the camp. Admittedly, the opportunity to assume a "privileged" position brought about a higher chance of survival, but maybe some people didn't know their limits. If someone did a bit too much to counter the Nazi supremacy, then she would be in greater danger than a woman who worked in the factory, for example. We were known by name. When I worked for Treite, everyone knew who I was. Some people crossed the line by thinking that they were more powerful than the overseer, for example. Not everyone can handle a modicum of power. For instance, the block senior had power over food – and that was power over life! If one person did a deal with the food, that meant someone else would get less. And if someone reported it, the punishment was severe. (Libusé Nachtmanová in Walz 2005b: 161)

What all prisoner functionaries had in common was that their work was always carried out at the behest of the SS, so even if it was not their intention, the functionaries became the henchmen and enforcers of the SS. Their proximity to the SS alone set these inmates apart from the mass of other prisoners. If they worked in the immediate physical vicinity of the SS on account of their position, then they would always have much better living conditions than the other regular prisoners – better accommodation, better hygienic conditions, better food and clothing – if for no other reason than that the SS feared contagious diseases and would not tolerate direct contact with louse-ridden, filthy, starving people in their offices or sick bays.

In addition to this privileged situation, which was often envied by the other inmates, the prisoner functionaries sometimes wielded a more or less significant degree of power over their fellow prisoners – both the power of punishment by order of and in accordance with the wishes of the SS, as was the case for a Kapo in a supervisory role, and the power to secretly make decisions in favor of certain other prisoners. At the same time, this proximity to the powerful posed a constant danger to the prisoner functionaries themselves. Since a prisoner functionary was frequently "a witness to the secrets of the SS-men [. . .], a *Lagergeheimnisträger*" (Feliks Mylyk in Shelley 1986: 301) and therefore knew a great deal about the internal plans, manipulations (such as those related to death records), and decisions of the SS, many functionaries were convinced that their knowledge would prevent them from ever leaving the camp alive. The SS undoubtedly made this abundantly clear to them. Regardless of how they carried out their duties or whether they did more to help than to harm their fellow prisoners – certain ones, anyway – they were in an exposed position and therefore faced special dangers.

What this meant personally to the prisoner functionaries in their everyday lives and while carrying out their high-profile activities can perhaps be explained best by the accounts of former prisoners who did not have a very strong ideological orientation. Because prisoners who had previously been involved in ideologically motivated and organized resistance movements would have already had some experience in acting strategically and occasionally taking serious personal risks, we can assume that the truly politically motivated inmates pursued specific intentions if they were assigned to special tasks. However, other prisoners who just happened to be assigned to such duties – because they could speak and write German, for example, and therefore seemed qualified to work as clerks for the SS or camp Gestapo – lived in a state of constant fear because of their proximity to the camp administration and worried continually about drawing negative attention to themselves. They often only gradually became aware that their insider knowledge placed them in a particularly precarious situation and that their fate appeared to have been determined long before.

This distinction is illustrated very clearly in the book *Secretaries of Death* edited by Lore Shelley (1986). The book consists largely of texts from former female prisoner functionaries in Auschwitz who worked in the registry and document section, secretariat, interrogation section (where they were forced to witness horrific scenes of torture and record or falsify the statements of the tortured), and the civil registry (where they habitually had to falsify causes of death). These prisoners had largely similar social backgrounds: The majority of them arrived in Auschwitz in 1942 on the first two transports from Slovakia, had been deported as Jews, and usually had a school education and some professional training which singled them out as being suitable to work in the offices of the SS. In addition to being able to type and write shorthand, most of them also had a very good knowledge of German and sometimes other foreign languages. Many of them had several years of experience working in offices, banks, or administrative positions (cf. ibid.). Although these women were Jewish and, for this reason alone, their ultimate fate in Auschwitz seemed to have been sealed, they were also armband wearers who were entrusted with administrative tasks for which their previous training had qualified them. Since they were Jewish, the SS did not have to think twice about involving them in secret procedures in the course of their duties and thus compromising them by making them witnesses because – just like the Jewish *Sonderkommando* (special detail) in the gas chambers of Auschwitz (cf. Levi 1989: 50) – their path to extermination had already been laid out. Some of them wound up surviving by chance, but this was never the intention of the SS. Both the tasks they were forced to carry out and the knowledge they could not avoid acquiring made them, in a sense, into unwilling accomplices.

The male prisoners who worked in the offices of Auschwitz, by contrast, were mostly political resistance fighters from Poland. The majority of them were among the very first inmates in Auschwitz and had been in the camp since it was established in the summer of 1940. They, too, had to have a knowledge of German, though the accounts published by Shelley give the impression that language skills were not as essential for them as they were for the female secretaries who arrived two years later (see below). At this early stage of the camp's existence, when there were fewer prisoners, the SS probably could not afford to be too particular. When the prisoner population expanded in the camp and the SS could choose more qualified workers, the prerequisites for a position in the offices became much stricter. On account of their political consciousness, these male prisoner functionaries from the Polish resistance were aware of the special position their roles placed them in, and it was their intention to take advantage of any opportunities which arose for the benefit of "their cause." They accepted the resulting danger because they never lost sight of their goal to fight the Nazi regime and harm it in any way possible (cf. Shelley 1986: 278–341).

Raya Kagan describes the relationship between the SS and these two groups of prisoner functionaries in Auschwitz as follows: "[T]he relations between the SS and the male non-Jewish prisoners were better than that between the SS and the women inmates. We represented a double danger in the eyes of the SS as women as well as Jews. We were considered inferior and they constantly made us aware of this" (Raya Kagan quoted in ibid.: 276).

Just as there were many ambivalences within the prisoner society, as described above, there were pronounced ambivalences among the SS as well with respect to the prisoner functionaries. While SS members tended to behave in a stereotypical and almost predictable way toward the anonymous mass of prisoners – by giving preferential treatment to prisoners with the green triangle, for example, while treating those with the pink triangle in a particularly disdainful way and preferring not to view those with the yellow triangle as fellow human beings at all (cf. Hermine Markovits in ibid.: 121) – they were more nuanced in their personal interactions with the prisoner functionaries. In many of the accounts by the Jewish secretaries in Auschwitz, we find that even the SS and Gestapo supervisors who were most feared as brutal torturers established something like a personal relationship with "their" prisoner functionaries and repeatedly took steps to protect them. For example, former secretary Lilly Hönig says:

> Kamphuis was not above killing prisoners in the street, yet once, when I had a terrible toothache, he took me immediately to the men's camp, where a male prison dentist extracted the offending tooth. Though no less an anti-Semite than the other SS-men, Kamphuis was protective of "his" Jews. Thus, Kamphuis could be dangerous for strangers. One Shabbat afternoon, we returned from the Stabsgebäude [i.e., general staff building] to the office in the barracks and found all drawers on the floor. Oberscharführer [i.e., Staff Sergeant] Quackernack (of the Standesamt [i.e., civil registry office]) and Boger (of the escape detail) had made a search and found a few biscuits and a little sugar in them. "You dirty Jews, you stuff your bellies while our courageous soldiers don't have anything to eat at the front," they screamed and began to hit us. But Kamphuis rushed to our aid and stopped them. "If you hit my Jews I am going to hit your Jews," he threatened both of them. (Lilly Hönig in ibid.: 89)

Maryla Rosenthal describes a different SS man from the interrogation section:

> Boger behaved very humanely toward me. He gave me his canteen filled with food from the SS kitchen, which was prohibited, ostensibly for cleaning purposes. Together with two friends, we locked ourselves in the restroom and shared the food. During the cold winter months, Boger provided shoes and warm clothing for me. (Maryla Rosenthal in ibid.: 149)

This same *Oberscharführer*, Wilhelm Boger, was notorious for his especially brutal interrogation methods. The most feared torture instrument of all was even named after him: the *Boger-Schaukel* or Boger swing (cf. Langbein 2004: 386; Shelley 1986: 105). Hermann Langbein describes it as follows:

> The swing is the Political Department's favorite form of torture. An inmate has to sit on the floor and draw up his knees. His hands are bound in front and pulled over his knees. A pole is placed under the hollows of his knees and over his lower arms, and the inmate is hung from this pole with his head down. Then he is rocked back and forth, and with each swing he gets a slap on his buttocks. All this would be bearable, but, worst of all, the tormentors hit his genitals. Boger, the notorious SS technical sergeant of the Political Department, takes direct aim at these. The inmates [. . .] have to strip and get only thin dungarees but no underwear. I never imagined that testicles could swell so horrendously and turn blue and green. (Langbein 2004: 178)

From our perspective today, it is difficult to comprehend how someone like Boger could be called "humane." However, it is likely that behavior such as giving food, shoes, and clothing to a Jewish woman, of all people, was all the more striking in such violent surroundings and would have seemed like a special personal reward and humane act to the prisoner who was otherwise both physically starved and starved for human acknowledgment. In Erving Goffman's terms, Maryla Rosenthal's perspective (see above) can be interpreted as evidence of "colonization" (Goffman 1961: 62f.), where the world of the camp is viewed as the entire world and the inmate tries to make a "home" there (ibid.). This strategy also shows the traits of a "divided" or "torn habitus" (Bourdieu 2007) in which completely contradictory influences are integrated and incorporated so that the contradictions do not become a pressing problem.

In another case, former secretary Hermine Markovits describes how she wrote a poem for a fellow prisoner's birthday and secretly typed it out. She had not finished typing it by the midday break, so she left the paper in the covered typewriter, where it was discovered by Quackernack, head of the civil registry office. When she returned from lunch with "the girls," they were all forced to stand at attention and were told that if the guilty party did not voluntarily step forward, every fourth person would be sent back to the Birkenau camp. The conditions were so catastrophic in Birkenau that being sent back there almost certainly meant a swift death, so this was a terrifying threat to the secretaries. Markovits then raised her hand as the guilty party:

> "You wrote this? All the others are dismissed! You come to my office." In his private room Quackernack delivered a long lecture on the prohibition of writing poems in camp. "Well, what should I do with you?" "I don't know, Herr Oberscharführer." Then he took his cane and hit the table. I looked at him and did not know how to react. "Why don't you scream so that those outside can hear you!" he exclaimed. (Hermine Markovits in Shelley 1986: 119)

Elsewhere she writes:

> Brose [an SS man] was a decent and gentlemanly man. He always treated me like a lady and frequently brought home-cooked food for me from his wife. When we had to go out for interrogations it was he who carried the typewriter. "I just don't want to be served by a lady. It's not your fault that you were born Jewish just as I cannot help it that I was born German." (Ibid.: 121)

On the way to a prisoner interrogation – during which the most horrific forms of torture were habitually used, frequently resulting in the death of the prisoner – the SS man Brose could not permit "a lady" to carry her typewriter herself, even though, from his ideological perspective, she should not have even been considered a human being. Rationally speaking, such behavior is difficult to understand and seems almost schizophrenic. But apparently the driving force here is not rationality but the fact that an actual person – who furthermore, on account of her privileged position, did not appear as inhuman as the regular prisoners in all of their filth, starvation, and despair – displayed not just human but personal traits which could not simply be ignored in the course of direct daily interaction. By remarking that she could not help being born Jewish, the SS man seems to imply that he feels something has gone amiss for her to not be like other Jews.

Former male secretary Aloiz Oskar Kleta recounts how he had resolved to respond to all orders and questions from the SS with a vigorous "*Jawohl!*" After reading in Kleta's file that he was from the Polish resistance, section head Quackernack asked Kleta if he was someone who wanted to kill SS men. Kleta did not fully understand the question because he had not learned the word "*umbringen*" (to kill) in school, so he answered with an energetic "*Jawohl!*" and clicked his heels together. Quackernack flew into a rage, threw chairs around, and finally repeated his question. Another "*Jawohl!*" from Kleta made the situation even worse. When the SS man asked Kleta whether he had even understood the question, Kleta again responded with "*Jawohl!*," at which point Quackernack stormed out of the room. Kleta, who thought he had ruined any chance of being assigned to the office and would probably be severely punished, was nonetheless taken on as a secretary without further comment and inducted into the operations in the department (cf. Aloiz Oskar Kleta in ibid.: 283).

Though very different from the situation described by the women above, this case also reveals a certain ambivalence toward a prisoner, a Pole, who, according to Nazi standards, was considered not only "racially inferior" but also an ideological opponent and thus a member of an "enemy category." All of the examples mentioned here are hard to explain rationally, but they show that along with the pronounced personal vanities of the SS ("my Jews"), and despite the tremendous imbalance of power between the SS and the armband wearers, a personal relationship could develop which lifted the prisoner functionaries out of anonymity. If we consider that such an "ennobled" prisoner would feel somewhat more like a human being again, then it is possible that, despite their fundamental condemnation of the SS, the inmates themselves might have been corrupted to the point that they developed a different – more humane? – image of their SS tormentors. It is also obvious that the improved position of the prisoner functionaries would be envied by the regular prisoners, who suspected the functionaries of collaboration with the SS and accused the armband wearers of not doing enough to help their fellow prisoners. Ultimately, then, whether they wanted to or not, the prisoners who were entrusted with special functions also occupied special, better positions at the interface between the prisoner society and the SS. Their privileged position was envied, even though it meant that they constantly faced additional dangers because of it.

On account of the exposed and somewhat corrupting position of the prisoner functionaries in the concentration camps, these prisoners were the focus of a very controversial and at times highly ideological debate after the end of the "Third Reich" (cf. Detlef Garbe in *Abgeleitete Macht* 1998: 13). Those from the political resistance movement emphasized the solidarity and cohesion of the prisoners who opposed the regime and declared that the rescue and aid efforts undertaken by the prisoner functionaries for the benefit of their fellow prisoners were humane acts in an inhumane environment. But immediately after the liberation of the camps, it became public knowledge that some prisoner functionaries had savored their power without reservation and used brute force against their fellow prisoners. We now know of a large number of cases in which the SS – with psychological cunning – deliberately chose green-triangle prisoners to violently enforce the strict regime among their subordinate prisoners. These cases contributed to the image of the "greens" as especially brutal and self-serving, and they also damaged the reputation of the armband wearers as a whole. However, a closer reading of prisoners' accounts and historical documents quickly reveals that their triangle color was not the determining factor in whether prisoner functionaries would abuse their power and employ violence to keep their fellow inmates in line. The image of the prisoner functionaries that emerged after the war was shaped less by historical facts than by the ideological debate surrounding them. In the post-war trials of Nazi perpetrators, some brutal Kapos were also accused of having viewed their position as *carte blanche* to kill and thus acted in the interests of the SS. Many of them – those with green as well as with red triangles – received prison sentences (cf. Brzezicki et al. 1987; Langbein 2004: 146).

In the wake of the "Third Reich," this strongly polarized (and polarizing) debate about the role of the prisoner functionary painted a black-and-white image of "red" prisoner functionaries as "good" and others – particularly "greens" – as "evil." This notion also found its way into the divergent discourse of the German Democratic Republic and the Federal Republic of Germany, in which the role of communists was judged in accordance with the ideological underpinnings of each state (cf. Detlef Garbe in *Abgeleitete Macht* 1998: 13). I do not intend to analyze this debate any further, however. Instead, I want to turn back to the prisoner society and consider what it meant for there to be a "preferred class" of prisoners who, as elites, stood apart from the mass of the damned.

In a chapter entitled "The Gray Zone" in his last book *The Drowned and the Saved* (Levi 1989: 36–69), Primo Levi discusses the "hybrid class of the prisoner-functionary" (ibid.: 42) and calls for a more nuanced view of camp life as a whole:

We also tend to simplify history; but the pattern within which events are ordered is not always identifiable in a single, unequivocal fashion [. . .]. Nevertheless, perhaps for reasons that go back to our origins as social animals, the need to divide the field into "we" and "they" is so strong that this pattern, this bipartition – friend/enemy – prevails over all others. [. . .] This is certainly the reason for the enormous popularity of spectator sports, such as soccer, baseball, and boxing: the contenders are two teams or two individuals, clearly distinct and identifiable, and at the end of the match they are vanquished and victors. If the result is a draw, the spectator feels defrauded and disappointed. [. . .]

This *desire* for simplification is justified, but the same does not always apply to simplification itself, which is a working hypothesis, useful as long as it is recognized as such and not mistaken for reality. The greater part of historical and natural phenomena are not simple, or not simple in the way that we would like. Now, the network of human relationships inside the Lagers was not simple: it could not be reduced to the two blocs of victims and persecutors [. . .] here the righteous, over there the reprobates. [. . .]

Instead, the arrival in the Lager was indeed a shock because of the surprise it entailed. The world into which one was precipitated was terrible, yes, but also indecipherable: it did not conform to any model; the enemy was all around but also inside, the "we" lost its limits, the contenders were not two, one could not discern a single frontier but rather many confused, perhaps innumerable frontiers [. . .]. (Ibid. 1989: 36–8)

The prisoners entrusted with functions no longer belonged solely to the prisoner society; instead, through their interactions with the SS, they were able to come to a kind of trade-off with the SS and achieve a different, better status beyond the usual stereotypical prejudgments of the prisoner groups. This was certainly one of the most unfathomable mysteries to the other regular prisoners. In the experience of the other prisoners, this "hybrid class" (ibid.: 42) was populated with both "good" and "evil" individuals; there were also unpredictable ones, and it was deemed best to get in good with them just to be on the safe side. The "hybrid" nature of these positions is clearly illustrated by Aloiz Oskar Kleta when he says that prisoners and Kapos alike both respected and feared the functionaries working in the political department because they believed the functionaries could help as well as harm them, and that he himself never dispelled this error (cf. Kleta in Shelley 1986: 285). It was obviously a good thing – and ultimately also a form of *symbolic power* – for others to think that you had an influence, even if this was not really the case.

In relation to the questions being explored in this work, I am less interested in clarifying the guilt issue – and there is no doubt that some of the prisoner functionaries were very guilty indeed, though it was the corrupting system of the Nazi concentration camps that put them in this position in the first place – and more interested in examining the effects of different power resources and their impact on the social structure of the prisoner society.

Anise Postel-Vinay, a French woman who was imprisoned in the Ravensbrück concentration camp for women, tells of the resulting division of the prisoner society:

> There was a hierarchy, like there was in every camp. There was the aristocracy on one side and the people on the other. The aristocracy were the women in blocks one, two, three, and four who had good jobs. Just like in normal society, the women who had clean office jobs also had access to the showers, while we who did the dirty work with coal and earth were not allowed to wash – just like in every normal society. (Walz 2005a: 43':11"ff.)

Primo Levi writes: "In history and in life one sometimes seems to glimpse a ferocious law which states: 'to he that has, will be given; from he that has not, will be taken away.' In the Lager, where man is alone and where the struggle for life is reduced to its primordial mechanism, this unjust law is openly in force, is recognized by all" (Levi 1995: 88–9). Eugen Kogon also emphasizes that the differences in the camps corresponded in principle to those of a normal society: "These classes in the concentration camps were not extraordinary in their social structure, for they developed on the basis of economic position and special function just as they do in the outside world. The prisoners in positions of power formed the camp aristocracy, the 'big shots.'" (Kogon 2006: 309). In this passage, Kogon names the prerequisites for the emergence of a camp elite – of aristocrats and dignitaries – who stood apart from the mass of regular prisoners. After their initial shock, most prisoners apparently developed a keen sense of whether someone was for or against them. As described in the preceding chapters, stereotypes seem to have been the dominant factor when it came to mutual judgments among the mass of concentration camp inmates; but in personal interactions, other things could become more important, like a shared language and culture, a similar profession, a comparable social background, the same world-view, and so on. These two forms of differentiation – stereotypical or based on personal experience – also came into play in the behavior of the prisoner functionaries toward their fellow prisoners. In a group discussion on the topic of prisoner functionaries, Tadeusz Hołuj says:

> In nearly any position, there could be someone who worked for the benefit of the prisoners or the benefit of the SS. Sometimes it was even the same person. He did a little for one side, a little for the other – that's why the criminal cases are so difficult. The accused sits there on the bench, and he has a hundred witnesses defending him as a hero and a hundred saying he was a murderer. And both things are true. For one group, he was the best person because he helped them. This might have been a group of people with a

similar profession, of the same age, from his transport, his region, or with the same interests. But another group was exterminated by him. There may have been national or social differences. He was interested in helping one group and destroying the other. This naturally complicates things, because the dividing lines ran through the people themselves and not just through their functions. (Tadeusz Hołuj in Brzezicki et al. 1987: 238)

Primo Levi stresses that most people, and consequently also the concentration camp prisoners, desire clarity and unambiguousness in their lives (see above). But for the prisoners, this desire was pitted against a highly complex reality in the concentration camps – just like in the prisoners' previous, normal lives – which was usually far from unambiguous. In the camps, however, this reality was all the more complex because it was played out in entirely unfamiliar terrain. And if an inmate did not have at least a rudimentary understanding of how this reality worked, the consequences were much more severe than in normal life because in the concentration camps, everything was a matter of life or death. After a period of familiarization, the prisoners usually had an intuitive grasp of the importance of differences and similarities. "Block elders and capos appointed as their assistants dormitory orderlies and foremen who were like them," Hermann Langbein says (2004: 162). In the concentration camps, to be like someone else meant two things: to be in danger, because you were like someone whom the powerful wanted to oppress, and also potentially to be advantaged, because you were like someone toward whom the powerful were well disposed. Individuals with power could be found not only among the SS but also in the prisoner society itself, in the "camp aristocracy," which was feared, admired, and respected for its power and thus had a prominent status. Borowski tells the story of a deathly ill prominent prisoner whom he got to know in his position as a medical orderly:

[O]ne of the "bigwigs" in our block fell ill; he felt terrible, had a high fever, and spoke more and more of dying. Finally one day he called me over. I sat down on the edge of the bed.

"Wouldn't you say I was fairly well known at the camp, eh?" he asked, looking anxiously into my eyes.

"There isn't one man around who wouldn't know you . . . and always remember you," I answered innocently.

"Look over there," he said, pointing at the window. Tall flames were shooting up in the sky beyond the forest.

"Well, you see, I want to be put away separately. Not with all the others. Not on a heap. You understand?"

"Don't worry," I told him affectionately. "I'll even see to it that you get your own sheet. And I can put in a good word for you with the morgue boys."

He squeezed my hand in silence. But nothing came of it. He got well, and later sent me a piece of lard from the main camp. I use it to shine my shoes, for it happens to be made of fish oil. And so you have an example of my contribution to the lowering of the camp's mortality rate. (Borowski 1992: 99–100)

One of the participants in this dialog is a prominent prisoner – "There isn't one man around who wouldn't know you" – someone who has a certain reputation in the camp, the nature of which is not revealed to us here, however. The other is also no longer a regular prisoner since he works as a medical orderly and therefore enjoys a few privileges himself. He can even afford to use the lard he is given to shine his shoes since it is apparently of a low quality and not to his taste. A regular prisoner would have treated this lard like a treasure or eaten it himself because there was very little other fat in his diet. Although these two conversational partners do not share the same social status, both of them – one more so than the other – have been set apart from the large mass of other prisoners. One is already an aristocrat, while the other is just growing into this role and already knows what it entails: creating dependencies and flaunting affluence – Detlef Garbe refers to it as "personal patronage and clientelism" (in *Abgeleitete Macht* 1998: 11).

It is obvious that the gulf between the aristocracy and the masses would be all the greater under these conditions, but the effect is not really any different here than in normal life: It results in disadvantaged classes who view the privileged with a mixture of envy and respect. In the "you up there and us down here" scenario in the concentration camps, however, the lives of prisoners were always at stake, so the consequences of belonging to either the elite or the faceless mass were drastically different than in a "normal society."

When Primo Levi says there was not a single frontier in the camp but rather many confused ones (Levi 1989: 38), he is vividly describing the lack of clarity regarding the actual complexity of the prisoner society in the Nazi concentration camps. There were the antagonistic SS, who imprisoned and tormented the prisoners, and there was the masses of prisoners, who were divided into a hierarchy of aristocrats and regular inmates. The prisoners were further differentiated according to categories which indicated the reason for their imprisonment and drew on socially prevalent stereotypes. Personal experiences with the representatives of particular prisoner categories, with certain prisoner functionaries, or even with certain SS members could completely contradict conventional assumptions about the aristocracy, the prisoner categories, or the SS and had to somehow be incorporated into the inmates' value system. This made it all the more difficult to describe who was "evil" and who was "good." Despite an understandable desire for clarity, we accept such complexity in normal life because our survival does not depend on our ability to make sense of the confusion. The demand for clarity regarding relations within the prisoner society in the Nazi concentration camps, by contrast, comes down to a simple and terrible alternative between survival and death. Nevertheless, any attempt to discern a structure in this complex reality and take advantage of it was nothing more than "groping in the dark" (Friedländer 2007), where every step could be your last – with fatal consequences.

6.3 Men, women, children or: What's still normal here?

The men loved us also, but wretchedly. They experienced the sting of the decline of strength and manly duty since they could do nothing for the women. If we suffered seeing them unhappy, hungry, deprived, they did even more so, realizing their inability to protect and defend us, to assume their destiny on their own.

(Charlotte Delbo 1995: 117)

In the preceding sections, I used empirical material as the basis for taking a micro-sociological look at the hidden social world in the Nazi concentration camps (see chapter 5.3 primarily) and considering both the overt and more subcutaneous social-structural "architecture" of the prisoner society (see sections 6.1 and 6.2). In the following, I would like to give some thought to the importance and impact of gender separation in the concentration camps. While there are a multitude of nuanced "classes and ways of life" (Halbwachs 2001) on the micro-sociological level, the traces of which can be found deep inside the concentration camps, the classification criteria on the social-structural level are much more coarse-grained. The first aspect to mention here are the prisoner categories, which were based on the reasons for an inmate's imprisonment but which also drew on socially prevalent attitudes and thus conveyed concepts to the prisoners with which they were familiar from their former lives. The further division of the camp into a privileged "camp aristocracy" and the "common people" was influenced only marginally by the prisoner categories. While the split between the mass and the elite determines the personal chances available to an individual in normal life outside the concentration camps, this familiar social structure within the camps largely determined a prisoner's chances of surviving at all. The binary gender distinction that individuals usually take for granted because it seems so natural and irreversible was yet another classification factor within the prisoner society.

With very few exceptions, the Nazi concentration camps were exclusively either men's or women's camps, or at least the men's and women's sections of a camp would be hermetically sealed off from each other.[40] If there were any children in the camp, they usually stayed with their mothers if they were quite young; as soon as they were somewhat older, however, boys would be transferred to a camp or camp section for men. Adolescents were initially interned in their own "juvenile education camps," but during the mass deportations later on they were sent to the respective camps for adults. Many larger children lied about their age – often at the recommendation of more experienced long-term inmates – so that they would be sent to the adults' camp and assigned to work, which usually meant that they could avoid selections for the time being (as was the case with Ruth Klüger [2001]).

One might assume that in this gender-homogeneous prisoner society, an inmate's gender affiliation would be so self-evident that it would not need to be emphasized in any way, nor would it play a particularly important role in the daily struggle for survival. Various accounts written by former concentration camp prisoners tell a different story, however. Comments about male honor and masculinity, female shame and female charm, about male protectiveness and female ministration and maternalism run through these accounts of the authors' terrible imprisonment, as do remarks about the predicament of the respective opposite sex and the reversal of "normality." The conditions of imprisonment in the camps were clearly intended to annul the usual gender order, but they actually compelled the inmates to put even more effort into maintaining a gender-based social differentiation at the very least. In the following, examples of such efforts will be analyzed to draw conclusions about the social and personal value of an individual's gender affiliation.

The autobiographical accounts of *men* who were imprisoned in concentration camps regularly emphasize the special importance of the characteristic described by Bourdieu as male honor (see also Suderland 2007). According to Bourdieu, the idea of "masculinity as nobility" (Bourdieu 2001a: 56) is a "historical transcendental" (ibid.: 33) which is active as a "hidden constant" in all known societies (ibid.: 54) and which manifests itself by transforming the relationship between men and women into a power relationship. In the context of Paul Martin Neurath's theories, male honor can therefore be considered one of the "basic concepts" of society (Neurath 2005: 261) which defines the relationship between the genders as a hierarchical one. The extent to which the concentration camps demanded special "rules of behavior" (ibid.) will be explored in more detail in the following on the basis of a few selected examples.

In the sociological dissertation that he submitted in New York in 1943 and later published under the title of *The Society of Terror*, Neurath describes life *Inside the Dachau and Buchenwald Concentration Camps* (the subtitle of his book). His sociological perspicacity and his focus on the social dimension of camp life form the foundation of his very stringent depiction of the prisoner society. The book is divided into two large sections, "The Scene" and "The Society"; the second section closes with a fairly lengthy chapter, the title of which addresses the issue of male honor: "Why Don't They Hit Back?" (ibid.: 245–67). Both the prominent position of this chapter – as the conclusion to the original version of the dissertation – and its scope draw the attention of the reader to the relevance of the topic of honor. The heart of the problem depicted by Neurath is the fact that a prisoner who was hit by SS henchmen – something which happened regularly and was a systematic practice on the part of the SS – was not able to do what it would have been normal for a man to do under other circumstances, namely, hit back. If a prisoner had done this, he would have been shot on the spot. The rules of behavior in the camp were therefore unambiguous: "In concentration camp [*sic*] they didn't hit back" (ibid.: 246).

But how could a man take this insult without utterly forfeiting his male honor? The "metamorphosis from 'man' to 'camp prisoner'" (ibid.: 247) usually took place very soon after an individual entered a concentration camp, and the SS systematically paved the way for this transition through their treatment of new arrivals (ibid.: 247ff.; see also chapter 5.1). Acceptance of the camp rule that you "don't hit back" was a key requirement for survival. But Neurath makes it very clear that a concentration camp prisoner could defend his male honor using strategies specially adapted to the camp. Two aspects appear to be particularly important here. The first entailed not viewing the violent SS man as a man at all:

> To the prisoner, the SS guard or officer who slaps him is not so much a man who humiliates him through an insult as a sort of low animal, unpleasant and dangerous. To be bitten by a snake or a mad dog brings many unpleasant consequences. One may even die of it. But it certainly does not arouse the contempt of one's fellow men. (Ibid.: 258)

Through a reversal of perspective, the prisoner himself – who was at best a sub-human in the eyes of the SS – was able to remain a man and thus a human being. Even under the most adverse conditions, the male honor to which he was entitled placed the prisoner in a superior position, though the situation may have demanded a great deal of him. Viewed from this perspective, it was the SS man who was excluded from human society:

> Both know that the civilian rights of the prisoner are not suspended but abolished. To his guards the prisoner is no longer a man whose personality has any meaning. He no longer has an "honor" that has to be respected. And to the prisoner the guard becomes part of a machine, or a dangerous beast whose every move he watches and studies carefully, in order to get hurt as little as possible, but to whom any concepts of honor simply do not apply. (Ibid.: 260)

The strategy described here by Neurath could be called a "secondary adjustment" in Goffman's terms (Goffman 1961: 54ff.), a move which creates "counter-mores" (ibid.: 56) that enable the inmate "to reject his rejectors rather than himself" (ibid.: 58).

The second important aspect of the prisoners' strategy to preserve their male honor entailed viewing the other prisoners as the sole social reference for their behavior.

> [I]t [the society] has to adjust its concepts of honor and social status to this routine. This adjustment is made by not letting an insult affect a man's status. No social pressure is put upon him to hit back. On the other hand, terrific social pressure is put on him to take it the right way, to remain silent and stolid, both before, during, and after the beating. (Ibid.: 258)

By orienting himself on the other prisoners and certifying his "membership of the group of 'real men'" (Bourdieu 2001a: 52), the humiliated prisoner could still feel like a man as long as he fulfilled the requirements that characterized a "real man" in the concentration camps: he was not allowed to wail or scream when he was hit.

> It is the society of the prisoners which fulfills this most important task for the individual: It provides him with the forum he needs; it approves and disapproves of his behavior, thus lending meaning to his actions and reactions. The man who is being whipped on the stand knows that his friends will consider him a good man if he does not scream. There is more chance of his screaming when nobody is around to hear it, not only because it hurts, but also because nobody cares and nobody appreciates it if he keeps silent. (Neurath 2005: 136)

In my view, Neurath's remarks clearly illustrate that "[m]anliness [. . .] is an eminently *relational* notion, constructed in front of and for other men" (Bourdieu 2001a: 53; emphasis in original), but it is also an essential concept and a driving force behind the "socially sexed libido" (ibid.: 58). The following example from Robert Antelme will show how hitting back could be important in other situations as well for "real men" in the concentration camps.

Antelme's book *The Human Race* (1998) was written in 1946–7 and is thus one of the earliest accounts of the life of the prisoners in Nazi concentration camps. Antelme was imprisoned in a concentration camp later than Neurath, however, in the final year of the "Third Reich." Antelme describes prisoner life in a remarkably direct, forthright manner. In the first chapter, which makes up the main portion of his book, he provides a detailed depiction of the conditions in the Gandersheim concentration camp, a small satellite camp of Buchenwald located west of the Harz Mountains near Braunschweig.[41]

Antelme returns to the topics of masculinity and real men a remarkable number of times in his account. Both issues were apparently extremely important to the interactions of the imprisoned men. Antelme primarily associates masculinity with physical characteristics, such as a good diet that keeps the male muscles defined, as can be seen in the following quote: "The *Stubendienst* [i.e., dormitory orderly] ate his fill, and he used sometimes to walk around in the block bare-chested, showing off the fact that he wasn't growing thin. [. . .] He knew that he reigned more through his torso than through his *Stubendienst* armband, which anyone could have torn off easily [. . .]" (Antelme 1998: 157–8). Only prisoners who held a special position and were able to procure additional food could be in such good physical shape. Strength was therefore the unmistakable mark of power in the camp. Physical strength also meant that a prisoner had not lost his sexual virility, something which could be signaled by an erection or sexual activity on the part of the prisoner in question.

> Felix was able to eat this way for a month. He'd gained weight. Felix slept not far from the stove. When he lay down for the night he would remain stretched out on his pallet, covered only with his shirt. His thighs were clean and almost normal. He would wrap his shirt-tail around his genitals, covering them carefully. [. . .] Sometimes he'd place both hands on his genitals and look around. [. . .] Waking up in the morning, he'd sometimes laugh and say, "Shit, did I ever put it away while I was sleeping . . . I'm stuffed." The guys had at first looked at Felix with astonishment, later with hatred. On account of his thighs; and on account of the potatoes he hid between the pallet and the frame of his bed. (Ibid.: 183–4)

Masculinity – that is, strength and virility – can be equated with *power and dominance* in Antelme's account. By contrast, the concept of a real man was associated with the notion of *male honor*, and in the purely male society of prisoners this was something that had to be demonstrated – "in front of and for other men" (Bourdieu 2001a: 53). In the extremely close quarters where the prisoners were held, conflicts regularly erupted when one inmate would feel aggravated, provoked, or attacked by another. Antelme makes it clear that the right way to respond to such a situation was to respond the way a man would – namely, by hitting back. While Neurath emphatically states that under no circumstances could a prisoner defend himself against an SS man by hitting back, Antelme indicates that in conflicts between the prisoners themselves, hitting back was an "exchange of challenges" (Bourdieu 2001a: 47) which was the only way to preserve male honor. Here, too, fearlessness and stoicism in the face of pain were the key elements of male honor. Antelme vividly describes a scene in which André, a young political prisoner who was already very weak, was robbed of a slice of potato by a prisoner with a green triangle. When André demanded that the thief give back the stolen potato, the other prisoners intervened and open conflict broke out. Because the thief was in a position of power, the others did not rebuke him but instead mocked the victim of the theft because he was unable to defend himself:

> "And I'm telling you that you're not a man, because, if you were a man, you'd have pasted him." [. . .] "The gentleman is from the Resistance, but he doesn't want to get his feet wet. So he complains, because some of us around here are men who are willing to take care of ourselves. The gentlemen of the Resistance are all afraid of getting their asses whopped." (Antelme 1998: 133)

A physical fight then erupted between two prisoners who were not involved in the original altercation: a political prisoner and a prisoner categorized as a criminal who had been sent to the concentration camp for black-marketeering. The former accused the latter of being a Gestapo snitch, and the latter fiercely denied it with the following words:

> "[. . .] I'm a man, that's what I am. I never ratted on anybody. I don't do that sort of stuff. [. . .] I don't take it in the ass, I've always been straight." Nobody was answering him. [. . .] "Did you hear that asshole? [. . .] I never ratted on anybody, never. You get me? Never. Because I'm a man." (Ibid.: 133–4)

Hitting back and male solidarity are the focus of this scene described by Antelme. Male solidarity as a frame of reference appears to be unquestioned, but it is occasionally revealed to be problematic as well. In another passage, Antelme writes: "In fact, what could never be obtained by collectively asking for it [. . .] could be had through trafficking, through ass-kissing, through bargaining, and through a kind of solidarity between real men, which might, however, turn the next instant into a fierce hatred, then back again into complicity" (ibid.: 129).

At various points in his account, Antelme shows that the demonstrative repudiation of anything feminine was also important to the concept of masculinity. Anything "gay" is repeatedly and explicitly rejected, as demonstrated both in the passage cited above and when Antelme writes: "Naked, we tried not to touch each other; when we brushed against an arm or a shoulder, we would pull back quickly" (ibid.: 122). Even work normally associated with women was viewed as ignominious:

> In the factory, since I couldn't find a job in any of the workshops, I took hold of a broom. I had to have something in my hands. Brooms, however, were reserved for the elderly. I walked around a while in the shed, and whenever a civilian came toward me, I'd sweep. [. . .] They looked at me as though, with the broom, I was making fun of them [. . .]. I was wandering around with a woman's implement, and their women were fashioning the metal for the fuselage [of aircraft] and weren't wandering around. I abandoned the

broom when I saw that I was becoming too much of a scandal and before they raised a fuss. (Ibid.: 68)

Masculinity is clearly viewed as a particular form of honor and power, but it is also always contrasted with femininity. "Manliness, it can be seen, is an eminently *relational* notion, constructed in front of and for other men and against femininity, in a kind of *fear* of the female, firstly in oneself" (Bourdieu 2001a: 53; emphasis in original).

Neurath (2005) and Antelme (1998) view the community of men as the sole effective and valid point of reference in their accounts. There is no contradiction in their differing remarks about hitting back. While one refers to the blows of the SS that a "real man" is expected to tolerate stoically, the other refers to the blows of fellow prisoners which must naturally be countered in an appropriate way. Though both Antelme and Neurath were intellectuals, lawyers who had led cultivated lives and who, despite their involvement in the political resistance, were certainly not continually involved in fights, they both focus their attention on the importance of physical strength, the power to resist, and, in certain situations, the usually unquestioned need to hit back. At the same time, both confirm that only the community of men could judge who was a man and who was not. In light of this, it is entirely understandable that in the gender-homogeneous society of male prisoners, male honor was of essential importance to personal identity. However, we can also see that "the sense of honor, virility, 'manliness' [. . .] is the undisputed principle of all the duties towards oneself" (Bourdieu 2001a: 48) and that "the impossible ideal of virility" could be "the source of an immense vulnerability" (ibid.: 51).

Male virility clearly had a powerful external effect, as seen above, but it apparently also played an important role in an inmate's self-image. This is illustrated in Loden Vogel's diary (2002), which he secretly wrote while he was imprisoned in Bergen-Belsen and then published (with additional commentary) in the mid-1960s. Remarks about the waning and waxing of his sexual libido can be found throughout the diary:

> The lack of a libido is unsettling. I can't even get an erection anymore. (Vogel 2002: 52)

> I had an emission last night [. . .] The combination of protein deficiency/emission astonishes me. (Ibid: 53)

> There is a lack of both normal sex drive with all of its ramifications (there is no shame, no one tells dirty jokes, no one flirts [. . .]) and the homoeroticism known as camaraderie. (Ibid.: 63)

> Today [. . .] I saw one of the pretty girls [. . .] naked; she did not think anyone could see her, but that just made the natural, healthy excitement all

the greater. It was the first time here that something like that has given me pleasure. If the objects were more desirable, maybe I wouldn't be so asexual anymore. [. . .] Tonight I had an emission. (Ibid.: 66)

Now that I'm eating more, I feel like a man again. [. . .] Two more weeks of the status quo, and maybe sexuality will be on the cards again? (Ibid.: 71)

My libido, which – and this made the connection with my previous life so weak – had pretty much disappeared since the testicular edema, is gradually returning. Gradually I'm able to imagine and remember the feelings and reactions I used to have. (Ibid.: 74)

Another subject is important as well:

Yesterday evening I saw her [Mrs van L.] again, and our conversation through the barbed wire revolved around the lower resistance of the men, and the fact that the wives here don't need their husbands, but the husbands rely on their wives. She said she had also noticed how many women here had lovers. Well, I said, the more you notice that, the less opportunity there is for it. (Ibid.: 43)

Loden Vogel ponders these issues from a variety of perspectives. He is unsettled by his purely physical changes, and he also feels that "the connection with [his] previous life" (ibid.: 74) could be preserved if he could maintain his image of himself as a virile young man with erotic ambitions. This is why every nightly emission is a noteworthy event which he records as a ray of hope in his diary. His masculinity is a crucial part of his self. If this disappears, then the other aspects that make him the person he is are in danger as well.

For one final example of the important – and to a certain extent universally negotiable – aspect of masculinity in the concentration camps, I would like to turn to Primo Levi and a passage in the chapter "The Drowned and the Saved" from his first book *Survival in Auschwitz* (1995). In this passage, Levi describes a "dwarf" from Warsaw who was held in particularly high esteem in Auschwitz (ibid.: 95ff.). The social position of this "dwarf" occupied Levi's thoughts throughout his life, as can be seen in the fact that he mentions him in many different contexts, even in the last book he published shortly before his suicide.[42] In his first book he presents this "dwarf" as a representative of a certain type of person in the camp, but in his later work he mentions the "dwarf" in reference to the need to hit back. Levi himself never felt that he was able to do so (cf. Levi 1989: 136ff.). He attempted it only once in his life, namely, when the "dwarf" insulted him:

I had a sudden upsurge of pride; conscious of betraying myself, and of transgressing a norm handed down to me by innumerable forebears alien to violence, I tried to defend myself and landed him a kick on the shin with my wooden clog. [The dwarf] roared, not from pain but from wounded dignity. (Ibid.: 137)

Levi alludes here to a tradition that has taught him not to strike back. He says that such a thing is "beyond my reach" (ibid.: 136). It was apparently particularly important to Levi to emphasize this because Jean Améry had once accused him of being a "forgiver" (ibid.: 137). Following Bourdieu's arguments (2001a), Améry's accusation could be a veiled reference to a lack of manliness on Levi's part.[43] Levi's response – that hitting back was not part of the tradition he had inherited from his forebears – could be explained as follows by Bourdieu:

> The construction of the traditional Jewish habitus in central Europe [. . .] can be seen as a kind of *perfect inversion* of the process of construction of the male habitus [. . .]: the explicit refusal of the cult of violence, even in its most ritualized forms, such as duelling or sport, led to a devaluing of physical exercises,[44] especially the most violent ones, in favor of intellectual and spiritual exercises, favoring the development of gentle, "peaceful" dispositions [. . .]. (Bourdieu 2001a: 51, footnote 81; emphasis in original)

In the chapter "The Drowned and the Saved" from *Survival in Auschwitz* (Levi 1995), Levi devotes four pages to the "dwarf," whom he depicts as an "atavism [. . .] better adapted to [. . .] primordial conditions" (ibid.: 97). What does Levi mean by "primordial conditions"? If we read his passage through the lens of Bourdieu, we might surmise that Levi is describing an emblematic man: bursting with strength, "physically indestructible" (ibid.), challenging, upright, and always in the public eye – one of the prisoners with power in Auschwitz.

> He was a dwarf, not more than five feet high, but I have never seen muscles like his. [. . .] A sense of bestial vigor emanates from his body. [. . .] Nothing seems impossible to him. [. . .] he can spit incredible distances [. . .]. I saw him fight a Pole a whole head taller than him and knock him down with a blow of his cranium into the stomach [. . .] I never saw him rest, I never saw him quiet or still [. . .]. Of his life as a free man, no one knows anything; [. . .] he usually says [. . .] that he has begot seventeen children – which is not unlikely. He talks continuously on the most varied of subjects; always in a resounding voice, in an oratorical manner, with the violent mimicry of the deranged [. . .] and as is natural, he never lacks a public. (Ibid.: 95–6)

Levi leaves no doubt that this dwarf was demented, though he also possessed a certain shrewdness which, combined with his strength, was the basis for his powerful position in the camp. "His help was requested directly by the *Meister* only for such work as required skill and special vigor. Apart from these services he insolently and violently supervised our daily, flat exhaustion [. . .]" (ibid.: 97). As to whether he was "a madman," "an atavism," or simply "a product of the camp itself" (ibid.: 97), Levi suspects that all three things applied:

> There is some truth in all three suppositions. [. . .] If [the dwarf] regains his liberty he will be confined to the fringes of human society [. . .]. In the Lager [he] prospers and is triumphant. [...He is] respected by both leaders and comrades. [. . . A]s far as we could judge from outside, and as far as the phrase can have meaning, [he] was probably a happy person. (Ibid.: 97–8)

The words that Levi uses to describe this "dwarf" unmistakably express a certain – distanced – admiration. Though he himself felt bound to a different tradition,[45] Levi was familiar with the commonly accepted values and therefore respected this man in his "atavism." All of the criteria mentioned here can be found in Bourdieu's exploration of masculine domination (Bourdieu 1997a, 2001a): physical strength, the ability to "spit incredible distances,"[46] his predominance over other men, a nearly legendary virility, his upright and self-confident attitude toward the public, and so on.

In normal life outside the camp, these masculine attributes alone would not have been enough for this "dwarf" to be accorded respect, but the "primordial conditions of camp life" (Levi 1995: 97) offered a unique opportunity for someone who would otherwise be disdained to lay claim to his rights as a man. He is therefore also an example of the possibility of social advancement that was available to some inmates in the camps, even leading some of them to look back on Auschwitz as a "great time" (Langbein 2004: 491). This type of advancement required the kind of "secondary adjustment" described by Goffman as "conversion" (Goffman 1961: 63f.), which prompted prisoners to copy their SS overseers and strive to perfectly carry out their orders.

Bourdieu writes that "the social world treats the body like a mnemonic device" (Bourdieu 1997a: 167). In the society of the camp, where the prisoners had been stripped of all other universally recognizable social characteristics, the body was the sole remaining mnemonic device. It is especially clear here that "the genders, far from being simple 'roles' that can be played at will [. . .] are inscribed in bodies and in a universe from which they derive their strength" (Bourdieu 2001a: 103). This is the only way to explain why, in the passages cited above – which were written by intellectuals who felt called upon to ponder the weighty problems of life – "hitting back" or nightly ejaculations were considered such significant topics. Bourdieu insists that "the paradoxical logic of masculine domination [. . .], which can, without contradiction, be described as both spontaneous and extorted, cannot be understood until one takes account of the durable effects that the social order exerts" on people (Bourdieu 2001a: 37–8).

The inmates' efforts to defend their male honor under any circumstances, which seem absurd when viewed from the outside, are described by Bourdieu as the "negative side" and "trap" of male privilege (cf. Bourdieu 2001a: 50). The inescapable duty to always appear to be a real man – to oneself and others – shows just how much "the dominant is also dominated, but by his own domination" (Bourdieu 1997a: 189). It is important to note, however, that "to bring to light the effects that masculine domination exerts on the habitus of men does not mean, as some would like to think, trying to exculpate men" (Bourdieu 2001a: 114, footnote 2).

> The social world [. . .] carries out a coup against each of its subjects in that it imprints their bodies with what amounts to a program for perception, appreciation and action [. . .]. In its gendered and gendering dimension, as well as all other dimensions, this program acts like a (second, cultivated) nature, that is, with the commanding and (apparently) blind force of the (socially constituted) impulse [. . .]. (Bourdieu 1997a: 168)

In the following, a few relevant examples will be used to illustrate how this mechanism of the social world affects each of its subjects and can therefore be found in a special form even among female concentration camp prisoners. Despite initial impressions to the contrary, the Nazi concentration camps were a social world in which the "basic concepts" of gender continued to apply. We have already seen evidence of this in the preceding exploration of masculinity in the gender-segregated environment of the camps. It is apparent that "the question of honor and shame" (Bourdieu 2001a: 6) analyzed by Bourdieu in connection with masculine domination is an aspect of a hierarchical gender order which must be considered a "basic concept" of society.

The memoirs written by *women* formerly imprisoned in Nazi concentration camps often emphasize a different aspect of honor, namely, shame as a helpless response to injured honor.[47] These accounts revolve around both physical and social aspects of femininity, which the authors always depict as being linked to one another and which will be examined in more detail in the following.

Many female former prisoners describe the process of undressing, being totally shaved, and then dressing again for entry into the camp as an especially humiliating experience. While it seemed that "the world there was naked, that is, natural" (Apostoł-Staniszewska 1987: 225) because the people in the camps were reduced solely to themselves, with no recourse to the achievements of civilization, the example of physical nudity shows the extent to which civilization infiltrates the body and how "the social world treats the body like a mnemonic device" (Bourdieu 1997a: 167). Nudity did not just leave the body completely defenseless, it also represented a kind of "social nakedness." It was therefore very important to the women to cover themselves:

We wanted to cover our nakedness, and unlike Eve in the Garden of Eden, we had to include our nude heads. The going rate for a ragged kerchief soon rose to a day's ration of bread. My family was spared the cost: [. . .] I ripped a band from the hem of my dress. [. . .] We women were a strange sex, I decided: we sustain our sanity with mere trifles. Even in hell. Yes, even in hell. (Isaacson 1991: 77)

Libusé Nachtmanová describes her confusion and subsequent shock when she arrived in Ravensbrück and realized that – contrary to her first impression – she was actually in a camp for women; she had naturally assumed the emaciated, bald figures in the camp were men or boys. When she was shaved and she and the other naked women had been assessed by the SS, "they were more ashamed of their lack of hair than of their nakedness" (in Walz 2005b: 149; see also Walz 2005a: 13':53"ff.). In a video interview, she uses gestures to vividly demonstrate how the naked women, who would normally have covered their breasts and genitals with their hands, instead tried to hide their freshly shaven heads under their hands because, for them, there was no greater nudity than a bare head (see also Walz 2005a: 14':49"ff.).

Other women also report that the loss of their hair was the worst part of the camp admission process for them, as this was when they first became aware that the aim was to dehumanize them. Ruth Glasberg Gold, for example, describes how she felt when she saw her bald head:

I watched in dismay as my lovely hair cascaded to the dirt floor, leaving me with a feeling of nakedness and shame. It was not only the vanished dream of looking pretty and feminine that hit me, but the fact that I no longer looked like a girl. I was robbed of my identity and humiliated. My only consolation was that even bigger girls had to suffer the same indignity, and whether man or woman, once our heads were shaved, we all looked alike in a strange, grotesque way. (Gold 2009: 69–70)

It was somewhat comforting to this girl that others were going through the same thing she was. But Annette Eekmann, a Belgian woman from the communist resistance movement, intuitively sensed that when she was stripped of her clothing and hair upon her arrival at the Ravensbrück concentration camp for women, she was also being stripped of her identity: "It was also a very unpleasant experience, and it made us feel somewhat less like individual people. We were a big group, all completely naked, all the same – and you realize: now we're like sheep" (Annette Eekmann in Walz 2005a: 13':15"ff.).

Margit Schultz, a Hungarian teacher of the Jewish faith, describes her deportation to Auschwitz in an interview. She was imprisoned in section B III in Birkenau, a part of the camp known in the prisoner jargon as "Mexico." The inmates there were not given special uniforms but were instead forced to clothe themselves in ill-fitting civilian rags. Because the clothing was inadequate, many of the inmates wrapped themselves in colorful blankets taken from the property store called "Canada." From a distance, the prisoners' multicolored blankets looked like Mexican ponchos, hence the nickname of this section of the camp (cf. Walter in Benz et al. 2007: 118). Schultz suffered acutely from the lack of privacy there and found it "terrible that everything had to be out in the open. There was no toilet, for example. There were these wooden crates outside next to each hut, and you had to sit on those" (Margit Schultz in Schmidt 2003: 80). She tells of a particularly humiliating episode relating to nudity and clothing in Auschwitz:

> Every three weeks, we were led to a washroom where there was a shower. First we had to take off our dresses, and we were told that they were going to be disinfected. We spent three minutes or so under the shower, and one after the other we went out on the other side; suddenly there were three hundred of us. We came out and everyone was given a dress again. I put the dress on. I still remember that it was white, made of thin silk, white with black dots, and it was pleated [. . .]. It had once been very elegant, I thought, in private life. And probably because it couldn't withstand the disinfection, it was just a shred of fabric. I put it on, my chest was exposed and I was totally naked in the dress. I turned around, and because everything had to be "fast, fast, fast," they were hitting us and yelling "fast," I said: "Look, I'm completely naked in this dress." An SS man was standing there, and he hit me in the chest so hard, he had such a big hand and his fingers cut into me when he hit my chest. Because I was naked, blood spurted out everywhere. Then I fell and I had to give back the rags, so I was totally naked. I marched back to the room with the group, and on the seventh day – it was a Saturday afternoon after roll call – a friend came to me and brought me a brown dress that she had taken off a dead woman. [. . .] Never in my life had I been so happy about a gift like that dress. It was horrible, at first I was scared to death that someone would see me naked, because the first sign of someone going crazy was that they undressed. A human being is an animal, only reason sets us apart; the body is an animal. I was happy with the dress. It was a bit big, long. I was glad that the brown dress covered my feet a bit at night. It must have belonged to a very old woman because it was so long and wide, and I was so happy with the dress. Could you ever forget something like that? (Ibid.: 82–3)

This passage from an interview shows that clothing was not just protection against nudity; it represented much more. Even "Eve in the Garden of Eden" (Isaacson 1991: 77) covered up her nudity, so a naked human being represents all that is not human – "the body is an animal" (see above). Among those who were clothed, voluntary nudity was a sign of being "crazy" and no longer the same as the others: "[T]he first sign of someone going crazy was that they undressed" (see above). Unlike in a normal society, however, a diagnosis of insanity was fatal in Auschwitz because "crazy" prisoners were selected and gassed. As the only naked person among the clothed, Schultz clearly stood apart from the other prisoners, so she was "scared to death."

But even in Auschwitz, a dress was not just a dress; it said something about the person who wore or had worn it. The tattered dress allocated to Schultz "had once been very elegant" and was a symbol of the violent destruction of a distinguished way of life. The long, wide, brown dress given to her by a friend who had taken it from a dead woman ultimately seemed like a mandate for her to go on living and at least save her own skin. By means of her clothing, the old woman to whom the dress had probably belonged literally saved Schultz's life.

The autobiographical accounts of men also include comments on nudity and shaving. However, these usually appear in different contexts than those of the women. While a shaved head was apparently not a real problem for men because they were still unquestionably men, the women associated baldness with being robbed of their femininity. And while physical nudity triggered feelings of defenselessness and of being "helpless prey" (Levi 1989: 113) among the men, the women in Nazi concentration camps were always subject to evaluation by men (cf. Amesberger et al. 2004). The feeling of being "helpless prey" also always had a sexualized dimension for the women, as we saw from these quotes in chapter 5.1: "It was awful for us young girls. We stood there [naked in the showers], and the men came in and watched us" (Emilie Neu in Walz 2005b: 115); "[Two Gestapo men] hit the breasts of the young girls with a cane and kicked the older women in the buttocks [. . .]" (Urzula Wińska in Walz 2005a: 15′:38″ff.).

It was not only their ability to work that was being assessed during a selection, it was their femininity as well. Men report that when they passed by the assessing physician during a selection, they used all their energy to contract their muscles in order to look masculine and energetic (cf., e.g., Levi 1995: 128). Women also write that they tried to file past with an upright posture and their heads held high because they knew that this made for a better, more lively impression. However, many women also describe efforts to make themselves appear more feminine by pinching and rubbing their cheeks to make them look flushed, tracing their eyebrows with coal, and even darkening their greying hair (cf., e.g., Apel 2005: 59). In an account by Liana Millu,[48] we find the following:

> "Selection, it's a selection!" cried the skeletal Elenka, and she straightened her kerchief and briskly rubbed her face to bring some color to her ashy cheeks. The women were frantically pulling themselves together, helping each other appear as alert and robust as possible. [. . .]; eyes brightened; cheeks turned rosy with violent pinching. "Lili, fix yourself up a little," called Elenka. (Millu 1991: 45)

Selections in the concentration camps were undoubtedly a matter of life and death. But something else is expressed in the behavior of the women mentioned above, something that is constitutive of femininity in a male-dominated society:

> Masculine domination, which constitutes women as symbolic objects whose being (*esse*) is a being-perceived (*percipi*), has the effect of keeping them in a permanent state of bodily insecurity, or more precisely of symbolic dependence. They exist first through and for the gaze of others, that is, as welcoming, attractive and available *objects*. [. . .] As a consequence, dependence on others (and not only men) tends to become constitutive of their being. (Bourdieu 2001a: 66; emphasis in original)

This description of self-perception as the anticipated perception of others is found over and over again in the memoirs of women. Two closely related aspects are important here: cleanliness and a neat and tidy appearance. Cleanliness and hygiene were very significant to all prisoners in the Nazi concentration camps because they heavily influenced the inmates' susceptibility to illness. This is the aspect that male former prisoners focus on when they mention the indescribable filth and lack of opportunities for personal hygiene in the camps. The filth does not seem to have impaired their self-image as men; it may have sometimes affected their notion of themselves as intellectuals who were not used to doing dirty work, but it did not detract from their manliness.

For women, by contrast, physical cleanliness was apparently associated with a figurative notion of purity: "We didn't wash ourselves in Auschwitz, and we suffered a lot from this as women. Periods weren't an issue, but we were women, after all, and we missed it – we were women back home and we were used to hygiene" (Margit Schultz in Schmidt 2003: 94). In memoirs by women, there are very frequent references to menstruation or the lack thereof in the camps. But while the passages about virility and libido found in the memoirs of men always entail an aspect of reassuring oneself of one's own masculinity, the memoirs of women mention the lack of menstruation in the camps with a certain sense of relief. Opinions differed as to why menstruation stopped in the camps, and though the reasons are still not entirely clear today, both of the suggested theories are plausible: Many women stopped menstruating because they were malnourished, but there were also suspicions that the SS had ordered something to be added to their food which would stop their menstruation (bromine is often mentioned in connection with this). Although the women sometimes expressed concern that they might be infertile for life, their relief at not having to deal with menstruation under the terrible hygienic conditions was greater: "There were no sanitary towels or cotton wool, and cotton napkins or folded cloth didn't absorb very well and were difficult to wash" (Bondy[49] 2003: 125). Katharina

Katzenmaier, who was imprisoned in Ravensbrück at the age of twenty-five, reports: "When someone had their period, there was no help for it and no protection – nothing, it all flowed out, just like that, everywhere. And then you were mocked for not being clean!" (Walz 2005a: 55':00''ff.). Désiré Haffner describes her impressions of the women's camp at Auschwitz as follows:

> Their skeletal appearance, their shaved skulls, their blood-streaked bodies, their scaly skin – all this made it hard for an observer to recognize them as women. The lack of any hygiene was even more perceptible among them than in the men's camp because of the pungent odor that came from their blocks, the smell of thousands of women who had not been able to wash for months. (Désiré Haffner quoted in Langbein 2004: 90)

Even though Haffner does not state it directly, it is clear what she means: menstruating women smell. Although all prisoners in the Nazi concentration camps – with the exception of a few prisoner functionaries – suffered equally under the catastrophic hygienic conditions, and although the lack of water and resources for coping with the widespread diarrheal diseases was a terrible problem for everyone, menstruation was an additional strain on the women. The fact that even men address this "women's issue" is, I believe, a sign that it was not solely a matter of literal uncleanliness. For example, Tadeusz Borowski, who spent some time laying roofs in the women's camp, makes the following comment about the inmates in this section of the camp: "The women greedily gulped down the soup which nobody in our blocks would even think of touching. They stank of sweat and female blood" (Borowski 1992: 92). It is not the reference to the filth and the smell that is noteworthy here, but rather the fact that women and men alike emphasize the "otherness" of women; women turn the male gaze upon themselves, and a sense of metaphorical impurity comes into play, of which menstruation is a visible sign. In light of this, it is understandable that women in the camps would express more relief than concern about the cessation of menstruation.

Combatting the filth that was actually harmful to their health was an important concern for every concentration camp prisoner. For many women, this additionally entailed maintaining a certain degree of grooming – to the extent that this was possible in the extremely restrictive conditions in the camps. They were aided in this by the skills that most of them had acquired in the course of being raised to be "capable housewives," an upbringing that had taught them to make use of everything available to them. Those who were clearly from a "background of means" and had never had to cope with the demands of running a household were either derided or pitied by the other prisoners; they attracted attention, and it did not surprise their fellow inmates that the deterioration of their physical appearance was particularly swift (cf., e.g., Tillion 1975: 36). The desire for neatness and tidiness was expressed in a wide range of activities. Ruth Bondy summarizes her impressions of the section of Auschwitz-Birkenau known as the "Theresienstadt family camp" as follows:

> Just one day after arrival, there was a marked difference between the sexes here in Birkenau: The men, in their brimless caps and random assortment of trousers and coats – too short, too long, too wide, too narrow – looked like sad black storks. But in the space of just twenty-four hours, the women had managed to alter their equally random clothing to fit their body measurements and to repair damaged spots; they used splinters of wood as sewing needles, and they pulled threads from a blanket they had been given. Some women learned how to iron with bricks heated in the stove. (Bondy 2003: 137)

Charlotte Delbo writes: "Although their distress was just as great, the women still had some resources, those always possessed by women. They could do the wash, mend the only shirt, now in tatters [. . .]" (Delbo 1995: 118). There are frequent remarks in accounts from the camps that some women used their meager rations of margarine as face cream and felt better and more well groomed because of it. Liana Millu writes: "[T]he same women [. . .] never neglected to dab their faces with leftover margarine [. . .]" (Millu 1991: 194). Other women rejected such cosmetic practices for rational reasons: "We didn't use the margarine as skin cream, like some did, we ate all of it instead – though sometimes with disgust – because we wanted to maintain our physical condition" (Kertesz[50] 2003: 166). These references to the cosmetic efforts of some imprisoned women give no indication of how widespread such practices actually were. However, they do reveal that this issue was relevant to women to a certain degree – even in the concentration camps, where the primary focus was mere survival. This "women's issue" is addressed by men, too, such as former Auschwitz prisoner Jan Wolny, who describes the final stage of physical deterioration in the camps:

> I noticed that there were certain differences in the behavior of men and women in the *Muselmann*[51] phase. Women spoke faster and louder, they made noise and were hysterical. They gossiped at length and maliciously about their comrades and acquaintances. They acted more aggressively toward each other than men. Despite their *Muselmann* state, they strove to make themselves attractive to the men they encountered – they straightened their clothing, tidied their hair and forced themselves to smile despite all of their misery. Prior to the doctor's rounds, they smoothed the blankets and lay down primly. (Jan Wolny in Ryn and Kłodziński 1987: 139)

It is not necessary to determine conclusively whether this description reflects a man's fundamental view of women or whether this phenomenon actually occasionally existed; either case, each in its own way, would indicate that entrenched concepts of femininity still held sway in the camps despite the fact that the external circumstances seemed to massively counteract them.

To illustrate the full complexity of this effect, I would like to mention an occasion described by Charlotte Delbo,[52] the organization of a Christmas celebration in the women's camp in Auschwitz:

> We meant to celebrate a traditional Christmas. A Polish Christmas, since there was a larger contingent of Polish women. The Russians, also numerous, were not invited. [. . .]
>
> At the end of the day, each one of us, perched on her cot, busied herself with presents, sewing, drawing, embroidering, knitting. The tiniest tatter, or bit of wool, was obtained by infinitely complex maneuvers. During that time, throughout the final evenings, the cooks, who had much planning to do, set up their pots on the laboratory stove,[53] so as merely to warm the courses on the great day just before the meal. It was so cold that conservation was assured. Wanda was taking care of the tree. [. . .]
>
> Finally, Christmas Eve came. We were through working at four. [. . .] We had little time for primping or ironing a dress when our turn came. Since there was only one iron, we had to wait while it was warmed on the stove (where could that iron have come from?), meanwhile combing our hair. A few experts devoted their efforts to setting hair. [. . .] We enjoyed the new growth of our hair which, however, did not enable the volunteer hairdressers to set large curls. Some of us slipped on silk stockings of mysterious provenance. [. . .] We put on white collars cut out of shirt bottoms to wear on our striped dresses. Dark-haired girls crinkled paper, making flowers to affix to their hair. We got vaseline from the infirmary to smear on our eyelids. In the dormitory everyone was getting edgy, as if waiting for a ball to begin. "Are you through with the needle? – Who can lend me a hair brush? – Did anyone see my belt? – Hurry up and pass the iron here, we haven't had it yet." [. . .]
>
> We could hardly recognize one another, hair coiffed, faces made up. The lab chemists had made cheek and lip rouge, as well as powder, but they produced a single shade, so that, seeing all these faces painted the same color, the same way, was strangely disturbing. The sameness of our striped dresses became even more apparent. Suddenly we were filled with the feeling that all our efforts had been made in vain, that our preparations, excitement, and expectation of a real Christmas Eve feast had been to no avail. We had dressed up with great care, as though to welcome guests, guests who were not forthcoming. We were still among ourselves, with faces that were not ours. A moment of sadness broken by somewhat strained bursts of laughter. [. . .]
>
> The cooks made their way between the groups, filling the plates – lab glassware. It would have been unseemly to serve a Christmas meal in our tin cups. [. . .]

The women kissed one another. They never stopped kissing and exchanging hosts and good wishes. Each had ninety-four accolades to give and to receive. As to us – the Frenchwomen – we were a bit ill at ease, because Polish women kissed each other on the mouth, as Slavs do. [. . .]

The meal was drawing to a close. Someone switched off the lights. [. . .] One by one, the candles were lit. The fir tree emerged from the shadows surrounded by a ghostly halo. And the chorus of Polish women raised their voices in song. [. . .]

The chorus grew silent. Lights were switched back on. Each one was joining in the merriment dictated by the feast day. The chorus was congratulated. Indeed, they had performed beautifully. Then, a lot of paper was ripped to uncover a cake of soap, a rag doll, a handmade lace bow, a woven rope belt, a colorfully bound memorandum book [. . .]. (Delbo 1995: 162–6)

What is Delbo telling us? First, it must be clear that the women mentioned here were not Jews but political prisoners who – when measured against the prisoners in other categories – enjoyed certain privileges, even in Auschwitz. For example, they were occasionally permitted to receive packages, and even though these packages were routinely plundered by the SS and Kapos, the prisoners still sometimes had goods to exchange or ingredients they could use for a Christmas dinner. Working in a laboratory was an additional privilege, one which also depended in part on their prisoner category since Jews and "Gypsies" were not assigned to work details like this. It is also important to note that the women comprised a mixed group of French and Polish nationals who clearly had a strained relationship with the Russians, who were not invited to take part in the festivities.

The description of the preparations for this special Christmas feast do not differ much from those of an entirely normal Polish Christmas celebration, apart from the adjustments and arrangements made to suit the situation in the concentration camp. During the preparations, the women took on traditionally female duties: planning and organizing the celebration, drawing up a menu, acquiring and cooking the food, decorating the room, making gifts using traditionally female techniques (sewing, embroidering, knitting, plaiting), and so on. "Infinitely complex maneuvers" were also necessary here.

According to Bourdieu, such maneuvers are a strategy of the "dominated," who "always see more than they themselves are seen" (Bourdieu 1997a: 163, footnote 13). The resulting "clear-sightedness," which is usually referred to in women as "feminine wiles" or – more positively formulated – "feminine intuition" (ibid.: 163), is a function of the "dominated" adopting the viewpoint of the "dominant" and turning this gaze upon themselves. Bourdieu also refers to this as "the weapons of the weak" (Bourdieu 2001a: 59). I therefore think it is no coincidence that female prisoners, like former Auschwitz inmate Jadwiga Apostoł-Staniszewska, make comments like the following: "The camp demanded an improvised approach from us based more on feeling and intuition than on rational premises" (Jadwiga Apostoł-Staniszewska in Jagoda et al. 1987a: 17).

Regardless of their national, regional, or cultural background or their specific social background, it seems to have been a boon in the concentration camps for women – traditionally the "weaker" sex in a male-dominated society – to have had recourse to the strategies of the "dominated" so that they could make the "infinitely complex maneuvers" necessary to find solutions to apparently impossible problems. This is presumably what Judith Magyar Isaacson means when she explains that even in this hell, women saved themselves from insanity with "trifles" (Isaacson 1991: 77; see above), or what Ruth Bondy means when she remarks that after just one day in the "Theresienstadt family camp," there were obvious differences between the men and the women (Bondy 2003: 137; see above). Charlotte Delbo herself formulates it most precisely in the sense intended by Bourdieu when she stresses that even in these dire circumstances, women had resources – namely, the ones they always possess (cf. Delbo 1995: 118; see above). Whether these advantages actually objectively existed is open to speculation. In the context of this work, however, it is important to note that even in the concentration camps, there was a widespread assumption that women had special – namely, "feminine" – strategies which were different from those of the men and which could benefit them in the camps. In extreme terms, one could say that the traditional female habitus, which is usually interpreted as "female weakness" in a "normal" society, was able to mutate, in the perception of this prisoner society, into a unique strength because the women clearly already had access to the strategies of the "dominated."[54]

The passage from Charlotte Delbo expresses something else as well: By putting such effort into tidying themselves up, the women were continuing a tradition of festively decorating not just the Christmas party itself but also themselves. There is another effect at work here, the one Bourdieu is referring to when he says that women exist in a state of continually being perceived. "They exist first through and for the gaze of others" (Bourdieu 2001a: 66). They anticipated the gaze that men would turn on them and strove to meet these expectations as best they could under the circumstances. These efforts were rewarding because they enabled the women to demonstrate an aspect of normality to themselves and each other. Although they were imprisoned in a concentration camp under dire conditions, and although they came from very different countries and cultures, they were still "normal women." Being a woman was a binding, universally conveyable element within this barracks community, and though the French women were uncomfortable with the Polish convention of kissing on the mouth "as Slavs do" (Delbo 1995: 165), the commonalities between the women were stronger than the differences. Another noteworthy aspect of Delbo's remark about kissing is that, in the original French, there is no accusative object here: "[. . .] *les Polonaises embrassaient sur la bouche, à la slave*" ("... the Polish women kissed on the mouth, as Slavs do") (Delbo 1970: 82). This hints that the unease was apparently so great that Delbo could not bring herself to write "they kissed *us* on the mouth" – and this single missing word makes the discomfort almost palpable. Something "very feminine" is expressed here as well, but it is only universal in the sense that it expresses a general rejection of same-sex sexuality. The fact that kissing on the mouth "as Slavs do" had no sexual connotations for the Polish women was a cultural difference which the French women tried to overlook for the benefit of the celebration they wanted to enjoy together.

There is a trace of something else in this passage, too: The desire for normality was evidently also a desire for "feminine beauty" among these women, but it was additionally a desire for individuality. The women had made themselves up because that was what you did for a normal Christmas party. In doing so, they emphasized their femininity, but they suddenly looked even more similar to each other than they had before because the shared makeup had turned their faces into masks in a way – their faces were not their own, as Delbo puts it. This concept of individuality is shaped by the notion that while the body is the medium of individuality to a certain extent, individuality must be expressed through added personal trappings. Therefore, a completely naked person does not appear to be an individual ("the body is an animal," as Margit Schultz says, or "all completely naked, all the same – [. . .] like sheep," according to Annette Eekmann; see above), but neither does a person who is all made up if there are others who look too much like her. Individuality is apparently expressed by navigating a very fine line between similarities and differences with the help of a few culturally based tools. In this account, Charlotte Delbo uses linguistic, literary tools to depict the amalgamation of physical and psychological aspects of social life in a striking, concrete way.

The number of situations in which femininity played a special role in the concentration camps is almost endless. Topics frequently mentioned in the literature include secret love affairs with male prisoners (see Delbo 1995; Millu 1991), sexual services provided in exchange for life-saving measures such as additional food or a safer work detail (see Birger 1992; Millu 1991), forced brothel work and sexualized violence by the SS and Kapos, and homosexual relationships among female prisoners (see, above all, Amesberger et al. 2004). The special "female networks" of the so-called "camp families" and their importance to the psychological stability of their members are also mentioned often, though it is a matter of scholarly debate as to whether these were specifically "female" forms of networks or whether the perception of what both women and men did in the camps – namely, banding together in small groups of friends who looked out for each other – differed depending on whether it was women or men doing it (cf. essays in Bock 2005). In the memoirs of men, such forms of sociality tend to be referred to as "resistance" or "the underground" (cf. ibid.: 13) and they thus acquire a political tinge because they are contextualized differently. If we view small networks like these as a "female" peculiarity, we also overlook their exclusive character and obscure the fact that belonging to a small group of women who looked after each other simultaneously entailed excluding other women. Magdalena Sacha has researched these exclusion processes among Polish Catholic and Polish Jewish women in the Hasag-Leipzig satellite camp (Sacha 2002) and found that, despite their common language and national background, the Catholic and Jewish women were very aware of and meticulously cultivated a sense of differentiation, that there were very few opportunities for contact between the two groups in the camp, and that each group accused the other of unfair patronage.[55]

An issue of much greater consequence to female prisoners was how to care for the small *children* who usually stayed with their mothers – if they were admitted to the camp at all instead of being selected immediately upon arrival. If the mothers fell ill or died, other women often adopted the children, so to speak, and became "camp mothers" (cf. Klüger 2001; Walz 2005a, 2005b). Relationships like this also formed with adolescents who had passed themselves off as being older in order not to be selected and subsequently had to cope with camp life entirely on their own (cf. ibid.). When small children were selected, their mothers often chose to die with them instead of being parted from them (see, e.g., Bondy 2003). However, in his nightmarish story "This Way for the Gas, Ladies and Gentlemen," Tadeusz Borowksi describes the exact opposite, namely, that a mother abandoned her child during a selection so that she would not be sent to her death as well (Borowski 1992: 43). There is no question that women in the camps – just like women in normal life – were considered to have a "natural" connection with (their) children, unlike fathers, who were only able to remain with their children if these children were adolescent boys (see, e.g., Frister 2001). Even in the concentration camps, therefore, the fate of women was closely intertwined with that of their children, and strong bonds formed on a micro-social level within the prisoner society when women took responsibility for children who were not their own (see, e.g., Klüger 2001). Many former prisoners remark in their memoirs that the women's practical concerns for their family members were a distraction from their own misery (e.g., Millu 1991; Vogel 2002).

It was especially problematic when women gave birth in the camp. During selections on the ramp, women who were visibly pregnant were either forced to have an abortion or sent directly to the gas chambers. If the pregnancy was first discovered inside the camp, the women were permitted to give birth, though generally under completely inadequate conditions;[56] no additional resources or baby foods were available, however, so newborns would die after just a few days or even hours (cf.

Elias 1999; Millu 1991; Walz 2005a, 2005b). But the pregnancy of a woman within the prisoner society was sometimes also viewed as a sign of female potency; giving life to another human being gave women the confidence and hope that they might survive the camp themselves (cf. Millu 1991; for a theoretical analysis of this, see also O'Brien 1983). Even "Gypsies" occasionally earned the sympathy that was withheld from them in other contexts because they usually had several children with them and they were unable to adequately care for them in the camp (see, e.g., Langbein 2004; Zywulska 2004). In these cases, the "maternal" impulse seems to have outweighed the unease otherwise felt toward these "savage" and seemingly alien women (see also section 6.1).

In addition to the aspects already mentioned – female sexuality, birth, and child-rearing – which would generally be considered "women's issues" in any other context as well because they are supposedly based on biological differences, I would like to look at one other aspect that seems to have played a different role for men and women in the camps, although it is not tied to any biological factors or their social after-effects: namely, *cooking*.

Because all concentration camp prisoners were drastically under-nourished, food was a matter of constant concern to them. They had to expend a great deal of their energy making sure they got their fair share when food was handed out, using every means available to them to acquire additional amounts and rationing what they received to ensure a relatively continual supply. As mentioned earlier, women were often additionally burdened with the practical care of their family members, something they viewed as their intrinsic responsibility and a duty they attempted to fulfill as long as they possibly could. To this end, they would embark on tortuous routes to make secret contacts and set complicated transactions in motion when necessary (see, e.g., Millu 1991). Hunger and food were therefore permanent topics of conversation among all concentration camp prisoners. Nonetheless, there tended to be differences in how these topics were approached by men and women. In the following, I would like to briefly outline these differences to show the variations in the social aspects of the same object of consideration (hunger and fantasies of food).

The prisoners' minds circled endlessly around thoughts of the freedom that they hoped for, eagerly anticipated and discussed in countless private conversations. These thoughts and discussions revolved around a future life which they described in dazzling detail, a life which naturally included bountiful meals prepared with good ingredients following traditional recipes. Almost all of the memoirs by women mention the nearly manic exchange of recipes,[57] during which the inmates discussed – and sometimes argued about – the tiniest details of ingredients and preparations. The prisoners talked about the meals that they themselves would someday plan and prepare for their families – and maybe their friends (see, e.g., Klüger 2001; Walz 2005a, 2005b). These conversations focused on meals, but through them the women were also reconstructing their former everyday lives, in which they were providers for their families, and reaffirming their *continuity as social beings*, at least on a communicative level. Maria Montuoro[58] wrote a story focusing on this:

> [You] could [. . .] always overhear comments like this: "Will you invite me to lunch?" "Gladly." "What will you make?" "How about this: chicken in aspic . . ." ". . . and how will you prepare it?" Then there would be a discussion about the preparation. The way things were made generated the most interest.
>
> And between the workplaces, under the glow of the lamps or in the cold light of day, on the paths between the gloomy huts and up and down the bunk beds there flowed endless rivers of sauces, mountains of butter appeared, piles of cheese, sugar, jam, all surrounded by a fully equipped kitchen. Never before had there been such excessive extravagance in a household. If you listened closely, the conversations merged into a bizarre symphony. "Take a pan, grease it, fill the cannelloni . . . slow-cooked pieces of liver . . . stir your mayonnaise well . . . a layer of dough, a layer of jam, then soak it with rum ..." [. . .] It was basically just a game played by the imprisoned girls who told each other wonderful tales. Eating was no longer viewed as an act necessary to keep the organism alive. It had become a mental pursuit, an intellectual pleasure. (Montuoro 2003: 143–4)

It is apparently so self-evident to Montuoro that only "imprisoned girls" could play an intellectual game like this that she does not feel the need to mention it specifically. Another passage describes an argument about the purpose and risks of sabotage, during which a female prisoner defends her view that the risks are too great with the following words: "'... I want to live, do you understand?' she nearly shouted. 'I want to go home . . . I want . . . I want to cook, do you understand? [. . .]'" (ibid.: 153). This inmate's expression of desire to lead the normal life of a normal woman, which culminates with the desperate cry "I want to cook," conflicted with the realization that even if you did survive the imprisonment, nothing would ever be as it had been before. For this reason, the secretly written recipes are eventually burned in a decisive gesture in Montuoro's account:

> The lights were extinguished in the room. In the fading light, Maia saw how her friend pulled the recipe booklet from under her dress, looked at it for a moment and pressed it to her chest with her bony hand. She briefly stroked it with her fingers as if she were parting with a beloved living creature. Then she resolutely threw it in the stove. The flames licked the thin pages, which were densely filled with tiny handwriting. In a single moment, these flames destroyed appetizers, jams, soups, homemade desserts, candied fruits and

other dishes: an entire artificial paradise – a lonely oasis in a bleak desert – Suzanne's only treasure. (Ibid.: 155)

In this story, Montuoro focuses her readers' attention on a topic that many female concentration camp survivors addressed in a seemingly incidental way only after they had described the horrific details of their imprisonment. It is clear that something other than indescribable hunger was of significance here, something that was associated with the prisoners' former lives. A secret cookbook could do nothing to stave off the torment of actual starvation; in fact, the paper and pencil that were needed to write the book had probably been acquired in exchange for bread. But the "oasis in a bleak desert" – even if it was actually more of a mirage – was reached by holding on to one's "normal" calling as a housewife, mother, and cook.

Men in the concentration camps also dreamed of a normal home life, lavish meals, and hospitality extended to guests. The men, too, planned entire menus in anticipation of this. The difference is that, in their imagined feasts, it is usually their wives or mothers doing the cooking. For example, Robert Antelme describes the following scene which occurred while the prisoners carried loads of lumber from one place to another:

He bitches because he's taller and is carrying more; he thinks we should have lined ourselves up differently. He talks while he carries. Where he comes from, in the Auvergne, people eat well. In the morning he has bread, butter, and coffee. During the day he serves a lot of apéritifs. He eats well at noon too. He has a few drinks on his day off. He is married. His wife bakes cakes for him. And when he goes to his mother's he also eats well. In the Auvergne, people eat well. There's pork, there's cheese. [. . .] If they'd move their asses a little, it wasn't impossible the whole thing would be over by Christmas. We could be home by January. Yes, I'll eat well if I visit him. I'm invited. [. . .] Each of us will already be with somebody else in a little while. He'll explain how his mother makes custard [. . .]. We'll invite each other over to dinner [. . .]. (Antelme 1998: 42–3)

Elsewhere he writes: "Yes, I'd go to Nice when I got back; we'd eat a *pambania*.[59] [. . .] We'd have a drink first, a Cinzano, sitting there in front of the sea; then we'd eat the *pambania* – his mother makes a great one" (ibid.: 165).

These conversations about eating fulfilled a similar purpose to those among the women. The inmates' terrible hunger drew their attention to anything that had to do with edibles, but at the same time, these men were also reaffirming their social position – as men (and also as experts in good food) who could certainly invite and entertain guests, but who would naturally not be involved in preparing the food themselves because they knew that their wives or mothers would handle this (as usual).[60]

Though this is by no means an exhaustive examination of the importance of gender differentiation among the prisoners in Nazi concentration
camps, I believe these examples show that traditional notions of one's
own gender and that of others played a very influential role in the camps.
Male honor and female shame were under fierce attack in the concentration camps, and this was viewed as an attack on both the prisoners'
human dignity and their individuality. Members of the opposite sex
were usually not in each other's presence in the camps, but the prisoners' habitus led them to perceive the social gender division as a real force
which was particularly important to observe under the extreme conditions because it was a reaffirmation of normality. As Charlotte Delbo
writes in the passage quoted as the epigraph to this section: "They [the
men] experienced the sting of the decline of strength and manly duty
since they could do nothing for the women. If we suffered seeing them
unhappy, hungry, deprived, they did even more so, realizing their inability to protect and defend us, to assume their destiny on their own" (Delbo
1995: 117). This clearly expresses the *reciprocity* of the gender relationship.
In principle, everyone had to look out for themselves in the concentration camps and get by as best they could even though they usually had
no useful prior experiences to draw on. Nonetheless, they reconstructed
the *social* space to which they felt they belonged based on their gender:
Women suffered because they knew that men had been robbed of their
"male superiority"; men suffered because it was obvious to them that
they were unable to fulfill their genuine "manly duty" to protect women.
This mutual referencing of the opposite sex worked on a very impersonal level – men protect women, women suffer knowing the men are
defenseless – and it took place even when the respective opposite sex was
not actually present. Whether women were ultimately in greater need of
protection in the concentration camps than men remains an open question. The historical evidence shows that many women were able to skillfully adapt their strategies to the circumstances, but no judgment will be
passed here on whether they were fundamentally better at doing this than
men. Comments to this effect in the memoirs of former prisoners can be
explained, upon closer analysis, in terms of a prisoner's own social position as a man or a woman.

Men and women did similar things in the camps – such as cultivating friendships with small groups of fellow prisoners – but they used
different words to describe these activities: Men referred to this as the
"underground" or "resistance," while women spoke of "camp families"
or "camp sisters." There is also evidence that older male prisoners sometimes "adopted" younger boys, though they often ran the risk of being
suspected of pederasty by their fellow prisoners for doing so. Among
women, by contrast, such "adoptions" were accepted as instances of
"camp motherhood" and were looked on very favorably by fellow prisoners. So even though men and women behaved in very similar ways, they

themselves stressed the differences and strove to embed their actions in a "male" or "female" social context in order to emphasize that they were still "real" men or "real" women in the camps.

With respect to the question posed in the title of this section – *What's still normal here?* – I would summarize the answer as follows: The strict gender separation and general lack of children in these camp societies meant that life in the concentration camps was in no way normal for the inmates. Most prisoners suffered the effects of this "topsy-turvy world." However, this did nothing to change the fact that they continued to view themselves and each other as completely normal people – as men and women – who at least tried to do what was considered normal for "real" men and women to do. Or, as Paul Martin Neurath would put it: They adjusted their "rules of behavior" to the dramatically different living situation in the concentration camps in order to hold onto the "basic concepts" of society (cf. Neurath 2005: 261) – and these concepts undoubtedly involved reciprocal gender relations.

6.4 Summary: An examination of the structure of the prisoner society or: The significance of similarity and difference

The sixth chapter of this work has focused on the prisoner society in the Nazi concentration camps. My main purpose here has been to illustrate the reciprocal relationships between the different groups of agents within this involuntary community. Though life in the camps was incomparable to anything else in many respects, a closer inspection reveals a number of fundamental distinctions among the apparently undifferentiated mass of thousands upon thousands of prisoners.

The first distinction to mention here is the classification based on the reasons for an inmate's imprisonment, which led to *prisoner categories* indicated by colored triangles worn on the clothing. Although this form of order was violently imposed by the Nazis, the categories themselves were based on a long tradition of dealing with these different groups of people in different ways. The triangle classification made it *easier for the SS to manage* the prisoners, but the inmates themselves also had a *social understanding* of what the categories represented and drew their own conclusions about the nature of the people identified in this way. The categories drew on existing social stereotypes and the inmates' own prejudices, so they aggravated relations between the groups of prisoners and cemented the prisoner hierarchy conceived by the SS. But if inmates encountered each other as individuals in the camps and their expectations of each other were not met, their prejudices could be cast aside and they could view each other simply as exceptions to a rule whose fundamental validity did not need to be questioned. I have explained how the prisoners perceived themselves and each other using the examples of *Jews, "Gypsies,"* and *homosexuals*. In doing so, it emerged that the prisoner categories could be the cause of *fragmentation* and *dissociation processes* but also the basis for *attempts at community-building*. The desire for differentiation was strong among the prisoners, and it was bolstered by their concept of and need to be perceived as individuals with unique characteristics. Prisoners could individually distance themselves from their assigned categories to achieve this, but they could also identify and emphasize shared traits within their own category, accept and endorse these traits for themselves, and view them as the basis for mutual understanding, the formation of groups and exclusionary mechanisms. In addition to the official prisoner categories, shared *"pre-concentrationary" experiences* (Pingel 1978: 10) played an important role; these could be based on mutual worldviews or on local, regional, national, or cultural influences which could be expressed through shared social practices (see also chapter 5.3). The prisoner categories and their supplemental national or geographic codes were based largely on established "schemes of perception, appreciation and action" (Bourdieu 1984: 100) and therefore did not need to be fleshed out by the Nazis. Which of these characteristics was perceived as dominant depended on a variety of factors in different situations. However, being a Jew or "Gypsy" usually dominated the other characteristics in the concentration camps, so these classifications stood apart from the other prisoner categories as well as the national, regional, and cultural classifications.

Additionally, *prisoner elites* emerged in the concentration camps, groups which were primarily drawn – sometimes independent of a prisoner's categorization – from the prisoner functionaries, who, on account of their special position, not only enjoyed noticeably better living conditions, but also had *power and influence*. Among the prisoner functionaries there were many cases of what Goffman refers to as "colonization" (Goffman 1961: 64), in which the "total institution" becomes the sole point of reference, along with – in very extreme cases – "conversion" (ibid.: 63), whereby inmates strove for perfection in the eyes of the SS and were therefore particularly brutal toward their fellow prisoners. The regular *mass of prisoners* viewed these elites as a kind of aristocracy and treated them as such: with both the contempt of the excluded in the face of the noblesse of the privileged and the deference that seemed due to those in positions of power. Just like in normal life outside the camps, they felt it was very unfair for those who already had more than others to be given additional benefits as well. Through their close personal contact with the SS, these elite prisoners sometimes started to view their captors through different eyes and recognize human traits in them – while other regular prisoners saw them only as brutal torturers. This shift in perspective can be explained by Goffman's concept of "colonization." Regular prisoners therefore frequently suspected the prisoner functionaries of having been corrupted by the privileges of their position and of being in collusion with the SS. Sometimes even members of the SS would begin to take a more nuanced view of the prisoner functionaries, whom they encountered not en masse but instead as individuals with personal characteristics – and even assets. The proximity of the elite prisoners to the SS sharpened the distinction between the prisoners' positions and alienated the inmates in classes that were far removed from each other. The occasional personal contact between the prisoner functionaries and the respective representatives of the SS led to a *"divided" habitus* (Bourdieu 2007), by means of which conflicting tendencies could be integrated and incorporated without being perceived as a direct contradiction.

The prisoner society was therefore divided into a variety of fractions who cast an appraising eye over themselves and each other and who each laid claim to a particular position in the social space. A second, coarser distinction emerged on the basis of functions carried out in the prisoner self-administration system, and this split the prisoner society into two opposing classes: the privileged and the underprivileged. These social structures were present in both the men's and women's camps and camp sections, and they had a concrete influence on the daily life of the inmates. A third aspect which was extremely important to everyone involved was whether a prisoner was a *man* or a *woman*. Though the camps, or at least the separate sections of the camps, were generally gender-homogeneous, gender identity lost none of its relevance for the inmates. Gender classification was *fundamental* to the prisoners' self-image and the appraisal of their fellow inmates, and one of the most confusing aspects of the concentration camp experience was that it was often impossible to distinguish the men from the women at first glance. Extreme malnutrition frequently obliterated the physical indicators of masculinity and femininity, and the prisoners' ill-fitting clothing and shaved heads meant that there were no differences whatsoever in their outward appearance. The memoirs of former concentration camp prisoners clearly show that *emphasizing the social aspects of gender identity* therefore became all the more important to the inmates. These aspects included "the question of *honor*" among the men and "*shame*" among the women (Bourdieu 2001a: 6) as well as the *anticipation of the male gaze* (cf. ibid.: 66) among the female prisoners. Although members of the opposite sex were not usually in each other's company in the camps, the prisoners made continual reference to the other gender as a way of reaffirming their own "proper" social position and reconstructing this position despite the absence of their respective counterpart. These reconstructions exhibited the features of the "*dominant*," on the one hand, and the "*dominated*," on the other, because even in the reality of "normal" life, gender relations are a power relationship. It is not surprising to find Bourdieu's criteria for this in the literature of memory considering "the durable effects that the social order exerts" on people (ibid.: 38).

Part IV
Social Libido

7

The Constitution of Social Identity in the Concentration Camps

The Concepts of Individuality and the Importance of Social Structures in a "Topsy-Turvy World"

In conclusion, I would like to return to my initial considerations and reflect on the questions that were raised. Theoretically supported answers to these questions have emerged in the course of this work, and I intend to gauge these against the empirical findings. Where necessary, we will also hear again from former concentration camp prisoners whose own words corroborate the sociological answers I have found.

The starting point for the questions addressed here was the widely held view – in both scholarly literature and other literature about the Holocaust – that the prisoners in Nazi concentration camps did *not* constitute a society because they were forced to live together in unprecedentedly inhumane conditions and were thus in a situation which would not normally be associated with a society. Numerous comments from former concentration camp prisoners containing a wealth of nuanced detail about social differentiation in the camps suggest that the opposite is true – namely, that *structural characteristics similar* to those of any *normal society* were prevalent in the camps. But above all, it was an observation by former Dachau and Buchenwald prisoner Paul Martin Neurath which prompted me to examine the inner life of the concentration camps in more detail from a sociological perspective. In his doctoral dissertation entitled "Social Life in the German Concentration Camps Dachau and Buchenwald" (published as Neurath 2005), which, as noted earlier, he submitted in 1943 after his release from Buchenwald and emigration to the USA, Neurath discussed the social status of the prisoners and their respective sense of honor: "The difference between the two societies, that outside and that inside the camp, seems [. . .] one of rules of behavior rather than basic concepts" (Neurath 2005: 261). The questions that were provoked by Neurath's proposition and that I have explored in this work revolve around these *"basic concepts" of society* and the special *"rules of behavior"* which had to be adapted to the circumstances in the camps so that the unchanging constituents of the social order could be reconstructed. What ideas could be considered "basic concepts" of society, and what measures were necessary in the camps to express these ideas in a way appropriate to the situation?

I suggest that the "basic concepts" of society must include those ideas that:

- first, pertain to the characteristics considered typical of individual members of a society or of social groups within it and their relations with one another;
- and, second, were so important to the prisoners, even in the extremely restricted and oppressive conditions in the concentration camps, that, once free, they continually addressed them in various ways in their accounts of their imprisonment.

If these concepts were inessential trivialities, they would have lost their significance under the enormous pressure of the situation and given way in the prisoners' autobiographical output to other subjects which were more important in this context. In fact, though such basic ideas about humanity and society are approached in different ways in the memoirs of former prisoners, they are a common thread running through many of these texts. There is no question that the prisoners endured horrendous suffering in the camps. But even as they were bewildered by the entirely unexpected circumstances in which they found themselves, and even under the mental and physical strain of the situation, their "schemes of perception, appreciation and action" (cf. Bourdieu 1984: 100 and *passim*) were apparently still shaped by their prior social experiences.

As *more or less spatially isolated outposts of "Third Reich" society*, the concentration camps functioned much like pressure cookers in which the destructive heat of National Socialist ideas was unleashed upon the alleged and actual opponents of National Socialism primarily through *violent demonstrations of the "dissymmetry of forces"* (Foucault 1995: 55). At the same time, because the prisoners were forced to focus solely on what was necessary for survival, *the "basic concepts" of society were boiled down to their non-reducible essence*. This claim is supported by Zygmunt Bauman, who views the extreme conditions of the Holocaust as a suitable "laboratory" for revealing key attributes of our society (cf. Bauman 1989: 12). Nevertheless, the concentration camp prisoners had to make "secondary adjustments" (Goffman 1961: 54ff.) to adapt their usual strategies to the new situation.

The prisoners had vastly different social backgrounds, however – they came from all over Europe, from cities and rural areas, from a variety of cultures and social milieus; they represented every imaginable profession and adhered to a wide range of world-views; they spoke different languages, and even those who shared a language would have different dialects and vernaculars. We can therefore assume that their formative social influences were just as varied. An analysis of their published memoirs confirms that the people in these camps reflected the full social diversity of humanity. Yet despite the evident *manifold disparities*, we seem to find *universal criteria for these "basic concepts" of society* in the prisoners' autobiographical accounts, though these criteria always exhibit a *certain degree of social distortion* owing to the divergent influences mentioned above. The prisoners' understanding of the world around them depended on their previous experiences, which were, in turn, shaped by a concrete perspective arising from their position in the social space of their society of origin.

Bourdieu's *concept of the social space* has great explanatory power in this context because the perspective associated with a physical location – a literal *view of the world* – concisely conveys something of the complex way in which individuals are cognitively, physically, and sensually influenced by this "social space." An individual's perceptions, evaluations, and actions are determined by his or her position in the social space. This position is also the reason that some things, people, and behaviors will seem familiar and obvious while others will seem alien. The resultant *practical sense* or *habitus* is intrinsic to humanity, and it distinguishes one person from another because these diverging positions ultimately give people different views of the world which they express through the means available to them. Social agents are socialized and shaped by their positions in the social space in such a way that they actually make distinctions corresponding to the objective differences between various living conditions and ways of life in this space. Bourdieu's sociological concepts show us that people have "socially constituted interests" associated with a social space – meaning that, depending on their position in this social space, some things will be important to them and others will be irrelevant – and that they intentionally pursue these interests without always having a conscious reason for doing so. Bourdieu coined the term *"social libido"* to describe this urge which, like a natural impulse, drives people to make social distinctions (cf. Bourdieu 1998: 78–9; see also chapter 1, note 6 above).

With regard to the subject of the work at hand, we must look for the distinctions made by the prisoners in Nazi concentration camps – distinctions made not solely on account of the particular situation in these camps, but because this type of differentiation represented the last thread of continuity with the prisoners' former lives. In this sense, even *concentration camp prisoners* can be viewed as *social agents* who were compelled by the horrors of the camps to attempt to maintain familiar social continuities, at least on a small scale and in their own personal judgments. The individual experiences in their lives prior to the camps represented the objectification of what was normal, and this was often the basis for reaching an understanding with fellow prisoners who had had similar experiences. The camp, in turn, was a counterworld for the prisoners in which everything appeared to be "topsy-turvy." At times, this strengthened the social forces among the prisoners through which they tried to restore or recreate normality as much as possible in the camps. They could do this – despite their isolation from the outside world and the camps' Dantesque surroundings, which were equally frightening and confusing – because the objective nature of society which supposedly no longer applied to them had been incorporated into their habitus. Bourdieu describes this relationship between the individual and society thusly: "'[T]he world encompasses me but I understand it.' Social reality exists, so to speak, twice, [. . .] *outside* and *inside* of agents" (in Bourdieu and Wacquant 1992: 127; emphasis added).

For the prisoners themselves, this incorporation of social reality had something fundamentally human about it, and their own words confirm this. Jadwiga Apostoł-Staniszewska, who was imprisoned in Auschwitz, insists that these incorporated principles cannot be destroyed as long as a person still lives:

> To annihilate the people in the concentration camp, the SS men needed only a heavy club, a hard boot heel, a fist, or the crematorium, but the Nazis did not have the means to destroy the human beings within the people. And this is the decisive truth about the concentration camp; it is attested to by those whom fate left alive, and by those whose ashes are scattered across the fields before the camp and whose memory will never perish. (Apostoł-Staniszewska 1987: 225)

Robert Antelme, whose book *The Human Race* returns again and again to this particular aspect of human existence, puts it this way (see also the opening epigraph to part III above):

> The SS who view us all as one and the same cannot induce us to see ourselves that way. They cannot prevent us from choosing. On the contrary: here the need to choose is constant and immeasurably greater. The more transformed we become, the farther we retreat from back home, the more the SS believe us reduced to the indistinctness and the irresponsibility whereof we do certainly present the appearance – the more distinctions our community does in fact contain, and the stricter those distinctions are. The inhabitant of the camps is not the abolition of these differences; on the contrary, he is their effective realization. (Antelme 1998: 88)

He goes even further when he says: "[There was] no way that you'd ever really become nobody for everybody" (ibid.: 173). Even regarding the final stage of life before death from starvation and exhaustion, Adolf Gawalewicz – who barely survived this stage himself – makes the following observation:

> In general, you can say that the same differences were apparent between the *Muselmänner*[1] as between people living in normal conditions, differences

which were both physical and psychological. Conditions in the camp made these differences more acute, and we often witnessed a reevaluation of the role of the physical and psychological factors. (Adolf Gawalewicz in Ryn and Kłodziński 1987: 122)

To use Erving Goffman's words, these statements show not only "what can be done to the self" (Goffman 1961: 12) in a "total institution" like a concentration camp, but also where the boundaries apparently lie and what consequently *cannot* be done to the self.

But what do the authors of the concentration camp memoirs quoted in this work believe are the key criteria which make a person a distinguishable being – the criteria that constitute this "self" and prevent one from "ever really [becoming] nobody for everybody" (Antelme 1998: 173)? What are these "basic concepts" of self and society that are referred to so often in the literature of memory?

Following the lines of argument in this genre of literature, the highest priority is placed on the idea of *human dignity* as something that must be accorded to every individual on account of their being part of the human race. The Nazis, however, tried to exclude certain groups from the human collective and, by definition, from the human race,[2] and they therefore deliberately created conditions in the concentration camps which were so inhuman that it was difficult for the prisoners to continue to act like human beings. Basic vital needs such as sufficient food and sleep, regularly alternating periods of rest and exercise, and physical integrity were so flagrantly disregarded that the prisoners who were relentlessly exposed to these conditions struggled to satisfy any needs beyond this. The prisoners perceived this situation to be beneath human dignity and therefore dehumanizing, and they developed a variety of strategies to cope with it.

The first criterion associated with human dignity was human *reason* or a person's ability to use his intellect and "influence his own fate by reasonable behavior" (Neurath 2005: 86). Even for "the most despised proletarian there is the reassurance of reason," Robert Antelme writes (1998: 51). But because the concentration camps sprang from a "concept" of society which its opponents rejected as being utterly absurd – the National Socialist concept of a "racially homogeneous people's community" destined for world domination (cf. Dumont 1992; Wildt 2007) – reason seemed to follow completely different rules for those who had been imprisoned in the camps to be "domesticated" or murdered than it did in normal life. The camps were therefore initially utterly incomprehensible to them. If the prisoners wanted to return to something corresponding to their notion of human reason, they had to adapt their coping strategies to these special circumstances. Only by doing so would they have the slightest chance of demonstrating their faculty of reason, to themselves if no one else. Erving Goffman calls such strategies "secondary adjustments"

(Goffman 1961: 54), which can function as a *"lodgment for the self"* (ibid.: 55) in "total institutions" by proving to prisoners that, despite everything, they are still capable of acting and have some degree of control over certain aspects of their lives (ibid.). The only way for prisoners to compensate for the apparent lack of reason in the concentration camps was to apply their own sense of reason by making "secondary adjustments" to their strategies. At the same time, the memoirs of former prisoners make it very clear that these adjustments were always made on the basis of the *habitus* brought to the camp by each prisoner. This habitus provided structures of perception, appreciation, and action and thus acted as a type of foundation. In actual social practice, the concrete notion of reason was not so much logical or (in a Kantian sense) theoretical as it was a *"practical reason"* (Bourdieu 1998) which follows the implicit logic of the social order and is thus "common sense" instead of rational strategic calculation. The adjustment strategy described as "colonization" by Goffman (Goffman 1961: 64), through which inmates largely come to terms with their situation, clearly reveals the resultant overlapping effect. Even imperial colonizers were incapable of entirely eradicating the cultural practices and organizational principles of their colonized social agents by enforcing their own organizational structures and patterns of thought. Instead, everything that was forbidden or undesirable within their imposed framework was simply driven into available niches or new channels. The Nazis were equally unable to completely annihilate the prisoners' existing habitus – the "human beings within the people." Their habitus could not be extinguished because it had been incorporated. Instead, the strange new experiences *overlaid* and *modified* their existing habitus, resulting in *strategies that were changed* but in which their old *schemes of perception, appreciation, and action were still embedded.* Sometimes a "secondary adjustment" could lead to irresolvable contradictions and discordances that are much better explained by Bourdieu's concept of the *"cleft"* or *"torn habitus"* (Bourdieu in Bourdieu and Wacquant 1992: 127; cf. also Bourdieu 2007: 100), which more clearly conveys the dissonance generated by these contradictions. Such dissonance could arise, for example, if a prisoner felt his or her human dignity had been restored through acknowledgment by an SS man even though the prisoner profoundly rejected both the SS man as a person and the ideas to which he adhered (cf. chapters 5.3 and 6.2).

In modern Westernized societies, the idea of human dignity is associated with the assurance of human reason. But implicit in this idea is also the notion that humans are *individuals* who are always members of a human *society* and who stand in a specific *relation* to that society. Although opinions on the nature of this interrelationship between individual and society varied depending on one's world-view and ranged from more individualistic outlooks to more holistic ones (cf. Dumont 1992), former concentration camp prisoners are largely in agreement in their memoirs that people are always to be viewed as entities who each make their own contribution to society in one way or another. Regardless of whether this contribution is subordinate to a "great common cause," such as a political or religious utopia, or whether it serves personal intellectual or artistic objectives, each individual is a part of the whole and thus accounts for some portion of the character of their society. Since people make different contributions to the constitution of their society, this *idea of individuality* implies that people are, in one way or another, *distinguishable* from one another. In the concentration camps, the Nazis vehemently challenged the modern Western world's deeply rooted belief in the individuality of each person by employing measures aimed at "leveling" the prisoners. The autobiographical accounts from former prisoners consequently offer numerous indications that the prisoners viewed this as a fundamental attack on their human dignity. But this attack merely compelled them to cling all the more tightly to the concept of their own individuality:

> We are being transformed. Our faces and bodies are going downhill, there's no more telling the handsome from the ugly. In three months' time we'll be more different still, we'll be even less distinguishable from one another. Yet each of us will continue, in a vague way, to maintain the idea of his own singularity. (Antelme 1998: 87)

The need to express one's individuality is also evident in the account of a Christmas party written by Charlotte Delbo, who describes her disappointment when, despite their best efforts, the women in her hut wound up looking even more alike than they previously did on account of their uniform clothing and living conditions (see also chapter 6.3):

> We could hardly recognize one another, hair coiffed, faces made up. The lab chemists had made cheek and lip rouge, as well as powder, but they produced a single shade, so that, seeing all these faces painted the same color, the same way, was strangely disturbing. The sameness of our striped dresses became even more apparent. Suddenly we were filled with the feeling that all our efforts had been made in vain, that our preparations, excitement, and expectation of a real Christmas Eve feast had been to no avail. (Delbo 1995: 164)

In the entry from July 26, 1944 in Loden Vogel's Bergen-Belsen diary, we find similar thoughts on the pursuit of individuality and distinguishability:

> And suddenly it's clear to me how much more interesting people are when they're in their own environment or they at least have their own environment. No one has that here. Because of this and the small number of possible actions and reactions, facial expressions become wrinkles, and any sign of individuality becomes a meaningless variation of something which, on

balance, is the same in most respects. The same food, the same place to sleep, the same work, the same ambitions [. . .], the same back story, to the extent that a back story matters here. I was so proud when Mechanicus told me that someone thought the two of us "stuck out." There's no greater compliment here. (Vogel 2002: 49)

Vogel not only expresses his claim to an individual identity here, he also provides us with a list of criteria for making one person distinguishable from another:

- one's own environment, or *material resources* such as a place to sleep and food to eat, as well as a profession and the work that one does – in other words, one's "way of life" (cf. Halbwachs 2001);
- and individual facial expressions, or a physiognomy which says something about one's nature or character, as well as one's ambitions and a personal back story which have left visible traces. He thus shifts the focus of identity to the *body as the bearer of individual traits and social characteristics* – and all of these are features of the habitus (cf. Bourdieu *passim*).

It seems to me that the words written by the young Vogel in Bergen-Belsen precisely express what Bourdieu means when he says "[s]ocial reality exists, so to speak, twice, [. . .] outside and inside of agents" (Bourdieu in Bourdieu and Wacquant 1992: 127). At the same time, Vogel's comment about individuality touches on the aspect of *social position*, since the criteria he mentions are in no way entirely neutral; instead, if these criteria are "extrapolated on," they can tell us something more about the position of a person in the social space of a society. With an eye to Bourdieu's theoretical concepts, Gunter Gebauer describes this relationship as follows:

The self formulates its intentions as a part of the societal whole. The subjectivity expressed in first-person statements is an instantiation of positions within the social realm. It is situated in the habitus of the person and manifests itself especially in the apparently purely subjective acts of an individual's decision-making behavior. [. . . I]n statements that declare singular intention, the agent often shows his own social position; he expresses himself as the representative of a social group, class, faction, and of gender, male or female. (Gebauer 2000: 71)

Summarizing to this point, we can see that the notion of an inalienable *human dignity* is the guiding principle behind the "basic concepts" of humanity in the memoirs of former concentration camp prisoners. This human dignity is coupled, in turn, with the idea that human beings are *individuals endowed with reason* who are unique and who *stand in a particular relation to society.* This relation is expressed in a concrete *social position* which is identified by several criteria.

Former concentration camp prisoners consistently mention three primary attributes as the central components of this social identity – which, as Jean-Claude Kaufmann points out, is "an invention from non-invented material" (Kaufmann 2005: 106). These attributes are *gender*, *class*, and a more difficult to define conglomeration of concepts that can relate to a person's regional or national background but may also include *"ethnic" attributions* with their inherent associated notions of heritage and genetic kinship. Even though differing social positions can lead to widely varying views on precisely which characteristics determine one's affiliation with a gender or class and what typical signs indicate affiliation with a particular "ethnic" group, there is general agreement that these are the fundamental criteria for social differentiation. Furthermore, these identity-defining social attributes always appear to go hand in hand with a *sense of honor* that stems from a *moral code* applicable to everyone within a society or social group and that demands *behavior appropriate* to one's class, gender, or "ethnic" identity. The right to be treated decently – i.e., with honor – is codified and thus enforceable by law in most societies, not least because honor is a strong driving force for human activity and an insult to one's honor must therefore be viewed as a potential point of conflict. In the memoirs of former concentration camp prisoners, too, we find lines of argumentation based on such codes of honor which can be used to explain certain behaviors and judgments.

The *top priority* for the concentration camp prisoners as regards both social position and a prisoner's respective code of honor seems to be *gender affiliation.* As gender is determined by the "biological reality" of the body (Bourdieu 2001a: 11), it is a universally identifiable criterion of a binary social order which can be *universally conveyed* beyond all linguistic differences, specific cultural conditioning, or affiliation with a class or milieu. While prisoners in the largely leveled society of the camps faced fierce challenges to the social position they had held in their previous lives (in the sense of belonging to a class or milieu), these challenges were even more acute in the case of gender identity. Since the prisoner community was generally gender-homogeneous, it is likely that there was less emphasis on accentuating one's own gender through contrast with the other gender. Additionally, the physically straining and extremely unhygienic conditions in the camps – where malnutrition, disease, and physical deterioration were a horrifyingly normal state of affairs – meant that the standards against which men and women are usually judged no longer applied. Even women had their heads shaved and were forced to carry out heavy physical labor while subsisting on an extremely poor diet, they lost their feminine curves and stopped menstruating; men became emaciated and as weak as small children, they struggled to control their bodies, and only the most privileged could still have an erection. This seems to have made it all the more important to the prisoners to affirm their gender identity as a *minimum component of social identity*, since gender could be universally understood regardless of one's origin, status, language, or culture.

The measures which expressed the priority of gender identity in the Nazi concentration camps were varied, and the "rules of behavior" were adapted to the circumstances. On the one hand, the more the physical unambiguity of one's gender was up for discussion, the more focus was placed on *physical attributes*. For example, signs of *masculinity* such as physical size and strength were emphasized even by those men who probably did not define themselves as men primarily through such criteria in their previous life (see chapter 6.3). Proof of masculinity was also always an indication of masculine domination in two respects: in terms of a man's self-mastery and in terms of his social position, which was always supposed to be superior to that of a woman's – even in the concentration camps. Masculine honor therefore demanded that male prisoners counter provocations or insults from fellow prisoners with demonstrations of physical strength before the eyes of everyone else – that is, "in front of and for other men" (Bourdieu 2001a: 53).

For female prisoners, the physical aspect of *femininity* stood in a special relation to forced nakedness and was expressed in female *shame*. Women tended to react defensively to injuries to their honor by employing *exit strategies* or attempting to make themselves invisible. For instance, while the women – unlike the men – were not forced to cover their heads according to the camp rules, scarves were considered essential because they hid the women's shaved heads and concealed the fact that they no longer had hair (see chapter 6.3). Depending on the situation, however, women would sometimes also try to emphasize their physical attributes. For example, the female body could be accentuated through the use of improvised make-up or the skillful alteration of clothing: "Lily took off her lab coat. Underneath she had on a striped, clean dress, tight-fitting, even a little short. Lily was twenty years old. Her stylishness triumphed over captivity. She had refashioned the striped dress" (Delbo 1995: 156). This *enactment of the female body* can also be interpreted as an attempt to *attract the dominant male gaze* and manifest one's social position as a woman, even in the concentration camp, in order to demonstrate normality (see chapter 6.3).

Both genders apparently engaged in recurrent *virtual enactments* in the camps involving the visualization of future scenarios which highlighted the social aspects of the male or female position. Examples of the virtual enactment of gender-related social positions can be found in conversations between the prisoners about satisfying, delicious meals. In companionable discussions anticipating their longed-for liberation, male prisoners would invite each other over to their respective houses to enjoy wonderful food prepared by their wives or mothers. In similar scenarios between female prisoners, by contrast, the women would imagine themselves as housewives and cooks who would provide ample food and hospitality to both their families and their guests. For both genders, these conversations were triggered by ceaseless hunger and they revolved around fantasies of fantastic food, but the social positions expressed here are clearly divided into male and female, and thus into *dominant* and *dominated* (see chapter 6.3). The discussions themselves were communication acts – meaning that the prisoners were social agents during them – but at the same time, they served almost exclusively to virtually create a situation in which the prisoners could finally reassume the social positions that seemed comfortable to them and appropriate to their conversational partners.

A remarkable number of prisoner memoirs mention the regular exchange of recipes or frequent mutual invitations to dinner for the period after liberation. This constant repetition seems to have also been a *ritual enactment*, the social dimension of which was comforting because it was an assurance of normality. Just like the shared profession of faith repeatedly renews the religious order, mutual invitations and planned feasts expressed a faith in one's own future – a future in which things would be in their proper order again, in which men would be able to be "like men" and women "like women" (see chapter 6.3).

Even in the camps, the genders were defined in reference to each other. This is especially clear in the passages in which male or female narrators express their discomfort at the inability of the opposite sex to perform the duties traditionally associated with their gender. For example, women say that they found it very difficult to see men so helpless and suffering. Aside from their own consequent lack of protection, these women appear to have been most upset by the fact that the weakness of the men was externally apparent, which disrupted what was felt to be the natural order of things.

> The men loved us also, but wretchedly. They experienced the sting of the decline of strength and manly duty since they could do nothing for the women. If we suffered seeing them unhappy, hungry, deprived, they did even more so, realizing their inability to protect and defend us, to assume their destiny on their own. (Delbo 1995: 117; see also epigraph to chapter 6.3)

This "strength" that was lacking in the men can be understood as genuine male potency here – potency in the sense of an inherent force, capability, or the capacity to achieve something (cf. *Merriam-Webster* online[3]), and thus also power. The men imprisoned in the concentration camps had been fundamentally robbed of this potency on account of their prisoner status. Meanwhile, the women's need for protection corresponded to their self-image in principle; it was a matter of great concern that the women in the camps could no longer be protected by the men. The ability "to assume their destiny on their own" is mentioned as a male prerogative.

Whether such self-determination was always realized in life outside the camp is irrelevant; what is significant is that it is acknowledged to be a male right in texts written by both men and women. This short passage from Charlotte Delbo, who complains about the "topsy-turvy" gender relations in the camp, also shows how describing the camp's deviation from normality simultaneously served to affirm the concept of what was normal (see chapter 1).

The prisoners could do very little to restore the usual gender order in the camps; they were restricted to nuances, but nuances which were very carefully observed. Robert Antelme, for example, describes the following situation: "I was wandering around with a woman's implement, and their women were fashioning the metal for the fuselage and weren't wandering around. I abandoned the broom when I saw that I was becoming too much of a scandal and before they raised a fuss" (Antelme 1998: 68; see also chapter 6.3). In addition to the obvious – and at times seemingly exaggerated – reaction to insults to honor where gender was concerned, it was the discussion of the "topsy-turvy world" of the concentration camps in conversations and diary entries which most effectively demonstrated that the prisoners felt that gender relations actually should have been different and that the "basic concept" of the "masculine domination" of the hierarchical gender order had not really been obliterated.

Reaching an understanding on social differentiation in terms of *belonging to a milieu or class* appears to have been more complicated in the Nazi concentration camps than reaching an understanding on the binary gender order. For a start, the material foundation of social distinctions based on different "ways of life" (Halbwachs 2001) appeared to have been eliminated for the prisoners, who were all in the same situation. Unlike gender differentiation, which is fundamentally based on physical traits that were still present – though not always immediately apparent – the material aspects of the prisoners' former class or milieu differences were more or less non-existent. Such distinctions could at best be created or restored on the basis of a prisoner's classification according to the reasons for their arrest, by assuming a prisoner functionary position with the authority and advantages that entailed, or through the subtle use of certain social, cultural, and economic practices. While in principle the inmates had no influence over their prisoner category,[4] it is apparent that the habitus the prisoners brought with them were critically important to the creation of new social distinctions in the camps. These habitus could come into play on the three distinct levels of sociality in the concentration camps (see chapter 5.3).

The "rules of behavior" here were strategies of self-assertion which depended directly on the prisoners' former lives. On the *first level of sociality*, which was oriented on *military models*, the prisoners' own experience of the military – through either observation or participation – could at least serve as a rough guideline for the behavior demanded of them.

Furthermore, the transparent regimentation of military practices some-times enabled the prisoners to find and exploit loopholes for primarily individualized strategies, though they always faced the threat of discovery and punishment for doing so.

Once the prisoners had become more familiar with camp life, options opened up to them in the *shadow zone* between their flouting of the regulations and the toleration of their transgressions by the guards. Above all, this *second level of sociality* created a space for the covert *camp economy* and *cultural activities*. Both of these areas were vital to the prisoners – though in different ways – so a great deal of inventiveness was exhibited here. Economic and cultural activities followed the same principles within the camps as they did outside of them, and this is the reason that so many prisoners were able to take part in them or even knew how they functioned in the first place. It is also why members of the SS, despite their ideological indoctrination, could be convinced to contribute to such activities as well, either through tacit toleration or through active participation to their own advantage, even though it meant that they were cooperating with the "internal enemy" (Sofsky 1997). The strategies employed in the shadow zone were mainly *collective* because nothing less than strategically planned cooperation between proper networks was usually required here.

The *third, most deeply hidden level of sociality* was the *latent social life of the prisoners*, the *diversity* of which is almost impossible to grasp. On this level, the concentration camp prisoners used self-determined strategies to distract themselves from the misery of camp life. One important task here was to bolster fellow prisoners who were particularly distressed and therefore at risk. The aspect of *self-determination*, which kept alive the prisoners' memory of their individuality, was heavily influenced by inmates' *abilities and experiences*, which documented both *where you came from* and *where you actually belonged*. This latent social life in the camps was therefore used to establish *prisoner communities within individual huts or throughout the entire camp*, on the one hand, and to define boundaries and *expose social lines of demarcation*, on the other. This particularly hidden level of sociality represented a "realm of possibilities" (Bourdieu 2000a) in two respects: The opportunities for such activities were extremely limited owing to the circumstances, but they were also influenced by the prisoners' prior experiences. It was not just a matter of recognizing opportunities and seizing them *spontaneously* or in a carefully *planned* way; when options did open up to them, the prisoners could generally only fall back on their existing body of experience. The interplay of the present situation and the prisoners' personal past did not exclude the possibility of forging new paths and taking advantage of options which had not been used before, but there was still a noticeable difference between those who could call on familiar routines and those who had to first acquire knowledge of a practice in order to make use of it.

These micro-sociologically distinct levels of sociality often overlapped in everyday camp life, thus generating a *very complex social reality*. This reality was either extremely contradictory or homogeneous depending on how one looks at it. The nameless, faceless mass of downtrodden and degraded creatures struggling to survive was at the same time – when examined from a different perspective – a complex society of individuals who joined together in groups at every possible opportunity and actualized socially relevant differences in order to affirm their human dignity. On the one hand, the SS succeeded in its strategy of turning the prisoners into bureaucratically managed numbers who would fight over a crust of bread; but, on the other hand, this strategy strengthened the desire of the dehumanized to assert their individuality both by expressing solidarity and by cultivating significant differences and nuances which harked back to their former ways of life. Here, too, we see virtual and ritual enactments which largely relied on the prisoners' imaginative capabilities and which, through constant repetition, took on the character of a ritual which was intended to document their self-assertion toward the Nazis. For the clandestine cultural activities in particular, *recourse to the prisoners' imagination* was often the basis and prerequisite for everything else (when running through musical scores or scripts, for instance), but a great deal of *physical effort* was also frequently required (such as when playing music, performing cabaret, or acting in a play).

Along with the economic activities in the shadow zone – which often, but not only, served to fulfill the prisoners' basic material needs – diverse cultural activities carried out on all three levels of sociality played an important role. Zygmunt Bauman reinforces the idea that *culture can be thought of as a survival strategy* for the concentration camp prisoners in that it both ties in with the past and uses innovative means to create something new, making it an expression of the "permanence and durability which life, by itself, so sorely misses" (Bauman 1992: 4). Cultural activity can therefore also be understood as a potency, an ability to generate something that connects with what has gone before and leaves a trace that shows that one has lived. Although the omnipresent "odors" (ibid.: 4) of death and dying in the Nazi concentration camps could not be "undone" (ibid.) through the prisoners' cultural activities, they could be concealed for a short while.

The behaviors exhibited on all three levels of sociality could be considered largely "contained" forms (Goffman 1961: 199) of "*secondary adjustments*" (ibid.: 54) where existing structures must be exploited in order "to obtain forbidden satisfactions or to obtain permitted ones by forbidden means" (ibid.: 54). When the employed strategies were not unique to individuals, the agents in the "underlife" (ibid.: 199) that emerged in the concentration camps had to call on existing social networks as well as establish new ones. Some of these hidden social activities showed the traits of "colonization" (ibid.: 62f.) since normal life outside of the camp was temporarily pushed out of the prisoners' spectrum of perception and the world within the camp became their sole reference point.

Additionally, the habitus of every agent involved – prisoners and SS alike – was instrumental in shaping all three levels of sociality. The possibilities and limits as well as the contradictory tendencies were rooted in the partially "forgotten history" (Bourdieu 1990) of the social agents and their social relationships. The terrifying new experiences in the world of the concentration camp could lead to a "cleft habitus" (Bourdieu 2007) which ran counter to the rational intentions of the agents and enabled the existence of a shadow zone. As examples of *"a logic in action"* (Bourdieu 2000b), most prisoners still felt the ambition to perform a task well if they had fundamentally positive associations with it, even if it was being carried out at the order of the SS, just as SS officers could not suppress feelings of vanity and unadulterated pleasure if a concentration camp prisoner sketched a flattering portrait of them. As "the active presence of the whole past of which it is the product," the habitus "gives practices their relative autonomy with respect to external determinations of the immediate present" (Bourdieu 1990: 56) – that is, it makes it possible for completely contradictory tendencies to exist simultaneously.

As a result, the Nazi concentration camps were the sites of differing realities, all of which were equally real. The daily sight of a mass of indistinguishable and pitiable faces was as much a part of this camp reality as the fact that there was "no way that you'd ever really become nobody for everybody" (Antelme 1998: 173). The state of being somebody was shaped both by *individual* aspects and by certain *social affiliations* – Neurath mentions the influence of "social background and concepts" on the individual prisoners (cf. Neurath 2005: 131).

As is the case with gender differentiation, the views on different social positions that are expressed in the memoirs of former prisoners depend heavily on each prisoner's own position – both the position in the social space that had been held in society outside of the camp and the position held in the social space within the camp. Loden Vogel, for example, who came from Amsterdam's upper middle class and had strong artistic ties, noted in his diary in Bergen-Belsen on February 22, 1945: "We came to the conclusion that we would have more to gain than to lose by returning in one piece (as if that were even possible!) than most of the others, as they were just simple folk and even their Sunday lives seemed unbearable to us" (Vogel 2002: 97).

Prisoners who had the chance to take on functionary positions in the camp would exploit the advantages available to them and subsequently look at the world of the camp through different eyes than those who did not have such opportunities (see chapter 6.2). A prisoner could even move up the social ladder by assuming a functionary position, and some people who experienced this viewed their period in the camp as a "great time" compared to their previous life (cf. Langbein 2004: 490).

This type of advancement required the kind of "secondary adjustment" described by Goffman as "conversion" (Goffman 1961: 63f.), which led prisoners to copy their SS overseers and strive to perfectly carry out their orders.

But former prisoners also vividly describe how the differences they brought with them to the concentration camps did not permanently disappear; they simply became (or were made) temporarily invisible. They continued to play a decisive role in direct encounters between people, and differing positions were expressed in a variety of ways on the microsocial level of camp life in particular (see chapter 5.3). *Social origins* were an important topic of conversation which enabled people to distinguish themselves by distancing themselves from the enforced sameness of prisoner life. Additionally, the *preferences and aversions* embedded in the prisoners' habitus helped shape the concrete structure of the hidden camp life, the diversity of which reflects a full spectrum of "lifestyles" (Bourdieu 1984) – though in a necessarily compressed form on account of the situation in the camps.

In their memoirs, former prisoners often describe the complex diversity of the prisoner society using the example of the prisoner community in their own huts, since they generally had a better insight into the origins and social position of their fellow prisoners in this context; people knew each other and knew a good deal about each other in the huts. In depicting this diversity, the *symbolic order of society* is frequently mentioned, in which the respective representatives of the lowest to the highest positions are listed (e.g., in Szalet 1945: 97f., see chapter 5.3, or Heger 1994: 30ff. and 34, see chapter 6.1). The terms used here are not neutral but convey the value judgments generally associated with them. For example, when Leon Szalet contrasts educated people and their knowledge with less educated people and their experience and explains that the two benefited from each other in the camp (cf. Szalet 1945: 97f.), it appears to me that he is symbolically denying the actual social significance of these differences (cf. Bourdieu 1994: 127) on account of the situation rather than acknowledging an equivalency between experiential knowledge and intellectual reflection. Bourdieu calls the symbolic denegation of social distance by agents in a higher position a "strategy of condescension" (ibid.). Symbolic denegation of the "fundamental powers" inherent in "social capital" conceals, but does not eliminate, the distance. Bourdieu explains these "strategies of condescension" as follows: "[O]ne can use objective distances in such a way as to cumulate the advantages of propinquity and the advantages of distance, that is, distance and the recognition of distance warranted by its symbolic denegation" (ibid.: 127). Because the SS imposed its own order on the camps, the "social capital" that existed and was recognized in society outside of the camps was not necessarily associated with "fundamental powers" within the camps. The *symbolic recognition* of each person's respective social position, which was an intrinsic part of interaction between the inmates, was therefore all the more important as it helped maintain the essential factors of the social order.

"[T]his sense of one's place, and the affinities of habitus experienced as sympathy or antipathy, are at the basis of all forms of cooptation, friendships, [. . .] associations, and so on" (ibid.: 128). So while the objective, substantial foundations of different "ways of life" (Halbwachs 2001) were largely non-existent in the camps, habitus – as incorporated social structure – ensured that a prisoner's sense of his or her own social position and that of others could continue to have an effect, as could forms of "symbolic mastery" (Bourdieu 1990).

In perceiving and evaluating fellow prisoners, contempt or respect for their position always came into play when this position was known. Leon Szalet, for example, talks about the excessive deference shown toward two professors:

> [. . .] Franz surprised us pleasantly [and did something completely out of character which we found difficult to explain]. He treated both professors with the greatest respect and procured them as many alleviations as were possible in a concentration camp. [. . .] The other comrades, too, outdid each other in showing their esteem for the two scholars. Everyone considered himself fortunate if he could do them a good turn, and would gladly have endured all kinds of hardships if by doing so he could have saved them any suffering. [...T]o the professor even the greatest boor replied promptly in a friendly voice: "You're very welcome, Professor. Don't mention it." [Everyone sensed how much coarseness and gruffness offended this sensitive scholar, how much he suffered under every crude word; and everyone wanted to spare him this distress as much as possible]. (Szalet 1945: 157; new translation from the German text in Szalet 2006: 242–3 in brackets)

The social distance remained between the "scholars" and the "boors" even after Professor Sternbach, the older of the two imprisoned professors, admitted to his fellow prisoners

> how much ashamed he was of the special privileges which had been given to him. [. . .] [His desire to be the same as us, to fully share our fate, went so far that he refused many of the courtesies we tried to extend to him.] [. . .] We all tried more than ever, against his will and often without his knowledge, to do him services and favors. (Szalet 1945: 211; new translation from the German text in Szalet 2006: 325 in brackets)

While the SS viewed these two professors merely as Polish Jews who were to be housed with others of their kind in the isolation hut of Sachsenhausen concentration camp (cf. Szalet 1945: 157), the Polish-Jewish prisoner community in this hut took it upon itself to actually cultivate a social distance and lavish the two professors with demonstrations of respect. This social practice is the exact opposite of symbolic denegation (cf. Bourdieu 1994: 127) since it entailed actualizing the social symbolic order of inequality and openly documenting social distance through acts of subservience. Nevertheless, this strategy could only be applied in a way that was "possible in a concentration camp" (Szalet 1945: 157).

While it previously would have been unthinkable for a university-educated businessman like Leon Szalet to discuss diseases of the digestive tract and sanitary conditions with a scholar (Szalet 2006: 462), other rules applied in the camp. In Sachsenhausen, it was almost an honor – if a deeply upsetting one – for Szalet to give Professor Sternbach his newspaper so that the professor, who was suffering from dysentery and had spent the night in the latrine in desperate and degrading circumstances, could clean himself. As a dysentery epidemic reached a climax in the camp, the block leaders ordered prisoners suffering from severe dysentery to sleep in the nauseatingly filthy latrines to prevent them from soiling the rest of the hut if they could not reach the toilets in time (Szalet 1945: 209ff.). When the honored Professor Sternbach eventually met this fate, Szalet became concerned and went to the latrines at night to check on him. Sternbach then made a request:

> "Could you lend me a little piece of newspaper? I will give you twice as much tomorrow."
>
> As it happened, I had managed to buy a whole newspaper that day, in exchange for half of my bread ration, and I ran into the dormitory to fetch my treasure from its hiding place in the straw sack. How frightfully he must be suffering from that foulness! If I could only get water for him. But that was impossible. At least I would offer to help him. But when I saw the poor smeared face before me again and laid the newspaper in the trembling hands, all I could say was a wretched, "Here, please."
>
> Professor Sternbach tore off the first page of the newspaper and held out the rest to me. "Thank you very much," he gasped, and tears ran over his besmirched face. [. . .] "No, it is all for you," I said. [. . .] "Really?" he asked, unbelieving. "Is it really all for me?" [. . .] I wanted to say something, but I could not even bring out a "yes" and could only nod my head.
>
> Then a blissful smile spread over his sunken face. He clutched the newspaper in both hands and said joyfully, with a liveliness unusual in him: "Ah, I am so very happy. This is something I will never forget. How much suffering it will save me! Oh, I cannot tell you how glad I am now."
>
> That was too much for me. An old dirty newspaper had become the supreme blessing of a man who a few months before had been the pride of Polish scholarship, honored wherever learning is prized. (Ibid.: 213)

This horrific, hopeless scene is moving proof of the extent to which the camps were a "topsy-turvy world" (Klüger 2001) resembling hell, and it is also an example of what Paul Martin Neurath means when he says that while the "rules of behavior" in the camps had to be adjusted, the "basic concepts" still applied (Neurath 2005: 261): *The circumstances were "topsy-turvy" but the social order had to endure.* The other "regular" prisoners who were also severely ill are completely overlooked by Szalet in this scene even though they shared the professor's fate. The scholar once again experienced the deference due to him on account of his elevated social status, and it was to Szalet's own credit that he offered up a sacrifice to the professor.

This episode can be interpreted in two different ways: Looking at the *ruptures*, readers see a hellish alternative world where human dignity had been obliterated; but looking at the *continuities*, it seems that even in the concentration camps it was not possible to completely annul the social order.

In the absence of closer personal contact or concrete knowledge about a person, the social impact of a prisoner's classification became all the more powerful. The memoirs of former concentration camp prisoners are therefore rife with blanket judgments about other groups of prisoners based on social stereotypes familiar from their own previous lives. Even though the hierarchical classifications cemented the inequality of the prisoners in a dramatic way, the prisoner categories were not the reason for this inequality. "Their ideological constructions were mutually compatible because it was possible to reach a consensus on the elements of these constructions [. . .]" (Eberle 2005: 93) – that is, these constructions were widely socially accepted and their effects were felt even in the concentration camps.

Communal life in the camps was shaped not only by the prisoners' preconceptions about the characteristics of those classified as "anti-social" or communist, for example – preconceptions which they often felt were confirmed – but also by their preconceived notions about nationalities, regional backgrounds, or *"ethnic"* predispositions.

Prisoners openly expressed their views on the *"heterogeneous composition"* and the "value" of certain "elements" (Kogon 2006: 35) of the prisoner society, which can be interpreted as a sign that there was a consensus regarding the prisoner classifications in the camps (cf. Eberle 2005: 93).

The perspectives which came into play here regarding such groups or factions were heavily influenced by a prisoner's own position in the social space of the prisoner society; that is, a prisoner's view of such groups varied according to his or her own nationality, regional background, or "ethnic" affiliation (see chapter 6.1 in particular).

However, classification as a *Jew* or *"Gypsy"* usually dominated the other (social, political, national, etc.) categories and was considered meaningful by the members of all other prisoner groups. This was undoubtedly the intention of the SS, but it was possible only because these socially relevant classifications had been used as a matter of course to draw boundaries in the "normal" society outside of the camps for many generations – and this practice was thus taken for granted by the prisoners as well. The habitus as the "forgotten history" and "active presence of the whole past of which it is the product" (Bourdieu 1990: 56) conveyed the criteria which were necessary for this type of distinction to dominate other differences (see also chapter 4.2.4). In the prisoners' minds, these assumptions became certainties that did not have to be checked against reality. Being viewed as a Jew or "Gypsy" had a *specific weight* which was always heavier than that of other social determining factors – gender and class could certainly never outweigh it (see chapter 6.1).

Stereotypical notions about classes and their associated "ways of life" (Halbwachs 2001), as well as clichés about nationalities or "ethnic" attributes, were usually put to the test in personal encounters between prisoners: that is, during their social interactions, the prisoners checked to see whether these notions were supportable. If the above-mentioned Professor Sternbach had not exhibited the noblesse expected from such a scholar, for example, his fellow prisoners would probably not have been so eager to demonstrate their respect for him.

However, if the usual clichés were not confirmed in the course of personal encounters and experiences, this was attributed to the irregularity of the situation and was assumed to be an exception to the rule which therefore did not need to be questioned. The reasoning used here was that sometimes a prisoner's category was wrong – as might be the case with prisoners wearing a pink triangle who were "actually" opponents of the regime whom the SS had falsely accused of being homosexual because they had no other grounds for arrest – or that someone was clearly "not true to type," such as a prisoner classified as a criminal who demonstrated solidarity with other prisoners (see chapter 6.1).

It was usually not a question of experiencing sympathy or antipathy when interacting with Jews and "Gypsies"; even if the majority harbored a general antipathy toward these groups, this could always be corrected in personal encounters. But the knowledge that someone was a Jew or a "Gypsy" could never be forgotten. It seems that both in the sense of the National Socialist world-view and according to a widespread social consensus, Jews and "Gypsies" were ultimately just "guilty of being accused" (Bauman 1995: 204). The prisoners in the other categories had also been "accused" by the Nazis, but whether they were actually "guilty" or not could be determined through personal encounters with them, when preconceived notions could be adjusted if necessary. There was apparently no question, however, that Jews and "Gypsies" were supposedly damaging to the community. Jews were thought to pose a danger primarily on account of their supposed "slyness" and "cunning," a certain intellectual capability that was aimed primarily at material benefits and led to extreme adaptability in every imaginable situation, which always worked to the advantage of "the Jews" (cf. Borowski 1992). "Gypsies," by contrast, were considered dangerous because of their "lack of civilization" and "savagery" combined with a type of "practical cunning" which they knew how to use for their own benefit, which other prisoners had to be wary of, and which was always coupled with total social non-conformance (cf. Delbo 1995 or Neurath 2005). The common factor in both cases is the apparently *non-negotiable certainty about a dangerous inferiority.*

The majority of society, and the concentration camp prisoners belonging to this majority, engaged in fundamentally different social practices with Jews and "Gypsies" than with other social groups. When dealing with other social groups, there were strong dependencies between the schemes of perception and appreciation resulting from a prisoner's own position. For example, the respect shown to the two professors mentioned above can be considered a special characteristic of members of the educated middle class, who, because they possess some knowledge and intellectual skills themselves, have a particular appreciation for the highest position achievable in this social arena. From the perspective of a manual laborer, by contrast, the professor may be a genteel man, but in a sense he comes from a different world to which the laborer has no connection. In fact, the professor's sophistication and resolutely polite manners even in the concentration camp could potentially cause a worker to feel nothing but contempt. An example of such an attitude can be seen in the case of the Goral mentioned in chapter 6.1, who, even in the moment of his death, felt compelled to express his disdain for his fellow Polish prisoners from the cities, whom he dismissed as "damned spoiled brats" with their "fancy talk" (cf. Daxelmüller 1998: 983f.; Suderland 2004: 128ff.). When it came to dealing with Jews and "Gypsies," however, there does not appear to have been a comparably wide range of perception and appreciation schemes shaped by one's own position in the social space. Instead, there was general agreement on the particular characteristics of these groups, and even when such characteristics were not apparent in personal encounters with individual members of these groups, the other prisoners' fundamental opinions of them remained unchanged.

Since classifying someone as a Jew or "Gypsy" is always a hierarchizing classification which is independent of the classified individual's way of life, this distinction is qualitatively different from other evaluation criteria. To be a Jew or a "Gypsy" amounts to having an irredeemable flaw which cannot be compensated for by other characteristics. I therefore believe it is not adequate to categorize this as an "ethnic" classification, as is usual in sociological contexts. In the Nazi concentration camps, the fact that fellow prisoners were Jews or "Gypsies" was fundamentally important to the interaction (or conflict) between prisoners across all social formations. This shows that this classification has its own inherent power and leads me to conclude that a new sociological term needs to be found to describe this qualitative difference. Following my analysis, I believe that the term *"caste"* as proposed by Max Weber (Weber 1978: 933f.) is suitable for expressing the quality of this particular social relation. The criteria associated with this notion of caste – separation, an inherited division of labor, and a pre-determined place in the social hierarchy (see also chapter 4.2.4) – are met in the sense that prevailing opinion unquestioningly assumes them to be facts, and they can never be forgotten.

Returning to the question of the "basic concepts" of society (Neurath 2005) which the prisoners strove to realize in the Nazi concentration camps, albeit through modified "rules of behavior" (ibid.), we can see that these "basic concepts" were made up of just a few components. The dominant notion is that of the right to *human dignity* which is accorded to every single person as an *individual endowed with reason*. Individuals make different contributions to society depending on their *social position*, and there appear to be four main criteria that determine one's position in the social space: *gender, class, "ethnic group," and caste*.

A closer analysis of the importance of these criteria, however, shows that they have differing "specific weights," meaning that some aspects are negotiable under certain circumstances, while others are considered to be irreversible. The apparently non-negotiable criteria undoubtedly include gender, which, as Bourdieu formulates it, is "a fundamental dimension of the habitus which, like the sharps and clefs in music, modifies all of the social qualities associated with the fundamental social factors" (Bourdieu 1997b: 222). Being identified as a Jew or "Gypsy" appears to be equally non-negotiable, as this aspect, too, "modifies all of the social qualities associated with the fundamental social factors" (ibid.). Looking through Max Weber's sociological lens, this can be viewed as a social mechanism of action arising from caste thinking. I therefore propose that even in Western societies, caste is a persistent "basic concept" with a formative influence on human interaction. Although we do not historically associate the term "caste" with Western societies, recent research shows that the social idea behind the caste concept may very well originate in Europe and that the strictness of this distinction in particular can be traced back to European ambitions (cf. Waligora 2006; see also chapter 4.2.4.). Regardless of the fact that we do not typically use the term caste to describe this distinction, it is absolutely clear that the idea behind the term is present in the prevailing opinions on social differentiation.

The two other social categorizations – class and "ethnic group" – have a different quality in social intercourse. Both awareness of "class and way of life" (Halbwachs 2001) and "ethnic" (self-)labeling certainly influence interactions depending on each person's respective position in the social space, but the possibility of modification appears to exist for these categories in the social practice of the concentration camps. In other words, based on specific experiences with people classified this way, the evaluations associated with these classifications were at least partly reversible.

This means that *two fundamental parameters initially determine the signs* which indicate social position, and both are based on a *social frame of reference with a binary structure*. In the case of *gender*, belonging to the male or female sex determines the signs in as much as to be a man means to occupy a fundamentally dominant position, while to be a woman means to be fundamentally dominated – namely, by men. With *caste*, too, there is a binary frame of reference which determines the social sign: If someone can be assigned to a caste – such as Jews or "Gypsies" – this is a minus sign that "modifies all of the social qualities associated with the fundamental social factors" (Bourdieu 1997b: 222). Once these two parameters have been determined – once it is clear to which gender someone belongs and whether they must be assigned to a caste – then the *precise positions in the social space* can be more finely adjusted in social interactions on the basis of *class- and lifestyle-related attributes* and *"ethnic" values.*[5]

Although the weighting was different on account of the situation in the concentration camps, the means of enforcing or demanding the familiar social order were basically the same in the camps as they were in normal life outside: The measures used were *individualistic* or *collective*, they were *strategically planned* or *spontaneously intuitive*, and both the *body* and the *mind* came into play in *virtual* and *ritual enactments*. It is difficult to judge whether the virtual and the ritual were actually considered more important in the camps than they were in normal life, but the memoirs of former prisoners suggest that this was the case. It is possible, however, that the prisoners were simply more aware of their strategies in the concentration camps because their usual "automatisms" had become impossible. It therefore also stands to reason that, in the camps, highly complex plans had to be developed to achieve relatively modest goals, where intuitive spontaneous action would probably have sufficed in normal life. The prisoners in this "topsy-turvy world" also seem to have been more aware of certain aspects of their habitus from their lives before imprisonment since the conditions in the forcible detention camps prevented them from simply carrying on as they had before. Establishing that others were different from oneself and that something was lacking was a first step toward realizing the normality that was so sorely missed here. This process was not necessary outside of the camps because, in normal life, it is usually sufficient for people to be guided by their habitus. But with a correspondingly adapted habitus, the social order becomes completely obvious. The prisoners had to find new ways of enacting their habitus in the camps, and this was a painful process since the necessary fit between their habitus and the social space did not initially exist here. The *"social libido"* (Bourdieu 1998: 78–9), this "impulse" toward the social, appears to be so powerful, however, that they made "secondary adjustments" in order to generate opportunities to surrender to this "impulse" and *create forms of expression for the "basic concepts" of society with the help of different strategies*. These forms of expression in the camps could differ radically from those in normal life – they could appear strange, imaginative, excessive, or very moving – but since "[t]he social space is indeed the first and last reality, [. . .] it still commands the representations that the social agents can have of it" (ibid.: 13). To put it another way: The "basic concepts" of society are expressed in diverse ways through recurring variations of social practices that create socially relevant, classifying distinctions, and no one who has a share in them can completely escape them. Since these "basic concepts" are embedded in the habitus, they are not merely familiar social practices – "schemes of perception, appreciation, and action" (Bourdieu *passim*) – they also define the "realm of possibilities" (Bourdieu *passim*) and thus the *thinkable* as well as the *unthinkable*. The social world is therefore an ongoing "performative discourse" (Bourdieu 1994: 137) which is conducted through deeds, words, and thoughts and which sets its boundaries in the same way.

Looking through the "window" of the Holocaust (Bauman 1989: viii), we can see the strength of the driving force of the "social libido" and thus the essential nature of this "performative discourse." In the exceptional situation in the Nazi concentration camps, the prisoners faced a constant struggle for bare survival, but they also went to every length and faced every conceivable hardship and risk in order to continue this *"performative discourse" as an expression of their genuine humanity*. I am astounded by the extent to which the differentiating criteria typical of modern Western societies had been internalized, despite the many disparities between the prisoners – who, after all, came not only from a wide range of social milieus but also from all over Europe and even other continents, and thus from a variety of societies which differed radically in many ways. It is perhaps least surprising that gender differentiation was apparently of primary importance. But fine social adjustments based on lifestyle and (internal) ethnic differentiation were also so significant that the prisoners drew on these aspects for the purposes of social distinction in the camps and seem to have effortlessly agreed on the nuances of them. Prisoners who came from communist societies or who had adopted this world-view and fought for its realization also took heed of the socially relevant nuances between different ways of life and "ethnic" dispositions – meaning that the "distinctions" (Bourdieu 1984) and similarities were socially relevant in the concentration camps even to those who strove for a society of equals. It seems that only by looking through the "window" of the Holocaust can we see that a type of caste thinking, with the strict notion of social inevitability which we thought had long been overcome, is still prevalent even in modern Westernized societies. In contemporary social analyses, we view this phenomenon as antisemitism and antiziganism, but we overlook the "social mechanism" of caste thinking that gives rise to both attitudes.

In closing, I would like to go back to the music metaphor mentioned at the start. The "basic concepts" (Neurath 2005) at the heart of the "performative discourse" (Bourdieu 1994) carried out in modern Western societies – human dignity, individuality, reason, and social position – also shape the individual and collective improvisations of the polyphonic and by no means always harmonious choir of concentration camp prisoners. The leitmotifs of "individuals endowed with reason" and "social position" harmonize with the ground bass[6] of "human dignity" which is the foundation of the unwritten musical score of society. There are sharps and clefs here which, even in the concentration camps, "[modify] all of the social qualities associated with the fundamental social factors" (Bourdieu 1997b: 222) and thus have a key influence on positions in the social space. This should prompt us to reconsider Bourdieu's theoretical model of the social space when we cast an analytical look at our society today. Expanding this model to include the dimensions of "gender" and "caste" that are present in social practice could help to reveal the tremendous power of these social "sharps" and "clefs."

Notes

Chapter 1 Topic and Research Question

1 The concept of a prisoner society has not played a significant role up until now, as can be seen in the fact that searching for the term *Häftlingsgesellschaft* (prisoner society) in the database of the German National Library results in just six hits, one of which is the German edition of this book (Suderland 2009) (last searched on August 4, 2012; catalog search for the German National Library at http://www.dnb.de/). The few publications listed there are evidence of the fragmentary approach to examining individual groups of prisoners (see Benz and Distel 2005b; Streibel and Schafranek 1996). Since the Holocaust archives of the International Tracing Service (ITS) in Bad Arolsen were opened in early 2008, more serious thought may now be given to the existence of a "prisoner society," as these archives hold thousands of as yet unresearched files and documents which could shed a light on the hidden social life of the inmates (cf. Kohl 2008; ITS archive at http://www.its-arolsen.org/en/homepage/index. html).

2 Considering that people are always born into a social situation not of their own choosing, the idea that societies typically have a voluntary basis is rather surprising and not terribly plausible from a sociological viewpoint.

3 For more on Pierre Bourdieu's sociological concepts, see below.

4 Paul Martin Neurath (1911–2001) was an Austrian-born American sociologist who was imprisoned in the Dachau and Buchenwald concentration camps from 1938 to 1939 for being Jewish and an opponent of the Nazi regime. Neurath, who had a doctoral degree in law, subsequently emigrated to the USA and recounted his experiences in a sociological dissertation submitted to Columbia University in New York in 1943 with the title of "Social Life in the German Concentration Camps Dachau and Buchenwald." This work was highly controversial – not because of its content, which was not deemed especially interesting, but because of his method of "participatory observation," which was viewed as scientifically unreliable and questionable in New York as it was associated with the methods of the competing Chicago School.

The dissertation was therefore not accepted until 1951 after a methodological appendix had been added (see the afterword by Christian Fleck, Albert Müller, and Nico Stehr in Neurath 2005: 279–311). Neurath's dissertation was published for the first time by Suhrkamp in Germany in 2004. On the basis of this German edition, the book finally appeared in English in 2005 (cf. Neurath 2005). Since Neurath's book deals with "The Society of Terror" in the concentration camps, as the title alone shows, I find it remarkable that it does not appear in the search results for the term *Häftlingsgesellschaft* (prisoner society) in the catalog of the German National Library (cf. note 1) – an indication of just how poorly established the concept of a "prisoner society" really is.

5 The concentration camps are not to be considered synonymous with the Holocaust as a whole. However, as key elements of the comprehensive extermination concept referred to by the term Holocaust, the camps were critical tools for, and the culmination of, the systematic realization of the Holocaust (for more on the term Holocaust, see chapter 3, note 3).

6 Libido is a term from the field of psychoanalysis that describes an eager striving for something. By "social libido," Bourdieu means the striving for social recognition. In *Practical Reason*, in a short section entitled "Investment" (Bourdieu 1998: 76–9), he discusses the term libido in the context of his sociological theories in connection with the question of *Is a disinterested act possible?* (ibid: 75ff.): "Having defended my usage of the notion of interest, I will now attempt to show how it can be replaced by more rigorous notions such as *illusio, investment,* or even *libido*" (ibid.: 76; emphasis in original). The different terms used by Bourdieu connote different aspects of human behavior. "Interest" and "investment" are terms relating to the economy, and Bourdieu always uses them in reference to the "economy of action." "Illusio," which is related to the Latin word *ludus,* meaning game, highlights the belief necessary for participating in social games that these are to be taken seriously and actually mean something. "Libido," by contrast, emphasizes the desire aroused by this belief to take part in the game, to pursue interests and make investments (cf. Suderland 2009a). Elsewhere, Bourdieu writes about social recognition thusly:

> One of the most unequal of all distributions, and probably, in any case, the most cruel, is the distribution [. . .] of *social importance* and of *reasons for living.* [. . .] Conversely, there is no worse dispossession, no worse privation, perhaps, than that of the losers in the symbolic struggle for recognition, for access to a socially recognized social being, in a word, to humanity. (Bourdieu 2000c: 241; emphasis added)

The struggle for "social importance" and "reasons for living" is a plausible explanation for why we feel the strong urge to seek recognition and why our desire to take part in these deadly serious social games, to pursue our own interests and make investments, apparently never disappears, regardless of our situation (cf. Suderland 2009a).

Chapter 2 The "Third Reich" and the Nazi Concentration Camps

1 The image of a laboratory appears frequently: see Roman Frister, for example: "Like myself, they were guinea pigs in a giant laboratory of human survival" (Frister 2001: 339).

2 For more on Pierre Bourdieu's terminology and concepts, see below.

3 Bajohr's study (2003) vividly explains which social and economic interests promoted the radicalization of antisemitism and silenced the objections initially voiced against these tendencies.

4 However, the term *Schutzhaft* does not appear until later amendments and implementing regulations (cf. Hensle 2005).

5 Wolfgang Benz and Barbara Distel refer to *Zwangslager* (forcible detention camps) in the foreword to the first volume of their multi-volume history of the Nazi concentration camps (Benz and Distel 2005a: 7-9). They argue that the term *Konzentrationslager* (concentration camp) is restrictive and therefore marginalizes – or even ignores – the equally horrendous conditions in other types of Nazi camps. The "world of the camps" (ibid.: 12) during the "Third Reich" also included numerous so-called work education camps, youth protection camps, Russians' camps, "Gypsy" camps and ghettos, etc., where the conditions were no less inhumane than they were in the camps known as concentration camps (cf. ibid.: 8). In an introductory essay, Benz defines "forcible detention camps" as institutions

> in which people had to live under guard and against their will, where they were forced into activities and behaviors determined neither by their own volition nor the standards of a constitutional state. [. . .] This parallel world of the concentration camps covers everything from "youth protection camps" [. . .] to the execution sites and extermination camps [. . .] whose sole purpose was to liquidate deportees. (Ibid.: 12)

All of these "sites of imprisonment and terror" served to "discipline, detain, subjugate, exploit [and] exterminate people" even if they did not fit the formal definition of a concentration camp – namely, a camp that was under the authority of the Concentration Camps Inspectorate or the SS Economic Administration Main Office (ibid.: 11f.). Since the work at hand is more concerned with the conditions in the camps than with their formal definition as concentration camps, in the following I use the terms "concentration camp" and "forcible detention camp" synonymously. The description of the organizational structure and personnel in the camps known in Nazi parlance as concentration camps also applies to the sparsely documented conditions in other forcible detention camps.

6 In 1933, Germany had 520,000 inhabitants of the Jewish faith, of whom around 109,000 were not German nationals. According to the criteria of the "Aryan paragraph" (first formulated in the "Law for the Restoration of the Professional Civil Service" of April 7, 1933; cf. Benz et al. 1997: 373f.), there were also around 380,000 "German Christians of Jewish descent" (cf. Rummel

and Rath 2001: 6). Even taking this racist assessment standard into account, the number of "Jewish persons" in Germany would have made up a maximum of one percent of the population: "Eighty million Germans and millions of Austrians feared a group of others who made up less than one percent of the population as soon as they could no longer distinguish these others from themselves" (Lind 1996: 156).

7 Collective term for the three laws passed on September 15, 1935 by the Nazi Party in Nuremberg: the "Reich Citizenship Law," the "Law for the Protection of German Blood and German Honor," and the "Reich Flag Law." The "Reich Citizenship Law" decreed that only people who could prove they were of "German or kindred blood" could be citizens of the German Reich. This definition stripped Jews of their German citizenship. The "Blood Protection Law" prohibited marriage or extramarital sexual relations between Germans and Jews under penalty of imprisonment. The "Reich Flag Law" declared the swastika flag to be the German national flag (cf. RGB1 1935 I: 1146).

8 This board game is like a combination of Parcheesi or Ludo and Coppit: A very simple drawing of a small town appears on the board. Jewish houses and businesses are marked on the streets of the town, which is surrounded by a wall with battlements. The winner is the first player to drive six Jews out of the town ("Off to Palestine!") and assemble them in one of the "collection areas" outside the city wall. The "Jew hunters" are represented by small, colorful wooden figurines which are reminiscent of the wooden toys typical of the Erz Mountains. The figures of the Jews resemble the conical pieces in the game of Coppit, but they have grotesque faces painted on them. The game board also features sayings like "Throw the die skillfully so you collect a lot of Jews!" and "If you drive out six Jews, you'll be the winner for sure!" Over a million copies of this board game were sold in 1938 alone (cf. picture and explanation in Rogasky 1988: 24; a clearer picture can be found in Barnavi 1992: 227 or in *Heimat und Exil* 2006: 19). Unlike other propaganda games of the time which served the purposes of warmongering, for example, hardly any copies of this game now exist, probably because such unpleasant reminders of widespread antisemitism were destroyed promptly before the de-Nazification process (information about the game was gratefully received from Mr. Urs Latus of the Nuremberg Toy Museum and Mr. Bernwart Thole of the German Games Archive in Marburg via telephone conversations with the author on October 13, 2003).

9 One example that has recently come to light is the Berlin-Schöneweide camp. This camp, consisting of fourteen stone huts, was a branch of the Sachsenhausen concentration camp and was located in the middle of a residential area on Köllnische Strasse and Britzer Strasse. Local residents had a clear view of the camp from the balconies of the surrounding houses. The camp held female forced laborers from various countries (Italy, Poland, France) as well as 200 women from the Ravensbrück concentration camp, most of whom were Polish. According to the building permit, the camp had been designed for 2,160 people, but current evidence indicates it was only

continuously occupied by around 500 prisoners. A documentation center has been established in the preserved stone buildings of this camp, the only former forced labor camp of its kind to have remained completely intact. See Benz and Distel 2006a: 120ff.; *Förderverein – Materialien* at http://www.zwangsarbeit-in-berlin.de/schoeneweide/foerderverein-texte.htm, accessed on April 25, 2013; Layer-Jung and Pagenstecher 2004; and Topography of Terror at http://www.topographie.de/en/nazi-forced-labor-documentation-center, accessed on April 25, 2013.

10 Kató Gyulai (2001) talks about the permanently unusable latrines in the Spandau camp (a satellite camp of Sachsenhausen; cf. Benz and Distel 2006a: 123ff.): "We had to do our business in the courtyard. Only a wire fence stood between the courtyard and the street, so people could see us clearly. At the request of local residents [*sic*], they started to build a little hut in the courtyard [. . .]" (Gyulai 2001: 60). Marianne Pintér, another prisoner in this camp, recalls: "We had to do our business along the fence on the side of the camp where the streetcar passed by. So there we sat, and the people on the streetcar, the people passing by could see us. That was the worst thing!" (quoted in ibid.: 108, footnote 42).

11 This dual subordination, which applied to the political department as well, was not uncommon in the "Third Reich" and frequently led to "wrangling over competencies" (Morsch 2005: 60f.; see also Sofsky 1997: 97ff.).

12 Prisoners who were selected for extermination immediately upon arrival at the camp and those who had died en route were not registered and were identified by the letter "B" in the confirmation of receipt on the admissions list for the transport. The rest were listed with an additional letter "A" in the *"Lebendregistratur"* (records of the living) (cf. Paczuła 1995: 29ff.).

13 In most cases, the causes of death were falsified when deaths were recorded. However, the prisoner functionaries assigned to the "production line" of filling out forms sometimes made telling errors. For example, the cause of death for a small child might be given as "decrepitude" (cf. Grotum and Parcer 1995: 218f.). In the births section of the registry office, children born in the camp were immediately given a prisoner number, and a corresponding file would be created for them in the "records of the living." The marriage section usually registered the marital status of SS personnel. The only documented prisoner wedding was that of a political prisoner in Auschwitz (Paczuła 1995: 32, footnote 28); this was also mentioned by former secretary Hermine Markovits (in Shelley 1986: 120) and was described in more detail by Borowski (Borowski 1992: 134f.). For detailed information on the register, see Paczuła (1995).

14 Images of the camp regulations and disciplinary code for Dachau can be found in Zámečník (2007: 402ff.).

15 After being released from the Sachsenhausen concentration camp, Leon Szalet went into exile in the USA. From 1942 to 1944 – while the Nazis were still in power – he wrote a report about his experiences as a prisoner in the Jewish blocks of Sachsenhausen (cf. Szalet 2006: 482). In a number of places, he vividly

portrays the unpredictable and extremely brutal regiment of block leaders (cf. ibid.: *passim*).

16 Quoted from the minutes of a meeting of the Berlin Chamber of Physicians from June 16, 1928 (cf. Winau 2005: 177, footnote 7).

17 Camp commandant Karl Otto Koch was actually sentenced to death and executed (cf. Orth 1998: 762f.).

18 For more details on different groups of prisoners, see chapter 6.1.

19 The potential forms of violence could vary widely depending on where someone was assigned – e.g., in the camp administration offices or on prisoner guard duty.

20 "In keeping with the ideal of a racial elite, there were strict fitness criteria for the *Totenkopf* units in the first few years, similar to those for the military SS-VT [*SS-Verfügungstruppe* – SS Combat Support Force]. SS men were supposed to be at least 1.72 meters tall (5 feet, 8 inches), and had to document their 'Aryan ancestry'; they had to be healthy and *blutjung* (in the prime of youth) – no older than twenty-three. No candidates could wear eyeglasses, and men from large urban areas were not accepted for regular positions. Intellectual abilities were secondary; the focus was on physical traits, ideological malleability, and the principle of voluntary enlistment" (Sofsky 1997: 109).

Chapter 3 Introductory Comments on the Disciplinary Context and Methods

1 Belgian artist René Magritte provides a vivid example of how the depiction of reality can be confused with the reality of what is being depicted. Magritte used a photorealistic technique to paint an apple that looks real enough to touch. The title of the painting, *Ceci n'est pas une pomme* (*This is not an apple*), which appears as a large caption at the top of the picture, reminds the viewer that this is merely a depiction of an apple (cf. image in Passeron 1971: 88).

2 The same applies to transcripts of interviews from oral history projects. Ulrike Jureit argues that the same methodological approach should be taken to "personal accounts, witness statements made in court, memoirs and autobiographies" as to statements made by survivors in oral history interviews (cf. Jureit 1998: 5).

3 As it is used here, the term Holocaust is not restricted to the extermination of the European Jews, as is usually the case, but instead describes the entirety of the extermination concept devised and implemented by the Nazis. It also does not refer solely to "annihilation on so massive and indiscriminate a scale as to render death void of all personal characteristics, and hence virtually anonymous or absurd. [. . .] 'Holocaust' suggests not only a brutally imposed death but an even more brutally imposed life of humiliation, deprivation, and degradation" (Rosenfeld 1980: 3). Regarding the history of the term Holocaust, see Stirn (2000) or, for more detail, Wyrwa (1999). See Agamben (2002: 28ff.) for criticism of the term Holocaust.

4 Eugen Kogon (1903–87), born in Munich, was a political opponent of the Nazi regime who was imprisoned in the Buchenwald concentration camp from 1938

to 1945. His book *The Theory and Practice of Hell*, originally published in 1946 as *Der SS-Staat*, is based on a report about Buchenwald that he was commissioned to write by the camp's American liberators (regarding the background to the report, see Kogon 2006: xiff.).

5 Regarding academic styles, see also Fleck (1999 [1935]).

Chapter 4 Sociological Orientations

1 Pierre Bourdieu (1930–2002) was a French sociologist. He studied philosophy in Paris, then moved to Algeria, where he carried out ethnographic research into the Kabyle people who were oppressed by colonial France. After returning to France, he applied his philosophical and ethnographic findings to sociological research projects there. He worked as an assistant professor at the Sorbonne in Paris and a lecturer in Lille before taking up a sociology professorship at the Collège de France in Paris, a position he held until his death. Cf. Krais (2004: 179ff.); *50 Klassiker der Soziologie* (http://agso.uni-graz.at/lexikon/klassiker/bourdieu/06bio.htm, accessed on April 25, 2013).

2 Bourdieu himself did not study the concentration camps. I am aware of only two passages in which he mentions them, both relating to specific people. The first is in relation to the French sociologist Maurice Halbwachs, who was arrested by the Nazis and imprisoned in the Buchenwald concentration camp, where he died of illness and exhaustion in January 1945 (cf. the homage to Halbwachs, Bourdieu 2003). The second time he mentions the camps is in a discussion with Franz Schultheis about his photographic and ethnographic work in Algeria. His experiences with the oppressed Kabyle people remind him of reports by the French anthropologist Germaine Tillion about the time she spent in German concentration camps (cf. Tillion 1975):

> I was very moved and sensitive to the suffering of the people there [in Algeria], but I also felt the distance of the observer. [. . .] All of this came to mind as I was reading Germaine Tillion, an anthropologist [. . .] who describes in her book *Ravensbrück* how she was forced to watch people die in the concentration camp, and that each time someone died, she made a notch. She was just doing her job as a professional anthropologist, and she says in her book that that helped her get through it. (Bourdieu in Schultheis 2003: 35–6)

3 He does repeatedly use the term "class racism" (e.g., in Schultheis 2003: 26). Although this term is commonly used in racism research as an antonym to "racial racism" to stress the social Darwinian component of racism (cf. Hund 2006, 2007; Traverso 2003), we must assume that it has a special nuance in the context of Bourdieu's concepts. One indication of this can be found in a passage in which Bourdieu explains his concept of racism in more detail, shedding light on the thinking behind the use of the term in connection with his sociological theories. In a very short essay entitled "The Racism of 'Intelligence,'" Bourdieu says: "The first point I would make is that there is

no single racism, there are *racisms* in the plural. There are as many racisms as there are groups who need to justify themselves in existing as they exist; this is the invariant function of all racisms" (Bourdieu 1993c: 177; emphasis in original). According to Bourdieu, one characteristic of all racisms is an "apparent scientificization" of discourse (ibid.: 178) which makes it possible to euphemize racism (cf. ibid.). He focuses less on obvious and brutal racism than on the hidden mechanisms of exclusion in everyday social life made possible through "second-degree legitimation" (ibid.: 179), such as those found in the educational system.

4 The politically correct expression would be Sinti and Roma. However, even these terms do not entirely accurately describe what they are supposed to represent (cf. Pohl 2003: 111). Furthermore, they are contentious among the people in question because Sinti is the name of the Romany-speaking people settled in Germany while Roma refers to the Romany-speaking people of southeastern Europe – but the Lalleri, Lovari, Manush, Kalderash, Kale, Arlia, Jenische, etc. (cf. Winter 2005), were also persecuted as "Gypsies," and as they have different traditions from the Sinti and Roma, they feel excluded by these terms as an identifier. Such an identifier is essentially the continuation of a centuries-old tradition of using *one* name for very different things (see also Zimmermann 1996). For this reason, I use the term "Gypsies" ("*Zigeuner*" in German, the term also employed by the Nazis) in distancing quotation marks in order to represent – but not uncritically reproduce – the popular understanding of these groups of people in society at the time and in Nazi thinking (for the correct terminology, particularly in relation to the debate about the controversial inscription originally proposed for the central memorial in Berlin that was to be dedicated to "those persecuted as Gypsies," see, e.g., Jäckel 2005). [*Translator's note*: The memorial that was finally unveiled in October 2012 is dedicated to "the Sinti and Roma of Europe murdered under National Socialism."]

5 All the more since the concept of "ethnicity" has recently experienced something of a revival in various contexts – either to express the special aspects of the social situation of immigrants or to give globalized culture a label that seems to make it possible to identify origins. The term "ethnic" as an adjective has positive connotations and is popularly used to express a certain longing for such origins. The fact that it is really nothing more than a disguised term for race is conveniently overlooked not only by the culture and fashion industries ("ethnic food," "ethnic look," etc.) but also in politics and science. The question of what an "ethnos" actually is remains largely unanswered, and attempts to define it based on "*Volksgruppen*" [*Translator's note*: literally "groups of peoples," often used synonymously for "ethnic groups" in German] are vague. See, for example, *Meyers Großes Taschenlexikon*: "Ethnos [Greek], a group of people who form a cultural, social, historical and genetic unit and are otherwise known as 'tribes' or 'peoples'" (*Meyers Großes Taschenlexikon* 2006: "Ethnie," p. 1999). Regarding the use of the term in sociology, Max Weber's definition still seems to be the most useful:

We shall call "ethnic groups" those human groups that entertain a subjective belief in their common descent because of similarities of physical type or of customs or both, or because of memories of colonization and migration; [. . .] it does not matter whether or not an objective blood relationship exists. Ethnic membership (*Gemeinsamkeit*) differs from the kinship group precisely by being a presumed identity, not a group with concrete social action, like the latter. (Weber 1978: 389)

Despite this precise definition based on social practice, the term "ethnicity" is still used in a remarkably undifferentiated way in academic language today (see also section 4.2.4.).

6 For example, there was a notion that certain "inferior races," such as the Slavic peoples, could be "improved" or "nordicized." This was unthinkable for Jews from the Nazi point of view, however (see section 4.2.4 on plans for the treatment of "*Judenmischlinge*," or "persons of mixed blood," at the Wannsee Conference and its official follow-ups).

7 For a detailed treatment of class, gender, and caste, see sections 4.2.2, 4.2.3, and 4.2.4.

8 Regarding race and nation, see section 4.2.4. Cf. also Weber (1978, volume I, part II, chapter V, section 4: "Nationality and Cultural Prestige," pp. 395–8).

9 For a detailed treatment of the concepts of the individual and society, see section 4.2.1.

10 Norbert Elias solves this problem in his comprehensive socio-historical study of *The Civilizing Process* by introducing the concepts of "external constraint" and "self-constraint" and the idea of social "figurations" in which individuals are enmeshed (cf. Elias 2000).

11 Regarding the diverse facets of the "life reform movement," see also the extremely informative exhibition catalog *Die Lebensreform. Entwürfe zur Neugestaltung von Leben und Kunst um 1900* (2001). For a long time there was very little discussion of this movement in academia or society because the early National Socialists adopted some of its ideology. A thorough analysis of the movement also reveals that it was partially entangled with the "*völkisch*" movement, which raises questions about the degree of responsibility to be borne by this group.

12 It is a little-known fact that there was also a Jewish youth movement in Germany which, aside from its religious orientation, had characteristics very similar to the German youth movement. Like the Christian and "*völkisch*" youth movements, the Jewish youth movement went in a number of different political directions, some of which were liberal and some of which were paramilitary in nature. The Zionist youth movement can be viewed as a counterpart to the "*völkisch*"-oriented German youth movement and a reaction to antisemitism and the signs of the times (cf. also Schüler-Springorum 2005b).

13 For contemporary views on the integration of German Jews in the "German people's community" from a Jewish perspective, see Cahnman (2005).

14 After Reich President Hindenburg died in 1934, Hitler had a new law passed that additionally made him Reich President and thus Commander of the

Army. From this point on, officers and soldiers no longer swore an oath of allegiance to the Constitution but rather to Hitler himself: "I swear by God this sacred oath that I will render unconditional obedience to Adolf Hitler, leader of the German Reich and people and supreme commander of the army, and that as a brave soldier I will be willing to give my life for this oath at any time" (cf. Kammer and Bartsch 2002: 281).

15 Daniela Münkel lists the annually recurring festivals and reveals that there were celebrations almost every month which, together with athletic events, the "Stew Sundays" of the *Winterhilfswerk* (Winter Relief), and local Nazi Party gatherings, led to a tremendous concentration of Nazi festivities taking place in succession throughout the year (cf. Münkel 2004: 165f.).

16 One of the first signs of this peak in activity could be seen as early as 1935 in the "processions of shame," during which people who had continued to interact with the "Jewish race enemy" and thereby supposedly harmed the "community of the people" were exposed and driven through the streets under a hail of insults and blows. On the orders of Himmler, antisemitic pogroms took place all over Germany throughout 1938, culminating in November (cf. Wildt 2007: 219ff. and 301ff.).

17 Maurice Halbwachs (1877–1945), French sociologist and philosopher; doctor of law; professor of sociology and pedagogy at the University of Strasbourg, 1919–35; professor of sociology at the Sorbonne in Paris, 1935–44, where he worked with Marcel Mauss among others; appointed Chair of Social Psychology at the Collège de France, Paris, in May 1944. In July 1944, Halbwachs was arrested by the Gestapo and deported to Buchenwald, where he died of illness and exhaustion in March 1945. Cf. *50 Klassiker der Soziologie* (http://agso.uni-graz.at/lexikon/klassiker/halbwachs/22bio.htm, accessed on April 25, 2013); see also Bourdieu (2003). Today Maurice Halbwachs is usually remembered for his social psychological work on "collective memory"; his writings on the class situation of laborers and the middle class, by contrast, remain largely unknown (cf. also Krapoth 2005).

18 In his works, Halbwachs extensively researched the "working class" and the "middle class." Above all, he used detailed consumer studies to show that, even with the same budget, different classes will set very different spending priorities. He also developed theories on the upper middle classes and entrepreneurs (cf. Halbwachs 1958, 2001).

19 It is not entirely clear what Halbwachs means here by "the deeper, more primordial aspects of human society," but the key aspect in this quotation is the reference to what Bourdieu calls the "taste for the necessary" and the "distance from necessity" (cf. Bourdieu 1984: 177ff. and 374ff.).

20 Halbwachs writes: "Class concepts [resolve into] individual concepts, and the socialized relationships in which the individual is integrated appear to be maintained solely through his deliberate force of will" (Halbwachs 2001: 44).

21 In an essay from 1920 ("Matière et société," or "Material and Society"), Halbwachs writes about prisoners of war: "Instead of losing their former social characteristics, they often seem to be even more aware of them [. . .].

The prisoners in the camps and fortresses usually form their own society with the same general traits of the peoples from whom they were separated" (Halbwachs 2001: 93).

22 From the 1970s in particular, the women's movement was able to raise a certain awareness in Western societies of the social constitution of the role of women. Recently, however, findings from the field of brain research have been used as a counterargument to emphasize the fundamentally different makeup of the two genders on the neuronal level. There is seldom any discussion of the fact that the differing structure of the male and female brain is also the product of social processes (cf., e.g., Schmitz 2005; von Bredow 2007). In his article on amnesia research, Jörg Michael Kastl (2004) discusses the social structuring of the brain and stresses that Bourdieu's habitus concept is supported by neuropsychology, meaning that human socialization has physiological effects on the brain.

23 Although sociology views people as agents – that is, acting individuals – the discipline has traditionally struggled with the significance of the body in social interaction. The notion of the dualism of body and mind is deeply rooted in European thought and can be found in most sociological theories, such as role theory. This opposition is not at all neutral, however, as greater significance is always attributed to the mind. With Pierre Bourdieu's habitus concept, this dualism can be abolished and people can be viewed not solely in terms of their mind, but also as material beings (cf. also Krais 2003).

24 *"Fremdartig"/"artfremd"* (foreign/alien) is an allusion to the *"Gleichartige"/ "Artgleiche"* (kindred/of the same type) wordplay of Michael Wildt (2007: 359).

25 The situation is entirely different in the USA, where the term "race" continues to be used in a relaxed way (cf. Bös 2005). However, Bös also criticizes the lack of exact definitions, the imprecise use of the terms "race" and "ethnicity," and the pedestrian understanding of these concepts in American social research (cf. ibid.: 21ff.). In Germany, the term "race" still appears in a few legal texts, but in this context it is used more in the sense of "racism" or "racist." The German Institute for Human Rights has therefore published a policy paper which recommends the avoidance of this term in legal texts (cf. Cremer 2008).

26 Bourdieu should have heeded this advice himself when he used the term "ethnic" in the comment cited above about the "space of ethnic groups." The fact that he does not do so in this case shows, above all, how words can be forms of "symbolic violence," as this violence functions first and foremost because "being born in a social world, we accept a whole range of postulates, axioms, which go without saying and require no inculcating. [. . .] Of all forms of 'hidden persuasion,' the most implacable is the one exerted, quite simply, by the *order of things*" (Bourdieu in Bourdieu and Wacquant 1992: 168; emphasis in original).

27 When the *Deutsche Volksliste* (DVL, German People's List) was drawn up by Himmler in 1941,

an insidious system of *völkisch* racist hierarchization was created. In 1944, the DVL listed 2.75 million people to be Germanized, while long-range plans called for 14 million over the course of thirty years. This was countered by 31 million people who were "unable to be Germanized" (50% of Czechs, 65% of Ukrainians, 75% of Byelorussians, 80% of Poles and 100% of Jews); the plans for these people consisted of resettlement [. . .], deportation [. . .] and extermination [. . .]. (Michael Hensle in Benz et al. 1997: 439)

28 The SS Special Camp in Hinzert near Trier has since come to light as an

assembly and test camp for checking the "Germanizability" mostly of Polish forced laborers. [. . .] On account of their "Aryan" appearance, these men were given a chance to survive in Hinzert by proving they were "able to be Germanized." [. . .] The Race and Settlement Main Office carried out the "racial" examination. When a prisoner was classified as able to be Germanized, preparations could be made for releasing him from imprisonment after six months and marrying him to a German woman. Prisoners who did not pass the review were transferred [. . .] to other concentration camps where they were usually executed. (Bader and Weiler 2007: 23)

29 The resolutions of the Wannsee Conference and the strategic talks that followed it (see also the following note) as well as the regulations applicable to "Gypsies" stated that the threat from "persons of mixed blood" was particularly great. The minutes from the Wannsee Conference, for example, include passages referring to "persons of mixed blood of the second degree," who, if they were the product of a "bastard marriage" where both parents were already "persons of mixed blood," were to be treated as Jews and deported. Equally, if one partner in a marriage was a "person of mixed blood of the first degree" and the other a "person of mixed blood of the second degree," this couple would be deported even if the marriage were still childless, "since possible children will as a rule have stronger Jewish blood than the Jewish person of mixed blood of the second degree" (Pätzold and Schwarz 1992: 109ff.; official US government translation of the Wannsee Conference for the Nuremberg Trials). Regarding "Gypsies," see Pohl (2003: 111f.).

30 Conference on January 20, 1942 held on the orders of Reichsmarschall Hermann Göring and at the invitation of Reinhard Heydrich in a villa in the Berlin suburb of Wannsee, which was to focus above all on clarifying the organization of the "final solution of the Jewish question" (cf. Kammer and Bartsch 2002: 272ff.; regarding the protocol of the Wannsee Conference, see Pätzold and Schwarz 1992: 102–12).

31 Before it had been scientifically proven that the Romany language is related to Sanskrit, making India a likely place of origin, it was thought that "Gypsies" might have come from Egypt. The word "Gypsy," short for Egyptian, is evidence of this presumed background (see also further below regarding the legend of refused succor). The German word *Zigeuner*, on the other hand, comes from the Ancient Greek *Athinganoi* (also the derivation of *Atsingan*,

Acigan, Cigan, Cingari) and refers to the caste of "untouchables" in India (cf. Maciejewski 1996: 16).

32 The fact that this was actually the case will be seen in the empirical section of this work (part III).

33 An analogy to the attitude toward Jews and "Gypsies" which is of interest to us here can be seen in the attitude toward people with dark skin, which was also viewed as an indelible blemish and a sign of "inferiority." Against the backdrop of colonial policy at the start of the twentieth century, apparently scandalous relationships between "white" German men and the native dark-skinned women in the colonies were fiercely debated, and there were calls for marriage prohibitions. Furthermore, the North African units stationed in the Rhineland during the French occupation after World War I were referred to as the "black shame." Even the social democratic Reich President Friedrich Ebert complained that "using colored troops of the basest culture to supervise a people of such great intellectual and economic importance as the Rhinelanders is a grave injury to the laws of European civilization" (Ebert quoted in Wildt 2007: 221). Relationships between these "black" occupying soldiers and German women were viewed as a defilement of the entire nation. The escalation from scandal to shame also clearly shows that gender relations in these misalliances intensified the problem, so the "defilement" of a white woman was considered much more serious than an "inappropriate" sexual relationship between a white man – the colonizer – and a black woman, who was subordinate to him on multiple levels (as a woman and as a "primitive") (cf. also Maß 2006; Wildt 2007: 220f.). In the "Third Reich," the children born of these relationships between dark-skinned French occupying soldiers and German women were referred to as "Rhineland bastards," and they played a part in the discussion of forced sterilization because the "Law for the Prevention of Genetically Diseased Offspring" of July 14, 1933 did not apply to them. It is thought that 800 so-called "Negro bastards" underwent illegal forced sterilization – often without their knowledge (cf. Ganssmüller 1987: 87ff.). This aspect will not be examined in any further detail in the work at hand because, unlike the treatment of Jews and "Gypsies," it is not relevant to the Nazi concentration camps (regarding the "race problem" in American society, see also Bös 2005).

34 Other minorities in the early modern period included religious refugees, who, according to the definition of "ethnic groups" mentioned above, could certainly be viewed as "ethnic minorities." In actuality, however, they were protected by sovereigns of the same faith (cf. Herzig 1996: 43).

35 Cautiously called "emergency bishops" to begin with (cf. Herzig 1996: 29).

36 Because of their small dimensions, they were called "miniature states," with a slightly sneering undertone (cf. *Meyers Großes Taschenlexikon* 2006: "Duodezstaat," 1702).

37 These are commonly depicted as effects of the Reformation in historical and sociological studies. But I think you could also turn the argument around and say that the diffusion of a new way of thinking – like that expressed in the concept of the individual – not only made something like the Reformation

possible in the first place, it also enabled it to develop such tremendous momentum that these far-reaching changes were triggered in all parts of society. The changes were political, economic, and cultural in nature and therefore influenced the entire social life of the individual. Moreover, in this view of the situation, it is the people themselves who, through mutual cooperation, are the historical *agents* in this process – not Luther or Calvin – and who thus drove these extensive social changes forward.

38 Subject = subjugated.

39 The most famous historical example is *"Jud Süß"* ("Jew Süss"), actually Joseph Süßkind Oppenheimer (1698–1738), who first held the position of treasurer at the court of Duke Charles Alexander of Württemberg and later initiated a number of very ambitious and far-reaching state reforms which made him many enemies. After the sudden death of Duke Charles Alexander, Oppenheimer was arrested, accused of "obtaining office by devious means, lese majesty, high treason, draining the country dry, and other crimes" (Breuer and Graetz 1996: 116), and finally sentenced to death by hanging. The fact that he was Jewish played a decisive role in his trial, and he was made the scapegoat for all those involved in unpopular policies who were not called to account for their actions because of their relationship with the deceased duke or other considerations (cf. ibid.). Even into the twentieth century, Oppenheimer was a symbol of "Jewish slyness," "greed," and "lust for power," and was the basis for the main character in the Nazi antisemitic propaganda film *Jud Süß* (1940) (cf. Schoeps 1992: 348). For a general introduction to Court Jews, see Battenberg (2001: 107ff.).

40 Historical proof of this can be found in special entry permits, residence permits, and similar documents relating to the purposes mentioned (cf. Herzig 1996).

41 For a general introduction to *Betteljuden* (Jewish beggars), see Battenberg (2001: 112ff.).

42 The lack of criteria for determining who exactly was a "Gypsy" makes it almost impossible to estimate what proportion of the population "Gypsies" accounted for. What we do know is that the fear of the harm they might do because of their lack of discipline was much greater than the "danger" they actually posed. For example, in his "Stricter Edict against the Gypsies" of 1710, King Frederick I of Prussia decreed that

> the unruliness of the Gypsies [. . .] was to be punished "for reasons of contagion," that is, because of the threat of potential contamination [. . .]. The severity of the measures does not correspond to the extent of deviant behavior on the part of a small minority; it can be explained, rather, by the fear that "disobedience and iniquity" could rub off on the majority population. They talk about the lawlessness of the Gypsies, but what they mean is the crumbling obedience of the subjugated. (Maciejewski 1996: 18f.).

The Jewish population seems to have reached a demographic peak after 1650, when Jews made up around one percent of the total population (cf. Herzig

1996: 40). Jewish court factors, in turn, represented a negligible proportion of this already marginal minority, but they played a disproportionately large role in public perception. Larger portions of the Jewish population became paupers particularly in the second half of the eighteenth century, but opinions differ widely on the actual extent of this pauperization (cf. Battenberg 2001: 112ff., especially 114; Herzig 1996: 40).

43 There is absolutely no scientific proof for this assumption because the lack of criteria for establishing who is actually a "Gypsy" makes it impossible to determine. The origins of the myth of the "traveling Gypsies," on the other hand, can now be almost seamlessly reconstructed. The myth is based mainly on early "Gypsy research" which became very popular in the eighteenth century through the works of Heinrich Grellmann, who largely copied older sources. The popular romantic image of the rustic traveling "Gypsies," for which there is no historical basis, and the assumption that this prototypical "Gypsy" no longer existed can be traced back to these early modern, pseudo-scientific fantasies (cf. above all Willems 1996; Zimmermann 1996).

44 The legend of Ahasver cannot be precisely dated but first appears in the literature around 1600. It has been a recurrent literary motif ever since, even to the present day. Prominent examples include Goethe (1774), von Arnim (1811), and Heym (1981), as well as Richard Wagner's romantic opera *Der fliegende Holländer* (1841) (cf. Baleanu 1992; Mayer 1979: 21ff.).

45 The word "usury" originally only meant "interest" in the sense of "augmentation" and was thus actually neutral (see *The Oxford Dictionary of English Etymology* 1966: 966). The term only takes on negative connotations when the demand for interest is considered fundamentally unjustified and therefore exorbitant or immoral.

46 In this case, integration in the sense of the assignment of a social function and position (cf. Endruweit and Trommsdorff 1989: 307f.).

47 Regarding the integration and exclusion of Jews in the early modern period, see Battenberg (1996, 1997) and Walz (1995). Regarding "Gypsies" in the early modern period, see Herzig (1996).

48 This belief appears to have had currency until recently. Even during the Nazi era, it was said that "the Jew and the Gypsy [. . .] are far removed from us today because their Asiatic ancestors were entirely different from our Nordic ancestors" (Robert Körber 1936, quoted in Willems 1996: 98).

49 The shrewd analyses of English social anthropologist Mary Douglas reveal that such notions of purity and impurity were prevalent and still are in our societies today (cf. Douglas 2002, 2003). "[I]f uncleanliness is matter out of place, we must approach it through order. Uncleanliness or dirt is that which must not be included if a pattern is to be maintained" (Douglas 2002: 50).

50 In Germany, this process started – after a few tentative preliminary attempts in Baden (1809) and Prussia (1812) – with the proclamation of the emancipation of the Jews by the constituent National Assembly in St. Paul's Church in Frankfurt in 1848 and was considered complete when equal rights were granted to Jews in Bavaria in 1872 (cf. Barnavi 1992: 159).

51 Especially from Galicia and Bukovina.

52 Berlin and Vienna were most affected by this influx. For more on Vienna, see the very informative essay by Hoffmann-Holter (2000).

53 For example, when I presented a paper on this subject at the University of Giessen in May 2005, a woman with Jewish parents told me that her mother and father always chuckled at and teasingly distanced themselves from their "stinking relatives from the East."

54 In contrast to traditional anti-Judaism, which is based not on racial but on theological grounds and classifies Jews as "the murderers of Christ." The extent to which racist considerations were a part of this is debatable.

55 Criticism in a similar vein – though much more conceptually nuanced and formulated from a pointedly Jewish perspective – can be found in Werner J. Cahnman's work in connection with Weber's use of the term "pariah." Cahnman argues instead for the concept of the "stranger," someone who is marginalized as an outsider but can still be an intermediary: "He is a neighbor, but he has the advantage of remoteness" (cf. Cahnman 1989b: 19ff.; also 24f.). This undoubtedly describes one possible aspect of the relationship between Jews and the rest of society, but it does not take into account or explain the aspect of remaining excluded.

56 *Jati* (type) denotes actual, empirically identifiable social groups and thus smaller, more manageable units such as occupational groups. *Varna* (color), on the other hand, refers to the fundamental categorization of society into four groups: "priests," "warriors," "merchants," and "servants." The so-called "untouchables" – incidentally, a term that is not Indian in origin – do not belong to any of the four *varnas* but can belong to a *jati* (cf. Bayly 1999; Reifeld 2001; Skoda 2003; Waligora 2006). This "system" is therefore nowhere near as coherent as we have long been led to believe (cf. especially Dumont 1980) and is clearly based far more on specific social practices than on an ideologically underpinned framework of ideas.

57 Waligora bases this primarily on the work of British historian Susan Bayly (1999), which has received a great deal of attention in recent years.

58 I believe the effect of this process is somewhat analogous to the formation of identity through bureaucratic registration as described by Kaufmann (2005; see also section 4.2.1.). There is no question that the separation of the Indian castes took on a life of its own as a result of this colonial development and became a real factor in Indian society, one which is hotly debated around the world today (cf. Reifeld 2001), but this does not need to be discussed in more detail in this context.

59 The word "caste" itself is used occasionally in the literature of the time by both the victims and the perpetrators. For example, it appears in a dissertation published in 1927 by "racial scientist" Robert Ritter, who played a decisive role in dealing with the "Gypsy question" in the "Third Reich." In this dissertation, entitled *Das geschlechtliche Problem der Erziehung. Versuch einer Sexualpädagogik auf psychologischer Grundlage* (The Gender Problem in Education. An Approach to Sex Education on a Psychological Basis), Ritter distinguishes between

"classes, tribes, castes, and denominations" (quoted in Zimmermann 1996: 128). Leon Szalet also talks about the *"Nazikaste"* (Nazi caste) and its "slaves" in the memoirs of his imprisonment in Sachsenhausen, which were written before the end of the war (Szalet 2006: 341). [*Translator's note*: In the abridged English version of Szalet's manuscript published in 1945, *"Nazikaste"* is translated as "Nazi elite" rather than "Nazi caste"; cf. Szalet 1945: 222.] Extreme notions of "impurity" were also rampant during this time, with some people going so far as to believe that "a single sexual encounter with a Jewish man was enough to forever 'contaminate' the children of an 'Aryan' woman even if they were sired by another man of 'pure blood'" (Wildt 2007: 223). This attitude was depicted in the very popular novel *The Sin against the Blood* by Arthur Dinter (1917) (cf. Wildt 2007: 222f.).

60 This is why even the way in which sociology has dealt with the question of the social implications of gender can be viewed as an expression of "symbolic violence" (Bourdieu 2001a). For a long time these implications were not questioned at all, and even today gender usually comes second in the sequence of "class and gender," despite the fact that this differentiation is the top priority in social interaction.

61 An analogy to this – which will not be described in detail here – can be found in the way in which the former colonial powers and the USA treated the colonial population and the people deported as slaves.

62 Since the non-negotiability of this affiliation and the traditional traits of castes – separation, hereditary division of labor, and a certain hierarchical position – fundamentally correspond to the characteristic aspects of the category of gender, it is highly likely that gender differentiation could be viewed from this perspective as well. In this case, affiliation with one of the two gender castes would be a differentiation principle of the highest priority. Theoretically interpreting gender in this way would reduce the number of fundamental social structural categories to just two: caste (which would comprise a dual affiliation with gender and "ethnic group," like in Indian society with its dual affiliation with *jati* and *varna*) and class (which can be identified by one's lifestyle). Although a theoretical intellectual game like this might heighten our awareness of the social significance of gender and more clearly illustrate the extent of the structural disadvantages or advantages associated with one's gender affiliation, I will not go into this thought experiment in any more detail here (cf. also chapter 7, note 5).

63 Michel Foucault (1926–84), French philosopher, sociologist, historian, and translator. His best-known works include *Surveiller et punir: Naissance de la prison* from 1975 (published in English in 1977 as *Discipline and Punish: The Birth of the Prison*), in which he explores the changing function of torture and punishment through history (cf. Foucault 1995). From 1970 until his death in 1984, Foucault was a Professor of the History of Systems of Thought, a post created specially for him at the Collège de France in Paris. Cf. *50 Klassiker der Soziologie* (http://agso.uni-graz.at/lexikon/klassiker/foucault/14bio.htm, accessed on April 25, 2013).

64 Torture here is not to be confused with interrogation under torture, where violence is used to coerce a confession. Instead, this is punishment through torture, where precisely dosed physical suffering is part of the punishment itself (cf. Foucault 1995).

65 In the camp regulations and disciplinary code for the Dachau concentration camp of October 1, 1933, which applied to all concentration camps from 1934 onward (reprinted in Zámečník 2007: 406ff.), paragraph 19 lists *"Pfahlbinden"* (being strung up from a post by the arms) as a potential "auxiliary punishment" (ibid.: 411). This form of torture is therefore not the product of a single sick mind; it was a common practice in all concentration camps.

66 In his brilliant book *The Origins of Nazi Violence* (2003), Enzo Traverso explores the various roots of the National Socialist idea.

> Some were *ideological* (racism, eugenics), *political* (Italian Fascism), or *historical* (imperialism and colonialism); others were *technological* and *social* (the rationalization of forms of domination, total warfare, serialized extermination, etc.) – but all had their origins in the context of the European civilization. From this point of view, the singularity of the genocide of the Jews seems to be [. . .] a unique synthesis of a vast range of modes of domination and extermination already tried out separately in the course of modern Western history. (Ibid.: 151; emphasis added)

While I wholeheartedly agree with Traverso, I also believe that he takes too narrow a view of modernity and therefore overlooks the fact that some of the roots of National Socialism were much older and that this is another distinguishing characteristic of the "singularity of the genocide."

67 Erving Goffman (1922–82), Canadian-born US sociologist; initially studied chemistry; earned a doctorate under Anselm Strauss and taught at various American universities (including in Chicago, Berkeley, and Philadelphia). His preferred method of research was anthropological fieldwork. Cf. *50 Klassiker der Soziologie* (http://agso.uni-graz.at/lexikon/klassiker/goffman/20bio.htm, accessed on April 25, 2013).

68 A book, incidentally, which has apparently attracted very little attention in Germany. The only German-language edition, published in paperback by Fischer in 1994, is long out of print and can only be found in the occasional second-hand bookshop. The other work I have cited here, *Culture as Praxis* (1999), has never been published in German and does not appear to have been very widely received in Germany. I have quoted from these two works frequently and at length in this chapter to give readers who may be unfamiliar with them an impression of the nature of Bauman's theories.

69 Zygmunt Bauman, born 1925 in Poznań, Poland; professor of sociology at the universities of Warsaw, Tel Aviv, and Leeds (cf. Bauman 1995). Although he is Jewish, he managed to escape the Holocaust because he was serving in the Polish army in Russia during the time in question (cf. Bielefeld 1993: 17). His wife, Janina Bauman, wrote an account of surviving the Warsaw Ghetto (Bauman 1986), which prompted him to delve more deeply into theories of

the Holocaust (cf. Bauman 1989: 208ff.). The important sociological work that resulted from this, *Modernity and the Holocaust*, was first published in 1989 – prior to the book *Mortality, Immortality and Other Life Strategies* discussed here (1992) – and provides sociological insights into the close connection between civilization and extermination (cf. Bauman 1989).

70 Bauman does not refer to the Holocaust or concentration camps in this book, but one can assume that they were very present in his mind while he was writing it.

Part III (introduction)

1 Robert Antelme (1917–90), born in Corsica, studied law. He was arrested in 1944 for being a member of the French Resistance and was eventually imprisoned in Buchenwald. He was severely ill at the time of his liberation. In 1946–7 he wrote an account of his experiences in German concentration camps, but his book *The Human Race* was not published in France until 1957, and it was first translated into German in 1987 and into English in 1998. (In the following, the other authors of the autobiographical literature discussed will be introduced in the notes as here: with a brief explanation of their background, the reasons for their imprisonment in a concentration camp, and how their works came to be written and published.)

2 "Unimaginable: a word that doesn't divide, doesn't restrict. The most convenient word. When you walk around with this word as your shield, this word for emptiness, your step becomes better assured, more resolute, your conscience pulls itself together" (Antelme 1998: 289–90).

3 I include the memoirs of former prisoners as well as scholarly literature based on primary sources for an empirical foundation.

Chapter 5 Camp Life

1 This is the title of the book he wrote in 1961 (Semprún 1990). Jorge Semprún (1923–2011) was a Spanish-French writer. After the Spanish Civil War he mostly lived in France. He was active in the French Resistance and was deported to Buchenwald. Cf. *Encyclopædia Britannica* online (http://www.britannica.com/EBchecked/topic/1786003/Jorge-Semprun, accessed on April 25, 2013).

2 Viktor Frankl (1905–97), Austrian, born into a Jewish family. Neurologist and psychiatrist with a focus on suicide prevention, founder of logotherapy, a form of existential analysis. In 1942 he was deported to Theresienstadt with his wife and family; he was later transferred to other camps, including Auschwitz. He was the only one in his family to survive the Holocaust. Frankl wrote about his experiences in the concentration camps immediately after he was liberated; his book was published in 1946 in Vienna (cf. Frankl 1985).

3 For Neurath, see chapter 1, note 4.

4 Primo Levi (1919–87), Italian chemist, son of Jewish parents, was arrested as a

resistance fighter in Italy in 1943 and imprisoned in Auschwitz in early 1944. His first book, *Survival in Auschwitz*, was written immediately after he was liberated and was published in 1947. His last work, *The Drowned and the Saved*, returned to the same themes and was published in 1986, a year before his suicide.

5 Ruth Elias, born in 1922 in Moravska Ostrava in what is now the Czech Republic, was persecuted for being Jewish and deported first to Theresienstadt in 1942, then to Auschwitz and Taucha. In Auschwitz, she gave birth to a child who died a few days later. After she was liberated, she initially returned home before emigrating to Israel in 1949. Elias did not talk about her concentration camp experiences with her children, but she wrote her memoirs for her grandchildren. Her book was published in German in 1988 (cf. Elias 1999).

6 Unfortunately, Bourdieu neglects to point out that the continuity of one's name has been (or was for a long time) traditionally only a guarantee for men in Western European societies. In this respect, Bourdieu himself displays a certain gender blindness and reveals that *his* view of the social world is a gendered view. However, even a law which stipulates (or stipulated) that women must take their husband's family name when they marry does not contradict Bourdieu's comment about the significance of one's own name. In fact, acknowledging the relevance of nominal continuity shows that the administrative act of changing a name entails a hefty dose of symbolic violence and that the traditionally expected name change after marriage causes (or caused) women to experience a loss of identity – a form of subjugation that is obscured by the fact that most marriages are assumed to be voluntary and that there is even sometimes a sense of pride in one's newly acquired family name.

7 Leviticus 19:28 (i.e., Pentateuch; third book of Moses): "You shall not [. . .] print any marks upon you" (cf. Wachten 2006).

8 [*Translator's note*: Levi points out here that in German, the word *Zugang* "is an abstract, administrative term, meaning 'access,' 'entry.'"]

9 Regarding the bureaucratic details of dispossession, see the very detailed examples in Meinl and Zwilling (2004) or Rummel and Rath (2001).

10 Jean Améry, pseudonym for Hans Mayer (1912–78): "The [. . .] autodidact Hans Mayer, who later called himself Jean Améry, was a blond Jew raised as a Catholic, a school dropout, fatherless, well read, and very ambitious" (Auffermann 2007). He emigrated to Belgium in 1938–9, was first imprisoned in 1940, and escaped from an internment camp in 1941. He was subsequently active in the resistance and arrested again in 1943, imprisoned, and tortured by the SS in the infamous Fort Breendonk. He was deported to Auschwitz in January 1944, where he was imprisoned at the same time as Primo Levi (see above). After Auschwitz was evacuated in January 1945, he was transferred to Mittelbau-Dora and Bergen-Belsen, where he was liberated in April 1945. After the war, he primarily worked as a journalist. He became known through his essays on the concentration camps in his book *At the Mind's Limits* (originally published in German in 1966); his book *On Suicide* (originally published in German in 1976) was very controversial. He committed suicide in a hotel

in Salzburg in the autumn of 1978 while on a book tour (cf. Auffermann 2007; Heidelberger-Leonard 2010; Pfäfflin 1996). [*Translator's note*: In addition to the pseudonym of Jean Améry, this author used variants of his name throughout his life (http://www.perlentaucher.de/vorgeblaettert/irene-heidelberger-leonard-jean-amery-teil-1.html, accessed May 3, 2013). He was actually born Hans Ma*i*er, as in the title of Steiner's (1996) collection, but at school he went by the names Hans, or Johann, Ma*y*er. As an adult he had official papers issued to him as both Hans Ma*i*er and Hans Ma*y*er, and would occasionally write as Han*n*s Mayer (cf. Mayer 1988). Readers should also note that Hans Mayer, author of the 1979 book on Richard Wagner, is a different author.]

11 This standardized classification system was used in all concentration camps from 1938 (cf. Eberle 2005: 93). We can assume that a size had been specified for the triangles, as in May 1942 the SS Economic Administration Main Office issued an order to "reduce the side length of the triangles to 6 cm to save fabric for the war effort" (ibid.: 107, footnote 11).

12 For a more detailed description of the effects of this classification system as viewed from different perspectives, see chapter 6.1.

13 The Society of International Bible Students is better known today as the Jehovah's Witnesses. As adamant conscientious objectors, they were a thorn in the side of the Nazi regime. On the other hand, the strong pressure to conform within their community of faith resulted in a pronounced self-discipline in the concentration camps accompanied by a high degree of social solidarity. Because Jehovah's Witnesses supported their ill or more hapless brethren, their huts usually met the fastidious standards of order and cleanliness demanded of the prisoners and were often shown to inspection committees, such as delegations from the International Red Cross, who visited the concentration camps (cf. Ernst and Jensen 1989 and Rahe 1998). Additionally, on account of their "patient faith in the end of the world" they were frequently "loyal and willing workers, for the SS as well as for their fellow prisoners" (Kogon 2006: 33).

14 According to the accounts of survivors, the pink triangle that identified homosexuals was much larger than the other triangles (cf. chapter 6.1).

15 In the Polish territories occupied by Germany, it had been mandatory since 1939 for Jews to wear the yellow star outside the concentration camps as well. In 1941 a police decree made this mandatory throughout the German Reich and the Protectorate of Bohemia and Moravia, and in 1942 it was extended to all territories occupied by German troops (cf. Kammer and Bartsch 2002: 118).

16 As an example of this, I would like to mention a documented case from my own family: My great-uncle Heinrich Suderland, an active communist, was arrested in the spring of 1939 while attempting to cross the German border near Waldshut. He was deported to Dachau and, since his mother was Jewish, was forced to wear both a red and a yellow triangle. In 1940 he was transferred to Buchenwald. However, his brother Leo managed to "convince" a Gestapo office – by paying them a sum of money – that my great-uncle had been arrested solely for political reasons. During a subsequent morning roll-call, my

great-uncle was notified of his Aryanization by an SS officer, and his yellow triangle was ripped from his clothing. This probably saved his life since he was then transferred to the "political block," where the conditions were different than in the huts for Jews. He remained in Buchenwald until the camp was liberated in 1945 (cf. Rummel and Rath 2001: 266).

17 There could be additional categories as well which were indicated by other special identifiers. In the context of this work, however, it is not necessary to discuss them all in detail; they will be explained on an individual basis as the need arises. An overview of all triangles, special identifiers, and additional abbreviations can be found in Eberle (2005: 102ff.).

18 Pictures of the different triangles can be found in the appendix of Egon Kogon's book (1946). Newer editions of the book unfortunately no longer include this overview.

19 For more on this, see chapter 6.1.

20 More detail on this can be found in chapter 6.2.

21 Ruth Klüger, born in 1931 in Vienna to a Jewish family; as a young girl, she was imprisoned with her mother in Theresienstadt, Auschwitz-Birkenau, and Christianstadt. In 1947 she emigrated to the USA, where she studied English and German literature. Klüger was a literature professor at Princeton University. Today she lives in California (cf. Klüger 1999, 2001, 2008).

22 Since nearly all surviving prisoner accounts depict these daily routines in detail, I will only describe them briefly here based on representative passages from the literature.

23 Charlotte Delbo (1913–85), French resistance fighter, was arrested in March 1942 with her husband and other members of the Resistance. She was sent to Auschwitz in January 1943 and later to Ravensbrück. Her husband and other fellow prisoners had already been shot in May 1942. After she was liberated, she began writing about her experiences in 1946, but on account of her own reservations, her memoirs were not published in France until the 1960s and 1970s. This was the start of her active life as a writer. After the war, Delbo first worked for the United Nations and was later an assistant to the philosopher Henri Lefebvre. She wrote essays, plays, and prose throughout her life (cf. Langer in Delbo 1995: ix–xviii).

24 For an example from Dachau, see Stanislav Zámečník in Benz and Distel (2005c: 239ff.); for Auschwitz, see Barbara Distel in Benz and Distel (2007: 101ff.).

25 Capo (or Kapo): shortened form of the French word *caporal* (corporal); German slang for chief, overseer; particularly used in prisons, etc., to describe inmates entrusted with supervising their fellow prisoners. In southern Germany, "Kapo" is also used to mean "foreman." (See "Kapo" in the *Encyclopaedia Judaica* 1971: Vol. 10, 754f.) With the exception of quotations in which a different spelling is used, I have used the more common "Kapo" throughout this work.

26 Tadeusz Borowski (1922–51), Polish resistance fighter, was arrested in 1943 and deported to Auschwitz. He was later transferred to other camps, finally ending

up in Dachau. After he was liberated, he lived in Munich, Berlin, and Warsaw and worked as an editor and correspondent. He committed suicide in 1951 in Warsaw. Even before his imprisonment he had written poems and prose pieces for the Polish underground press. Immediately after his liberation he began to process his experiences in a literary form. The first of these texts were published as early as 1946 in Poland. Borowski's works are particularly revealing because, as a prisoner functionary, he had opportunities that were not open to regular prisoners. He used these opportunities to his own advantage and recounts these experiences without sugarcoating them. His literary style combined with his forthrightness pose a challenge to readers in terms of the "unimaginability" of the experiences in the camps (cf. Lustiger 2007a, 2007b).

27 For example, if it was extremely frosty or snowy, digging operations could not be carried out (cf., e.g., Szalet 1945, 2006).

28 Primo Levi wrote this *Report on the Sanitary and Medical Organization of the Monowitz Concentration Camp for Jews (Auschwitz–Upper Silesia)* together with his fellow countryman Leonardo De Benedetti, a physician. The report was written at the request of the Red Army immediately after Levi was liberated in the spring of 1945, while he was still in the Katowice "holding camp." A revised version of the report, which was the basis for the translation cited here, was written after Levi and De Benedetti returned to Italy in 1946 and published in an Italian medical journal (cf. Mesnard 2006).

29 Kató Gyulai, a Hungarian Jew, was deported as a young girl together with her sister Evi in October 1944. She was imprisoned in a number of different camps, including a satellite camp of Dachau (where she was forced to work for BMW) and later Ravensbrück and a satellite camp of Sachsenhausen in Spandau. She was extremely ill and weak at the time of her liberation; her sister did not survive her imprisonment and probably died in Ravensbrück. After returning to Budapest, Gyulai wrote her memoirs in 1947; they were published for the first time in 1995 (cf. Apel and Jaiser in Gyulai 2001: 111–20).

30 The prisoners had neither soap nor towels available to them and had to return to their huts wet and naked in all kinds of weather (cf. Levi and De Benedetti 2006: 45).

31 Leon Szalet (1892–1958), a Jewish Pole, was arrested in Berlin, where he lived and worked, in mid-September 1939 after Germany invaded Poland and was sent to the Sachsenhausen concentration camp. He spent 237 days there, mostly in isolation huts, until he was finally freed in May 1940 after his daughter intervened on his behalf. Immediately afterwards, Szalet emigrated with his daughter via Shanghai to the USA, where he began to write an account of his imprisonment. An English version of this account was published in 1945, but a German version was not published until 2006 (cf. Szalet 1945, 2006).

32 Sleep deprivation is classified as a modern method of torture; it causes psychological and physical instability which can lead to serious illness (cf. *Meyers Großes Taschenlexikon* 2006: 2279).

33 Himmler said this in reference to the risk that the masculinization of German women could lead to more widespread homosexuality in general.

34 Hans Reichmann (1900–64), a Jewish lawyer, was working as the legal advisor to the Central Association of German Citizens of Jewish Faith in Berlin when he was arrested during the pogrom in November 1938 and deported to Sachsenhausen. At the end of 1938 he was released along with many other people seized during this wave of arrests. He emigrated to London and immediately wrote an account of his experiences in the spring of 1939. Reichmann did not return to Germany after the end of the "Third Reich" but remained in contact with people there throughout his life. He became one of the leading lawyers representing the interests of German Jews in reparation affairs (cf. Michael Wildt in Reichmann 1998: 1ff.).

35 The prisoners' uniforms also had insignia in the form of the colored triangles (see section 5.1), though these were more a symbol of shame than honor. However, the triangles were sometimes viewed as badges of honor by the prisoners if the respective inmates were proud of their classification (as opponents of the regime, for example).

36 Loden Vogel, pseudonym for Louis Tas (1920–2011), a Dutch Jew. In September 1943, while he was a medical student, he was deported with his parents from Amsterdam to Westerbork and finally sent to Bergen-Belsen in April 1944. He was able to secretly continue writing a diary in the camp, and he managed to keep the diary with him when he was liberated and after he returned to the Netherlands. A stylistically revised version of his account was first published in 1946 in The Hague under the pseudonym Loden Vogel ("leaden bird"). The original text of the diary, with additional commentary by the author, was published in 1965. A German translation of the diary approved by the author and based on the annotated version from 1965 was published in 2002 (cf. Rahe in Vogel 2002: 7–12).

37 I believe that similar strategies are probably used in military practices in entirely different contexts as well. It is beyond the scope of this work to investigate this in more detail, but it would be interesting to find out what regular German soldiers today actually think about or do during their drills.

38 *Mahorca* (or *makhorka*) is the Russian name for a high-nicotine pipe and cigarette tobacco (cf. *Meyers Großes Taschenlexikon* 2006: 4635).

39 The Auschwitz-Monowitz camp in which Levi was imprisoned was sometimes called the Buna camp because it had been part of the Buna industrial facilities on the huge construction site of I.G. Farbenindustrie AG since October 1942. The company planned to build a large hydrogenation and synthesis plant to manufacture fuel and synthetic rubber for the war economy. Concentration camp prisoners were mostly forced to carry out construction and railway work there, but some were assigned to specialist work details (cf. Willems 2007), including Levi himself, who worked in the so-called Chemical Kommando toward the end of his imprisonment (cf. Levi 1995: 101ff. and *passim*). "The work quota and working conditions were determined and controlled by I.G. Farben, whose plant management refused all safety provisions for the laborers and was also responsible for the starvation rations distributed on the construction site and in the camp" (Willems 2007: 277).

40 For a more detailed discussion of Kapos and prominent prisoners, see chapter 6.2.

41 This refers to the camp brothel.

42 A similarly detailed description can be found under the heading of "Corruption" in Neurath (2005: 201ff.).

43 Roman Frister, born in 1928 in Bielsko, Poland, was arrested as a boy with his parents for being Jewish. His mother was murdered by an SS man shortly afterwards, while Frister himself was deported with his father to the Starachowice concentration camp, where his father died. Frister survived Auschwitz and death marches in a severely ill and weakened state. After the end of the war, he worked as a journalist in Poland until he was arrested by the communist authorities. In 1957 he emigrated to Israel, where he became head of a journalism school. His book *The Cap: The Price of a Life* was written much later (1993). In his memoirs, Frister declares that his purpose is to portray the dehumanization of the inmates in all of its horror by making any type of heroization appear to be an inappropriate distortion of reality. He depicts himself in particular as relentlessly calculating and ruthless toward his fellow prisoners (cf. Frister 2001: 5; Hogrefe 1997).

44 For more detail on this, see chapter 6.2.

45 Krystyna Zywulska (1918–92), born in Lodz, studied law in Warsaw and was active in the resistance. In 1943 she was arrested by the Gestapo and sentenced to death but was instead imprisoned in Auschwitz, where she managed to keep her Jewish identity a secret. She worked for a long time in the personal effects department known in the prisoner jargon as "Canada." This department collected and sorted the personal possessions taken from those who had been selected for immediate gassing. The department was called "Canada" with a degree of sarcasm owing to the wealth that one could acquire here with the right amount of skill and luck, much like a Canadian gold miner. Zywulska wrote her memoirs in 1946 (cf. Zywulska 2004; for more on "Canada," see Walter 2007).

46 "Canada" was the name of the prisoners' personal effects department (see previous note for further details).

47 The limits of this common basis in the prisoner society will be discussed in chapter 6.

48 Individual, solitary cultural activities or ones which took place surreptitiously on a small scale involving very few people in the camps will be discussed later in this section in connection with the third level of sociality, "latent camp life."

49 See Adler (1955) or Wlaschek (2001) regarding culture in Theresienstadt, or Fénelon (1997) regarding the women's orchestra in Auschwitz. Constanze Jaiser has researched the creation and use of poetry in the Ravensbrück concentration camp for women (Jaiser 2000). Works by Rolf D. Krause (1989) and Torsten Seela (1992) look at the approach to books and reading among the prisoners. For an examination of art in the concentration camps – primarily visual arts, but also music and literature – see the overview by Stefanie Endlich (2005). Daxelmüller (1998) deals systematically with the importance of cultural

activities in the concentration camps, covering both the performances ordered by the SS in order to mock and humiliate the prisoners and the inmates' own secretly planned and executed cultural initiatives which strengthened their personal and cultural identity.

50 The film became known by this cynical title – which probably originated with the prisoners who were forced to work as extras – after the end of the "Third Reich." The only authentically documented title is *Theresienstadt. Ein Dokumentarfilm aus dem jüdischen Siedlungsgebiet* (Theresienstadt: A Documentary Film from the Jewish Settlement Area). See also Margry (1992: 149ff.).

51 In a documentary about the director of this film, Kurt Gerron (see also note 53), the Czech cameraman used by the Nazis recounts that one scene had to be shot countless times: A teacher handed out apples and bread with margarine to a group of children, who were supposed to politely eat them with a happy expression on their faces. But because the children being filmed were practically starved, they devoured the fruit and bread before the scene could be shot. The process had to be repeated until the children were no longer as hungry and the scene could be filmed to the end (cf. *Kurt Gerron's Karusell* 1999).

52 The performances and café scenes in the film deliberately featured prominent, often internationally known cultural figures and scholars whose disappearance had been noted by the general public. Portraying them attending concerts in Theresienstadt was supposed to have a generally placatory effect on the public (cf. also Margry 1992: 152).

53 Kurt Gerron was known primarily for his portrayal of the magician Kiepert in the film *The Blue Angel* (based on the book *Professor Unrat* by Heinrich Mann; filmed in Germany in 1929–30; main roles played by Marlene Dietrich and Emil Jannings) (cf. Felsmann and Prümm 1992).

54 For more on the common preconception among concentration camp prisoners that "Gypsies" were uncooperative, see chapter 6.1.

55 It was at these rehearsals that Elias met her future husband, Kurt (cf. Elias 1999: 184ff.).

56 For more on exchanging recipes in the concentration camps, see chapter 6.3.

57 A very nuanced examination of the different aspects of religious practices in the camps can be found in Rahe (1998).

58 In general, however, we must assume that "the guards and SS members, as non-religious and non-churchly as they may have been, nonetheless stemmed from a culture and society influenced by Christianity, even if only in a limited, secularized way. This situation was not without consequence for religious life in the camp" (Rahe 1998: 1016). This means that on the side of the SS, the prohibited and unacknowledged acceptance of the hidden religious practices of the prisoners was one of the aspects of a "divided habitus" (Bourdieu 2007: 100) which led the guards to be more lenient in their punishment of the individual activities of the inmates – as long as these were Christian in nature and represented familiar values from their own social background.

59 For more on the visual arts in the concentration camps, see the essays in Benz and Distel (2002) and the summary in Endlich (2005).

60 The portraits by the Dutch artist Aat Breuer, who was imprisoned in Ravensbrück from 1943 to 1945, are relatively well known. She depicted both living and dead prisoners as well as scenes of everyday life in the camp. For thirty-four years after her liberation, Breuer hid her own pictures from herself because she did not want to be reminded of Ravensbrück. Encouraged by her daughter, she finally published the pictures in 1982 (cf. Gyulai 2001: 36; also Walz 2005a and 2005b).

61 A nuanced analysis of musical activities – both coerced and voluntary – in the Sachsenhausen concentration camp can be found in the book by Juliane Brauer (cf. Brauer 2009; for a more general overview, see also Fackler 2000 or Gilbert 2005).

62 When they were held in isolation, the inmates had to spend the whole day standing motionless in their hut or lying cramped on the bare floor instead of working. Later they were allowed to sit cross-legged, but this was no less stressful than any other position because their backs and legs would grow stiff (cf. Szalet 1945: *passim*).

63 The "window polishers" were prisoners who were ostensibly responsible for cleaning the windows but who actually kept watch to see whether a block leader was approaching so that they could warn the other prisoners to cease their prohibited activities (such as stretching their legs) (cf. Szalet 1945: 93).

Chapter 6 Prisoner Society

1 As was described in more detail in chapter 2.4.

2 Exceptions to this included the Theresienstadt camp, an "*Altersghetto*" (old-age ghetto) and later primarily a transit camp in the garrison town of Theresienstadt where the conditions were much different from those in most other camps (cf. Adler 1955; Benz et al. 1997: 757f.). In Auschwitz, the so-called "Theresienstadt family camp" and the "Gypsy family camp" (sections B IIb and B IIe in Auschwitz-Birkenau) were not divided according to gender, nor were parts of Bergen-Belsen at certain times.

The reason for this in Bergen-Belsen was that this camp initially served as a transit camp for specific groups of Jewish prisoners, such as those with dual citizenship or "Palestine certificates," who were to be exchanged for Germans interned in other countries (cf. Thomas Rahe in Vogel 2002: 7f.).

It is not entirely clear why the gender separation that was common in other camps was not put into practice throughout Auschwitz, though various theories have been put forward. The "Theresienstadt family camp" held deportees from Theresienstadt; these prisoners were housed in different huts according to gender, but the families and the men and women still had contact with each other because they were all held in the same section of the camp. The inmates here engaged in lively (and conspiratorial) activities in an attempt to educate their children and adolescents as well as they could (cf. Mandl 1966). The SS probably wanted to keep this section of the camp presentable for potential inspections. Most of the inmates of the "Theresienstadt family camp" were later gassed (cf. Jahn 2007). In the "Gypsy family camp," families were housed together in the blocks, though only one bed and two blankets were available for each family, regardless of the number of family members. Because many of these families had a large number of children, up to ten people often had to share a single bed. The hygienic conditions were particularly dire in this section of the camp, so the mortality rate was extremely high. These families were probably kept together because the SS shied away from the massive resistance they expected to face from the imprisoned "Gypsies" if they attempted to separate them. Hardly any of the prisoners in the "Gypsy family camp" survived (cf. Bistrović 2007).

3 See also chapters 2.1. and 2.2.

4 These stereotypical views of other prisoner groups are particularly apparent in the early texts about the Nazi concentration camps, such as those by Kogon (2006), Adler (1955) or even Améry (1980a), to mention just a few examples. After the end of the "Third Reich," resentments and mutual reservations between the different groups of victims made themselves felt in two ways in the context of questions about compensation, and they are a latent presence to this day. On the one hand, compensation practices in both the Federal Republic of Germany and the German Democratic Republic were oriented for a very long time on the prisoner categories, so former concentration camp prisoners were considered "eligible" or "ineligible" for compensation based on their prisoner classification. This meant that former prisoners persecuted on racial, political, or religious grounds were compensated, while those categorized as "anti-social elements," "Gypsies," or homosexuals received nothing – so the internal camp hierarchy was perpetuated (in part) (cf. Eberle 2005: 102). On the other hand, the survivors' associations did not have good relations with one another on account of their own traditional prejudices as well as these compensation practices. It was not until 1992 that the various victims' associations finally came together under the umbrella of the *Bundesverband Information und Beratung für NS-Verfolgte* (German Federal Information and Advisory Association for Victims of Nazi Persecution) in order to provide the affected individuals with a more effective advisory infrastructure (see http://www.nsberatung.de).

5 Primo Levi and Jean Améry are prominent examples of how the prosecuting authorities proceeded in these cases.

6 Placing two equilateral triangles on top of each other, one pointing up and one pointing down, forms the so-called Star of David or Shield of David, which appeared in Hebrew manuscripts as early as the eleventh century as "Solomon's seal" (cf. Barnavi 1992: 86).

7 "Magen David" (*Encylopaedia Judaica* 1971: Vol. 11, 687–97); "Badge, Jewish" (*Encylopaedia Judaica* 1971: Vol. 4, 62–74).

8 "Hundreds of these men, singled out as Jews, were married to non-Jewish women, or were the sons of mixed marriages, and their children were treated

as non-Jews outside. So far had the mixture of races [*sic*] gone that some of the men who were forced to wear the Star of David in the camp had been fervent anti-Semites outside [. . .]. I still remember the grotesque sight of a man with the star of the Jewish professional criminal on his trousers – which were held together by the belt of the SA unit of which he had been a member before he wound up in Dachau" (Neurath 2005: 69–70).

9 They were identified solely as Jews in the camp statistics as well, with the cynical result that historians today cannot help but adhere to this classification because it is no longer possible to determine the original nationality of these prisoners. Despite the best efforts of scholars researching the concentration camps, it is all but impossible to break through the type of thinking that was cemented by Nazi ideology.

10 Even before he was arrested, however, Szalet was confronted with the fact that the United Kingdom, which was allied with Poland, made a distinction between Poles and Polish citizens of the Jewish faith: He attempted to emigrate from Berlin to England in early September 1939 but was put on a plane again in London and sent straight back to Berlin (cf. Szalet 1945: 3ff.).

11 Regarding the significance of hitting back, see further below in section 6.3.

12 These latter clichés, which are more philosemitic – but which, like antisemitic sentiments, still imply that Jews are different somehow – can be found in many places in the literature of memory; frequent references are also made to the artistic and, in particular, musical abilities and talents of Jews.

13 For more detail on this, see chapter 4.2.4.

14 The guidelines for confining "Gypsies" in concentration camps were established in 1938 and 1939 (cf. Eberle 2005: 104).

15 For more detail on this, see chapter 4.2.4.

16 Hermann Langbein (1912–95), Austrian historian, was arrested for resistance activities and imprisoned in several different concentration camps, where he continued to participate in the resistance. After 1945 he served for many years as general secretary of the International Auschwitz Committee. In the mid-1960s he, along with Fritz Bauer, played a key role in bringing about the Frankfurt Auschwitz Trials (cf. Meisels 1996).

17 Regarding estimated numbers of victims from Germany, Austria, and various other countries, see Zimmermann (1996: 382f.). Many "Gypsies" became victims of systematic murder outside the camps when they were liquidated by the notorious *Einsatzgruppen* (mobile killing units) which moved through Europe carrying out mass executions. According to current research, these victims numbered between 200,000 and half a million (cf. Widmann 2003: 212f.).

18 This may have been the result of whether or how others attempted to involve them in such cooperative activities – otherwise it would be impossible to explain how such supposedly uncooperative people could work together to organize a successful armed uprising against the SS in the "Gypsy family camp" in May 1944 to prevent the complete liquidation of that section of the camp – at least temporarily (cf. Bistrović 2007: 117; Czech 1990: 626; Smoleń and Zimmermann 1995: 142).

19 Josef Kohout (1917–94) was born into a well-to-do Catholic household and arrested as a homosexual in 1939 in Vienna. After spending six months in prison, he was deported first to Sachsenhausen as a "protective custody prisoner" and later to Flossenbürg and its satellite camps. He was imprisoned in concentration camps until the end of the "Third Reich." His memoirs, one of the very few personal testimonies by an individual persecuted as a homosexual, were published in 1972 under the pseudonym Heinz Heger. After his death, his identity was revealed by his longtime companion, enabling many of the events and facts mentioned in his memoirs to be verified (cf. Müller 2002).

20 Germaine Tillion (1907–2008), French ethnologist and member of the Resistance, was arrested during the so-called "Night and Fog" campaign in 1942 (cf. Eberle 2005: 100, 105; see also Trouvé 2005) and eventually deported to Ravensbrück. Immediately after she was released, she wrote the first reports about the concentration camp, in which she records the data and information she had systematically compiled and reconstructed (Tillion 1975; see also Bourdieu in Schultheis 2003: 35f.).

21 Though we now know full well how dire the conditions actually were, this image of the "Gypsy camp" in Auschwitz persists to this day. For example, in 2005, an article in *Der Spiegel* about Dr. Mengele stated:

> [T]he doctor spent most of his time in a separate section near crematorium V – the "Gypsy camp." A "sea of huts" without toilets, with streets you would sink in up to your ankles – this is how the prisoners described the inferno. Nonetheless, a whiff of romanticism seems to have surrounded this section of the camp, where around 10,000 Sinti and Roma were penned in. The "Gypsies" were permitted to live together with their families. (Schulz 2005: 149)

22 For an overview of the history of the persecution of homosexuals in general, see *Die Geschichte des § 175* (1990).

23 Nonetheless, the memoirs of former prisoners frequently mention homosexual practices between women in the concentration camps as well (e.g. in Amesberger et al. 2004).

24 Homosexual activities between adults were punishable in Germany until 1969, and Paragraph 175 was not completely abolished until 1994 in the course of German reunification and the legal harmonization of the two German states. In 2002, individuals who had been convicted of homosexuality under the Nazi regime were finally pardoned so that they no longer had a criminal record (cf. Steinke 2002; see also Müller 2002).

25 After the German edition of the book at hand was published, another biography of a homosexual concentration camp prisoner was released based on forty hours of interviews and intensive source material research (Zinn 2011). The former prisoner in question was Rudolf Brazda, who survived the Buchenwald concentration camp and died in August 2011 at a very advanced age. (Cf. Hevesi 2011.)

26 These figures vary so drastically because the men imprisoned as homosexuals

were sometimes categorized differently; only a note in their files would have revealed their actual status – and many of these concentration camp files no longer exist.

27 They were sometimes given the green triangle of criminals on account of the criminalization of homosexuality or if they had a criminal record.

28 Prior to this, the prisoners had been forced to write letters to their families telling them that they were being subjected to harsher conditions and that if their relatives in foreign countries did not stop spreading "atrocity stories" about how badly the Jews were being treated in German concentration camps, the prisoners would face worse conditions still (cf. Neurath 2005: 66). Zámečník (2007) dates this incident with the "atrocity stories" to 1936 (ibid.: 103).

29 Regarding the importance of rumors in the prisoner society of the concentration camps, see also Michel (2002). When Neurath wrote his manuscript, he naturally did not have the opportunity to check his dates and facts; the work had already been submitted as a dissertation in the US in 1943 (cf. Neurath 2005: 279ff.).

30 Stanislav Zámečník (1922–2011), born in Moravia, was arrested by the Nazis when he was seventeen for political activities and incarcerated in a number of different prisons. In 1941 he was deported to Dachau, where he was imprisoned until the liberation of the camp in 1945. He subsequently earned a doctorate in history and worked at the Military History Institute in Prague. He was banned from employment in 1968 in the wake of the "Prague Spring" and was not able to continue his research again until 1989. His comprehensive book about Dachau, based both on his extensive study of historical sources and on his own experiences, was completed in 2000 and published for the first time in 2002 (cf. Zámečník 2007).

31 Stanislav Zámečník dates this period of isolation to the year 1936 (see note 28), and he does not mention any court proceedings relating to homosexual practices (cf. Zámečník 2007: 103). Like Neurath, Zámečník associates the alleged suicide of two Jewish communists – which was probably actually a case of murder following torture by the SS – with apparent "atrocity propaganda," but he dates this to the year 1934 (cf. Zámečník 2007: 42ff.).

32 Szalet reports that in Sachsenhausen,

> "The Latrine Courier" [. . .] soon came to have great influence. [. . .] Of course, a few of us pretended to have nothing but contempt for "The Latrine Courier." When a comrade announced that he had something of general interest to tell, they would say with superior shrugs: "Aha, a new latrine dispatch." All the same, they pricked up their ears and did not miss a syllable. One day it occurred to me that we might use "The Latrine Courier" as a means of keeping up morale [. . .]. Often when the general mood had reached a dangerous low, we invented reports that dispelled the depression. (Szalet 1945: 110–11)

33 In his book *The Cap: The Price of a Life*, Roman Frister is unusually open in his description of a particularly dramatic incident from the perspective of a *"Pipel"*

(Frister 2001: 237ff.): One night, a privileged prisoner raped the sixteen-year-old Frister while simultaneously shoving bread into the starving boy's mouth. He subsequently stole Frister's cap, knowing full well that the boy would be shot at the morning roll call for not having a cap, so there would be no one to testify to the rape. When Frister's seemingly inescapable fate dawned on him, he crept through the hut until he found a sleeping prisoner whose carelessly hidden cap he could steal. The following morning, he experienced the privileged prisoner's astonishment that Frister still had his cap – and then the gunshot during the roll call which felled the prisoner whose cap Frister had taken. Frister expresses the humiliation he felt at not having resisted the rape because of the bread, and he acknowledges that he brought about the death of another person to save his own life. Testimonies of this kind, particularly those which make reference to homosexual activities, are extremely rare in the literature of memory.

34 Not all prisoners were allowed to receive the bonus coupons that permitted them to visit the brothel; Jews in particular were excluded from this (cf. Langbein 2004: 405; Levi 1995: 80). German prisoners with the pink triangle were also forced to pay visits to the brothel, as this was expected to cure them of their "perverse disposition" (see, e.g., Heger 1994: 98).

35 In a letter to Himmler, the Minister of Justice explained the advantages of mixing the prisoners in this way: "This principle aims to distribute the homosexuals in such a way that they are always surrounded by a large majority of individuals who are not sexual perverts and who will keep both the homosexuals and each other under control on account of the abhorrence of homosexuality that is very widespread even among convicts" (quoted in Müller et al. 2002: 35).

36 Regarding the mass and the elite in the concentration camps, see section 6.2.

37 We know, for instance, that the "reigning" camp librarian in the prisoner library in Dachau was the social democrat Kurt Schumacher, who was "very distant" toward fellow anti-fascists who were not also social democrats and made no effort to support them (cf. Seela 1992: 103f.).

38 The Gorals self-identify as a rebellious highland people from the Beskid Mountains in Poland who have preserved their own customs for centuries (cf. *Meyers Großes Taschenlexikon* 2006: 2772).

39 In the camp jargon, prisoner functionaries were known as *Bindenträger* (armband wearers) on account of the armbands they wore, which signaled their position to the other prisoners.

40 Exceptions to this, as explained in the introduction to this chapter, included the Theresienstadt camp as well as the "Theresienstadt family camp" and the "Gypsy family camp" (camp sections B IIb and B IIe) in Auschwitz-Birkenau. The Bergen-Belsen concentration camp also temporarily had certain sections in which families or men and women could come into contact with each other.

41 Antelme and his fellow prisoners were first housed in a church and forced to construct the camp of huts and work in an aircraft parts plant. After the huts were completed in early 1945, Antelme was imprisoned in the camp until it

was evacuated. He was sent on a death march at the start of April 1945 and was finally liberated in Dachau at the end of the same month. For more on the Bad Gandersheim satellite camp, see Benz and Distel (2006a: 374–6).

42 It is also worth noting that the title of the chapter in his first book in which he describes the "dwarf" ("The Drowned and the Saved" in Levi 1995) is the same as the title of his entire last book (*The Drowned and the Saved*, Levi 1989). This shows that the question of why some survived while others did not plagued him his entire life.

43 Améry himself viewed returning a blow as a "reasoned revolt against the perverted world of the Lager" and considered Levi's "forgiveness" to be a sign of political weakness (cf. Levi 1990: 135). However, this does not necessarily mean that the issue of insufficient manliness did not implicitly play a role in Améry's criticism of Levi.

44 In the course of the Zionist movement, this "traditional Jewish habitus" also changed, and physical training became an important part of the preparation for the tasks to be faced in Erez Israel. Key aspects worth mentioning here include the "*Muskeljudentum*" ("muscular Jewry") called for by Max Nordau at the Second Zionist Congress in Basle in 1898 (cf. Nordau 1900) and the Maccabi athletic movement (cf. also Schoeps 1992: 431). Since Levi neither was a Zionist nor had any ambition to emigrate to Palestine, we can assume on the basis of his personal biography and his family customs that he was influenced by the "traditional Jewish habitus" described by Bourdieu. Améry was also Jewish, but following his father's early death, he was raised by his mother in a traditionally rural Catholic way, so it is likely that this "Jewish habitus" was alien to him. For more on Levi's biography, see Anissimov (1998); for Améry's biography, see Heidelberger-Leonard (2010); regarding sports in Judaism, see Schoeps (1992: 431f.).

45 This was the "traditional Jewish habitus" (Bourdieu 2001a: 51), which had always been the tradition of a minority in his home country of Italy, meaning that he must have been sufficiently familiar with the dominant notion of masculinity of the majority. In Auschwitz, by contrast, the Jewish tradition was the majority tradition among the prisoners in this late phase of the "Third Reich." However, this majority was very underprivileged within the camp hierarchy and therefore had very little scope to influence the "camp culture" (if there was such a thing). Regarding the composition of the prisoner society in Auschwitz at various times, see Piper (1998), for example.

46 A game played by boys which prepares them for the antagonistic world of men.

47 Shame is a common topic in autobiographical accounts of the Holocaust. Survivors felt ashamed because they had lived while others had died (see, e.g., Levi 1989). In the context of gender, however, shame was the result of honor which had been injured – in the case of women, usually through sexualized (symbolic and physical) violence.

48 Liana Millu (1912–2005), Italian resistance fighter, was imprisoned in Auschwitz-Birkenau and elsewhere for being Jewish. Shortly after she returned

home, she wrote about her time in the concentration camps. Her book, consisting of six stories, was published in 1947 by a small Italian publishing company and is probably the first depiction of everyday life in a concentration camp from a female perspective (cf. Jäger 2001).

49 Ruth Bondy, born in 1923 in Prague, survived Auschwitz and Bergen-Belsen. Since 1948 she has lived in Israel and worked as a journalist and author (cf. Distel 2003: 424).

50 Julia Kertesz, born in 1921 in Klausenburg/Romania, survived Auschwitz, Bergen-Belsen, and Neuengamme. She subsequently worked as a language teacher in Romania before emigrating to the Federal Republic of Germany in 1974 together with her husband (cf. Distel 2003: 424f.).

51 *Muselmann* (literally: Muslim) was the conventional term in all camps for prisoners in the final stage before death. The origin of the word is unclear, though there are various theories (cf. Agamben 2002: 44ff.; Benz et al. 1997: 590f.; Ryn and Kłodziński 1987). The less common female counterpart to the *Muselmann* was the *Schmuckstück* (trinket) (cf. Tillion 1975: 15, 23f.). Regarding "*Muselmänner*," Primo Levi writes the following:

> [T]hey, the *Muselmänner*, the drowned, form the backbone of the camp, an anonymous mass, continually renewed and always identical, of non-men who march and labor in silence, the divine spark dead within them, already too empty to really suffer. One hesitates to call them living: one hesitates to call their death death, in the face of which they have no fear, as they are too tired to understand. (Levi 1995: 90)

The conventional image of the *Muselmänner* has been heavily influenced by Levi's observations. Since *Muselmänner* (or *Schmuckstücke*) very rarely survived, the state of research into their actual circumstances and manifestations is desolate. This makes the attempt by Zdzisław Ryn and Stanislaw Kłodziński (1987) to systematically compile information and assessments from former concentration camp prisoners regarding this subject all the more commendable. In many ways, the empirical findings tend to support Giorgio Agamben's argument that even when "on the threshold between life and death" (the title of the work by Ryn und Kłodziński: *An der Grenze zwischen Leben und Tod*), the *Muselmänner* were still human beings (cf. Agamben 2002: 63) and that there was even a social life among them.

52 It is worth mentioning that this story, the title of which is "The Teddy Bear," has a chilling punchline (cf. Delbo 1995: 166), but this will not be discussed in detail here because it is not relevant to the question of the continuity of gender concepts.

53 The women worked in an experimental laboratory which was involved in producing synthetic rubber; they were also able to acquire some food on the black market by trading bread for dried peas, for example (cf. Delbo 1995: 162).

54 There has been a great deal of academic discussion about whether women really had better strategies in the concentration camps or whether, on account of their particular "female constitution," they actually suffered more than

men (cf., e.g., several essays in Bock 2005). This question cannot be definitively answered, and it is also not the focus of this work, which is primarily interested in how these aspects were perceived and expressed by the inmates themselves. Nonetheless, original source materials have revealed significant differences in the survival rates of men and women imprisoned at the same time in the same camp under the same conditions and forced to do work of the same difficulty. Hans Ellger, for example, researched the Neuengamme camp system and concluded that the mortality rate among the male prisoners was 15.2 percent while that of the female prisoners was only 0.8 percent. He attributes this both to "socialization-related gender differences" (Ellger 2005: 177), which assisted in the acquisition and use of additional foodstuffs and the fabrication of additional clothing (ibid.: 178f.), and to the establishment of traditionally female social networks in the form of "camp families" (ibid.: 179f.). Ellger also suspects, however, that individual male guards behaved differently toward female and male prisoners; in their personal accounts, male and female former prisoners sometimes refer to the same guard as either especially "violent" toward prisoners or as "invariably peaceable and good-natured" (ibid.: 181). It is therefore possible that it was easier for women to smuggle things into the camp undetected.

55 In this context, it should actually be "matronage."

56 One exception was the Ravensbrück camp for women, which had its own maternity ward where the women were able to give birth under relatively hygienic conditions. However, this did not change the fact that the babies born there died shortly afterwards because they could not be adequately cared for (cf. Walz 2005a, 2005b).

57 Exceptions to this are the texts by women whose declared intention is to depict the crimes committed in the camps and which therefore have a more political slant, such as the book by Germaine Tillion (1975).

58 Maria Montuoro was an Italian woman who was imprisoned in Ravensbrück and forced to carry out slave labor there (cf. Distel 2003: 426).

59 I was able to make only a provisional attempt to find out what kind of dish *"pambania"* is. After fruitlessly perusing a comprehensive French–German dictionary, an internet search led me to a recipe forum which mentioned *"pain bagnia"* or *"pan bagna,"* apparently a popular type of sandwich in southern France featuring boiled eggs and a variety of Mediterranean salad ingredients. In the context of this work, the specific meal discussed by Antelme and his comrade is not important. However, if *"pambania"* is, in fact, merely a type of sandwich, I find it all the more remarkable that in the fantasy scenario described here, his mother has to make it for him.

60 There are a few examples of a different male attitude toward cooking, such as that found in the memoirs of Yves Béon, which describe a professional cook who gives his fellow prisoners verbal "samples" of his culinary skills (Béon 1997: 35–6). The inmate says: "I'm a cook by profession. With anything, I'll make up a feast. [. . .]. Me, I've looked after ministers, famous actresses, and people of whom you have no idea [. . .]" (ibid.: 36). In light of Bourdieu's

theories (Bourdieu 1997a, 2001a), this attitude can also be viewed as an explicitly male perspective in which women are associated with the ordinary while men are associated with the extraordinary and the spectacular (in relation to kitchens and cooking, see in particular Frerichs and Steinrücke 1997).

Chapter 7 The Constitution of Social Identity in the Concentration Camps: The Concepts of Individuality and the Importance of Social Structures in a "Topsy-Turvy" World

1 Regarding the term "*Muselmann*," see also chapter 6, note 51.
2 For example, Hermine Markovits, who had to work as a secretary in Auschwitz, reports that she asked a camp physician who was responsible for gassing prisoners and whom she occasionally dealt with in the administrative offices how he could reconcile taking the Hippocratic Oath with killing human beings instead of helping them. He responded by curtly questioning whether Jews were actually human beings (cf. Hermine Markovits in Shelley 1986: 121).
3 http://www.merriam-webster.com/dictionary/potency accessed on April 29, 2013.
4 Exceptions prove the rule. Prisoners were sometimes able to bribe the Gestapo into removing their yellow triangle for Jews and categorizing them "merely" as enemies of the state, which undoubtedly improved their chances of survival (cf. Rummel and Rath 2001: 266; see also chapter 5, note 16).
5 Beyond these theoretical conceptual considerations, the idea that classification by gender was similar in character to being classified as a Jew or "Gypsy" can be found in an interview with Ruth Klüger (see also chapter 5, note 21), who makes interesting observations on "being a woman" and "being a Jew":

> I'm very unsure about the relationship between being a woman and being a Jew in our society today. People always reject the idea of comparing the two. [. . .] Both prejudices are abating, and both still exist. When someone talks down to you, you never know if it's because of the one reason or the other. (Klüger 2008: 146)

The comment by Raya Kagan quoted elsewhere (cf. chapter 6.2) – "We represented a double danger in the eyes of the SS as women as well as Jews" (cited in Shelley 1986: 276) – also indicates that to be a woman and a Jew was to be indelibly tarnished.
6 Ground bass or *basso ostinato* (obstinate bass) is the constant repetition of a musical phrase, motif, or harmonic pattern in the bass line of a piece of music, such as in a chaconne or a passacaglia. Cf. *Encyclopædia Britannica* online (http://www.britannica.com/EBchecked/topic/246877/ground-bass, accessed on April 29, 2013).

Bibliography

Abgeleitete Macht. Funktionshäftlinge zwischen Widerstand und Kollaboration (1998), published by the Neuengamme Concentration Camp Memorial. Bremen: Edition Temmen.

Adler, Hans G. (1955) *Theresienstadt 1941–1955. Das Antlitz einer Zwangsgemeinschaft. Geschichte, Soziologie, Psychologie.* Tübingen: Mohr.

Adorno, Theodor W. (1971) "Erziehung nach Auschwitz," in: *Erziehung zur Mündigkeit. Vorträge und Gespräche mit Hellmut Becker 1959–1969.* Frankfurt am Main: Suhrkamp, pp. 88–104.

Agamben, Giorgio (2002) *Remnants of Auschwitz: The Witness and the Archive.* Translated by Daniel Heller-Roazen. New York: Zone Books. [*Quel che resta di Auschwitz. L'archivio e il testimone*, 1998]

Aly, Götz and Karl Heinz Roth (2000) *Die restlose Erfassung. Volkszählung, Identifizieren, Aussondern im Nationalsozialismus.* [Revised version of edition from 1984, Berlin: Rotbuch]. Frankfurt am Main: Fischer Taschenbuchverlag.

Améry, Jean [pseudonym of Hans Mayer] (1978) "Fernsehgespräch" (recorded on July 20, 1978) in: *Hermannstraße 14. Halbjahresschrift für Literatur*, edited by Helmut Heißenbüttel and Bernd Jentzsch. Stuttgart: Klett-Cotta, pp. 45–8.

Améry, Jean [pseudonym of Hans Mayer] (1980a) *At the Mind's Limits: Contemplations by a Survivor on Auschwitz and its Realities.* Translated by Sidney Rosenfeld and Stella P. Rosenfeld. Bloomington and Indianapolis: Indiana University Press. [*Jenseits von Schuld und Sühne. Bewältigungsversuche eines Überwältigten*, 1966]

Améry, Jean [pseudonym of Hans Mayer] (1980b) *Örtlichkeiten.* Stuttgart: Klett-Cotta.

Améry, Jean [pseudonym of Hans Mayer] (1999) *On Suicide: A Discourse on Voluntary Death.* Translated by John D. Barlow. Bloomington: Indiana University Press. [*Hand an sich legen. Diskurs über den Freitod*, 1976]

Amesberger, Helga, Katrin Auer, and Brigitte Halbmayr (2004) *Sexualisierte Gewalt. Weibliche Erfahrungen in NS-Konzentrationslagern.* Vienna: Mandelbaum.

Anissimov, Myriam (1998) *Primo Levi: Tragedy of an Optimist.* Translated by Steve Cox. London: Aurum Press Ltd. [*Primo Levi ou la tragédie d'un optimiste*, 1996]

Antelme, Robert (1998) *The Human Race*. Translated by Jeffrey Haight and Annie Mahler. Evanston, IL: The Marlboro Press. [*L'espèce humaine*, 1957]

Apel, Linde (2005) "Judenverfolgung und KZ-System. Jüdische Frauen in Ravensbrück," in: *Genozid und Geschlecht. Jüdische Frauen im nationalsozialistischen Lagersystem*, edited by Gisela Bock. Frankfurt am Main: Campus, pp. 44–65.

Apostoł-Staniszewska, Jadwiga (1987) "Reflexionen aus dem Frauenlager Birkenau," in: *Die Auschwitz-Hefte. Texte der polnischen Zeitschrift "Przegląd Lekarski," über historische, psychische und medizinische Aspekte des Lebens und Sterbens in Auschwitz*, Vol. 1, published by the Hamburger Institut für Sozialforschung. Weinheim; Basel: Beltz, pp. 219–25.

Appelfeld, Aharon (2005) "Kindheit im Holocaust," in: *Le Monde diplomatique* (international supplement to the *taz*), February 11, pp. 1 and 10.

Arendt, Hannah (1951) "Die Konzentrationslager," in: *Elemente und Ursprünge totaler Herrschaft. Antisemitismus, Imperialismus, Totalitarismus*. Frankfurt am Main: EVA, pp. 644–71.

Arnold, Heinz Ludwig (ed.) (1988) *Text und Kritik. Zeitschrift für Literatur*. Issue 99: *Jean Améry*.

Auffermann, Verena (2007) "Die Stürme des Lebens," in: *Die Zeit* 31, p. 53.

Die Auschwitz-Hefte. Texte der polnischen Zeitschrift "Przegląd Lekarski" über historische, psychische und medizinische Aspekte des Lebens und Sterbens in Auschwitz, 2 volumes, published by the Hamburger Institut für Sozialforschung. Weinheim; Basel: Beltz 1987.

Bader, Uwe and Beate Weiler (2007) "Das SS-Sonderlager/KZ-Hinzert," in: *Der Ort des Terrors. Geschichte der nationalsozialistischen Konzentrationslager*, Vol. 5: *Hinzert – Auschwitz – Neuengamme*, edited by Wolfgang Benz and Barbara Distel. Munich: Beck, pp. 17–42.

Baier, Lothar (1996) "Die zarte Haltung. Die Kritik des schreibenden Lesers Jean Améry," in: *Jean Améry (Hans Maier)*, edited by Stephan Steiner. Basel; Frankfurt am Main: Stroemfeld, pp. 217–33.

Bajohr, Frank (2003) *"Unser Hotel ist judenfrei." Bäder-Antisemitismus im 19. und 20. Jahrhundert*. Frankfurt am Main: Fischer Taschenbuchverlag.

Bajohr, Frank (2004) "Über die Entwicklung eines schlechten Gewissens. Die deutsche Bevölkerung und die Deportationen 1941–1945," in: *Die Deportation der Juden aus Deutschland. Pläne – Praxis – Reaktionen 1938–1945*, edited by Birthe Kundrus and Beate Meyer. Göttingen: Wallstein, pp. 180–194.

Baleanu, Avram A. (1992) "Ahasverus, ewiger Jude," in: *Neues Lexikon des Judentums*, edited by Julius Schoeps. Gütersloh: Bertelsmann Lexikon Verlag, pp. 19–22.

Baranowski, Frank (2006) "Bad Gandersheim," in: *Der Ort des Terrors. Geschichte der nationalsozialistischen Konzentrationslager*, Vol. 3: *Sachsenhausen – Buchenwald*, edited by Wolfgang Benz and Barbara Distel. Munich: Beck, pp. 374–6.

Barhai, Avraham and Paul Mendes-Flohr (2000) *Aufbruch und Zerstörung: 1918–1945*, Vol. 4 of *Deutsch-jüdische Geschichte in der Neuzeit*, edited by Michael A. Meyer. Munich: Beck.

Barnavi, Eli (1992) *A Historical Atlas of the Jewish People: From the Time of the Patriarchs to the Present.* New York: Schocken Books.

Bastian, Till (2000) *Homosexuelle im Dritten Reich. Geschichte einer Verfolgung.* Munich: Beck.

Battenberg, Friedrich (1996) "Zwischen Integration und Segregation. Zu den Bedingungen jüdischen Lebens in der vormodernen christlichen Gesellschaft," in: *Aschkenas* 6(2), pp. 421–54.

Battenberg, Friedrich (1997) "Grenzen und Möglichkeiten der Integration von Juden in der Gesellschaft des Ancien Régime," in: *Migration und Integration. Aufnahme und Eingliederung im historischen Wandel,* edited by Mathias Beer, Martin Kintzinger, and Marita Krauss. Stuttgart: Franz Steiner Verlag, pp. 87–110.

Battenberg, Friedrich (2001) *Die Juden in Deutschland vom 16. bis zum Ende des 18. Jahrhunderts.* Munich: Oldenbourg.

Bauman, Janina (1986) *Winter in the Morning.* London: Virago.

Bauman, Zygmunt (1989) *Modernity and the Holocaust.* Cambridge: Polity.

Bauman, Zygmunt (1992) *Mortality, Immortality and Other Life Strategies.* Stanford: Stanford University Press.

Bauman, Zygmunt (1995) *Life in Fragments: Essays in Postmodern Morality.* Oxford: Blackwell.

Bauman, Zygmunt (1999) *Culture as Praxis.* London: Sage Publications. [Originally published 1973]

Bayly, Susan (1999) *Caste, Society and Politics in India from the Eighteenth Century to the Modern Age.* Cambridge: Cambridge University Press.

Beaufaÿs, Sandra (2003) *Wie werden Wissenschaftler gemacht? Beobachtungen zur wechselseitigen Konstitution von Geschlecht und Wissenschaft.* Bielefeld: Transcript.

Beckermann, Ruth (1996) "Unter der Bank gelesen," in: *Jean Améry (Hans Maier),* edited by Stephan Steiner. Basel, Frankfurt am Main: Stroemfeld, pp. 165–82.

Benz, Wolfgang (2005) "Nationalsozialistische Zwangslager. Ein Überblick," in: *Der Ort des Terrors. Geschichte der nationalsozialistischen Konzentrationslager,* Vol. 1: *Die Organisation des Terrors,* edited by Wolfgang Benz and Barbara Distel. Munich: Beck, pp. 11–29.

Benz, Wolfgang and Barbara Distel (eds) (2005ff.) *Der Ort des Terrors. Geschichte der nationalsozialistischen Konzentrationslager.* Munich: Beck.

Benz, Wolfgang and Barbara Distel (eds) (2005a) *Die Organisation des Terrors.* [Vol. 1 of Benz and Distel 2005ff: *Der Ort des Terrors. Geschichte der nationalsozialistischen Konzentrationslager*]. Munich: Beck.

Benz, Wolfgang and Barbara Distel (eds) (2005b) *Häftlingsgesellschaft. Dachauer Hefte* 21. Dachau: Verlag Dachauer Hefte.

Benz, Wolfgang and Barbara Distel (eds) (2005c) *Frühe Lager – Dachau – Emslandlager.* [Vol. 2 of Benz and Distel 2005ff: *Der Ort des Terrors. Geschichte der nationalsozialistischen Konzentrationslager*]. Munich: Beck.

Benz, Wolfgang and Barbara Distel (eds) (2006a) *Sachsenhausen - Buchenwald.* [Vol. 3 of Benz and Distel 2005ff: *Der Ort des Terrors. Geschichte der nationalsozialistischen Konzentrationslager*]. Munich: Beck.

Benz, Wolfgang and Barbara Distel (eds) (2006b) *Flossenbürg – Mauthausen – Ravensbrück*. [Vol. 4 of Benz and Distel 2005ff: *Der Ort des Terrors. Geschichte der nationalsozialistischen Konzentrationslager*]. Munich: Beck.

Benz, Wolfgang and Barbara Distel (eds) (2006c) *Realität – Metapher – Symbol. Dachauer Hefte* 22. Dachau: Verlag Dachauer Hefte.

Benz, Wolfgang and Barbara Distel (eds) (2007) *Hinzert – Auschwitz – Neuengamme*. [Vol. 5 of Benz and Distel 2005ff: *Der Ort des Terrors. Geschichte der nationalsozialistischen Konzentrationslager*]. Munich: Beck.

Benz, Wolfgang, Hermann Graml, and Hermann Weiß (eds) (1997) *Enzyklopädie des Nationalsozialismus*. Munich: dtv.

Béon, Yves (1997) *Planet Dora: A Memoir of the Holocaust and the Birth of the Space Age*. Translated by Yves Béon and Richard L. Fague. Boulder, CO: Westview Press. [*La planète Dora*, 1985]

Bettelheim, Bruno (1980a) "Individuelles und Massenverhalten in Extremsituationen," in: *Erziehung zum Überleben*. Stuttgart: DVA, pp. 58–95. [*Surviving and Other Essays*, 1979]

Bettelheim, Bruno (1980b) "Überlegungen zur Privatsphäre," in: *Erziehung zum Überleben*. Stuttgart: DVA, pp. 366–78. [*Surviving and Other Essays*, 1979]

Bielefeld, Ulrich (1993) "Gespräch mit Janina und Zygmunt Bauman," in: *Mittelweg 36* 2(4), pp. 17–22.

Bielefeld, Ulrich (2001) "Ethnizität und Existenz," in: *Geschlecht – Ethnizität – Klasse. Zur sozialen Konstruktion von Hierarchie und Differenz*, edited by Claudia Rademacher and Peter Wiechens. Opladen: Leske + Budrich, pp. 129–43.

Biller, Maxim (2006) "Die Hölle ist ein guter Stoff. Der Schriftsteller Maxim Biller über die Neuauflage von Tadeusz Borowskis 'Bei uns in Auschwitz,'" in: *Der Spiegel* 47, pp. 214–16.

Birger, Trudi (1992) *A Daughter's Gift of Love: A Holocaust Memoir*. Written with Jeffrey M. Green. Philadelphia: The Jewish Publication Society. [*Im Angesicht des Feuers*, 1990]

Bistrović, Miriam (2007) "Das Zigeunerlager (B IIe) in Birkenau," in: *Der Ort des Terrors. Geschichte der nationalsozialistischen Konzentrationslager*, Vol. 5: *Hinzert – Auschwitz – Neuengamme*, edited by Wolfgang Benz and Barbara Distel. Munich: Beck, pp. 115–18.

Blanchot, Maurice (1969) *L'entretien infini*. Paris: Gallimard.

Bock, Gisela (ed.) (2005) *Genozid und Geschlecht. Jüdische Frauen im nationalsozialistischen Lagersystem*. Frankfurt am Main: Campus.

Bondy, Ruth (2003) "Frauen in Theresienstadt und im Familienlager Auschwitz-Birkenau," in: *"Wir konnten die Kinder doch nicht im Stich lassen!" Frauen im Holocaust*, edited by Barbara Distel. Cologne: Komet, pp. 117–41.

Borowski, Tadeusz (1992) *This Way for the Gas, Ladies and Gentlemen*. Translated by Barbara Vedder. New York: Penguin Classics. [*Wybór Opowiadan*, 1959; selections from *Kamienny swiat* and *Pożegnanie z Marią*]

Borowski, Tadeusz (2008) *Bei uns in Auschwitz. Erzählungen*. Translated by Friedrich Griese. Frankfurt am Main: Schöffling. [*Utwory Wybrane*, 1991]

Bös, Mathias (2005) *Rasse und Ethnizität. Zur Problemgeschichte zweier Begriffe in der amerikanischen Soziologie.* Wiesbaden: VS.

Bourdieu, Pierre (1984) *Distinction: A Social Critique of the Judgement of Taste.* Translated by Richard Nice. Cambridge, MA: Harvard University Press. [*La Distinction: Critique sociale du jugement*, 1979]

Bourdieu, Pierre (1985) "The Social Space and the Genesis of Groups," in: *Theory and Society* 14(6), pp. 723–44.

Bourdieu, Pierre (1986) "The Forms of Capital," translated by Richard Nice, in: *Handbook of Theory and Research for Sociology of Education*, edited by John G. Richardson. Westport, CT: Greenwood Press, pp. 241–58. ["Ökonomisches Kapital, kulturelles Kapital, soziales Kapital," 1983]

Bourdieu, Pierre (1990) *The Logic of Practice.* Translated by Richard Nice. Stanford: Stanford University Press. [*Le sens pratique*, 1980]

Bourdieu, Pierre (1991a) "Genesis and Structure of the Religious Field," translated by Jenny B. Burnside, Craig Calhoun, and Leah Florence, in: *Comparative Social Research* 13, edited by Craig Calhoun, pp. 1–44. ["Genèse et structure du champ religieux," 1971]

Bourdieu, Pierre (1991b) *Language and Symbolic Power*, edited by John B. Thompson, translated by Gino Raymond and Matthew Adamson. Cambridge: Polity Press. [*Ce que parler veut dire*, 1982]

Bourdieu, Pierre (1993a) "The Paradox of the Sociologist," in: *Sociology in Question.* Translated by Richard Nice. London: Sage Publications Ltd., pp. 54–9. [*Questions de Sociologie*, 1984]

Bourdieu, Pierre (1993b) "The Linguistic Market," in: *Sociology in Question.* Translated by Richard Nice. London: Sage Publications Ltd., pp. 78–89. [*Questions de Sociologie*, 1984]

Bourdieu, Pierre (1993c) "The Racism of 'Intelligence,'" in: *Sociology in Question.* London: Sage Publications Ltd., pp. 177–80. [*Questions de Sociologie*, 1984]

Bourdieu, Pierre (1994) *In Other Words: Essays Towards a Reflexive Sociology.* Translated by Matthew Adamson. Stanford: Stanford University Press. [*Choses dites*, 1987]

Bourdieu, Pierre (1996) "Was bin ich? Ein Interview mit Pierre Bourdieu von Isabelle Graw," in: *THE THING Vienna.* http://www.homme-moderne.org/societe/socio/bourdieu/entrevue/was.html, accessed on April 29, 2013.

Bourdieu, Pierre (1997a) "Die männliche Herrschaft," in: *Ein alltägliches Spiel. Geschlechterkonstruktion in der sozialen Praxis*, edited by Irene Dölling and Beate Krais. Frankfurt am Main: Suhrkamp, pp. 153–217.

Bourdieu, Pierre (1997b) "Eine sanfte Gewalt. Pierre Bourdieu im Gespräch mit Irene Dölling und Margareta Steinrücke," in: *Ein alltägliches Spiel. Geschlechterkonstruktion in der sozialen Praxis*, edited by Irene Dölling and Beate Krais. Frankfurt am Main: Suhrkamp, pp. 218–30.

Bourdieu, Pierre (1998) *Practical Reason: On the Theory of Action.* Translated by Gisele Sapiro, Randal Johnson, Loïc Wacquant, Samar Farage, and Richard Nice. Stanford: Stanford University Press. [*Raisons Pratiques*, 1994]

Bourdieu, Pierre (1999) "Understanding," in: *The Weight of the World*, Pierre

Bourdieu et al. Translated by Priscilla Parkhurst Ferguson. Stanford: Stanford University Press. [*La Misère du monde*, 1993]

Bourdieu, Pierre (2000a) "The Biographical Illusion," translated by Yves Winkin and Wendy Leeds-Hurwitz, in: *Identity: A Reader*, edited by Paul du Gay, Jessica Evans, and Peter Redman. London: Sage Publications Ltd., pp. 299–304.

Bourdieu, Pierre (2000b) "A Logic in Action," in: *Pascalian Meditations*. Translated by Richard Nice. Stanford: Stanford University Press, pp. 142–6. [*Méditations pascaliennes*, 1997]

Bourdieu, Pierre (2000c) "Symbolic Capital," in: *Pascalian Meditations*. Translated by Richard Nice. Stanford: Stanford University Press, pp. 240–5. [*Méditations pascaliennes*, 1997]

Bourdieu, Pierre (2000d) "Habitus and Incorporation," in: *Pascalian Meditations*. Translated by Richard Nice. Stanford: Stanford University Press, pp. 138–42. [*Méditations pascaliennes*, 1997]

Bourdieu, Pierre (2001a) *Masculine Domination*. Translated by Richard Nice. Stanford: Stanford University Press. [*La domination masculine*, 1998]

Bourdieu, Pierre (2001b) "Teilen und herrschen. Zur symbolischen Ökonomie des Geschlechterverhältnisses," in: *Geschlecht – Ethnizität – Klasse. Zur sozialen Konstruktion von Hierarchie und Differenz*, edited by Claudia Rademacher and Peter Wiechens. Opladen: Leske + Budrich, pp. 11–30.

Bourdieu, Pierre (2003) "Die Ermordung des Maurice Halbwachs," in: *Maurice Halbwachs – Aspekte des Werks*, edited by Stephan Egger, translated by Jörg Ohnacker. Constance: UVK, pp. 229–34.

Bourdieu, Pierre (2004) *Schwierige Interdisziplinarität. Zum Verhältnis von Soziologie und Geschichtswissenschaft*, edited by Elke Ohnacker and Frank Schultheis. Münster: Westfälisches Dampfboot.

Bourdieu, Pierre (2005) "Principles of an Economic Anthropology," translated by Chris Turner, in: *The Handbook of Economic Sociology*, edited by Neil J. Smelser and Richard Swedberg. Princeton: Princeton University Press, pp. 75–89.

Bourdieu, Pierre (2007) *Sketch for a Self-Analysis*. Translated by Richard Nice. Cambridge: Polity Press. [*Esquisse pour une auto-analyse*, 2004]

Bourdieu, Pierre and Jean-Claude Passeron (1990) "Foundations of a Theory of Symbolic Violence," in: *Reproduction in Education, Society and Culture*. Translated by Richard Nice. London: Sage Publications Ltd., pp. 1–68. [*La Reproduction. Éléments pour une théorie du système d'enseignement*, 1970]

Bourdieu, Pierre and Loïc Wacquant (1992) *An Invitation to Reflexive Sociology*. Chicago: University of Chicago Press.

Brandenburg, Rainer (1990) "Zum Verhältnis von Subjekt und Geschichte im Werk Jean Amérys," in: *Über Jean Améry*, edited by Irene Heidelberger-Leonard. Heidelberg: Winter Universitätsverlag, pp. 59–68.

Brauer, Juliane (2009) *Musik im Lager Sachsenhausen*. Berlin: Metropol.

Brenner, Michael (1996) *The Renaissance of Jewish Culture in Weimar Germany*. New Haven, CT: Yale University Press.

Breuer, Mordechai and Michael Graetz (1996) *Tradition and Enlightenment 1600–1780*, Vol. I of *German-Jewish History in Modern Times*, edited by Michael

A. Meyer, translated by William Templer. New York: Columbia University Press.

Brzezicki, Eugeniusz, Adolf Gawalewicz, Tadeusz Hołuj, Antoni Kępiński, Stanisław Kłodiński, and Władysław Wolter (1987) "Die Funktionshäftlinge in den Nazi-Konzentrationslagern. Eine Diskussion," in: *Die Auschwitz-Hefte. Texte der polnischen Zeitschrift "Przegląd Lekarsk" über historische, psychische und medizinische Aspekte des Lebens und Sterbens in Auschwitz*, Vol. 1, published by the Hamburger Institut für Sozialforschung. Weinheim; Basel: Beltz, pp. 231–9.

Bundesverband Information und Beratung NS-Verfolgter. http://www.ns-beratung. de, accessed on April 30, 2013.

Burke, Peter (2005) *History and Social Theory*, 2nd edition. Ithaca, NY: Cornell University Press.

Cahnman, Werner J. (1989a) "In the Dachau Concentration Camp: An Autobiographical Essay," in: *German Jewry: Its History and Sociology*, edited by Joseph B. Maier, Judith Marcus, and Zoltán Tarr. New Brunswick, NJ: Transaction Publishers, pp. 151–8.

Cahnman, Werner J. (1989b) "Pariahs, Strangers, and Court Jews," in: *German Jewry: Its History and Sociology*, edited by Joseph B. Maier, Judith Marcus, and Zoltán Tarr. New Brunswick, NJ: Transaction Publishers, pp. 15–28.

Cahnman, Werner J. (2005) "Judentum und Volksgemeinschaft," in: *Deutsche Juden. Ihre Geschichte und Soziologie*. Münster: Westfälisches Dampfboot, pp. 20–6.

Christin, Olivier (2005) "Geschichtswissenschaften und Bourdieu," in: *Pierre Bourdieu: Deutsch–französische Perspektiven*, edited by Catherine Colliot-Thélène, Étienne François, and Gunter Gebauer. Frankfurt am Main: Suhrkamp, pp. 195–207.

Cremer, Hendrik (2008) *"... und welcher Rasse gehören Sie an?" Zur Problematik des Begriffs "Rasse" in der Gesetzgebung*. Published by the German Institute for Human Rights, Berlin. *Policy Paper No. 10*.

Czech, Danuta (1990) *Auschwitz Chronicle 1939–1945*. Translated by Barbara Harshav, Martha Humphreys, and Stephen Shearier. New York: Henry Holt & Company. [*Kalendarium wydarzen w obozie Koncentracyjnym Auschwitz-Birkenau 1939–1945*, 1958–63]

Daxelmüller, Christoph (1998) "Kulturelle Formen und Aktivitäten als Teil der Überlebens- und Vernichtungsstrategie in den Konzentrationslagern," in: *Die nationalsozialistischen Konzentrationslager. Entwicklung und Struktur*, Vol. 2, edited by Ulrich Herbert. Göttingen: Wallstein, pp. 983–1005.

de Montlibert, Christian (2003) "Maurice Halbwachs über soziale Klassen," in: *Maurice Halbwachs – Aspekte des Werks*, edited by Stephan Egger. Constance: UVK, pp. 29–44.

Death Books from Auschwitz. Remnants. Vol. 1: Reports (1995) Edited by the State Museum of Auschwitz-Birkenau. Translated by Michael Jacobs, Georg Mayer, and Jacek Plesniarowicz. Munich: K.G. Saur.

Delbo, Charlotte (1970) *Auschwitz et après II: Une connaissance inutile*. Paris: Les Éditions de Minuit.

Delbo, Charlotte (1995) *Auschwitz and After*. Translated by Rosette C. Lamont. New Haven, CT: Yale University Press. [*Auschwitz et après*, written 1946–7, published 1970]

Distel, Barbara (1998) "Das Zeugnis der Zurückgekehrten. Zur konfliktreichen Beziehung zwischen KZ-Überlebenden und Nachkriegsöffentlichkeit," in: *Die nationalsozialistischen Konzentrationslager. Entwicklung und Struktur*, Vol. 1, edited by Ulrich Herbert. Göttingen: Wallstein, pp. 11–16.

Distel, Barbara (ed.) (2003) "*Wir konnten die Kinder doch nicht im Stich lassen!*" *Frauen im Holocaust*. Cologne: Komet.

Distel, Barbara (2005) "Frauen in nationalsozialistischen Konzentrationslagern – Opfer und Täterinnen," in: *Der Ort des Terrors. Geschichte der nationalsozialistischen Konzentrationslager*, Vol. 1: *Die Organisation des Terrors*, edited by Wolfgang Benz and Barbara Distel. Munich: Beck, pp. 195–209.

Dölling, Irene (1999) "'Geschlecht' – eine analytische Kategorie mit Perspektive in den Sozialwissenschaften?" in: *Potsdamer Studien zur Frauen- und Geschlechterforschung* 3(1), pp. 17–26.

Dölling, Irene and Beate Krais (2007) "Pierre Bourdieus Soziologie der Praxis: ein Werkzeugkasten für die Frauen- und Geschlechterforschung," in: *Prekäre Transformationen. Pierre Bourdieus Soziologie der Praxis und ihre Herausforderungen für die Frauen- und Geschlechterforschung*, edited by Ulla Bock, Irene Dölling, and Beate Krais. Göttingen: Wallstein, pp. 12–37.

Douglas, Mary (2002) *Purity and Danger: An Analysis of the Concepts of Pollution and Taboo*. London: Routledge. [Originally published 1966]

Douglas, Mary (2003) "Pollution," in: *Implicit Meanings: Selected Essays in Anthropology*. London, New York: Routledge, pp. 106–15. [Originally published 1968]

Duby, Georges (ed.) (1992) *A History of Private Life*, 4 volumes. Translated by Arthur Goldhammer. Cambridge, MA: Belknap Press. [*Histoire de la vie privée*, 1985]

Duesterberg, Julia (2002) "Von der 'Umkehr aller Weiblichkeit.' Charakterbilder einer KZ-Aufseherin," in: *Gedächtnis und Geschlecht. Deutungsmuster in Darstellungen des nationalsozialistischen Genozids*, edited by Insa Eschebach, Sigrid Jacobeit, and Silke Wenk. Frankfurt am Main: Campus, pp. 227–43.

Dumont, Louis (1980) *Homo Hierarchicus: The Caste System and Its Implications*. Translated by George Weidenfeld and Nicolson Ltd. and by the University of Chicago. Chicago: University of Chicago Press. [*Homo hierarchicus: Le système des castes et ses implications*, 1966]

Dumont, Louis (1992) *Essays on Individualism: Modern Ideology in Anthropological Perspective*. Translated by Paul Hockings, Joseph Erhardy, and Louis Dumont. Chicago: University of Chicago Press. [*Essais sur l'individualisme: Une perspective anthropologique sur l'idéologie moderne*, 1983]

Dupont, Marc (2002) "Biologische und psychologische Konzepte im 'Dritten Reich' zur Homosexualität," in: *Nationalsozialistischer Terror gegen Homosexuelle. Verdrängt und ungesühnt*, edited by Burkhard Jellonnek and Rüdiger Lautmann. Paderborn: Schöningh.

Eberle, Annette (2005) "Häftlingskategorien und Kennzeichnungen," in: *Der Ort des Terrors. Geschichte der nationalsozialistischen Konzentrationslager*, Vol. 1: *Die Organisation des Terrors*, edited by Wolfgang Benz and Barbara Distel. Munich: Beck, pp. 91–109.

Elias, Norbert (1996) *The Germans: Power Struggles and the Development of Habitus in the Nineteenth and Twentieth Centuries.* Translated by Eric Dunning and Stephen Mennell. New York: Columbia University Press. [*Studien über die Deutschen*, 1989]

Elias, Norbert (2000) *The Civilizing Process: Sociogenetic and Psychogenetic Investigations.* Translated by Edmund Jephcott. Oxford: Blackwell; therein "Postscript" (1968), pp. 449–83. [*Über den Prozess der Zivilisation*, 1939]

Elias, Ruth (1999) *Triumph of Hope: From Theresienstadt and Auschwitz to Israel.* Translated by Margot Bettauer Dembo. New York: John Wiley & Sons Inc. [*Die Hoffnung erhielt mich am Leben. Mein Weg von Theresienstadt und Auschwitz nach Israel*, 1988]

Ellger, Hans (2005) "Die Frauenaußenlager des KZ Neuengamme. Lebensbedingungen und Überlebensstrategien," in: *Genozid und Geschlecht. Jüdische Frauen im nationalsozialistischen Lagersystem*, edited by Gisela Bock. Frankfurt am Main: Campus, pp. 169–84.

Encyclopaedia Judaica (1971) 16 volumes, edited by Cecil Roth and Geoffrey Wigoder. New York: The Macmillan Company.

Endlich, Stefanie (2005) "Kunst im Konzentrationslager," in: *Der Ort des Terrors. Geschichte der nationalsozialistischen Konzentrationslager*, Vol. 1: *Die Organisation des Terrors*, edited by Wolfgang Benz and Barbara Distel. Munich: Beck, pp. 274–95.

Endruweit, Günter and Gisela Trommsdorff (eds) (1989) *Wörterbuch der Soziologie.* Stuttgart: Enke; Munich: dtv.

Ernst, Christoph and Ulrike Jensen (eds) (1989) *Als letztes starb die Hoffnung. Berichte von Überlebenden aus dem KZ Neuengamme.* Hamburg: Rasch/Röhring.

Eschebach, Insa, Sigrid Jacobeit and Silke Wenk (eds) (2002) *Gedächtnis und Geschlecht. Deutungsmuster in Darstellungen des nationalsozialistischen Genozids.* Frankfurt am Main: Campus.

Faber, David (2001) *Because of Romek: A Holocaust Survivor's Memoir.* El Cajon, CA: Granite Hills Press.

Faber, Erwin and Imanuel Geiss (1992) *Arbeitsbuch zum Geschichtsstudium.* Wiesbaden: Quelle & Meyer.

Fackler, Guido (2000) *Des Lagers Stimme – Musik im KZ.* Bremen: Edition Temmen.

Felsmann, Barbara and Karl Prümm (1992) *Kurt Gerron – gefeiert und gejagt: 1897–1944. Das Schicksal eines deutschen Unterhaltungskünstlers.* Berlin: Edition Hentrich.

Fénelon, Fania (1997) *Playing for Time.* Translated by Judith Landry. Syracuse, NY: Syracuse University Press. [*Sursis pour l'orchestre*, 1976]

Fleck, Ludwik (1999) *Entstehung und Entwicklung einer wissenschaftlichen Tatsache. Einführung in die Lehre vom Denkstil und Denkkollektiv.* Frankfurt am Main: Suhrkamp. [Originally published 1935]

Flick, Uwe (1996) *Qualitative Forschung. Theorie, Methoden, Anwendung in Psychologie und Sozialwissenschaften*. Reinbek: Rowohlt.

Flick, Uwe, Ernst von Kardoff, Heiner Keupp, Lutz von Rosenstiel, and Stephan Wolff (eds) (1991) *Handbuch qualitative Sozialforschung*. Munich: Psychologie Verlags Union.

Förderverein für ein Dokumentations- und Begegnungszentrum zur NS-Zwangsarbeit in Berlin-Schöneweide. http://www.zwangsarbeit-in-berlin.de, accessed on April 25, 2013.

Förderverein – Materialien. "Dokumentation 2003: Blicke auf das Lager." http://www.zwangsarbeit-in-berlin.de/schoeneweide/texte/nsw-2003-dokumentation.pdf, accessed on April 25, 2013.

Foucault, Michel (1995) *Discipline and Punish: The Birth of the Prison*. Translated by Alan Sheridan. New York: Vintage Books. [*Surveiller et punir: Naissance de la Prison*, 1975]

Fowler, Bridget (2007) "Pierre Bourdieus *Die männliche Herrschaft* lesen. Anmerkungen zu einer intersektionellen Analyse von Geschlecht, Kultur und Klasse," in: *Prekäre Transformationen. Pierre Bourdieus Soziologie der Praxis und ihre Herausforderungen für die Frauen- und Geschlechterforschung*, edited by Ulla Bock, Irene Dölling, and Beate Krais. Göttingen: Wallstein, pp. 141–75.

Frankl, Viktor E. (1985) *Man's Search for Meaning*. Translated by Ilse Lasch. New York: Washington Square Press. [... *trotzdem Ja zum Leben sagen. Ein Psychologe erlebt das Konzentrationslager*, 1946]

Frei, Norbert, Sybille Steinbacher and Bernd C. Wagner (eds) (2000) *Ausbeutung, Vernichtung, Öffentlichkeit. Neue Studien zur nationalsozialistischen Lagerpolitik*. Munich: Saur.

Frerichs, Petra and Margareta Steinrücke (1997) "Kochen – ein männliches Spiel? Die Küche als geschlechts- und klassenstrukturierter Raum," in: *Ein alltägliches Spiel. Geschlechterkonstruktion in der sozialen Praxis*, edited by Irene Dölling and Beate Krais. Frankfurt am Main: Suhrkamp, pp. 231–55.

Freytag, Nils and Wolfgang Piereth (2004) *Kursbuch Geschichte*. Paderborn: Schöningh.

Friedländer, Saul (2007) "Wenn wir den Schreien lauschen," in: *Frankfurter Rundschau*, October 15, 2007. http://www.fr-online.de/literatur/wenn-wir-den-schreien-lauschen,1472266,2689202.html, accessed on April 30, 2013.

Frister, Roman (2001) *The Cap: The Price of a Life*. Translated by Hillel Halkin. New York: Grove Press. [*Deyokan 'atsmi 'im tsaleket*, 1993]

Fritz Bauer Institut (2000–6) *Cinematography of the Holocaust: Documentation and Record of Moving Image Materials*. http://www.cine-holocaust.de/eng/, accessed on April 30, 2013.

Fröbe, Rainer (1998) "KZ-Häftlinge als Reserve qualifizierter Arbeitskraft. Eine späte Entdeckung der deutschen Industrie und ihre Folgen," in: *Die nationalsozialistischen Konzentrationslager. Entwicklung und Struktur*, Vol. 2, edited by Ulrich Herbert. Göttingen: Wallstein, pp. 636–81.

Ganssmüller, Christian (1987) *Die Erbgesundheitspolitik des Dritten Reiches. Planung, Durchführung und Durchsetzung*. Cologne: Böhlau.

Garbe, Detlev (2005) "Selbstbehauptung und Widerstand," in: *Der Ort des Terrors.* *Geschichte der nationalsozialistischen Konzentrationslager,* Vol 1: *Die Organisation des Terrors,* edited by Wolfgang Benz and Barbara Distel. Munich: Beck, pp. 242–57.

Gebauer, Gunter (2000) "Habitus, Intentionality, and Social Rules: A Controversy between Searle and Bourdieu," translated by Jennifer Marston William, in: *SubStance* 29(3), Issue 93, pp. 68–83.

Gebauer, Gunter and Christoph Wulf (1998) *Spiel – Ritual – Geste. Mimetisches Handeln in der sozialen Welt.* Reinbek: Rowohlt.

Gehring, Petra (2004) *Foucault – Die Philosophie im Archiv.* Frankfurt am Main: Campus.

Die Geschichte des § 175. Strafrecht gegen Homosexuelle (1990), published by the Freunde eines Schwulen Museums in Berlin. Berlin: Verlag Rosa Winkel.

Giere, Jaqueline (ed.) (1996) *Die gesellschaftliche Konstruktion des Zigeuners. Zur Genese eines Vorurteils.* Frankfurt am Main; New York: Campus.

Gilbert, Shirli (2005) *Music in the Holocaust: Confronting Life in the Nazi Ghettos and Camps.* Oxford: Clarendon Press.

Gilcher-Holtey, Ingrid (1996) "Kulturelle und symbolische Praktiken: Das Unternehmen Pierre Bourdieu," in: *Geschichte und Gesellschaft. Zeitschrift für Historische Sozialwissenschaft.* Sonderheft 16: Kulturwissenschaft heute. Göttingen: Vandenhoeck & Ruprecht, pp. 111–30.

Gilcher-Holtey, Ingrid (2001) "'Kritische Ereignisse' und 'kritischer Moment.' Pierre Bourdieus Modell der Vermittlung von Ereignis und Struktur," in: *Struktur und Ereignis,* edited by Andreas Suter and Manfred Hettling. Göttingen: Vandenhoeck & Ruprecht, pp. 120–37.

Goffman, Erving (1961) *Asylums: Essays on the Social Situation of Mental Patients and Other Inmates.* New York: Anchor Books.

Goffman, Erving (1971) "The Territories of the Self," in: *Relations in Public: Microstudies of the Public Order.* New York: Basic Books, pp. 28–61.

Gold, Ruth Glasberg (2009) *Ruth's Journey: A Survivor's Memoir.* Bloomington, IN.: iUniverse, Inc. [Originally published 1996]

Goldstein, Jacob, Irving F. Lukoff, and Herbert A. Strauss (1991) *Individuelles und kollektives Verhalten in Nazi-Konzentrationslagern. Soziologische und psychologische Studien zu Berichten ungarisch-jüdischer Überlebender.* Frankfurt am Main: Campus.

Grau, Günter (ed.) (1995) *Hidden Holocaust? Lesbian and Gay Persecution in Germany, 1933–1945.* Translated by Patrick Camiller. Chicago: Fitzroy Dearborn Publishers. [*Homosexualität in der NS-Zeit. Dokumente einer Diskriminierung und Verfolgung,* 1993]

Grotum, Thomas and Jan Parcer (1995) "Computer-Aided Analysis of the Death Book Entries," in: *Death Books from Auschwitz. Remnants. Vol. 1: Reports,* edited by the State Museum of Auschwitz-Birkenau. Translated by Michael Jacobs, Georg Mayer, and Jacek Plesniarowicz. Munich: K.G. Saur, pp. 203–31.

Günter, Manuela (2003) "'Mich gibt es nicht – welche Erleichterung!' Zu einer Poetik der 'Autodemolition' bei Jean Améry," in: *Jüdische Intellektuelle im 20.*

Jahrhundert, edited by Ariane Huml and Monika Rappeneder. Würzburg: Königshausen & Neumann, pp. 191–206.

Gyulai, Kató (2001) *Zwei Schwestern. Geschichte einer Deportation*, edited by Linde Apel and Constanze Jaiser. Berlin: Metropol.

Hájková, Anna (2002) "Spezifika im Verhalten der niederländischen Juden in Theresienstadt," in: *Abgeschlossene Kapitel? Zur Geschichte der Konzentrationslager und der NS-Prozesse*, edited by Sabine Moller, Miriam Rürup, and Christel Trouvé. Tübingen: Edition Diskord, pp. 88–103.

Hájková, Anna (2005) "Strukturen weiblichen Verhaltens in Theresienstadt," in: *Genozid und Geschlecht. Jüdische Frauen im nationalsozialistischen Lagersystem*, edited by Gisela Bock. Frankfurt am Main: Campus, pp. 202–19.

Halbwachs, Maurice (1958) *The Psychology of Social Class*. Translated by Claire Delavenay. Glencoe, IL: The Free Press. [*Analyse des mobiles dominants qui orientent l'activité des individus dans la vie sociale*, 1938]

Halbwachs, Maurice (2001) *Klassen und Lebensweisen. Ausgewählte Schriften*, edited by Stephan Egger and Franz Schultheis. Constance: UVK. [Essays from 1905–39]

Heger, Heinz [pseudonym of Josef Kohout] (1994) *The Men with the Pink Triangle*. Translated by David Fernbach. New York: Alyson Books. [*Die Männer mit dem rosa Winkel*, 1972]

Heidelberger-Leonard, Irène (1988) "Das Problem der Neinsage, ihrer Herkunft und Zukunft. 'Die Schiffbrüchigen' als Vorübung zu 'Lefeu oder Der Abbruch,'" in: *Text und Kritik. Zeitschrift für Literatur*, Issue 99: *Jean Améry*, pp. 33–9.

Heidelberger-Leonard, Irène (ed.) (1990) *Über Jean Améry*. Heidelberg: Winter Universitätsverlag.

Heidelberger-Leonard, Irène (1996) "Zur Dramaturgie einer ästhetischen Existenz. Brüche und Kontinuitäten," in: *Jean Améry (Hans Maier)*, edited by Stephan Steiner. Basel; Frankfurt am Main: Stroemfeld, pp. 235–48.

Heidelberger-Leonard, Irène (2010) *The Philosopher of Auschwitz: Jean Améry and Living with the Holocaust*. Translated by Anthea Bell. London: I.B. Taurus & Co. Ltd. [*Jean Améry. Revolte in der Resignation*, 2004].

Heimat und Exil. Emigration der deutschen Juden nach 1933 (2006), published by the Stiftung Jüdisches Museum Berlin and the Stiftung Haus der Geschichte der Bundesrepublik Deutschland. Frankfurt am Main: Jüdischer Verlag of Suhrkamp Verlag.

Heinemann, Lars (2001) "Ethnizität und Geltung. Möglichkeiten und Grenzen konstruktivistischer Theorien bei der Erklärung ethnischer Vergemeinschaftung," in: *Geschlecht – Ethnizität – Klasse. Zur sozialen Konstruktion von Hierarchie und Differenz*, edited by Claudia Rademacher and Peter Wiechens. Opladen: Leske + Budrich, pp. 111–28.

Heißenbüttel, Helmut and Bernd Jentzsch (eds) (1978) *Hermannstraße 14. Halbjahresschrift für Literatur*. Sonderheft *Jean Améry*. Stuttgart: Klett-Cotta.

Hensle, Michael P. (2005) "Die Verrechtlichung des Unrechts. Der legalistische Rahmen der nationalsozialisitischen Verfolgung," in: *Der Ort des Terrors. Geschichte der nationalsozialistischen Konzentrationslager*, Vol. 1: *Die Organisation des Terrors*, edited by Wolfgang Benz and Barbara Distel. Munich: Beck, pp. 76–90.

Herbert, Ulrich (ed.) (1998) *Die nationalsozialistischen Konzentrationslager. Entwicklung und Struktur*, 2 volumes. Göttingen: Wallstein.

Herzig, Arno (1996) "Die Fremden in der Frühmoderne," in: *Die gesellschaftliche Konstruktion des Zigeuners. Zur Genese eines Vorurteils*, edited by Jaqueline Giere. Frankfurt am Main; New York: Campus, pp. 29–45.

Herzog, Hanna and Adi Efrat (2005) "'Wir Griechinnen wurden *klepsi klepsi* genannt.' Jüdisch-griechische Frauen im Konzentrationslager Ravensbrück," in: *Genozid und Geschlecht. Jüdische Frauen im nationalsozialistischen Lagersystem*, edited by Gisela Bock. Frankfurt am Main; New York: Campus, pp. 85–102.

Heuß, Herbert (1996) "Die Migration von Roma aus Osteuropa im 19. u. 20. Jahrhundert. Historische Anlässe und staatliche Reaktion – Überlegungen zum Funktionswandel des Zigeuner-Ressentiments," in: *Die gesellschaftliche Konstruktion des Zigeuners. Zur Genese eines Vorurteils*, edited by Jaqueline Giere. Frankfurt am Main; New York: Campus, pp. 109–31.

Hevesi, Dennis (2011) "Rudolf Brazda, Who Survived Pink Triangle, Is Dead at 98," in: *The New York Times*, August 5, 2011. http://www.nytimes.com/2011/08/06/world/europe/06brazda.html, accessed on April 25, 2013.

Hitler, Adolf (2009) *Mein Kampf*. Translated by James Murphy. London: Hurst and Blackett. [*Mein Kampf*, 1923]

Hockerts, Hans Günter (1993) "Zeitgeschichte in Deutschland. Begriff, Methoden, Themenfelder," in: *Aus Politik und Zeitgeschichte* B29–30/93, pp. 3–19.

Hockerts, Hans Günter (2002) "Zugänge zur Zeitgeschichte. Primärerfahrung, Erinnerungskultur, Geschichtswissenschaft," in: *Verletztes Gedächtnis. Erinnerungskultur und Zeitgeschichte im Konflikt*, edited by Konrad H. Jarausch and Martin Sabrow. Frankfurt am Main; New York: Campus, pp. 39–73.

Hoffmann-Holter, Beatrix (2000) " 'Ostjuden hinaus!' Jüdische Kriegsflüchtlinge in Wien 1914–1924," in: *Die Stadt ohne Juden*, edited by Guntram Geser and Armin Loacker. Vienna: Filmarchiv Austria, pp. 311–46.

Hogrefe, Jürgen (1997) "Hinrichtung der Seele: Die Mütze oder Der Preis des Lebens. Mit seiner hemmungslosen KZ-Beichte schockiert der jüdische Autor Roman Frister die Israelis – weil sie die dunkle Seite der Opfer aufdeckt," in: *Der Spiegel* 28. http://www.spiegel.de/spiegel/print/d-8741953.html, accessed on April 30, 2013.

Hund, Wulf D. (2006) *Ungleichheit und Untermenschen. Perspektiven des Rassismus*. Discussion paper for the workshop "Konjunkturen des Rassismus" at the "Ungleichheit als Programm" conference of the Bund demokratischer Wissenschaftlerinnen und Wissenschaftler. Frankfurt, November 24–6. http://www2.bdwi.de/uploads/wulfdhund_ungleichheit_und_untermenschen.pdf, accessed on April 30, 2013.

Hund, Wulf D. (2007) *Rassismus*. Bielefeld: Transcript.

Hutter, Jörg (1998) "'Sie sind ja schon wieder hier!' Ein ehemaliger Rosa-Winkel-Häftling berichtet. Karl Gorath: Schwul und verfolgt." Interview in *die tageszei-*

tung, June 27–8. [Also available at http://www.joerg-hutter.de/karl_b_.htm, accessed on April 30, 2013]

Hutter, Jörg (2000) "Konzentrationslager Auschwitz: Die Häftlinge mit dem rosa Winkel," in: *Homosexuelle in Konzentrationslagern*, edited by Olaf Mussmann. Bad Münstereifel: Westkreuz-Verlag. [Also available at http://www.joerg-hutter.de/auschwitz.htm, accessed on April 30, 2013]

Isaacson, Judith Magyar (1991) *Seed of Sarah: Memoirs of a Survivor*. Champaign: University of Illinois Press.

Jäckel, Eberhard (2005) "Sinti, Roma oder Zigeuner?" in: *Frankfurter Allgemeine Zeitung* 31, February 7, p. 31.

Jäger, Gudrun (2001) "Liana Millu. Jüdin, Partisanin, frühe Feministin." Lecture given during a seminar on "Jüdischer Widerstand und Hilfe für Verfolgte" on November 24 in Frankfurt. http://www.resistenza.de/content/view/50/37/, accessed on April 30, 2013.

Jagoda, Zenon, Stanislaw Kłodziński, and Jan Masłowski (1987a) "Das Überleben im Lager aus der Sicht ehemaliger Häftlinge von Auschwitz-Birkenau," in: *Die Auschwitz-Hefte. Texte der polnischen Zeitschrift "Przegląd Lekarski" über historische, psychische und medizinische Aspekte des Lebens und Sterbens in Auschwitz*, Vol. 1, published by the Hamburger Institut für Sozialforschung. Weinheim; Basel: Beltz, pp. 13–51. [Originally published 1971]

Jagoda, Zenon, Stanislaw Kłodziński, and Jan Masłowski (1987b) "Selbsthilfe und 'Volksmedizin' im Konzentrationslager," in: *Die Auschwitz-Hefte. Texte der polnischen Zeitschrift "Przegląd Lekarski" über historische, psychische und medizinische Aspekte des Lebens und Sterbens in Auschwitz*, Vol. 2, published by the Hamburger Institut für Sozialforschung. Weinheim; Basel: Beltz, pp. 149–87. [Originally published 1982]

Jahn, Franziska (2007) "Das 'Theresienstädter Familienlager' (B IIb) in Birkenau," in: *Der Ort des Terrors. Geschichte der nationalsozialistischen Konzentrationslager*, Vol. 5: *Hinzert – Auschwitz – Neuengamme*, edited by Wolfgang Benz and Barbara Distel. Munich: Beck, pp. 112–15.

Jaiser, Constanze (2000) *Poetische Zeugnisse. Gedichte aus dem Frauen-Konzentrationslager Ravensbrück 1939–1945*. Stuttgart; Weimar: Metzler.

Jaiser, Constanze (2005) "Repräsentationen von Sexualität und Gewalt in Zeugnissen jüdischer und nichtjüdischer Überlebender," in: *Genozid und Geschlecht. Jüdische Frauen im nationalsozialistischen Lagersystem*, edited by Gisela Bock. Frankfurt am Main: Campus, pp. 123–48.

Jarausch, Konrad H. (2002) "Zeitgeschichte und Erinnerung. Deutungskonkurrenz oder Interdependenzen?" in: *Verletztes Gedächtnis. Erinnerungskultur und Zeitgeschichte im Konflikt.*, edited by Konrad H. Jarausch and Martin Sabrow. Frankfurt am Main; New York: Campus, pp. 9–37.

Jarausch, Konrad H. and Martin Sabrow (eds) (2002) *Verletztes Gedächtnis. Erinnerungskultur und Zeitgeschichte im Konflikt*. Frankfurt am Main; New York: Campus.

Jellonnek, Burkhard and Rüdiger Lautmann (eds) (2002) *Nationalsozialistischer Terror gegen Homosexuelle. Verdrängt und ungesühnt*. Paderborn: Schöningh.

Joas, Hans (2003) "Sociology after Auschwitz: Zygmunt Bauman's Work and the Problems of German Self-Understanding," in: Hans Joas, *War and Modernity*. Translated by Rodney Livingstone. Cambridge: Polity Press, pp. 163–70. [*Kriege und Werte. Studien zur Gewaltgeschichte des 20. Jahrhunderts*, 2000]

Jureit, Ulrike (1998) *Konstruktion und Sinn. Methodische Überlegungen zu biographischen Sinnkonstruktionen*. Oldenburg: bis. [Oldenburger Universitätsreden 103]

Kaienburg, Hermann (2005) "Zwangsarbeit. KZ und Wirtschaft im Zweiten Weltkrieg," in: *Der Ort des Terrors. Geschichte der nationalsozialistischen Konzentrationslager*, Vol. 1: *Die Organisation des Terrors*, edited by Wolfgang Benz and Barbara Distel. Munich: Beck, pp. 179–94.

Kammer, Hilde and Elisabet Bartsch (2002) *Lexikon Nationalsozialismus. Begriffe, Organisationen, Institutionen*. Reinbek: Rowohlt.

Kantor, Alfred (1971) *The Book of Alfred Kantor: An Artist's Journal of the Holocaust*. London: Piatkus.

Kastl, Jörg Michael (2004) "Habitus als non-deklaratives Gedächtnis. Zur Relevanz der neuropsychologischen Amnesieforschung für die Soziologie," in: *Sozialer Sinn* 2, pp. 195–226.

Kaufmann, Jean-Claude (2005) *Die Erfindung des Ich. Eine Theorie der Identität*. Translated by Anke Beck. Constance: UVK. [*L'invention des soi. Une théorie de l'identité*, 2004]

Kavčič, Silvija (2002) "Kollektive Erinnerungen? Berichte von slowenischen Überlebenden des KZ Ravensbrück," in: *Abgeschlossene Kapitel? Zur Geschichte der Konzentrationslager und der NS-Prozesse*, edited by Sabine Moller, Miriam Rürup, and Christel Trouvé. Tübingen: Edition Diskord, pp. 104–17.

Kershaw, Ian (1997) "Führer und Hitlerkult," in: *Enzyklopädie des Nationalsozialismus*, edited by Wolfgang Benz, Hermann Graml, and Hermann Weiß. Munich: dtv, pp. 22–33.

Kertész, Imre (2004) *Fatelessness*. Translated by Tim Wilkinson. New York: Vintage. [*Sorstalanság*, 1975]

Kertész, Imre (2011) *The Holocaust as Culture*. Translated by Thomas Cooper. Kolkata: Seagull Books. [*A holocaust mint kultúra*, 1993]

Kertesz, Julia (2003) "Von Auschwitz ins Volkswagenwerk. Erinnerungen an KZ-Haft und Zwangsarbeit," in: *"Wir konnten die Kinder doch nicht im Stich lassen!" Frauen im Holocaust*, edited by Barbara Distel. Cologne: Komet, pp. 157–85.

Kinder im KZ Theresienstadt – Zeichnungen, Gedichte, Texte. Exhibition in the Hessisches Staatsarchiv Darmstadt from January 28–February 15, 2002.

"Kinder im KZ Theresienstadt – Zeichnungen, Gedichte, Texte. Materialien und Hinweise zur neuen Ausstellung" (2001) In: *Informationen* 25(53), published by the Studienkreis Deutscher Widerstand 1933–1945, pp. 4–17.

Klieger, Bernard (1960) *Der Weg, den wir gingen. Reportage einer höllischen Reise*. Brussels: Codac Juifs. [*Le Chemin que nous avons fait*, 1946]

Klüger, Ruth (1999) *weiter leben. Eine Jugend*. Munich: dtv.

Klüger, Ruth (2001) *Still Alive: A Holocaust Girlhood Remembered*. New York: The Feminist Press at CUNY. [*weiter leben. Eine Jugend*, 1999]

Klüger, Ruth (2008) "Man ist irrsinnig indiskret," in: *Der Spiegel* 33, pp. 144–7.

Klüver, Reymer (2007) "Mengeles Malerin," in: *Süddeutsche Zeitung*, January 16. http://www.sueddeutsche.de/leben/auschwitz-zeichnungen-mengeles-malerin-1.255756, accessed on April 30, 2013.

Kogon, Eugen (1946) *Der SS-Staat. Das System der nationalsozialistischen Konzentrationslager*. (Auflage für Großhessen; published under the Military Government). Frankfurt am Main: Verlag der Frankfurter Hefte.

Kogon, Eugen (2006) *The Theory and Practice of Hell*. Translated by Heinz Norden. New York: Farrar, Straus and Giroux. [*Der SS-Staat. Das System der nationalsozialistischen Konzentrationslager*, 1946]

Kohl, Christiane (2008) "Holocaust-Archiv Bad Arolsen. Das gesammelte Grauen. Im Holocaust-Archiv Bad Arolsen lagern Tausende Akten über die Opfer des Nationalsozialismus – nun konnten Forscher sie erstmals auswerten," in: *Süddeutsche Zeitung*, June 27. http://www.sueddeutsche.de/politik/holocaust-archiv-bad-arolsen-das-gesammelte-grauen-1.190460, accessed on April 30, 2013.

Köhler-Zülch, Ines (1996) "Die verweigerte Herberge. Die heilige Familie in Ägypten und andere Geschichten von 'Zigeunern' – Selbstäußerungen oder Außenbilder?" in: *Die gesellschaftliche Konstruktion des Zigeuners. Zur Genese eines Vorurteils*, edited by Jaqueline Giere. Frankfurt am Main; New York: Campus, pp. 46–86.

Kolmer, Felix (2002) *Expert opinion* on manuscript of "Der Blick nach innen. Bildung im Konzentrationslager als Ressource für das tägliche Überleben" by Maja Suderland. Prague: November 15 (Ms).

Komenda, Janina (1987) "Frauen im Revier von Birkenau," in: *Die Auschwitz-Hefte. Texte der polnischen Zeitschrift "Przegląd Lekarski" über historische, psychische und medizinische Aspekte des Lebens und Sterbens in Auschwitz*, Vol. 1, published by the Hamburger Institut für Sozialforschung. Weinheim; Basel: Beltz, pp. 185–207. [Originally published 1982]

Königseder, Angelika (2005) "Die Entwicklung des KZ-Systems," in: *Der Ort des Terrors. Geschichte der nationalsozialistischen Konzentrationslager*, Vol. 1: *Die Organisation des Terrors*, edited by Wolfgang Benz and Barbara Distel. Munich: Beck, pp. 30–42.

Koren, Yehuda and Eilat Negev (2004) *In Our Hearts We Were Giants: The Remarkable Story of the Lilliput Troupe – A Dwarf Family's Survival of the Holocaust*. New York: Carroll & Graf.

Körte, Mona (2005) "Zeugnisliteratur. Autobiographische Berichte aus den Konzentrationslagern," in: *Der Ort des Terrors. Geschichte der nationalsozialistischen Konzentrationslager*, Vol. 1: *Die Organisation des Terrors*, edited by Wolfgang Benz and Barbara Distel. Munich: Beck, pp. 329–44.

Koselleck, Reinhart (1977) "Standortbindung und Zeitlichkeit. Ein Beitrag zur historiographischen Erschließung der geschichtlichen Welt," in: *Objektivität und Parteilichkeit in der Geschichtswissenschaft*, edited by Reinhart Koselleck. Munich: dtv, pp. 17–46.

Krais, Beate (1993) "Gender and Symbolic Violence: Female Oppression in the Light of Pierre Bourdieu's Theory of Social Practice," in: *Bourdieu: Critical Perspectives*, edited by Craig Calhoun, Edward LiPuma, and Moishe Postone. Chicago: University of Chicago Press, pp. 156–77.

Krais, Beate (2001a) "Die feministische Debatte und die Soziologie Pierre Bourdieus: Eine Wahlverwandtschaft?" in: *Soziale Verortung der Geschlechter. Gesellschaftstheorie und feministische Kritik*, edited by Gudrun-Axeli Knapp and Angelika Wetterer. Münster: Westfälisches Dampfboot, pp. 317–38.

Krais, Beate (2001b) "'Gesellschaft in Indien: Die Soziologie des Kastenwesens' von Louis Dumont," in: *Lexikon der Soziologischen Werke*, edited by Georg W. Oesterdiekhoff. Opladen: Westdeutscher Verlag, pp. 159–60.

Krais, Beate (2001c) "'Homo aequalis' von Louis Dumont," in: *Schlüsselwerke der Soziologie*, edited by Sven Papcke and Georg W. Oesterdiekhoff. Opladen: Westdeutscher Verlag, pp. 117–20.

Krais, Beate (2003) "Körper und Geschlecht," in: *Aufs Spiel gesetzte Körper*, edited by Thomas Alkemeyer, Bernhard Boschert, Robert Schmidt, and Gunter Gebauer. Constance: UVK, pp. 157–68.

Krais, Beate (2004) "Soziologie als teilnehmende Objektivierung der sozialen Welt. Pierre Bourdieu," in: *Französische Soziologie der Gegenwart*, edited by Stephan Moebius and Lothar Peter. Constance: UVK, pp. 171–210.

Krais, Beate (2006a) "Gender, Sociological Theory and Bourdieus' Sociology of Practice," in: *Theory, Culture, Society* 23(6), pp. 119–34.

Krais, Beate (2006b) "Über einige theoretische Probleme der Soziologie des Geschlechterverhältnisses. Geschlechterrollen, Gender und Bourdieus 'Die männliche Herrschaft,'" in: *Journal Phänomenologie* 25(1), pp. 13–22.

Krais, Beate and Gunter Gebauer (2002) *Habitus*. Bielefeld: Transcript.

Krapoth, Hermann (ed.) (2005) *Erinnerung und Gesellschaft. Hommage à Maurice Halbwachs (1877–1945)*. Wiesbaden: VS.

Krause, Rolf D. (1989) "Vom kalten Wind. Leseverhalten und Literaturrezeption in den nationalsozialistischen Konzentrationslagern," in: *Alltag, Traum und Utopie. Lesegeschichten – Lebensgeschichten*, edited by Rainer Noltenius. Essen: Klartext Verlag, pp. 124–40.

Krausnick, Michail (ed.) (1983) *"Da wollten wir frei sein!" Eine Sinti-Familie erzählt*. Weinheim; Basel: Beltz & Gelberg.

Kreckel, Reinhard (1989) "Klasse und Geschlecht. Die Geschlechtsindifferenz der soziologischen Ungleichheitsforschung und ihre theoretischen Implikationen," in: *Leviathan* 3, pp. 305–21.

Kurt Gerron's Karussel (1999). A documentary film by Ilona Ziok. Germany, the Netherlands, the Czech Republic. Broadcast on PHOENIX on August 23, 2008 (20:15–21:15).

Kuzmics, Helmut and Gerald Mozetič (2003) *Literatur als Soziologie. Zum Verhältnis von literarischer und gesellschaftlicher Wirklichkeit*. Constance: UVK.

Kwiet, Konrad (1997) "Rassenpolitik und Völkermord," in: *Enzyklopädie des Nationalsozialismus*, edited by Wolfgang Benz, Hermann Graml, and Hermann Weiß. Munich: dtv, pp. 50–65.

Lammel, Inge (1995) "Das Sachsenhausen-Liederbuch," in: *Sachsenhausen-Liederbuch. Originalwiedergabe eines illegalen Häftlingsliederbuches aus dem Konzentrationslager Sachsenhausen*, edited by Günter Morsch. Berlin: Edition Hentrich, pp. 14–31.

Lamnek, Siegfried (1993) *Qualitative Sozialforschung*, Vol. 2: *Methoden und Techniken*. Weinheim: Beltz, Psychologische Verlagsunion.

Langbein, Hermann (1979) "Im Zigeunerlager von Auschwitz," in: *In Auschwitz vergast, bis heute verfolgt. Zur Situation der Roma (Zigeuner) in Deutschland und Europa*, edited by Tilman Zülch. Reinbek: Rowohlt.

Langbein, Hermann (1995) "SS Physicians in KL Auschwitz," in: *Death Books from Auschwitz. Remnants. Vol. 1: Reports*, edited by the State Museum of Auschwitz-Birkenau. Translated by Michael Jacobs, Georg Mayer, and Jacek Plesniarowicz. Munich et al.: K.G. Saur, pp. 61–76.

Langbein, Hermann (1996) "Auschwitz III – Monowitz," in: *Jean Améry (Hans Maier)*, edited by Stephan Steiner. Basel; Frankfurt am Main: Stroemfeld, pp. 25–32.

Langbein, Hermann (2004) *People in Auschwitz*. Translated by Harry Zohn. Chapel Hill: University of North Carolina Press. [*Menschen in Auschwitz*, 1995]

Lasker-Wallfisch, Anita (1996) *Inherit the Truth*. New York: St. Martin's Press.

Layer-Jung, Gabriele and Cord Pagenstecher (2004) "Das Pertrix-Außenlager in Berlin Schöneweide," published by the *Förderverein für ein Dokumentations- und Begegnungszentrum zur NS-Zwangsarbeit in Berlin-Schöneweide.* layerjung-pagenstecher-2004-pertrix.pdf. http://www.zwangsarbeit-in-berlin.de/schoeneweide/foerderverein-texte.htm, accessed on April 30, 2013.

Die Lebensreform. Entwürfe zur Neugestaltung von Leben und Kunst um 1900 (2001) 2 volumes. Darmstadt: Häusser.

Lentin, Ronit (2002) "Chaotic Girlhood: Narratives of Jewish Girl Survivors of Transnistria," in: *Childhood and Its Discontents: The First Seamus Heaney Lectures*, edited by Joseph Dunne and James Kelley. Dublin: The Liffey Press, pp. 123–58.

Levi, Primo (1989) *The Drowned and the Saved*. Translated by Raymond Rosenthal. New York: Vintage International. [*Sommersi e i salvati*, 1986]

Levi, Primo (1990) *The Mirror Maker: Stories and Essays*. Translated by Raymond Rosenthal. New York: Schocken Books. [*Il fabbricante di specchi: Racconti e saggi*, 1971]

Levi, Primo (1993) *The Reawakening*. Translated by Stuart Woolf. New York: Macmillan. [*La tregua*, 1963]

Levi, Primo (1995) *Survival in Auschwitz*. Translated by Stuart Woolf. New York: Touchstone. [*Se questo è un uomo*, 1947]

Levi, Primo (2000) *The Periodic Table*. Translated by Raymond Rosenthal. London: Penguin Books. [*Il sistema periodico*, 1975]

Levi, Primo (2001) "Return to Auschwitz," in: *The Voice of Memory: Interviews 1961–87*, edited by Marco Belpoliti and Robert Gordon, translated by Robert Gordon. Cambridge: Polity Press, pp. 208–17. [*Primo Levi: Conversazioni e interviste 1963-87*, 1997; interview from 1982]

Levi, Primo and Leonardo De Benedetti (2006) "Report on the Sanitary and Medical Organization of the Monowitz Concentration Camp for Jews (Auschwitz–Upper Silesia)," in: *Auschwitz Report*. Translated by Judith Woolf. London: Verso, pp. 31–78. [*Rapporto sull'organizzazione igienico-sanitaria del campo di concentramento per ebrei di Monowitz (Auschwitz–Alta Silesia)*, 1946]

Liebau, Eckart (1990) "Laufbahn oder Biographie? Eine Bourdieu-Lektüre," in: *BIOS Zeitschrift für Biographieforschung und Oral History* 1, pp. 83–9.

Liebrand, Claudia (2003) "'Das Trauma der Auschwitzer Wochen in ein Versmaß stülpen' oder: Gedichte als Exorzismus. Ruth Klügers *weiter leben*," in: *Jüdische Intellektuelle im 20. Jahrhundert*, edited by Ariane Huml and Monika Rappeneder. Würzburg: Königshausen & Neumann, pp. 237–49.

Lind, Jakov (1996) "Zweifel und Verzweiflung," in: *Jean Améry (Hans Maier)*, edited by Stephan Steiner. Basel: Stroemfeld, pp. 153–63.

Longerich, Peter (2006) *"Davon haben wir nichts gewusst." Die Deutschen und die Judenverfolgung 1933–1945*. Munich: Siedler.

Louis, Chantal (2007) "Lesben unterm Hakenkreuz. Die Zeit der Maskierung," in: *EMMAonline* 1. http://www.emma.de/lesben_ns_zeit_1_2007.html, accessed on April 30, 2013.

Ludewig-Kedmi, Revital (2001) *Opfer und Täter zugleich? Moraldilemmata jüdischer Funktionshäftlinge in der Shoa*. Gießen: Psychosozial.

Lustiger, Arno (2007a) "Bitte, die Herrschaften zum Gas," in: *Die Welt*, January 20. http://www.welt.de/print-welt/article709925/Bitte-die-Herrschaften-zum-Gas.html, accessed on April 30, 2013.

Lustiger, Arno (2007b) "Wer war Tadeusz Borowski? Pole, KZ-Häftling, Wahrheitsfanatiker, Kommunist, Kulturattaché, Selbstmörder: Ein kurzes Leben im 20. Jahrhundert," in: *Die Welt*, January 20. http://www.welt.de/print-welt/article709924/Wer-war-Tadeusz-Borowski.html, accessed on April 30, 2012.

Maciejewski, Franz (1996) "Elemente des Antiziganismus," in: *Die gesellschaftliche Konstruktion des Zigeuners. Zur Genese eines Vorurteils*, edited by Jaqueline Giere. Frankfurt am Main; New York: Campus, pp. 9–28.

Mandl, Thomas (1966) *Das kulturelle Leben und die erzieherische Tätigkeit im Ghetto Theresienstadt (1941–1945) und im Familienlager der Juden aus Theresienstadt in Auschwitz (1943–1944)*. Interview with Ben-David Gershon. Cologne (typed manuscript, 84 pages). [The Hebrew University of Jerusalem, The Institute of Contemporary Jewry, Oral History Division; Nr. 3/392]

Margry, Karel (1992) "'Theresienstadt' (1944–1945): The Nazi Propaganda Film Depicting the Concentration Camp as Paradise," in: *Historical Journal of Film, Radio and Television* 12(2), pp. 145–62.

Martschukat, Jürgen and Olaf Stieglitz (2005) *"Es ist ein Junge!" Einführung in die Geschichte der Männlichkeit in der Neuzeit*. Tübingen: Edition Diskord.

Maß, Sandra (2006) *Weiße Helden, schwarze Krieger. Zur Geschichte kolonialer Männlichkeit in Deutschland 1918–1964*. Cologne: Böhlau.

Matthäus, Jürgen (2005) "Quellen," in: *Der Ort des Terrors. Geschichte der nationalsozialistischen Konzentrationslager*, Vol. 1: *Die Organisation des Terrors*, edited by Wolfgang Benz and Barbara Distel. Munich: Beck, pp. 363–76.

Mayer, Hanns [pseudonym of Hans Mayer alias Jean Améry] (1988) "'Die Schiffbrüchigen' (Inhalts-Umriss)," in: *Text und Kritik. Zeitschrift für Literatur* Issue 99: *Jean Améry*, pp. 30–2.

Mayer, Hans (1979) *Richard Wagner in Selbstzeugnissen und Bilddokumenten.* Reinbek: Rowohlt.

Meinl, Susanne and Jutta Zwilling (eds) (2004) *Legalisierter Raub. Die Ausplünderung der Juden im Nationalsozialismus durch die Reichsfinanzverwaltung in Hessen.* Frankfurt am Main; New York: Campus.

Meisels, Mosche (1996) "Keine vollwertigen Menschen. Hermann Langbein – 1967," in: *Die gerechten Österreichs. Eine Dokumentation der Menschlichkeit,* published by the Austrian Embassy in Tel Aviv, pp. 50–3. http://gd.auslandsdienst. at/deutsch/gerechte/inhalt.php, accessed on April 30, 2013.

Memorial Book: The Gypsies at Auschwitz-Birkenau (1993) Edited by the State Museum of Auschwitz-Birkenau and the Documentary and Cultural Center of German Sinti and Roma in Heidelberg. Munich: Saur.

Mesnard, Philippe (2006) "Ein Text ohne Belang?" in: *Bericht über Auschwitz,* written by Primo Levi and Leonardo De Benedetti. Translated by Jutta Waldner and Ulrich Zieger. Berlin: BasisDruck, pp. 11–56.

Meuser, Michael (2006) *Geschlecht und Männlichkeit. Soziologische Theorie und kulturelle Deutungsmuster,* 2nd revised and updated edition. Wiesbaden: VS.

Meyer, Michael A. (ed.) (2000) *Deutsch-jüdische Geschichte in der Neuzeit,* 4 volumes. Munich: Beck. [Beck'sche Reihe 1401]

Meyers Großes Taschenlexikon in 24 Bänden (2006) 10th revised edition. Leipzig; Mannheim: Bibliographisches Institut & Brockhaus.

Michel, Antje (2002) "Gerüchte im KZ Sachsenhausen. Ein Paradigma für die Kommunikationssituation einer Zwangsgesellschaft von Konzentrationslagerhäftlingen," in: *Abgeschlossene Kapitel? Zur Geschichte der Konzentrationslager und der NS-Prozesse,* edited by Sabine Moller, Miriam Rürup, and Christel Trouvé. Tübingen: Edition Diskord, pp. 59–68.

Millu, Liana (1991) *Smoke over Birkenau.* Translated by Lynne Sharon Schwartz. Philadelphia: The Jewish Publication Society [*Il fumo di Birkenau,* 1947]

Moll, Michael and Barbara Weiler (eds) (1991) *Lyrik gegen das Vergessen. Gedichte aus Konzentrationslagern.* Marburg: Schüren.

Moller, Sabine, Miriam Rürup, and Christel Trouvé (2002) *Abgeschlossene Kapitel? Zur Geschichte der Konzentrationslager und der NS-Prozesse.* Tübingen: Edition Diskord.

Montuoro, Maria (2003) "Schicht 'B,'" in: *"Wir konnten die Kinder doch nicht im Stich lassen!" Frauen im Holocaust,* edited by Barbara Distel. Cologne: Komet, pp. 142–56.

Morsch, Günter (2005) "Organisations- und Verwaltungsstruktur der Konzentrationslager," in: *Der Ort des Terrors. Geschichte der nationalsozialistischen Konzentrationslager,* Vol. 1: *Die Organisation des Terrors,* edited by Wolfgang Benz and Barbara Distel. Munich: Beck, pp. 58–75.

Morton, Frederic (1996) "Amérys zweite Fremde. Eine kritische

Auseinandersetzung mit Jean Amérys Doppelexil," in: *Jean Améry (Hans Maier)*, edited by Stephan Steiner. Basel; Frankfurt am Main: Stroemfeld, pp. 209–16.

Müller, Christian (2003) "Review of *Wilhelminism and Its Legacies. German Modernities, Imperialism, and the Meaning of Reform, 1890–1930. Essays for Hartmut Pogge von Strandmann* (2003) edited by Geoff Eley and James Retallack. Oxford: Berghahn," in: *H-Soz-u-Kult*, November 26. http://hsozkult.geschichte.hu-ber lin.de/rezensionen/id=3105&count=20&recno=1&type=rezbuecher&sort=dat um&order=down&search=Eley+Christian+M%FCller, accessed on April 30, 2013.

Müller, Joachim, Andreas Sternweiler, and Fred Brade (eds) (2000) *Homosexuelle Männer im KZ Sachsenhausen*. Berlin: Verlag Rosa Winkel.

Müller, Klaus (2002) "Totgeschlagen, totgeschwiegen? Autobiographische Zeugnisse homosexueller Überlebender," in: *Nationalsozialistischer Terror gegen Homosexuelle. Verdrängt und ungesühnt*, edited by Burkhard Jellonnek and Rüdiger Lautmann. Paderborn: Schöningh. [Also available at http://kmlink. home.xs4all.nl/09newarticles/01saarbruecken.htm, accessed on April 30, 2013]

Münkel, Daniela (2004) "'Volksgenossen' und 'Volksgemeinschaft.' Anspruch und Wirklichkeit," in: *Die Deutschen im 20. Jahrhundert*, edited by Edgar Wolfrum. Darmstadt: Primus, pp. 159–68.

Naor, Simha (1986) *Krankengymnastin in Auschwitz. Aufzeichnungen des Häftlings Nr. 80574*. Freiburg im Breisgau: Herder.

Neurath, Paul Martin (2005) *The Society of Terror: Inside the Dachau and Buchenwald Concentration Camps*. Boulder, CO: Paradigm Publishers. ["Social Life in the German Concentration Camps Dachau and Buchenwald," dissertation written in 1943]

Niethammer, Lutz (1990) "Kommentar zu Pierre Bourdieu: Die biographische Illusion," in: *BIOS Zeitschrift für Biographieforschung und Oral History* 1, pp. 91–3.

Nordau, Max (1900) "Muskeljudentum," in: *Jüdische Turnzeitung* June. http:// www.zionismus.info/grundlagentexte/gruender/nordau-2.htm, accessed on April 30, 2013.

Nyiszli, Miklós (1993) *Auschwitz: A Doctor's Eyewitness Account*. Translated by Tibére Kremer and Richard Seaver. New York: Arcade Publishing Inc. [*Dr. Mengele boncolóorvosa voltam az auschwitzi krematóriumban*, 1960]

O'Brien, Mary (1983) *The Politics of Reproduction*. Boston; London; Henley: Routledge & Kegan Paul.

Orth, Karin (1998) "Die Kommandanten der nationalsozialistischen Konzentrationslager," in: *Die nationalsozialistischen Konzentrationslager. Entwicklung und Struktur*, Vol. 2, edited by Ulrich Herbert. Göttingen: Wallstein, pp. 755–86.

Orth, Karin (2000) "Gab es eine Lagergesellschaft? 'Kriminelle' und politische Häftlinge im Konzentrationslager," in: *Ausbeutung, Vernichtung, Öffentlichkeit. Neue Studien zur nationalsozialistischen Lagerpolitik*, edited by Norbert Frei, Sybille Steinbacher, and Bernd C. Wagner. Munich: Saur, pp. 109–33.

Orth, Karin (2005) "Bewachung," in: *Der Ort des Terrors. Geschichte der national-*

sozialistischen Konzentrationslager, Vol. 1: *Die Organisation des Terrors*, edited by Wolfgang Benz and Barbara Distel. Munich: Beck, pp. 126–40.

The Oxford Dictionary of English Etymology (1966) Edited by C.T. Onions. Oxford: Oxford University Press.

Paczuła, Tadeusz (1995) "Office Procedures in KL Auschwitz," in: *Death Books from Auschwitz. Remnants. Vol. 1: Reports*, edited by the State Museum of Auschwitz-Birkenau. Translated by Michael Jacobs, Georg Mayer, and Jacek Plesniarowicz. Munich: K.G. Saur, pp. 25–60.

Passeron, René (1971) *René Magritte*. Berlin: Rembrandt Verlag.

Pätzold, Kurt (2005) "Häftlingsgesellschaft," in: *Der Ort des Terrors. Geschichte der nationalsozialistischen Konzentrationslager*, Vol. 1: *Die Organisation des Terrors*, edited by Wolfgang Benz and Barbara Distel. Munich: Beck, pp. 110–25.

Pätzold, Kurt and Erika Schwarz (1992) *Tagesordnung: Judenmord. Die Wannseee-Konferenz am 20. Januar 1942*. Berlin: Metropol.

Pfäfflin, Friedrich (1996) "Jean Améry – Daten zu seiner Biographie," in: *Jean Améry (Hans Maier)*, edited by Stephan Steiner. Basel; Frankfurt am Main: Stroemfeld, pp. 265–80.

Pfeffer, Gottfried (1985) "Das fehlende Positive. Sozialdeterministische Aspekte bei Bourdieu und ihr möglicher 'Aufklärungswert,'" in: *Neue Sammlung* 25, pp. 283–99.

Pingel, Falk (1978) *Häftlinge unter SS-Herrschaft: Widerstand, Selbstbehauptung und Vernichtung im Konzentrationslager*. Hamburg: Hoffmann und Campe.

Piper, Franciszek (1998) "Die Rolle des Lagers Auschwitz bei der Verwirklichung der nationalsozialistischen Ausrottungspolitik. Die doppelte Funktion von Auschwitz als Konzentrationslager und als Zentrum der Judenvernichtung," in: *Die nationalsozialistischen Konzentrationslager. Entwicklung und Struktur*, Vol. 1, edited by Ulrich Herbert. Göttingen: Wallstein, pp. 390–414.

Pohl, Dieter (2003) *Verfolgung und Massenmord in der NS-Zeit 1933–1945*. Darmstadt: Wissenschaftliche Buchgesellschaft.

Pollak, Michael (1988) *Die Grenzen des Sagbaren. Lebensgeschichte von KZ-Überlebenden als Augenzeugenberichte und als Identitätsarbeit*. Frankfurt am Main; New York: Campus.

Quack, Sybille (2003) *Dimensionen der Verfolgung. Opfer und Opfergruppen im Nationalsozialismus*. Munich: DVA.

Rademacher, Claudia and Peter Wiechens (eds) (2001) *Geschlecht – Ethnizität – Klasse. Zur sozialen Konstruktion von Hierarchie und Differenz*. Opladen: Leske + Budrich.

Rahe, Thomas (1998) "Die Bedeutung von Religion und Religiosität in den nationalsozialistischen Konzentrationslagern," in: *Die nationalsozialistischen Konzentrationslager. Entwicklung und Struktur*, Vol. 2, edited by Ulrich Herbert. Göttingen: Wallstein, pp. 1006–1022.

Rakytka, Ján (2001) *Life Forbidden*. Self-published. [*Žít zakázáno*, 1999]

Raphael, Lutz (2004) "Habitus und sozialer Sinn. Der Ansatz der Praxistheorie Pierre Bourdieus," in: *Handbuch der Kulturwissenschaften*, Vol. 2: *Paradigmen und Disziplinen*. Stuttgart: Metzler, pp. 266–276.

Reemtsma, Jan Philipp (1996) "172364. Gedanken über den Gebrauch der ersten Person Singular bei Jean Améry," in: *Jean Améry (Hans Maier)*, edited by Stephan Steiner. Basel; Frankfurt am Main: Stroemfeld, pp. 63–86.

Régnier-Bohler, Danielle (1988) "Imagining the Self," in: *A History of Private Life*, Vol. II, edited by Philippe Ariès and Georges Duby. Translated by Arthur Goldhammer. Cambridge, MA: Belknap Press, pp. 311–93. [*Histoire de la vie privée, vol. II: De l'Europe féodal à la Renaissance*, 1985]

Reichmann, Hans (1998) *Deutscher Bürger und verfolgter Jude. Novemberpogrom und KZ Sachsenhausen 1937 bis 1939*. Munich: Oldenbourg.

Reichsgesetzblatt RGBl. Issued by the Reich Ministry of the Interior. Berlin: Reichsverlagsamt, 1922–45.

Reifeld, Helmut (2001) *Die Bedeutung der UN-Weltkonferenz gegen Rassismus für Indien*. Bonn: Konrad-Adenauer-Stiftung. http://www.kas.de/wf/de/ 33.3653/, accessed on April 30, 2013.

Reinhardt, Fritz (1937) "Vom Wesen der Volksgemeinschaft," in: *Grundlagen, Aufbau, und Wirtschaftsordnung des nationalsozialistischen Staates* 8 [17 pages].

Riedel, Dirk (2006) "'Arbeit macht frei.' Leitsprüche und Metaphern aus der Welt des Konzentrationslagers," in: *Realität – Metapher – Symbol. Dachauer Hefte* 22, edited by Wolfgang Benz and Barbara Distel. Dachau: Verlag Dachauer Hefte, pp. 11–29.

Rieger, Else (2002) "'… aber ihr seid nicht besser als wir.' Überlegungen zur Stellung der jüdischen Sonderkommandos in Auschwitz," in: *Abgeschlossene Kapitel? Zur Geschichte der Konzentrationslager und der NS-Prozesse*, edited by Sabine Moller, Miriam Rürup, and Christel Trouvé. Tübingen: Edition Diskord, pp. 118–33.

Rieger-Ladich, Markus (2005) "Weder Determinismus, noch Fatalismus: Pierre Bourdieus Habitustheorie im Licht neuerer Arbeiten," in: *Zeitschrift für Soziologie der Erziehung und Sozialisation* 25(3), pp. 281–96.

Rogasky, Barbara (1988) *Smoke and Ashes: The Story of the Holocaust*. Oxford: Oxford University Press.

Rosenfeld, Alvin (1980) *A Double Dying: Reflections on Holocaust Literature*. Bloomington: Indiana University Press.

Rost, Nico (1983) *Goethe in Dachau*. Frankfurt am Main: Fischer. [Originally published 1948]

Roviello, Anne-Marie (1990) "An den Grenzen des Geistes," in: *Über Jean Améry*, edited by Irene Heidelberger-Leonard. Heidelberg: Winter Universitätsverlag, pp. 49–58.

Rummel, Walter and Jochen Rath (2001) "'Dem Reich verfallen' – 'den Berechtigten zurückzuerstatten.' Enteignung und Rückerstattung jüdischen Vermögens im Gebiet des heutigen Rheinland-Pfalz 1938–1953*. Koblenz: Verlag der Landesarchivverwaltung Rheinland-Pfalz.

Ryn, Zdzisław and Stanisklaw Kłodziński (1987) "An der Grenze zwischen Leben und Tod. Eine Studie über die Erscheinung des 'Muselmanns' im Konzentrationslager," in: *Die Auschwitz-Hefte. Texte der polnischen Zeitschrift "Przegląd Lekarski" über historische, psychische und medizinische Aspekte des Lebens und Sterbens in Auschwitz*, Vol. 1, published by the Hamburger Institut für Sozialforschung. Weinheim; Basel: Beltz, pp. 89–154.

Sacha, Magdalena (2002) "Polinnen und polnische Jüdinnen im Außenlager Hasag-Leipzig. Zusammen, aber getrennt," in: *Abgeschlossene Kapitel? Zur Geschichte der Konzentrationslager und der NS-Prozesse*, edited by Sabine Moller, Miriam Rürup, and Christel Trouvé. Tübingen: Edition Diskord, pp. 69–87.

Safranksi, Rüdiger (1997) *Das Böse: oder Das Drama der Freiheit*. Munich: Carl Hanser Verlag.

Said, Edward W. (2001) "Kultur, Identität und Geschichte," translated by Ina Schröder, in: *Kulturtheorien der Gegenwart. Ansätze und Positionen*, edited by Gerhart Schröder and Helga Breuninger. Frankfurt am Main; New York: Campus, pp. 39–58.

Schmidt, Monika (2003) "'Das sind Sachen, von denen man sich nicht befreien kann.' Margit Schultz. Erinnerungen an Auschwitz und Peterswaldau," in: *"Wir konnten die Kinder doch nicht im Stich lassen!" Frauen im Holocaust*, edited by Barbara Distel. Cologne: Komet, pp. 70–104.

Schmitz, Sigrid (2005) "Frauen – Männer – Hirne. Wie Wissenschaft Fakten schafft," in: *Wissenschaft und Kritik. Beiträge zu Bildung und Gesellschaft*, published by the Hans-Böckler-Stiftung and the Gewerkschaft Erziehung und Wissenschaft, Frankfurt, pp. 33–9.

Schneider, Karlheinz (1996) "Ni bourgois – ni citoyen – Zum Modell der Emanzipation und Selbstemanzipation von Juden," in: *Die gesellschaftliche Konstruktion des Zigeuners. Zur Genese eines Vorurteils*, edited by Jaqueline Giere. Frankfurt am Main; New York: Campus, pp. 132–46.

Schoeps, Julius (ed.) (1992) *Neues Lexikon des Judentums*. Gütersloh: Bertelsmann Lexikon Verlag.

Schoppmann, Claudia (1991) *Nationalsozialistische Sexualpolitik und weibliche Homosexualität*. Pfaffenweiler: Centaurus.

Schoppmann, Claudia (1995) "The Position of Lesbian Women in the Nazi Period," in: *Hidden Holocaust? Gay and Lesbian Persecution in Germany 1933–45*, edited by Günter Grau. Translated by Patrick Camiller. Chicago: Fitzroy Dearborn Publishers, pp. 8–15. [*Homosexualität in der NS-Zeit. Dokumente einer Diskriminierung und Verfolgung*, 1993]

Schüler-Springorum, Stefanie (2005a) "Masseneinweisungen in Konzentrationslager. Aktion 'Arbeitsscheu Reich,' Novemberpogrom, Aktion 'Gewitter,'" in: *Der Ort des Terrors. Geschichte der nationalsozialistischen Konzentrationslager*, Vol. 1: *Die Organisation des Terrors*, edited by Wolfgang Benz and Barbara Distel. Munich: Beck, pp. 156–64.

Schüler-Springorum, Stefanie (2005b) "Die 'Mädelfrage.' Zu den Geschlechterbeziehungen in der deutsch-jüdischen Jugendbewegung," in: *Jüdische Welten. Juden in Deutschland vom 18. Jahrhundert bis in die Gegenwart*, edited by Marion Kaplan and Beate Mayer. Göttingen: Wallstein, pp. 136–54.

Schulte, Jan Erik (2005) "Das SS-Wirtschaft-Verwaltungshauptamt und die Expansion des KZ-Systems," in: *Der Ort des Terrors. Geschichte der nationalsozialistischen Konzentrationslager*, Vol. 1: *Die Organisation des Terrors*, edited by Wolfgang Benz and Barbara Distel. Munich: Beck, pp. 141–55.

Schultheis, Franz (2003) "Bilder aus Algerien. Ein Gespräch," in: *Pierre Bourdieu in Algerien. Zeugnisse der Entwurzelung*, edited by Franz Schultheis and Christine Frisinghelli. Graz: Edition Camera Austria, pp. 21–51.

Schulz, Matthias (2005) "Teufel im Barackenmeer. War der KZ-Arzt Josef Mengele ein Spitzenforscher der Genetik?" in: *Der Spiegel* 12, pp. 146–50.

Schützeichel, Rainer (2004) *Historische Soziologie*. Bielefeld: Transcript.

Schwarz, Gudrun (1997) *Die nationalsozialistischen Lager*. Frankfurt am Main: Fischer Taschenbuchverlag.

Schwarz, Gudrun (1998) "Frauen in Konzentrationslagern – Täterinnen und Zuschauerinnen," in: *Die nationalsozialistischen Konzentrationslager. Entwicklung und Struktur*, edited by Ulrich Herbert. Göttingen: Wallstein, pp. 800–21.

Sebald, Winfried Georg (1990) "Jean Améry und Primo Levi," in: *Über Jean Améry*, edited by Irene Heidelberger-Leonard. Heidelberg: Winter Universitätsverlag, pp. 115–23.

Seel, Pierre (1995) *I, Pierre Seel, Deported Homosexual*. Translated by Joachim Neugroschel. New York: Basic Books. [*Moi, Pierre Seel, déporté homosexuel*, 1994]

Seela, Torsten (1992) *Bücher und Bibliotheken in nationalsozialistischen Konzentrationslagern. Das gedruckte Wort im antifaschistischen Widerstand der Häftlinge*. Munich: K.G. Saur.

Semprún, Jorge (1990) *The Long Voyage*. Translated by Richard Seaver. New York: Schocken Books. [*Le grand voyage*, 1964]

Setkiewicz, Piotr (1998) "Häftlingsarbeit im KZ Auschwitz III-Monowitz. Die Frage nach der Wirtschaftlichkeit der Arbeit," in: *Die nationalsozialistischen Konzentrationslager. Entwicklung und Struktur*, Vol. 2, edited by Ulrich Herbert. Göttingen: Wallstein, pp. 584–605.

Shelley, Lore (1986) *Secretaries of Death: Accounts by Former Prisoners Who Worked in the Gestapo of Auschwitz*. New York: Shengold Publishers.

Shik, Na'ama (2005) "Weibliche Erfahrungen in Auschwitz-Birkenau," in: *Genozid und Geschlecht. Jüdische Frauen im nationalsozialistischen Lagersystem*, edited by Gisela Bock. Frankfurt am Main: Campus, pp. 103–22.

Skoda, Uwe (2003) "Kaste, das Kastensystem und die Scheduled Castes," in: *Suedasien.info*. http://www.suedasien.info/laenderinfos/461, accessed on April 30, 2013.

Smoleń, Kazimierz and Michael Zimmermann (1995) "The Gypsies in KL Auschwitz," in: *Death Books from Auschwitz. Remnants. Vol. 1: Reports*, edited by the State Museum of Auschwitz-Birkenau. Translated by Michael Jacobs, Georg Mayer, and Jacek Plesniarowicz. Munich: K.G. Saur, pp. 133–44.

Sofsky, Wolfgang (1995) "Analyse des Schreckens. Eugen Kogons 'Der SS-Staat' und die Perspektiven der KZ-Forschung," in: *Polis 15: Analysen – Meinungen – Debatten*. Schriftenreihe der Hessischen Landeszentrale für politische Bildung.

Sofsky, Wolfgang (1997) *The Order of Terror: The Concentration Camp*. Translated by William Templer. Princeton: Princeton University Press. [*Die Ordnung des Terrors: Das Konzentrationslager*, 1993]

"SS 'Medical Services' in KL Auschwitz" (1995) In: *Death Books from Auschwitz. Remnants. Vol. 1: Reports*, edited by the State Museum of Auschwitz-Birkenau. Translated by Michael Jacobs, Georg Mayer, and Jacek Plesniarowicz. Munich: K.G. Saur, pp. 77–80.

Steinberg, Paul (2001) *Speak You Also: A Survivor's Reckoning*. Translated by Linda Coverdale with Bill Ford. New York: Picador USA. [*Chroniques d'ailleurs*, 1996]

Steiner, Stephan (ed.) (1996) *Jean Améry (Hans Maier)*. Basel; Frankfurt am Main: Stroemfeld.

Steinke, Ron (2002) "'Ein Mann, der mit einem anderen Mann ...' Eine kurze Geschichte des § 175 in der BRD," in: *ForumRecht*, 60–3. http://www.forum-recht-online.de/2005/205/205steinke.htm, accessed on April 30, 2013.

Stirn, Aglaja (2000) "Überleben und Auseinandersetzung mit dem Holocaust-Trauma in einer Auswahl literarischer Zeugnisse jüdischer Schriftsteller," in: *Kölner Zeitschrift für Soziologie und Sozialpsychologie* 52(4), pp. 720–60.

Streibel, Robert and Hans Schafranek (1996) *Strategie des Überlebens. Häftlingsgesellschaften in KZ und GULag*. Vienna: Picus.

Suderland, Maja (2003) "Bildung, Distinktion und Habitus. Überlebensressourcen in der sozialen Welt der nationalsozialistischen Konzentrationslager," in: *ZSE Zeitschrift für Soziologie* 23(3), pp. 302–19.

Suderland, Maja (2004) *Territorien des Selbst. Kulturelle Identität als Ressource für das tägliche Überleben im Konzentrationslager*. Frankfurt am Main; New York: Campus.

Suderland, Maja (2005) "'Ist das ein Mensch?' Erfahrungen in der sozialen Welt nationalsozialistischer Konzentrationslager," in: *Wissenschaft und Kritik. Beiträge zu Bildung und Gesellschaft*, published by the Hans-Böckler-Stiftung and the Gewerkschaft Erziehung und Wissenschaft, Frankfurt am Main, pp. 13–23.

Suderland, Maja (2007) "Männliche Ehre und menschliche Würde. Über die Bedeutung von Männlichkeitskonstruktionen in der sozialen Welt der nationalsozialistischen Konzentrationslager," in: *Prekäre Transformationen. Pierre Bourdieus Soziologie der Praxis und ihre Herausforderungen für die Frauen- und Geschlechterforschung*, edited by Ulla Bock, Irene Dölling, and Beate Krais. Göttingen: Wallstein, pp. 118–40.

Suderland, Maja (2008) "Die schlafende Kraft des Habitus. Über verborgene Herrschaftsstrukturen in der Häftlingsgesellschaft nationalsozialistischer Konzentrationslager," in: *Symbolische Gewalt. Herrschaftsanalyse nach Bourdieu*, edited by Robert Schmidt and Volker Woltershoff. Constance: UVK, pp. 245–68.

Suderland, Maja (2009a) "Libido," in: *Bourdieu-Handbuch. Leben – Werk – Wirkung*, edited by Boike Rehbein and Gerhard Fröhlich. Stuttgart: Metzler, pp. 169–70.

Suderland, Maja (2009b) "Hysteresis," in: *Bourdieu-Handbuch. Leben – Werk – Wirkung*, edited by Boike Rehbein and Gerhard Fröhlich. Stuttgart: Metzler, p. 127.

Szalet, Leon (1945) *Experiment "E": A Report from an Extermination Laboratory*. New York: Didier.

Szalet, Leon (2006) *Baracke 38. 237 Tage in den "Judenblocks" des KZ Sachsenhausen*. Berlin: Metropol.

Szymański, Tadeuz, Danuta Symańska, and Tadeusz Śniesko (1987) "Das 'Spital' im Zigeuner-Familienlager in Auschwitz-Birkenau," in: *Die Auschwitz-Hefte. Texte der polnischen Zeitschrift "Przegląd Lekarski" über historische, psychische und medizinische Aspekte des Lebens und Sterbens in Auschwitz*, Vol. 1, published by the Hamburger Institut für Sozialforschung. Weinheim; Basel: Beltz, pp. 199–207. [Originally published 1965]

Taylor, Charles (1992) *Sources of the Self: The Making of Modern Identity.* Cambridge: Cambridge University Press.

"Theresienstadt. Ein Dokumentarfilm aus dem jüdischen Siedlungsgebiet" (2003) (information and data) from: *Cinematography of the Holocaust*, project by the Fritz Bauer Institut. http://www.cine-holocaust.de/cgi-bin/gdq?dfw00fbw000812. gd, accessed on April 30, 2013.

Tillion, Germaine (1975) *Ravensbrück.* Translated by Gerald Satterwhite. New York: Anchor Press. [*Ravensbrück*, 1973]

Topography of Terror Documentation Center. URL http://www.topographie. de/en/topography-of-terror/ accessed on April 25, 2013.

Traverso, Enzo (2000) "Als Intellektuelle in Auschwitz: Jean Améry und Primo Levi," in: *Auschwitz denken.* Hamburg: Hamburger Edition, pp. 246–80. [*L'Histoire déchirée*, 1997]

Traverso, Enzo (2003) *The Origins of Nazi Violence.* Translated by Janet Lloyd. New York: The New Press. [*La Violence nazie: une généalogie européene*, 2002]

Trouvé, Christel (2005) "Die 'Nacht- und Nebel'-Häftlinge 1942–1945," in: *Häftlingsgesellschaft. Dachauer Hefte* 21, edited by Wolfgang Benz and Barbara Distel. Dachau: Verlag Dachauer Hefte, pp. 50–65.

Tuchel, Johannes (2005) "Organisationsgeschichte der 'frühen Konzentrationslager,'" in: *Der Ort des Terrors. Geschichte der nationalsozialistischen Konzentrationslager*, Vol. 1: *Die Organisation des Terrors*, edited by Wolfgang Benz and Barbara Distel. Munich: Beck, pp. 43–57.

United States Holocaust Memorial Museum (USHMM) (n.d.) "Decree of the Reich President for the Protection of the People and the State." In: *Holocaust Encyclopedia.* http://www.ushmm.org/wlc/en/article.php?ModuleId=10007889, accessed on April 30, 2013.

van Dülmen, Richard (ed.) (2001) *Entdeckung des Ich. Die Geschichte der Individualisierung vom Mittelalter bis zur Gegenwart.* Darmstadt: Wissenschaftliche Buchgesellschaft.

Villa, Paula-Irene (1996) "Spürbare Zugehörigkeiten. Klasse und Geschlecht als zweifache Positionierung des Leibes," in: *Kategorie: Geschlecht? Empirische Analysen und feministische Theorien*, edited by Ute Luise Fischer, Marita Kampshoff, Susanne Keil, and Mathilde Schmidt. Opladen: Leske + Budrich, pp. 141–62.

Vogel, Loden [pseudonym of Louis Tas] (2002) *Tagebuch aus einem Lager.* Translated by Miriam Pressler and Randolf Wörner. Göttingen: Vandenhoek & Ruprecht. [*Dagboek uit een kamp*, 1965]

von Bredow, Rafaela (2007) "Das gleiche Geschlecht," in: *Der Spiegel* 6, pp. 142–9.

Wachten, Johannes (2006) "Körperbilder im Judentum," *journal-ethnologie. de* 3. http://www.journal-ethnologie.de/Deutsch/Schwerpunktthemen/ Schwerpunktthemen_2006/Hautzeichen_-_Koerperbilder/Koerperbilder_im_ Judentum/index.phtml, accessed on April 30, 2013.

Waligora, Melitta (2006) "Unberührbar heißt rechtlos. Das Kastensystem – eine Erfindung der kolonialen Moderne," in: *Das Parlament* 32–3. http://webarchiv. bundestag.de/archive/2010/0824/dasparlament/2006/32-33/Thema/027. html, accessed on April 30, 2013.

Walter, Verena (2007) "Raub," in: *Der Ort des Terrors. Geschichte der nationalsozialistischen Konzentrationslager*, Vol. 5: *Hinzert – Auschwitz – Neuengamme*, edited by Wolfgang Benz and Barbara Distel. Munich: Beck, pp. 128–30.

Walz, Loretta (2005a) *Die Frauen von Ravensbrück. Überlebende des Frauenkonzentrationslagers Ravensbrück erinnern sich*. Berlin: Loretta-Walz-Videoproduktion [DVD].

Walz, Loretta (2005b) *"Und dann kommst du dahin an einem schönen Sommertag."* Die *Frauen von Ravensbrück*. Munich: Kunstmann.

Walz, Rainer (1995) "Der nahe Fremde. Die Beziehungen zwischen Christen und Juden in der frühen Neuzeit," in: *Essener Unikate. Berichte aus Forschung und Lehre. Geisteswissenschaften* 6/7, pp. 56–63.

Weber, Max (1978) *Economy and Society*, edited by Guenther Roth and Claus Wittich. Berkeley: University of California Press. [*Wirtschaft und Gesellschaft*, 1922]

Welzer, Harald (2007) "Die Deutschen und ihr 'Drittes Reich,'" in: *Aus Politik und Zeitgeschichte* 14/15 ("Nationalsozialismus"), pp. 21–8.

Wendt, Bernd Jürgen (1995) *Deutschland 1933–1945. Das Dritte Reich. Handbuch zur Geschichte*. Hanover: Fackelträger.

Widmann, Peter (2003) "Fortwirkende Zerrbilder. Sinti und Roma im Nationalsozialismus und im Nachkriegsdeutschland," in: *Dimensionen der Verfolgung. Opfer und Opfergruppen im Nationalsozialismus*, edited by Sybille Quack. Munich: DVA, pp. 203–21.

Wildt, Michael (2007) *Volksgemeinschaft als Selbstermächtigung. Gewalt gegen Juden in der deutschen Provinz 1919 bis 1939*. Hamburg: Hamburger Edition.

Willems, Susanne (2007) "Monowitz (Monowice)," in: *Der Ort des Terrors. Geschichte der nationalsozialistischen Konzentrationslager*, Vol. 5: *Hinzert – Auschwitz – Neuengamme*, edited by Wolfgang Benz and Barbara Distel. Munich: Beck, pp. 276–84.

Willems, Wim (1996) "Außenbilder von Sinti und Roma in der frühen Zigeunerforschung," in: *Die gesellschaftliche Konstruktion des Zigeuners. Zur Genese eines Vorurteils*, edited by Jaqueline Giere. Frankfurt am Main; New York: Campus, pp. 87–108.

Winau, Rolf (2005) "Medizinische Experimente in den Konzentrationslagern," in: *Der Ort des Terrors. Geschichte der nationalsozialistischen Konzentrationslager*, Vol. 1: *Die Organisation des Terrors*, edited by Wolfgang Benz and Barbara Distel. Munich: Beck, pp. 165–78.

Winkler, Heinrich August (2006) *Germany: The Long Road West, Volume 1:*

1789–1933. Translated by Alexander J. Sager. Oxford: Oxford University Press. [*Der Lange Weg nach Westen,* 2000]

Winter, Balduin (2005) "Schwarzes Loch in der Zivilgesellschaft. Apartheid in der EU: Aus diskriminierten Roma lassen sich nicht einfach Normalverbraucher machen," in: *Das Parlament* 42. http://webarchiv.bundestag.de/cgi/show. php?fileToLoad=2228&id=1149, accessed on April 30, 2013.

Wippermann, Wolfgang (1993) *Geschichte der Sinti und Roma in Deutschland. Darstellung und Dokumente.* Working papers. Berlin: Pädagogisches Zentrum.

Wippermann, Wolfgang (1997) "Ideologie," in: *Enzyklopädie des Nationalsozialismus,* edited by Wolfgang Benz, Hermann Graml, and Hermann Weiß. Munich: dtv, pp. 11–21.

Wlaschek, Rudolf M. (ed.) (2001) *Kunst und Kultur in Theresienstadt.* Gerlingen: Bleicher.

Wolbring, Barbara (2006) *Neuere Geschichte studieren.* Constance: UVK.

Wulf, Christoph (2005) *Zur Genese des Sozialen. Mimesis – Performativität – Ritual.* Bielefeld: Transcript.

Wüllenkemper, Cornelius (2007) "Ende eines Sonderwegs. Berliner Historikertagung entkräftet die Theorie historischer Kontinuität zwischen den Weltkriegen," in: *Süddeutsche Zeitung,* January 20–1, p. 17.

Wustlich, Reinhart (2006) "Kampf gegen das Vergessen. Im Umfeld eines Konzentrationslagers," *Frankfurter Rundschau,* August 25.

Wyrwa, Ulrich (1999) "'Holocaust.' Notizen zur Begriffsgeschichte," in: *Jahrbuch für Antisemitismusforschung,* Vol. 8, edited by Wolfgang Benz, pp. 300–11.

Young, James Edward (1988) *Writing and Rewriting the Holocaust: Narrative and the Consequences of Interpretation.* Bloomington: Indiana University Press.

Zámečník, Stanislav (2007) *Das war Dachau.* Frankfurt am Main: Fischer Taschenbuch.

Zimmermann, Michael (1996) *Rassenutopie und Genozid. Die nationalsozialistische "Lösung der Zigeunerfrage."* Hamburg: Christians.

Zimmermann, Moshe (2002) "Täter–Opfer-Dichotomien als Identitätsformen," in: *Verletztes Gedächtnis. Erinnerungskultur und Zeitgeschichte im Konflikt,* edited by Konrad H. Jarausch and Martin Sabrow. Frankfurt am Main; New York: Campus, pp. 199–216.

Zinn, Alexander (2011) *"Das Glück kam immer zu mir." Rudolf Brazda – Das Überleben eines Homosexuellen im Dritten Reich.* Frankfurt am Main: Campus.

Zywulska, Krystyna (1980) *Wo vorher Birken waren. Überlebensbericht einer jungen Frau aus Auschwitz-Birkenau.* Darmstadt: Verlag Darmstädter Blätter. [*Przezylam Oswiecim,* 1946]

Zywulska, Krystyna (2004) *I Survived Auschwitz.* Translated by Krystyna Cenkalska. Warsaw: tCHu. [*Przezylam Oswiecim,* 1946]

Index